PAUL *and the*
COMPETING MISSION
in CORINTH

PAUL *and the* COMPETING MISSION *in* CORINTH

Michael D. Goulder

LIBRARY OF PAULINE STUDIES

Stanley E. Porter, *General Editor*

HENDRICKSON
PUBLISHERS

Copyright © 2001 Hendrickson Publishers, Inc.
P.O. Box 3473
Peabody, Massachusetts 01961-3473

ISBN 1-56563-379-2

Printed in the United States of America

First printing — October 2001

Cover image: El Greco (1541–1614). *Saints Peter and Paul.* Museu d'Art de
Cataluna, Barcelona, Spain. Scala / Art Resource, N.Y.

Library of Congress Cataloging-in-Publication Data

Goulder, M. D.
    Paul and the competing mission in Corinth / Michael D. Goulder.
       p. cm. — (Library of Pauline studies)
    Includes bibliographical references and indexes.
    ISBN 1-56563-379-2 (pbk. : alk. paper)
    1. Bible. N.T. Corinthians—Criticism, interpretation, etc. 2. Corinth
(Greece)—Church history. I. Title. II. Series.
    BS2675.52 .G68 2001
    227'.206—dc21
                                                            2001004817

TABLE OF CONTENTS

PREFACE

IN 1994 I published a short book, *A Tale of Two Missions* (republished in America under the title *St. Paul versus St. Peter*). It was intended for a broad audience, offering an explanation of the situation behind our New Testament and some documents from the second century. I therefore eschewed footnotes and pledged my respectability merely by listing a dozen articles I had published on the subject in learned journals and Festschriften. But sensing that I would not be likely to carry my professional colleagues with so brief an array of arguments, I added a defiant and ill-considered note in the introduction: "If they would prefer an 800-page statement, I am preparing one."

Reflection soon made clear that neither I nor anyone could hope to examine the entire New Testament, let alone the second-century documents, and offer a new and satisfying explanation in a mere eight hundred pages. Besides, my explanation was not entirely new. It was a much revised and elaborated form of a theory going back to the eighteenth century and made notorious by Ferdinand Christian Baur. Almost all scholars had been taught in their youth that it was based on a fundamental fallacy, and there was, in consequence, a heavy weight of prejudice against it that I would need to overcome. I saw, therefore, that I would have to concentrate attention on a limited part of the subject.

Baur's theory and mine supposes that behind the New Testament lies a basic rivalry between two missions, that is, two evangelizing communities sending out a series of emissaries to win converts to the Christian faith: the one headed in the 40s and 50s C.E. by James (Jesus' brother), Peter, and John; and the other by Paul. Galatians 2.7–8 refers to this dichotomy in so many words: "but when they saw that I had been entrusted with the gospel to the uncircumcision, just as Peter had been with that to the circumcision, for he who worked in Peter for the mission to the circumcision worked also in me for the Gentiles." There is evidence that some such rivalry underlies the letters to the Galatians, the Romans, and the Philippians. First Thessalonians is too early, and Philemon too short, for us to expect any such controversy. But our major Pauline documentation is the twenty-nine-chapter correspondence with the Corinthian church, and it is here that the attacks on Baur have been concentrated. Where, it has been asked, is the mention of circumcision, so hotly disputed in the other three letters? Why is there no discussion of the law? Where, apart from one or two neutral references, is there any mention of James and Peter?

The first topic to be tackled, therefore, was the Corinthian letters, with a determined effort to find out who the opposition were and if they were the same in both Epistles. My conclusion is that in fact the opponents were, in both letters, evangelists sent by the "pillars" in Jerusalem. We need a name for such people, and in some ways it would be most accurate to speak of them as Jacobites, since James was the moving spirit behind them. But 1 Cor 1.12[1] suggests that they spoke of themselves as "of Cephas," and Paul responds to this appellation. So it has seemed best to let them have their own self-identification, and I have called them the Petrines.

There will need to be a second volume to my apologia, if I live so long. I have argued here that the issues that divided Paul and the Petrines were far from limited to the law and circumcision. They extended to many practices in everyday life, such as attitudes about sex, work, money, idol food, and the behavior of women, and to major doctrinal issues such as the incarnation, the atonement, the resurrection, and the Parousia. It should be possible to trace, without trespassing into a third volume, the development of these disputes in the century following Paul.

I am grateful to the editor of *Novum Testamentum* for permission to reprint passages from my article "Libertines?" (1999), in ch. 8. The reader should note that the translations of the NT and other Greek texts are usually my own.

I would like to record my thanks to colleagues who have helpfully criticized parts of my thesis, especially in Britain and in Scandinavia; to Professor Kingsley Barrett for help and encouragement; to Dr. Christine Trevett, Dr. Stephen Chester, and above all to my Birmingham colleagues and friends David Parker and Mark Goodacre.

August 1999
Michael Goulder

---

[1]Hereafter such citations to 1 and 2 Corinthians will usually be expressed in a shorthand format so that 1 Cor 1.12 will be merely I,1.12.

ABBREVIATIONS

GENERAL

ca.	circa
ch(s).	chapter(s)
esp.	especially
frg.	fragment
mg.	margin
MSS	manuscripts
n.	note
no.	number
pc	*pauci,* a few
s.v.	*sub verbo,* under the word
v(v).	verse(s)

BIBLE TEXTS AND VERSIONS: DIVISIONS OF THE CANON AND ANCIENT VERSIONS

LXX	Septuagint
MT	Masoretic Text
NT	New Testament
OT	Old Testament

BIBLE TEXTS AND VERSIONS: MODERN EDITIONS AND VERSIONS

NA[26]	*Novum Testamentum Graece,* Nestle-Aland, 26th ed.
ASV	American Standard Version
BF[2]	British and Foreign Bible Societies, 2d ed.
Bover	*Novi Testamenti Biblia Graeca et Latina,* J. M. Bover
JB	Jerusalem Bible
KJV	King James Version

Luth	*Das Neue Testament, nach der Übersetzung Martin Luthers,* rev. ed., 1956
NEB	New English Bible
NRSV	New Revised Standard Version
RSV	Revised Standard Version
RV	Revised Version
Segond	*Le Nouveau Testament,* L. Segond, rev. ed., 1962
UBS	*The Greek New Testament,* United Bible Societies [UBS4]
WH	Wescott-Hort
Zür	*Die Heilige Schrift,* Zürich, 1942

OLD TESTAMENT PSEUDEPIGRAPHA

Apoc. Ab.	*Apocalypse of Abraham*
Apoc. Mos.	*Apocalypse of Moses*
2 Bar.	*2 Baruch (Syriac Apocalypse)*
3 Bar.	*3 Baruch (Greek Apocalypse)*
1 En.	*1 Enoch (Ethiopic Apocalypse)*
2 En.	*2 Enoch (Slavonic Apocalypse)*
3 En.	*3 Enoch (Hebrew Apocalypse)*
Jub.	*Jubilees*
Pss. Sol.	*Psalms of Solomon*
T. Levi	*Testament of Levi*
T. Reu.	*Testament of Reuben*
T. Naph.	*Testament of Naphtali*

DEAD SEA SCROLLS AND RELATED TEXTS

1QSa	*Rule of the Congregation* (Appendix a to 1QS)
1QSb	*Rule of the Blessings* (Appendix b to 1QS)
CD	Cairo Genizah copy of the *Damascus Document*

MISHNAH, TALMUD, AND RELATED LITERATURE

b.	Babylonian
m.	Mishnah
t.	Tosefta
ᶜAbod. Zar.	*ᶜAbodah Zarah*
Ber.	*Berakot*
Ḥag.	*Ḥagigah*
Ketub.	*Ketubbot*

Meg.	*Megillah*
Neg.	*Nega^cim*
Qidd.	*Qiddušin*
Šabb.	*Šabbat*
Sanh.	*Sanhedrin*
Ta^can.	*Ta^canit*
y.	Jerusalem
Yebam.	*Yebamot*

ANCIENT PAPYRI

P.Tebt.	Tebtunis Papyri

ANCIENT CHRISTIAN WRITINGS

1 Clem.	*1 Clement*
Acts Paul	*Acts of Paul*
Acts Thom.	*Acts of Thomas*
Epiphanius	
Pan.	*Panarion*
Eusebius	
Hist. eccl.	*Historia ecclesiastica*
Gos. Eb.	*Gospel of the Ebionites*
Gos. Thom.	*Gospel of Thomas*
Herm. *Vis.*	Shepherd of Hermas, *Vision*
Hippolytus	
Haer.	*Refutatio omnium haeresium (Philosophoumena)*
Ign. *Eph.*	Ignatius, *To the Ephesians*
Ign. *Phld.*	Ignatius, *To the Philadelphians*
Ign. *Rom.*	Ignatius, *To the Romans*
Irenaeus	
Haer.	*Adversus haereses*
Justin	
Dial.	*Dialogus cum Tryphone*
Origen	
Cels.	*Contra Celsum*
Ps.-Clem. Hom.	Pseudo-Clementine *Homilies*
Ps.-Clem. Rec.	Pseudo-Clementine *Recognitions*
Tertullian	
Val.	*Adversus Valentinianos*
Virg.	*De virginibus velandis*

OTHER ANCIENT WRITINGS

Appian
  Hist. rom.   *Historia romana*
Cicero
  Rab. Post.   *Pro Rabirio Postumo*
  Corp. herm.   *Corpus hermeticum*
Dio Chrysostom
  Tyr.   *De tyrannide*
Herodian
  Hist.   *History of the Emperors after Marcus*
Josephus
  A.J.   *Antiquitates judaicae*
  B.J.   *Bellum judaicum*
Philo
  Conf.   *De confusione linguarum*
  Congr.   *De congressu eruditionis gratia*
  Contempl.   *De vita contemplativa*
  Deus   *Quod Deus sit immutabilis*
  Leg.   *Legum allegoriae*
  Migr.   *De migratione Abrahami*
  Mos.   *De vita Mosis*
  Opif.   *De opificio mundi*
  QG   *Quaestiones et solutiones in Genesin*
  Spec.   *De specialibus legibus*
Ps.-Plato
  Ax.   *Axiochus*
Plutarch
  De laude   *De laude ipsius*
Quintilian
  Inst.   *Institutio oratoria*
Tacitus
  Germ.   *Germania*

SECONDARY SOURCES

AB   Anchor Bible
ANRW   *Aufstieg und Niedergang der römischen Welt: Geschichte und Kultur Roms im Spiegel der neueren Forschung.* Edited by H. Temporini and W. Haase. Berlin, 1972–
ANTC   Abingdon New Testament Commentaries

BAG	Bauer, W., W. F. Arndt, and F. W. Gingrich. *Greek-English Lexicon of the New Testament and Other Early Christian Literature.* Chicago, 1957
BAGD	Bauer, W., W. F. Arndt, F. W. Gingrich, and F. W. Danker. *Greek-English Lexicon of the New Testament and Other Early Christian Literature.* 2d ed. Chicago, 1979
BETL	Bibliotheca ephemeridum theologicarum lovaniensium
BFCT	Beiträge zur Förderung christlicher Theologie
BFT	Biblical Foundations in Theology
BHT	Beiträge zur historischen Theologie
Bib	*Biblica*
BNTC	Black's New Testament Commentaries
BU	Biblische Untersuchungen
BZ	*Biblische Zeitschrift*
BZNW	Beihefte zur Zeitschrift für die neutestamentliche Wissenschaft
CBQ	*Catholic Biblical Quarterly*
ConBNT	Coniectanea biblica: New Testament Series
EKKNT	Evangelisch-katholischer Kommentar zum Neuen Testament
ExpTim	*Expository Times*
FB	Forschung zur Bibel
FRLANT	Forschungen zur Religion und Literatur des Alten und Neuen Testaments
HNT	Handbuch zum Neuen Testament
ICC	International Critical Commentary
JBL	*Journal of Biblical Literature*
JJS	*Journal of Jewish Studies*
JSNT	*Journal for the Study of the New Testament*
JTS	*Journal of Theological Studies*
KEK	Kritisch-exegetischer Kommentar über das Neue Testament (Meyer-Kommentar)
LCL	Loeb Classical Library
LSJ	Liddell, H. G., R. Scott, and H. S. Jones. *A Greek-English Lexicon.* 9th ed. with revised supplement. Oxford, 1996
MM	Moulton, J. H., and G. Milligan, *The Vocabulary of the Greek Testament.* London, 1930. Reprint, Peabody, Mass., 1997
NCB	New Century Bible
NICNT	New International Commentary on the New Testament
NIGTC	New International Greek Testament Commentary
NovT	*Novum Testamentum*
NTG	New Testament Guides
NTS	*New Testament Studies*

OTP	*Old Testament Pseudepigrapha.* Edited by J. H. Charlesworth. 2 vols. New York, 1983, 1985
RB	*Revue biblique*
SBLDS	Society of Biblical Literature Dissertation Series
SBT	Studies in Biblical Theology
SJud	*Studies in Judaism*
SNTSMS	Society for New Testament Studies Monograph Series
SP	Sacra pagina
StPB	Studia post-biblica
Str-B	Strack, H. L., and P. Billerbeck. *Kommentar zum neuen Testament aus Talmud und Midrasch.* 6 vols. Munich, 1922–1961
TDNT	*Theological Dictionary of the New Testament.* Edited by G. Kittel and G. Friedrich. Translated by G. W. Bromiley. 10 vols. Grand Rapids, 1964–1976
TS	*Theological Studies*
TUGAL	Texte und Untersuchungen zur Geschichte der altchristlichen Literatur
VC	*Vigiliae christianae*
WBC	Word Biblical Commentary
WMANT	Wissenschaftliche Monographien zum Alten und Neuen Testament
WUNT	Wissenschaftliche Untersuchungen zum Neuen Testament
ZNW	*Zeitschrift für die neutestamentliche Wissenschaft und die Kunde der älteren Kirche*
ZTK	*Zeitschrift für Theologie und Kirche*

∼ 1 ∽

GODS ASCENDING

IN 1797, a little over two hundred years ago as I write, one J. E. C. Schmidt published an argument that behind the NT lay a struggle between the followers of Peter and of Paul.[1] The idea was taken up by Ferdinand Christian Baur, professor of church history and dogmatics in the University of Tübingen from 1826 till his death in 1860; he did so first in 1831, in an article of 146 pages,[2] and later in full-length works, most notably *Paulus, der Apostel Jesu Christi* in 1845.[3] Baur's powerful advocacy of the thesis drew widespread agreement but not without some sharp criticism, and in one form or another it became the dominant scholarly view for the rest of the nineteenth century; it was not effectively criticized until the work of W. Lütgert in 1908.[4]

Anyone writing a book with such a title as mine, *Paul and the Competing Mission in Corinth,* is calling up the ghost of Baur as surely as Saul called up the ghost of Samuel. In the KJV the witch of Endor said, "I saw gods ascending out of the earth. And [Saul] said unto her, What form is he of? And she said, An old man cometh up" (1 Sam 28.13–14). ("Gods" is a mistranslation of אלהים; I should say instead "a divine spirit.") Granted, Baur made many

---

[1] J. E. C. Schmidt, *Bibliothek für Kritik und Exegese* (2 vols.; 1797–1803), 1:91. Baur himself refers to Schmidt in F. C. Baur, "Die Christuspartei in der korinthischen Gemeinde, der Gegensatz der petrinischen und paulinischen Christentums in der ältesten Kirche, Petrus in Rom," *Tübinger Zeitschrift für Theologie* 4, no. 3 (1831): 61–206, here 76; but in fact the idea was widespread in the late eighteenth century. Both J. Semler and F. von Schelling were influential on Baur (L. M. White, "Baur, Ferdinand Christian, 1782–1860," in *Dictionary of Biblical Interpretation* [ed. J. H. Hayes; 2 vols.; Nashville: Abingdon, 1999], 1:112–13), with the suggestion that Petrine Christianity had developed into Catholicism, while Paul had introduced a superior faith now represented by Protestantism.

[2] Baur, "Christuspartei."

[3] F. C. Baur, *Paulus, der Apostel Jesu Christi—sein Leben und Wirken, seine Briefe und Lehre: Ein Beitrag zu einer kritischen Geschichte des Urchristentums* (Stuttgart, 1845; 2d ed.; ed. E. Zeller; Leipzig, 1866–1867); ET of 2d ed., *Paul, the Apostle of Jesus Christ* (Edinburgh, 1876).

[4] W. Lütgert, *Freiheitspredikt und Schwarmgeister in Korinth: Ein Beitrag zur Charakteristik der Christuspartei* (BFCT 12.3; Gütersloh: Bertelsmann, 1908).

mistakes, ~~like other scholars,~~ but he has been unjustly criticized for mistakes he did not make, and this book is an attempt to restate his central hypothesis on a somewhat different basis. Many NT critics have contributed insights to the meaning of the text, but it falls to the occasional genius, or divine spirit, to scent the outline of a true understanding from the mass of distracting detail. For all his errors, Baur was such a spirit. I shall begin, therefore, with a brief restatement of the part of his thesis that I believe to be well grounded.

Our closest insight into the history of the church in the 40s comes from the second chapter of Galatians.[5] Visitors to Paul's church at Antioch ("false brethren secretly brought in") had been alarmed at the failure to keep Jewish kashruth rules ("to spy out our freedom that we have in Christ Jesus, that they might enslave us") and had protested, causing a public altercation ("to whom we did not submit even for a moment"). It became clear to Paul that there would be trouble, and he went up to Jerusalem ("I went up by revelation") to get an agreement on the question from the leadership there ("I laid before them the gospel that I preach among the Gentiles, lest I should in any way run, or have been running, in vain"). He took Barnabas with him, his fellow pastor and trusted friend of the senior apostles, "taking Titus also with us," because he wanted to have a clear piece of evidence that a Gentile Christian did not have to be circumcised and that the "pillars" accepted this. Paul was nobody's fool.

The meeting was held privately (v. 2) and was a success. Paul explained his message and practice ("the gospel that I preach among the Gentiles"), and the pillars did not impose any conditions on him (οὐδὲν προσανέθεντο, v. 6) either about food and purity laws at the Eucharist or about circumcision. Titus's presence was a masterstroke ("Titus, who was with me, being a Greek, was not forced to be circumcised"), for Paul was able to appeal to this fact in fighting off the circumcisers of Galatians. The pillars were impressed by the success of Paul's work ("when they saw that I had been entrusted with the gospel to the uncircumcision") and shook hands ("they gave me and Barnabas the right hands of fellowship"). Hitherto there had been one mission (ἀποστολή), led by Peter to the Jews ("He that worked

---

[5]Baur expounds Gal 2.1–14 in *Paul,* 105–45, much of the argument being a rebuttal of claims of harmony with Acts. He does not argue that the false brethren were introduced at Antioch (rather than Jerusalem) but assumes it: "Why should [Paul] have gone to Jerusalem himself [in Gal 2.1–10]? Why did he so especially wish to treat of the matter with the Apostles if he had not good grounds for supposing that [they] were by no means ignorant of the attempts made by the παρείσακτοι ψευδάδελφοι?" (p. 121). This conclusion is disputed in modern times, e.g., by J. D. G. Dunn, *The Epistle to the Galatians* (BNTC; London: Black, 1993); but see F. Watson, *Paul, Judaism, and the Gentiles: A Sociological Approach* (Cambridge: Cambridge University Press, 1986), 50–51; and F. F. Bruce, *The Epistle to the Galatians: A Commentary on the Greek Text* (NIGTC; Grand Rapids: Eerdmans, 1982), 115–17, with a list of distinguished scholars.

in Peter for the circumcision mission"); now they recognized that there was a second, parallel mission ("had been at work also in me for the Gentiles"). The meeting ended on a high note of agreement ("that we should go to the Gentiles, and they to the circumcision"). The pillars were in some financial difficulty with their open-purse policy and requested Paul to help them with a collection from his wealthy Gentile converts ("only that we should remember the poor people," τῶν πτωχῶν, v. 10). Paul took up the request with enthusiasm ("which also I was eager to do"): if they accepted his money, they would be less likely to be critical of his liberalism.

The text makes clear that both parties accepted a division of the world into two missions, one of Peter (and John and James) to the Jews, the other of Paul (ἐμοί) to the Gentiles. This is not to assert that there were no independent missionaries; we know, for example, of Stephen and Philip and Apollos. But a mission, whether to Jews or Gentiles, required a sending community with finances to cover traveling and supporting personnel, and in the long run, independent missionaries would be drawn into one or other of the great missions, as Apollos was into the Pauline, or Barnabas (it seems) into the Petrine. Nor is it implied that all within a certain mission were united on all points of doctrine and practice. Peter took a softer line than James in Gal 2.11–12, and the circumcisers of Galatians took a harder line still; Luke is at pains to distance the apostles from the Pharisaic Judaizers of Acts 15.1–5. But difference of opinion is a natural state of affairs in any organization; all these people were part of the Petrine mission, even if they overstepped the mark.

Unfortunately, this was not the end of the story. Peter came to visit the Antioch church, sent by the others after second thoughts on their concessions. At first he was impressed by the warmth of his welcome and the church's spirit of devotion, and he fell in with the Pauline ways ("he ate with the Gentiles"); but after a while he was joined by a further deputation from Jerusalem ("before certain men came from James . . . but when they came . . ."). This forced the issue, and Peter succumbed to their pressure ("fearing those of the circumcision"). He told the church that the food laws were in the Bible and must be observed and that the Eucharist was for those who were prepared to do what God said ("he withdrew and separated himself"). This produced a catastrophe for Paul. The Jewish members of the church had long felt uncomfortable about the purity laws, and they sided with Peter, including even Barnabas ("the rest of the Jews joined in their hypocrisy, so that even Barnabas was led astray by their hypocrisy"). Paul made an angry expostulation ("I withstood [Cephas] to the face, because he was condemned"—by his own shilly-shallying), but the day was lost. Paul had either to bow and accept kashruth rules for his church or to strike out and found a Gentile church of his own. He was wise enough to accept the first alternative and to fight another day.

The incidents so described took place around 48, and the issue of whether Gentile converts should keep the law, including circumcision, was a live one seven years later when Paul wrote Galatians, and again in Romans, and in Philippians, perhaps Paul's last letter ("Beware of the dogs, beware of the evil workers, beware of those who mutilate the flesh," 3.2). It does not arise, apparently, in the Corinthian letters, but the tension between the Pauline converts and the Petrines seems evident.[6] In the opening verses of 1 Corinthians, Paul complains of what seem to be four factions in the church. One is of his own followers, and another of Apollos's; but I,3 appears to show that the two missionaries saw each other as colleagues, planting, watering, building together. This is confirmed by I,16.12, "I strongly urged [Apollos] to visit you with the other brothers, but it was not at all God's will for him to come now."[7]

But there is a third group, claiming to be "of Cephas." We need not think that Peter had himself visited Corinth or that he would have sanctioned their attitude, but their label is likely to be a claim to the authority of the Jerusalem leaders. This is strongly suggested by Paul's repeated defense of his apostleship both in the First Letter (3.21–4.15; 9.1–27) and in much of the Second Letter.[8] It becomes clear in II,11.22 that his critics are in fact Jewish Christians who think that they are the only true ministers of Christ and that Paul is no true apostle; the obvious contrast is with Peter and the other Jerusalem leaders, who were Jesus' chosen apostles.

In the long run, it was the Pauline version of Christianity that had the upper hand, for neither circumcision nor purity laws were accepted in the Catholic Church, and Paul was canonized as an apostle. Still, Jerusalem Christianity did not fade away. Peter was accepted as the first apostle, in Rome and elsewhere, and he has been a figurehead for faith far more than Paul. Jewish Christianity did not die with Peter and James, but its continuing life may be seen in the Pseudo-Clementines, the *Homilies* and *Recognitions,* in which Peter often disputes with Simon Magus, a code name for Paul. The two missions of Gal 2.8 in fact grew together into the Great Church. The leader of this reconciling movement was Luke. In his Gospel every opportunity is taken to draw the sting from the Markan account of Peter's (and the disciples') follies, stupidities, and disloyalties. His Acts divides into two approximate halves, in the first of which Peter is the hero, in the second Paul.

---

[6]For Baur's exposition of the Corinthian letters, see his *Paul,* 168–94, 258–307.

[7]οὐκ ἦν θέλημα: the Greek noun is a rendering of the common רצון for the will of God in rabbinic writing; cf. the proud Jew apostrophized in Rom 2.18, γινώσκεις τὸ θέλημα.

[8]It was this feature of the Corinthian letters that first suggested to Baur his overarching theory of Pauline-Petrine rivalry; see F. C. Baur, "Die Einleitung in das Neue Testament als theologische Wissenschaft," *Theologische Jahrbücher* 10 (1851): 294.

Moreover, in Acts 15 the private conference of Gal 2.1–10 is turned into a massive assembly in which both Peter and James give unqualified support to the Pauline mission on Pauline terms. In more than one sense Acts is an account of the road to the church of Rome.[9]

THE CHARGES AGAINST BAUR

Such an account of the history of the early church may seem innocuous, apart from the comments on the Corinthian letters; but the association with Baur will be enough to stir the reader's suspicions. For almost all modern scholars have been brought up in the belief that Baur was not only wrong on the major issues[10] but also wrongheaded—that is, that his judgments on questions of NT exegesis were determined not by the texts but by philosophical presuppositions. Probably the most important modern influences leading to the dismissal of Baur have been Werner Kümmel's *Das Neue Testament: Geschichte der Erforschung seiner Probleme* (1970)[11] and Stephen Neill's *Interpretation of the New Testament, 1861–1961* (1964).[12] Those who write the history of a subject take the power to direct the perspective of their readers in decades to come.[13] We may add the various introductions to the NT written to guide the student—for example, Philipp Vielhauer's *Geschichte der urchristlichen Literatur*.[14]

Credit is conceded to Baur today for his insistence on posing the historical question, for seeking an answer to it in the history of the developing churches, and for initiating *Tendenzkritik*. He is not allowed credit for his view that the early history of the church was determined by a rivalry between a Pauline and a Jerusalem mission, and it is this question that I wish to reopen.

Kümmel cites nineteenth-century critics of Baur for three points of fact: (i) there was not a single Jewish-Christian movement in the first two centuries but at least a firmer line and a more liberal line, and probably a

---

[9]Baur, *Paul,* 12, thought Acts was so full of tendentious distortions that it could not be by Luke.

[10]Although this is generally true, there has been a persevering respect for Baur's overall position by a minority of scholars; we may think of Ernst Käsemann, C. K. Barrett, Jacob Jervell, and Gerd Lüdemann.

[11]The English translation is W. G. Kümmel, *The New Testament: The History of the Investigation of Its Problems* (trans. S. M. Gilmour and H. C. Kee; Nashville: Abingdon, 1972).

[12]The second edition, revised by N. T. Wright, continues the account to 1986: Stephen Neill and N. T. Wright, *The Interpretation of the New Testament, 1861–1986* (2d ed.; New York: Oxford University Press, 1988).

[13]Cf. T. S. Kuhn, *The Structure of Scientific Revolutions* (2d ed.; Chicago: University of Chicago Press, 1970), 1–22.

[14]P. Vielhauer, *Geschichte der urchristlichen Literatur* (Berlin: de Gruyter, 1975).

great variety of views; (ii) the Jewish-Christian movement had no permanent influence on the Great Church, and the Pauline theology had little influence; and (iii) Paul was friendly to Peter in the Epistles and cites him as an ally. More significant, and damning, is Kümmel's own (and common) criticism (iv) that Baur's exegesis is determined by his Hegelianism. Not mentioned by Kümmel but historically important are the criticisms of Lütgert: (v) the Corinthian letters show no interest in the questions raised by the Judaizers in Galatians and Romans—neither circumcision nor kashruth is an issue—and (vi) on the contrary, the opposition in 1 Corinthians is principally of enthusiasts, who are likely to be Paul's own converts, more radical than he.

THE CHARGES REBUTTED

Jewish-Christian Diversity.   Albert Ritschl wrote in 1850,

> It is necessary to make many more distinctions [than Baur does] if we are to draw valid conclusions. So we point out that the original apostles, who lived as Jews, must be distinguished from the Jewish Christians; also various sects of Jewish Christians must be distinguished; and further the Gentile Christianity that was in process of becoming Catholic was not identical with the group influenced by Paul. These observations lead to more probable conclusions, as they do not compel us to regard every Christian phenomenon of the spirit during the period as either Jewish Christian, or Pauline, or neutralizing.[15]

Ritschl's idea of the complexity of first-century Judaism, and so of Jewish Christianity, will find a ready response today. But it is important to be fair to Baur, since he is often represented as identifying the Jerusalem apostles and the Judaizers. Vielhauer, for example, says, "According to the Judaist hypothesis in its classic [i.e., Baur's] formulation, the agitation in Galatia does not represent an isolated event but part of a big conscious countermission against Paul's mission, planned and organized by Peter, which has also left its traces in Corinth (Cephas party, 1 Cor 1:12; 3:22) and in Philippi."[16]

Baur, however, from his "Christuspartei" article of 1831 till the posthumous second edition of his *Paulus* in 1866–1867, does distinguish the apostles from the Judaizers. The main opposition was indeed "between the Paulinists and Petrinists or Judaizers."[17] But in 1831 he wrote, "Peter had no part in the faction at Corinth that bore his name . . . itinerant pseudoapostles who in-

---

[15]A. Ritschl, *Die Entstehung der altkatholischen Kirche* (Bonn, 1850), 22; my translation.

[16]Vielhauer, *Geschichte,* 118–19. For Baur as the classic statement of this position, p. 104.

[17]Baur, "Einleitung," 294.

voked the name of Peter had also come to Corinth. . . . [They] appealed above all to the authority of James and of Peter, though we can scarcely believe that the [Jerusalem] Jewish apostles approved them and could give recognition to sham emissaries of this sort."[18] And in his *Paulus* (1845) he says,

> There grew up within Jewish Christianity itself a strict and a liberal party. The stricter one wished to impose on Gentile Christians also the general principle that there was no salvation apart from Judaism. . . . The more liberal party was in principle in harmony with the stricter one—only after the concessions made by the Jewish Apostles to the Apostle Paul, they could not oppose him practically. . . . We cannot but think that the Jewish apostles were at the head of this [more liberal] party.[19]

I do not wish to dispute that Judaism was variegated in the first century or that several nuanced opinions may have been available: Essenes, Pharisees, Sadducees, Diaspora liberals, those who spoke of Noachian commandments, allegorists, and others. But even so, a further distinction seems to be required. The Gentile mission raised a crucial question on which every Christian had to take a stand: were the kashruth provisions in the OT, and as interpreted in Jewish tradition, to be required of the Gentile converts? Paul clearly felt that the Gentile mission would be inhibited, even crippled, if they were required, especially circumcision; living like Jews would, for potential converts, be bondage. The problems would extend to calendrical observance (Gal 4.10; Rom 14.5), since the employment of many Gentiles must have required Sabbath working. Whether from such pragmatic considerations or from more theological ones, he insisted that Gentiles were free of kashruth rules. We see the compulsiveness of the issue gradually dawning in the narrative of Gal 2. At first, when the pillars heard of procedures at Antioch, they were scandalized and sent the "false brethren" to remonstrate.[20] Then, when Paul appeared, they thought his liberalism was justified by his success. When he had gone, however, they had second thoughts and sent Peter to settle matters. When Peter came, he thought kashruth less important than the Christian spirit of the church. But then, when certain ones from James came, Peter thought the word of God was important after all. It was similar with the Antiochene Jewish Christians and even Barnabas. There was presumably a Gentile host providing a weekly Saturday supper with nonkosher

[handwritten margin note: But did Paul only later come to this conclusion? (cf. Gal. 5.11)]

---

[18]Baur, "Christuspartei," 61–62.

[19]Baur, *Paul*, 127–28.

[20]Gal 2.4 seems to imply that the "false brethren" were not just casual visitors. As ψευδάδελφοι, they are involved in some deceit; they are παρείσακτοι, a passive verbal adjective suggesting that a third party has introduced them; they come with intention, "to spy out our freedom," and with an ulterior motive, "that they might bring us into bondage." All this could be Paul's misunderstanding or his rhetoric, but the words imply a mission from the pillars, and this construction is historically plausible.

meat, and the Jewish Christians must have felt uncomfortable about joining in. Still, one does not want to make a fuss in a church meeting, and the host would be hurt, and the animal would have had its throat slit, so there was no question of blood . . . Thus is the human conscience lulled by half-truths. But the arrival of the certain men from James brought the issue to a head. Peter spoke up and posed the central question in Gal 2.12: "Brothers [and sisters], we cannot ignore the commandments of God, given us in the Bible and interpreted for us by the sages. Are you coming with me to honor them, or are you not?" The Antiochene Christians had to take a stand for one side or the other, and the remaining Jews joined in Peter's "hypocrisy," even Barnabas. But the central question was unavoidable, and we can watch Peter posing it.

We may even think that Baur has weakened by so steadily making a division between the pillars and the Judaizers, in a quest for "harmony." When the chips were down, the apostles and the "sham emissaries" were on one side of the fence, and Paul on the other. In modern discussion, the "classic position" of Baur is regarded as a long-discarded error, but the force of his argument is liable to bring his conclusion in by the back door. As Vielhauer concedes, "A connection of Paul's Galatian opponents with Peter and/or James may be neither proved nor convincingly disproved."[21]

We lack adequate evidence of any rivalry between a Pauline and a Jewish-Christian mission in the late second century, but we do have a first-hand account of such a conflict toward the end of the NT period. Ignatius writes to the Philadelphians in the twelfth decade of our era:

> For even though certain persons desired to deceive me after the flesh, yet the spirit is not deceived. . . . I cried out when I was among you; I spake with a loud voice, with the voice of God, Give ye heed to the bishop and the presbytery and deacons. Howbeit there were those who suspected me of saying this because I knew beforehand of the division of certain persons. . . . For I heard certain persons saying, If I find it not in the charters (ἀρχεῖα), I believe it not in the Gospel. And when I said to them, It is written, they answered me, That is the question. (Ign. *Phld.* 7–8, trans. B. F. Westcott)

Ignatius is a faithful Pauline: he constantly writes reminiscences of the Pauline Epistles in his letters and calls the Ephesians "fellow-mystics with the sainted Paul" (Ign. *Eph.* 12.3). The Philadelphian church is under the influence of those who "propound Judaism" to them (Ign. *Phld.* 6.1), and it is they who in the following chapter suspect Ignatius (correctly) of having known about the tensions from his friends the church officers. Then in ch. 8 they refuse the authority of "the Gospel," to which he appeals as Scripture ("It is written"). They will accept nothing but the ἀρχεῖα, the original Scriptures, the OT. It is the same basic tension that we have in the Antiochene church in Gal 2 and in the Epistle to the Galatians itself. So far at least, Baur was right.

---

[21]Vielhauer, *Geschichte,* 120.

The Influence of Jewish and Pauline Views. Ritschl also pointed to the diffi- culty of seeing any influence of Jewish Christianity—or, for that matter, any influence of Pauline thought—on second- or third-century Catholicism:

> We can now emphasize more strongly the inability of Jewish Christianity to develop. . . . Catholic Christianity did not issue from a reconciliation of Jewish and Gentile Christians but is a phase of Gentile Christianity alone. . . . We are far from presupposing a fundamental conflict between Paul and the original apostles. If such a conflict had existed, they could not have belonged to the same church, as they did, according to the documents that no one questions.

Paul and the pillars in fact, according to Ritschl, shared Jesus' insights: the transcending of the law by the principle of love, and the Lord's imminent return.[22]

To Ritschl, Jewish Christianity was, for all its possible variety, basically an insistence on the law; there was no insistence on the law in Catholic Christianity, so Jewish Christianity has left no mark on the future church. Similarly, Paul taught a gospel of justification by faith, and this teaching was submerged for fourteen centuries; hence, other movements in Gentile Christianity have been more influential on the Great Church than has Paul. But such simplicities cannot stand today. This study will note how many aspects of Jewish Christianity there were, an apocalyptic form of Judaism, with visionaries and ascetics and a realized eschatology that was to have a considerable input into the future, while the Pauline response was to be regulative for the early history of dogma. Baur was wrong on many details, but on the central issue he was more right than Ritschl.

Relations between Peter and Paul. Some of the same points were made by Adolf Jülicher a generation later, but Jülicher also noted the general courtesy that Paul shows to Peter:

> What the sequel was to this painful dispute [Gal 2.11–14] we do not learn, but we should have no justification for asserting that it resulted in a definite breach between the parties concerned. Even in the Epistle to the Galatians Paul speaks of Barnabas and Peter in far too friendly a way to leave room for the supposition that a dissolution of the agreement described in 2.8, 10 was contemplated on the ground of some serious difference. Paul does not relate the occurrence for the purpose of prejudicing his readers against Peter, or of lowering him in their eyes, but simply to illustrate in the most striking way his own unchanging steadfastness.[23]

---

[22]Ritschl, *Entstehung,* 22–23, 46–52, 107; I owe the references to Kümmel, *History,* 163–64.

[23]A. Jülicher, *Einleitung in das Neue Testament* (Freiburg im Breisgau, 1894), 5.

It is no occasion for surprise that Paul normally treats Peter with courtesy, and this for two reasons. First, Peter held a position of unassailable prestige in the church. He had been Jesus' leading disciple; Jesus had singled him out by giving him the name of destiny, *Kepha'* [Aramaic]; it was he who had led the church through the bleak days after the crucifixion, who had first had an experience of the risen Lord, who had (it was believed) led the first public preaching of the word and nearly suffered martyrdom for it. He was the anchor man who had continued to preside over the mission into the 50s and to whom the Jewish mission had specifically been entrusted (Gal 2.7). So no Christian could afford to be against Peter. The "Cephas party" at Corinth claimed his name because it was the highest on offer. Even the Fourth Evangelist, who wishes to subordinate Peter to his own hero, the beloved disciple, gives him the second-highest profile. Paul would have been insane to go public on any dissensions between him and Peter; it would be like a modern Catholic theologian disagreeing with the pope.

Second, it is likely that Paul and Peter normally got on very well. The problem was James, a man of principle, who was liable to insist on policies inconvenient in the Gentile mission. Peter, on the other hand, appears in the tradition as a weak and friendly man. He is not the stuff of which martyrs are made (Mark 14); he was "flexible" over eating with the Gentiles (Gal 2.12); Paul could not have persuaded the pillars to give him authority for the Gentile mission unless Peter had been willing; Luke can represent Peter as the man who first accepted a Gentile into the church without conditions (Acts 10). Hence Paul is happy to tell of his welcome by Peter in Gal 1.18 and to join his resurrection experience with that of Peter and the others. It is only when the Galatian Judaizers threaten to ruin his mission that he feels obliged to draw the curtain back and reveal the tensions of Gal 2.11–14, with some acid sarcasms in 2.6, 9. Later the Pauline movement will produce two pseudonymous letters disseminating Pauline doctrines under the name of Peter.

Hegelianism.   By far the most frequent and damaging charge against Baur, however, has been his Hegelianism. Kümmel writes,

> During the same years [after 1833] the philosophy of Hegel won predominant influence over him [Baur]. Hegel's view of history as a dialectic process of the resolution of the "being-in-itself" and the "being-for-itself" in the "being-in-and-for-itself" combined in Baur's thought with the opposition of Petrine and Pauline Christianity which he had observed by historical method which was settled in postapostolic Christendom, and this triple beat of thesis, antithesis, and synthesis now becomes the clue to the understanding of early Christianity. And history for him becomes the self-unfolding of the spirit in which the particular has to retire behind the general.[24]

---

[24]Kümmel, *History*, 132.

The same accusation is made more aggressively by Neill and Wright in their similar history of NT scholarship:

> It was just here that Baur believed that Hegel had given him the needed illumination. Judaic Christianity, Pauline Christianity, the reconciliation of both in the Catholic Church—these things run like a King Charles's head through the whole of Baur's researches; and this means that from 1833 onwards his work was gravely vitiated by an irrelevant and unproved presupposition . . . "a dialectical force of arm, which would twist a bar of iron to its purposes; and all brought to bear to prove a perverse and preposterous position. . . ."—There is Baur to the life, in so far as incautious assumptions at the start lead him into error on every principal point of New Testament criticism.[25]

Several things need to be said about Baur's "Hegelianism."

(i) Both Kümmel and Neill-Wright concede that Baur first effectively read Hegel in 1833; in this they accept the conclusions of P. C. Hodgson.[26] But the outline of Baur's theory of a basic Pauline-Petrine conflict underlying the NT, and in particular the troubles at Corinth, had already been published in 1831 in his "Christuspartei" article. So it was not an incautious assumption of Hegelian philosophy "at the start" that was the problem at all: Baur's dialectical theory was grounded in straightforward exegesis from the beginning. Kümmel is more just in saying that Baur had observed the basis of his theory by historical method.

(ii) No one reading Baur, for example, his *Paul, the Apostle of Jesus Christ* (the second German edition was virtually completed by 1860),[27] would have the least impression that he was dominated by an *idée fixe* ("a King Charles's head") that was "gravely vitiating" his judgment. The discussion reads just like a modern work of criticism, constantly checking the narrative of Acts against the Paulines, for instance, and using impressive logical argument to settle questions; the German style is more ponderous than we are used to, and the scholars with whom he disputes are often rationalists such as Neander, but the feel of the work is exclusively exegetical. Hodgson wrote, "We have Baur's direct and unequivocal testimony that his critical procedure was in no way a priori. Although he believed that history . . . is the outward patterning of an inward idea, the idea of reconciliation . . . , he also

---

[25]Neill and Wright, *Interpretation,* 23–24. Neill, who wrote this passage in 1962, takes Baur by the beard to kiss him ("Baur was a heroic figure" [p. 21], "Baur's industry and erudition" [p. 25]), but there is a sword in his left hand, and he smites him in the belly to the hilt.

[26]Ibid., 22–23, 196, and esp. Kümmel, *History,* 427 n. 177. P. C. Hodgson, *The Formation of Historical Theology: A Study of Ferdinand Christian Baur* (New York: Harper & Row, 1966), 23, gives 1834–1835 as the likely date for Baur's involvement with Hegel, citing a letter to his son.

[27]Hodgson, *Formation,* 32.

insisted that independent critical or positive historical research alone determines the shape of our understanding."[28]

(iii) In these circumstances an author's attachment to a philosophical or religious position is irrelevant. All scholars are subtly influenced in judgment by their presuppositions from life more generally, but we deal with the issues raised on the basis of the arguments advanced, not by attacking those presuppositions. For example, many Roman Catholic scholars may believe that Jesus' virginal conception is a historical fact, a conclusion congenial to Vatican theologians. I should not think it proper (or effective) to dismiss this claim on the ground that they are Catholics: the discussion is about the dating and relating of the traditions in Matthew and Luke, and similar matters. Similarly, Baur's presuppositions suggested to him, no doubt, that the Pastorals, with their incipient anti-Gnosticism, were later than the authentic Paulines, and in this case the presuppositions were helpful.

(iv) Of course, there is a limit to this. If we found a modern scholar proposing an Ophite interpretation of the Bible, we would say so and expose his or her irrationality without further discussion. But Hegel and Baur were extremely intelligent men, not crackpots. I would be unwilling to go all the way with Hegel and allow that everything in history (and beyond) must develop according to the thesis-antithesis-synthesis principle. But the idea is not, if applied selectively, "a perverse and preposterous position" at all. On the contrary, it is in many cases obviously true, as when the development of capitalism in the nineteenth century called communism into being and the two ultimately achieved some reconciliation in social democracy. In such matters the great Hegelian dialectic is but a complex statement, tricked out with impressive-sounding Greek assonance, of the truism that history advances with swings of the pendulum.[29]

It is not to be disputed that Baur got many things wrong, but his errors did not extend to "every principal point of New Testament criticism." He was correct in seeing a basic tension between Paul and the Jerusalem apostles in Gal 2 and in seeing this tension extended by followers of the latter in a Judaizing mission to Galatia and in the Pseudo-Clementines. He was also correct in seeing Acts as a later attempt to bring the two missions into

---

[28]Ibid., 3–4. Cf. his citation from Emanuel Hirsch on the framework into which Baur ordered his history of the NT period, "a framework not imposed on it a priori out of philosophical dialectic, but which rather gradually emerged and was clarified by many years of careful study" (p. 209).

[29]Baur did not, in any case, accept the neat thesis-antithesis-synthesis formula as governing the early history of the church. Hegel's philosophy was not so simple; but Baur saw Pauline Christianity as an antithesis of Petrine, with which it made a gradual reconciliation in the period of the Synoptics, and a final accommodation by the end of the second century. And reconciliations were not invariable; Catholicism simply overcame Gnosticism (ibid., 208).

harmony. He was wrong to see the Catholic Church as a straightforward synthesis of the two missions, though, as we shall see, not so wrong as appeared to Ritschl. But the central question that concerns us, whether the Pauline-Petrine tension lies at the root of the Corinthian troubles, is not to be settled by aspersions on Baur's philosophizing, but by exegesis of the two epistles.

Modern students of Baur have often shared my rejection of the assault on his "Hegelianism." Peter Addinall reproduces many of the points I have made and argues that Neill is unfair to Hegel as well as to Baur.[30] There is also an extended defense of Baur by R. C. Morgan.[31] An impressive apologia in German was written by Ulrich Köpf, who cites a comment of Baur in 1853, "My standpoint is, in a word, purely historical, in which the sole concern is, as far as it is at all possible, to present the historical data in their pure objectivity."[32] Baur was in this much influenced by the historian Niebuhr. He fearlessly treated Scripture like other human works and had no fear of doubt; D. F. Strauss was his colleague and caused his work to be suspect on religious grounds in his lifetime.

The Corinthian Problem.   As mentioned, the most significant critique of Baur and his followers was made by Lütgert in a short book, *Freiheitspredigt und Schwarmgeister in Korinth,* in 1908. Lütgert highlighted the differences between the opposition in Galatia and that in Corinth. In the latter there is no pressure to circumcise nor any reference to the church being forced to keep the law. On the contrary, the law is dramatically bypassed: sexual immorality and participation in idol worship alike are both practiced and defended. The opposition are certainly not "nomistic" Jews; they are pneumatics, gnostics, with an extravagant doctrine of Christian freedom. If we ask where this doctrine comes from, the most likely answer is Paul himself, for he had preached freedom from the law and the authority of the Spirit. They had outgrown his limited freedom, and they despised him as weak, both in person and in the ability to do wonders: he was no true pneumatic.

For Lütgert, Paul's mention of himself, Apollos, and Cephas as faction leaders is misleading. The pneumatics said they were "of Christ"—that is, they accepted no human leadership, only a divine one; Paul dislikes this and says they worship a different Jesus, with a different Spirit. They exalted their gnosis as a wisdom that Paul could not rival and derided his preaching of the cross as stupidity. Their gnosis tended in fact toward libertinism: incest,

[30]P. Addinall, "Why Read the Bible?" *ExpTim* 105 (1994): 136–40.
[31]R. C. Morgan, "Ferdinand Christian Baur," in *Nineteenth Century Religious Thought in the West* (3 vols.; ed. N. Smart et al.; New York: Cambridge University Press, 1985), 1:261–89.
[32]U. Köpf, "Ferdinand Christian Baur als Begründer einer konsequent historischen Theologie," *ZTK* 89 (1992): 440–61, here 453.

litigiousness, fornication, idolatry, chaotic worship with undisciplined women ranting on, greed and drunkenness at the meal, an unreal belief that the kingdom had arrived and the resurrection already taken place. Paul regarded this with alarm: it was a human wisdom, a far cry from Galatians. But the gnosis might also lead to an exaggerated spirituality, with demands for sexual ascesis, the other side of the same penny.

Lütgert's analysis was widely convincing and underlies all modern discussion of the two epistles, even when parts of it are rejected, and it is due to his clear thinking that the Tübingen theory has lost its position among the wise and understanding. The situation revealed at Corinth is clearly different from that implied in Galatians, and no sensible person will deny that the main Corinthian opposition are pneumatics with gnosticizing tendencies. In a sense, the present book is an attempt to reconcile the conclusions of Baur and Lütgert, and this attempt will have to be undertaken slowly. Nevertheless, it may be useful to indicate the outline of my proposal:

(i) Lütgert was right to see the main Corinthian problem, in both letters, as pneumatics boasting of their gnosis, with consequent moral and social behavior, but he was wrong to equate gnosis with wisdom, from which it is differentiated in I,12.8 and elsewhere. In I,1–2 the context indicates a Jewish wisdom, and σοφία was the normal term used by Diaspora Jews to commend their way of life to Gentiles (i.e., "words of wisdom," a halakah based on the law).

(ii) Neither scholar gives an analysis of gnosis. There are a series of indications that some of the opposition were visionaries and that they gained their gnosis in their visions. The visions that justified aberrant moral behavior may well have been as shocking to other Jewish Christians as to Paul.

(iii) Contemporary Judaism experienced the tension between two authorities, that of torah and that of the visionary, and took defensive measures against the latter, with its deviant doctrine and praxis. Paul faces both these claims to authority in Corinth, of "wisdom" and of "knowledge," buttressed in some cases by the stance of well-to-do and influential church members. Lütgert was right to see both ascetic and deviant movements among the Corinthian pneumatics, but the "knowledge" inspiring the latter is a long way from Paul's thinking.

(iv) Baur explained the slogan "of Christ" as a Petrine claim to have known Christ in the flesh; Lütgert, as a symbol of independence from any human missionary. Neither is convincing. The title of the group arises from its Christology, which was of an Ebionite, possessionist kind; they reverenced the divine Christ, not a human Jesus.

(v) The references in both letters to "examining" Paul, and depreciating his claim to apostolicity, are most easily understood as the attempt of a Cephas party to destroy his credibility. So Baur was right to see Paul and Apollos as allies and those "of Christ" as overlapping the Cephas party. In this respect we have the same lineup as in Galatians, Paul versus the followers of (James and) Peter,[33] although the issue of the law has not yet reached its crisis. Many of the texts in the two letters to which Baur appeals justify his exegesis rather than Lütgert's.

In the following chapters, I have, in an important measure, followed Baur's method against that of contemporary scholarship. To undertake a commentary today even on one of the Corinthian letters is liable to lead to a thousand pages, or perhaps four volumes; to attempt both epistles may seem rash. But Baur thought that a plausible exegesis could not be established on a narrow front: a persuasive picture must grow out of a consideration of the development of discussion over many decades in the church. He described the growth of Christian doctrine and practice: first over two centuries, and later over nineteen in his projected five-volume *Geschichte der christlichen Kirche*. Baur published the first volume in 1853. The remaining four volumes were put together from his notes in 1865–67 by his son, F. F. Baur. I have tried to follow him in this endeavor, to understand the two letters in their own right and to infer the opposition's stances against which Paul is writing. Second Corinthians was written only about a year after the First Letter, and I have been open to the possibility that it may have been written in the face of similar problems from a similar group of opponents. In a second work I hope to inquire whether the same questions recur in further documents of the NT and the Fathers. Sometimes it may be that totally new pressures arose, but the most plausible picture will include more development than fits and starts. Tertullian was right to say dismissively, "Apud Marcionem omnia fiunt subito" ("With Marcion everything happens suddenly").

So I am happy to have the ghost of Ferdinand Baur to preside over my studies. The criticisms of his historical work can be answered, and the attack on his philosophical presuppositions was misguided. He was a master spirit.

---

[33]Jesus entrusted the Jewish mission to Peter (Gal 2.7), but James, Jesus' brother, has taken over much of the authority in Gal 2.9, 12. Peter is the flag-carrier in 1 Corinthians also, with Jesus' brothers shadowy in the background at I,9.5.

CEPHAS IN 1 CORINTHIANS

THE STATUS QUAESTIONIS

BAUR THOUGHT that underlying the NT was a struggle between the Pauline and the Jerusalem churches, and the key evidence for this theory was Paul's insistent defense of his apostolicity. The attacks on it, reflected especially in the Corinthian letters, could best be explained as coming from the Jerusalem mission, and this seemed to be implied by references to Cephas in I,1.12 and 3.22. Baur saw the "slogans" of 1.12, "I am of Paul" and so forth, as coming from "parties," and he thought there were fundamentally only two parties at Corinth. Paul and Apollos were colleagues, and their converts were basically at one. The Cephas party claimed an authority that these two missionaries did not possess; Peter had been chosen by the historical Christ, and so his followers might also say, "I am of Christ." The same tension may be observed through most of I,1–4 and again in I,9, and at various points in 2 Corinthians, culminating in II,10–12. The numerous issues touched upon in the two letters are the matters on which the two parties divided.

Some of this outline has been maintained, especially in England,[1] and Vielhauer treats it sympathetically[2] while distancing himself from much of it. He would have broad support in saying the following: (i) Second Corinthians should not be treated with 1 Corinthians. Cephas is not named in the Second Letter, and it presents a new situation from the first; II,3.1 speaks of visiting evangelists with letters of commendation, and it is against these that II,10–12 polemicizes. Only by treating the two letters separately can one arrive at a position from which to inquire into the relations between the two. (ii) While the word *parties* may be too strong, it may be used for

---

[1]T. W. Manson, "The Corinthian Correspondence," in *Studies in the Gospels and Epistles: Essays in Memory of T. W. Manson* (ed. M. Black; Manchester: Manchester University Press, 1962), 190–207; C. K. Barrett, "Cephas and Corinth" and "Christianity at Corinth," in *Essays on Paul* (London: SPCK, 1982), 28–39, 1–27.

[2]P. Vielhauer, "Paulus und die Cephaspartei in Korinth," *NTS* 21 (1975): 341–52.

lack of another, and we should not minimize the σχίσματα and ἔριδες of the text, as Johannes Munck does.[3] They are Paul's initial topic in 1 Corinthians, and they take up much of I,1–4, even before the Corinthians' own letter is considered. But it is generally recognized that the significance that Baur gave to the parties was mistaken: there is no link with the Judaist countermission in Galatia. (iii) The various tensions in 1 Corinthians cannot all be ascribed to two parties. Paul addresses the Corinthians throughout as a unity and is opposed not to individual parties but to parties of any kind. When it comes to particular issues, he is often fighting on two fronts, not one: there are libertines in 6.12–19 and ascetics in ch. 7, and the "strong" and the "weak" in chs. 8 and 10. (iv) The Christ party remains a mystery. In Vielhauer's view, it never existed, and no one perhaps would support Baur's view of it today.

The consensus view that Vielhauer articulates does offer a necessary corrective to some of Baur's claims, especially those related to the identity of the Christ party. However, I would challenge this consensus on at least three points.

The Relation between 1 and 2 Corinthians.   While one must naturally be cautious in aligning the two Corinthian letters, Vielhauer exaggerates the danger in so doing. It may not be important that Cephas's name does not occur in 2 Corinthians. My daughter may write to me one week, "John Smith took me out to dinner," and the next week, "A lovely bunch of red roses appeared at the door today." I would be a poor interpreter if I did not infer that the roses were from Mr. Smith and that he had romantic aspirations. The two Corinthian letters are written to the same community at not much more than a year's interval, and it is more plausible that the same problems underlie both than that an entirely new group of troublemakers has arrived. We may not assume that the problems are the same, but we should inquire whether they seem to be.

The Presence of Parties at Corinth.   Prima facie, parties are what Paul is speaking of, even if he exaggerates their number. There are concerted attempts by a group with a different personal loyalty to depreciate Paul's position. Vielhauer thinks that those doing this are a party loyal to Cephas; if this were so, it is difficult to see how one can avoid the troublesome problem of their relation to the "Judaizers" of Galatians and Romans. Here again we should leave some questions for further discussion, as the last word has not been spoken on the law and circumcision in the different Pauline communities.

---

[3]J. Munck, *Paul and the Salvation of Mankind* (trans. F. Clarke; Richmond, Va.: John Knox, 1959).

The Identities of the Parties. Paul does not address particular groups at Corinth separately, and this has led many commentators to see the church as not beset by serious party divisions. Gordon Fee, for instance, denies that there were any parties and often speaks of "the Corinthians."[4] Not too much should be made of this, however. Paul normally addresses the church as a unity; but then, as any principal knows, this is the way to run a school. The principal knows the names of a few miscreants, and knows that there are a good number more. He or she understands that most of the school is innocent, but still speaks sharply to the united assembly. Then the guilty tremble at approaching justice, their friends fear lest they too be known, and the innocent stand smug but aware that future sins may be discovered. By being treated as a single community, everyone is edified, and there is a united will for a more virtuous future. If a humble principal knows this, how much more the apostle, whose foundation is in serious peril of fission or, worse, of being taken over by the misguided! Unity must be his watchword (I,1.10), and he wisely treats the church as a unity, so far as he may.

Moreover, it is not obvious that there are more than two effective parties, if we define *party* broadly. Any group is united by some issues and divided by others: the Conservative Party in Great Britain is united by a desire to resume power but divided over many practical policies. Mr. Major, the former prime minister, ran a moral crusade, Back to Basics, but his government was discredited in part by a series of sexual and financial scandals. The same may have been true of parties at Corinth, though a special feature there is that the deviant justified their behavior.

Scholars have dealt with the issue of the Corinthian parties in various ways. On the one hand, Johannes Munck effectively denied their existence. Munck argued that the σχίσματα were squabbles and bickering, to be distinguished from the factions (αἱρέσεις, I,11.19) that were to come as one sign of the end.[5] Thus, it is no great surprise that the divisions that critics had supposed in 1–4 disappear completely after 1–4. In addition, much has been made of the "Christ party," but it is quite unclear what the Christ party taught. Likewise, an Apollos party is widely supposed, largely on hints from Acts—Apollos was an Alexandrian and λόγιος—but the inference that he taught a Hellenistic wisdom gospel is a speculation. We may agree with Munck on the last point, but his main thrust seems misguided, for reasons to be elaborated in the chapters ahead.

Nils Dahl maintained a less drastic cut in the opposition: there were Paulines who said, "I am of Paul," and there were anti-Paulines who held a loyalty to other teachers, or just to Christ, as an objection to domination of

---

[4]G. D. Fee, *The First Epistle to the Corinthians* (NICNT; Grand Rapids: Eerdmans, 1987), 7–15 and passim.

[5]Munck, "The Church without Factions," in *Paul and Salvation*, 135–67.

the church by its human founder.[6] Dahl is right to see a dichotomy at Corinth, with Paulines on one side and anti-Paulines on the other, as I shall argue; but we can improve on his view of the Apollos and Christ groups.

A more common view of the issue of parties in Corinth has been that in I,1.10–17 Paul is opposing not factions but factionalism. It is true that Paul is decrying the quarrelsome spirit in the church, but there is clearly a faction or party that is "examining" him, "judging" him, not esteeming him as a servant of Christ or a steward of the mysteries of God (4.1–5), and that is generally dismissive of his standing as an apostle and his gospel of the cross. This is not just factionalism.

We may conclude then that there is no obviously cogent objection to Baur's theory. The evidence suggesting that he was right will be explored in the next two chapters.

A Petrine Opposition in 1 Corinthians

I,1.11–12.   Chloe's group gave Paul the impression that the whole church at Corinth (ἕκαστος) had divided into parties, primarily on the basis of the missionaries who had converted them. Neither they nor Paul can have seriously misrepresented the situation, because the Corinthians receiving the letter knew their church's situation.

Paul had founded the church, and Apollos had been an effective missionary after his departure (3.5–6; Acts 18.24–28). There is no adequate evidence for claims that Peter himself came to Corinth. He had been entrusted with the mission to the circumcised (Gal 2.8) and for fifteen years or so had limited his travels to Palestine; he was prompted to go to Antioch only after a visit to Jerusalem by Paul. Paul had founded many churches in Asia Minor and Greece, and we never hear of Peter's calling on any other of them. It is best, therefore, to think of the "Cephas party" in terms of a group of emissaries from Jerusalem, like the "false brethren" of Gal 2.4 or "those from James" of Gal 2.12. They might then appeal to Cephas's authority and cause divisions in the church. Despite Cephas's eminence, Paul mentions him only in the third place in 1.12, presumably because his mission was the third to come to Corinth. This is perhaps also implied by I,3.5, "I planted, Apollos watered." Luke says that Apollos had been influenced by Paul's friends Priscilla and Aquila, and his mention of Apollos's mission implies that he approved of it, as in line with Paul. Thus, we already have a first suggestion that the trouble did not start until the Petrine party arrived.

---

[6]N. Dahl, "Paul and the Church at Corinth according to 1 Corinthians 1–4," in *Christian History and Interpretation: Studies Presented to John Knox* (ed. W. R. Farmer et al.; Cambridge: Cambridge University Press, 1967), 313–35.

A visit by Cephas himself to Corinth was maintained by C. K. Barrett and is supported by Vielhauer.[7] But the evidence is not strong, and if Peter had been there in person, we might have expected a less kid-gloves response from Paul, as in Gal 2.

A fourth group is said to have maintained, "I am of Christ"; they are not likely to be the fruit of a fourth mission. I will argue in ch. 14 below that this is our first hint of a profound christological cleft between Paul and Jerusalem Christians. Jewish Christians later held that Christ was a heavenly power who entered Jesus at his baptism and left him before his crucifixion. In their view, Jesus was a sheerly human being, possessed like a prophet by divine power for a period, while Christ was the possessing spirit. Hence, only Christ was divine to them, and "I am of Christ" would be a challenge to any Pauline who thought that "Jesus is Lord." It is noteworthy that Paul has, in the first ten verses of the letter, used *Christ Jesus* three times and *Jesus Christ* five times, thereby stressing the unity of the single being. Moreover, the statement of 1.6, "as the witness of Christ was confirmed in you," shows that Paul spoke of Christ, too, before they came, though with a different meaning. He means to win them over if he can. Thus, "I belong to Christ" should be understood in this context as a defiant (and meaningful) statement made by members of the Cephas party.

I,1.13–17.   Because all Christians belong to Christ (3.23), the absurdity of a single group laying claim to his name draws the apostle's mockery. But he knows he will not win votes by sarcasm, so he turns the wit against himself: he was not crucified for his converts, nor were they baptized in his name. Of course, all Christians were baptized in the name of Jesus Christ (Acts 2.38; 8.16; 10.48), but Paul's stress on the small number he baptized suggests that it was important in Corinth to have been baptized by the right mission. How, then, could this come about?

Luke says that Paul spent eighteen months at Corinth (Acts 18.11), but his accounts of Paul's missions in Galatia and Macedonia suggest extensive evangelical mobility. Paul himself addresses 1 Corinthians to the church at Corinth "with all who call on the name of the Lord Jesus Christ in every place" (1.2), and 2 Corinthians to the same "with all the saints who are in the whole of Achaia" (1.1). Both of the two supplementary phrases probably imply the same public, a penumbra of Achaean churches in Cenchreae, Patras, Thebes, and so forth. In Rom 15.19 Paul says he fulfilled the gospel of Christ as far as Illyricum, which implies a mission at least as far as the region of Nicopolis, as was inferred by Titus 3.12. Paul, then, was often away from Corinth on Saturday nights. His calling was to evangelize; Timothy or Aquila or someone else could do the baptisms.

---

[7]Barrett, "Cephas and Corinth"; Vielhauer, "Paulus."

The NT draws a distinction between the baptism of John and Christian baptism, although the evangelists have some problem explaining the difference, and Luke says that Apollos himself knew only the baptism of John until Priscilla and Aquila took him in hand (Acts 18.25). But the issue in I,1 can hardly be that Apollos's baptism is inferior. The point alleged throughout the letter is, rather, that *Paul* is not a proper apostle, and in any case Apollos is quite sound on baptism by the time he has left Ephesus. We would, however, have a plausible scenario if the Cephas converts were told, "You will be receiving the authentic *apostolic* baptism, authorized by Cephas, not like these half-Christians baptized by Paul and Apollos." We would thus have a link with the party divisions of 1.12 and an explanation for Paul's distancing himself from the baptismal act. The last thing that the efficacy of baptism depended on was the person baptizing, but the phrase "the baptism of John" shows that different baptisms were around, and it might be significant who authorized one's baptism. We would also be in first touch with a pervasive theme of both letters, the attempt by another group to depreciate Paul as not being a true apostle.

I,3.4–17. With 1.17 Paul turns to the substantive difference between the two "gospels," his own gospel of the cross and his opponents' "wisdom of a word"/"taught words of human wisdom." This topic will occupy ch. 4, below, but it is useful to note that Paul makes no attempt to engage with three other "gospels" advocated by the three apparent parties (or even two, if we omit the Christ party). We have the impression that he is up against a single opposition. Nor can it be said that the parties of 1.12 have been forgotten, for, when the wisdom issue is settled (for the moment), Paul returns, in his characteristic way, to what led up to it: "For when one says, 'I belong to Paul,' and another, 'I belong to Apollos,' are you not merely human?" (3.4). Their quarrels show that all the talk of being spiritual is vapid.

Paul goes tactfully about his problem. Apollos had been schooled by his friends in Ephesus (Acts 18.26–27), and Paul was sufficiently at one with him that he could "strongly urge him" to go to Corinth and settle things (I,16.12); in short, there would have been no trouble between the two of them. The account of their relations in 3.5–9 is therefore straightforward. Paul had founded the church, so he had "planted"; Apollos had followed and expanded the church, so he had "watered." They had been colleagues, working on "God's field, God's building" (3.9).

Paul does not mind the field as an image for the church, though he prefers the body. More tricky is the building/temple image; the Jerusalem apostles used it, speaking of themselves as "pillars" (Gal 2.9), and it is not long before they are "foundations" (Eph 2.20). Paul wants to leave no doubt that the foundation he has laid is Jesus Christ (I,3.11), and in 3.11–17 he takes on a more menacing tone. He laid the foundation, and "someone else is building on it." "If anyone builds on" it, the quality of that person's work will become plain on judgment day. It will be tested with fire, and if it burns, the builder will lose out (ζημιωθήσεται, 3.15). Granted, the builder will be saved, but only as through fire. And even more threateningly: "If anyone destroys God's temple, God will destroy that man" (3.17).

The temple image is used for the church only twice in the accepted Pauline Epistles, here and at II,6.16, again a controversial passage that may reflect opposition teaching. This raises the question whether Paul may have avoided it because it suggests the position held by his opponents. As mentioned, they called themselves pillars, and I,3.11 could imply that they spoke of Peter as the foundation: "other foundation can no one lay than that which is set, which is Jesus Christ." How could any missionary, one might ask, think of a different foundation? But Simon was already called Cephas when Paul was taught the central gospel tradition ("he appeared to Cephas," I,15.5) and when he visited Jerusalem in the middle 30s (Gal 1.18). Furthermore, the church was unlikely to have made Jesus' name for Simon into his name of reference unless it was felt to be a positive theological symbol. It is difficult to think that it was understood to mean anything other than what Matthew thought it meant—"upon this rock I will build my church" (Matt 16.18)—even if the formulation is clearly Matthew's own. It is, then, only too plausible that a group that said, "I am of Cephas," that stressed the importance of a particular baptism, and that boasted of human leaders (3.21) would also have claimed that Peter was the foundation of the church.[8]

Who, then, is this "someone else" of whom Paul is speaking? It is not him, and it is not Apollos; the suggestion must be that it is the leader of the Cephas group. It is not at all likely that Peter was still in Corinth, if he had ever been there; nor would Paul be keen to threaten Peter, the leading apostle, with fire or destruction. But his party is there, and this is what is causing the trouble. Apollos built on Paul's foundation, but with durable materials—gold, silver, precious stones, so to speak, like Solomon of old[9]—

---

[8]So Barrett, "Cephas and Corinth." The conclusion is disputed by W. Schrage, *Der erster Brief an die Korinther* (3 vols. to date; EKKNT 7; Zürich/Neukirchen-Vluyn: Benziger/Neukirchener Verlag, 1991–), 1:295; G. Sellin, "Hauptprobleme des ersten Korintherbriefes," *ANRW* 25.4:2940–3044, here 3013; and all who dispute a Petrine opposition. Schrage appeals to Peter Lampe's brilliant article, "Das Spiel mit der Petrus-Namen—Matt. XVI.18," *NTS* 25 (1979): 227–45, which argues that *Cephas* originally meant a stone, not a rock, and that the Matthean logion was produced in the Greek church in Antioch years later. But this leaves open at what point the name was *understood* to mean a rock. Sellin's comment that Paul uses θεμέλιος and not πέτρα is not to the point: Paul needs to say that Jesus Christ was the *foundation*, not just the *rock/stone*.

[9]Gold, silver, and (precious) stones are mentioned in 1 Chron 22.14, 16; 29.2; 2 Chron 3.6. Haggai foresaw the new temple as made with gold and silver (2.8), and Isa 54.11–12 prophesied jewels for the walls of the city (cf. Fee). Schrage, on the other hand, sees the point of the materials in their durability. As building materials, however, gold and silver do not resist fire well, even if it is used to purify them.

and he will receive a reward (3.14). It is the promoter of the Cephas group who is building with combustibles—wood, hay, straw—and his work is worthless. Worse, he may even wreck the Corinthian church and destroy it; and if that happens, by God, he will answer for it.

I,3.18–23. This impression is confirmed in the following paragraph. The opposition is still linked with the wisdom gospel: "if anyone among you seems to be wise in this age . . ." (3.18). God exposes the vanity of such wise people, "so let no one boast in men." Paul rounds the passage off with a rhetorical flourish: "For all things are yours, whether Paul or Apollos or Cephas, or the world or life or death." Grandiloquent verbiage of this kind is not an accident. It is a smokescreen to hide the dangerous chasm that has opened up within the church. One of the groups at Corinth has been "boasting in men" (μηδεὶς καυχάσθω ἐν ἀνθρώποις), and Paul hastens to affirm that all the leaders belong equally to the whole church, and so belong to Christ, and so to God. Which group, then, has most to boast about "in men"? Paul and Apollos were discounted; they were not reckoned to be genuine apostles. But "I belong to Cephas" means something: "I was baptized as a member of the full apostolic church that Jesus committed to Peter and the Jerusalem apostles; these Paulines and Apollonians have no proper authorization from Jerusalem at all. Their teaching is different from the Petrine gospel: they never talk about words of wisdom."

We may notice here what Vielhauer has called "an eloquent silence."[10] If Paul were on as good terms with Peter as he says he is with Apollos, why does he not say so? Peter was a far more significant "fellow worker" than Apollos, and any tensions with a Cephas party could be immediately relaxed if Paul wrote, "I planted, [those of] Cephas watered." The obvious reason for his not so writing is that he did not see Peter as a fellow builder; on the contrary, the Cephas mission was a menace.

I,4.1–7. As so often, Paul approaches a difficult situation with tact and circumlocution but returns later to make the matter plain. He and his fellow missionaries should all alike be treated as "servants of Christ and stewards of the mysteries of God," but what has really been happening is that he has been "examined by you" (ὑφ' ὑμῶν ἀνακριθῶ, 4.3) and in fact judged by them, too ("judge nothing before the time, till the Lord comes," 4.5). The underlying situation becomes clear with 4.6–7: "These matters, brothers, I have transformed (μετεσχημάτισα) on to myself and Apollos for your sake (δι' ὑμᾶς) so that none of you will be puffed up for the one against the other (ἵνα μὴ εἷς ὑπὲρ τοῦ ἑνὸς φυσιοῦσθε κατὰ τοῦ ἑτέρου). For who distinguishes you? (τίς γάρ σε διακρίνει;) And if you received it too, why do you boast as if you did not receive it?"

---

[10]Vielhauer, "Paulus," 346–47.

"These matters" are the tensions between the missions, which have occupied the apostle hitherto. μετασχηματίζειν is a verb Paul uses four times
elsewhere, with the meaning "to change the form [of something]" (μετα–,
σχημα–). Three times in II,11.13–15 he speaks of other, false apostles, servants of Satan, "transforming" themselves, like their master, into apostles of
Christ or angels of light. In Phil 3.21 Christ will "transform" our lowly body
to be "of like form" with his glorious body. So here Paul has "transformed"
the discussion, which was really about another relationship, on to himself
and Apollos. He did this for pastoral reasons: "for your sake, brothers." Paul
was avoiding confrontation with the "someone else," which would have
made matters worse. Paul was an intelligent man. His enemies called him a
clever bastard (πανοῦργος δόλῳ, II,12.16); he preferred the term "wise master builder" (I,3.10).

Not only is μετασχηματίζειν always used by Paul elsewhere to mean
"transform"; it is never found in any Greek text with the meaning "apply" or
"treat metaphorically," according to David R. Hall, who documents this
with citations from Philo, Plutarch, Josephus, and 4 Maccabees.[11] Such
translations are often given, and the standard apologetic is to say that "transform" yields no sense and to appeal to LSJ for a meaning, "to transfer as in a
figure" (so, e.g., B. Fiore);[12] but I,4.6 is the only passage cited for this meaning, so the appeal is circular.

J. S. Vos produces a small number of passages to justify the meaning
"exemplify, apply the general to the specific."[13] Cyril of Alexandria cites the
psalmist's ἐπὶ τῷ κυρίῳ . . . πέποιθα and says that he is transferring
(μετασχηματίσας) the saying "on to us" (ἐφ᾽ ἡμᾶς), that is, applying the lesson to us. Origen says that Paul is here transforming, that is, applying, what
is valid for all generations on to Paul and Apollos. Vos limits the context to
I,3.5–4.5 and takes Paul to be applying or exemplifying what he holds about
all the apostles to Paul and Apollos. Such an interpretation must seem surprising if the context is broadened to include the quarrels of 1.10–17, and
particularly the final clause at the end of 4.6, to which Vos does not refer;
even the hostile tone over the τίς and ἄλλος in ch. 3 is difficult to fit in. The
weakened meaning of μετασχηματίζειν in Vos's texts does constitute an

---

[11]D. R. Hall, "A Disguise for the Wise: ΜΕΤΑΣΧΗΜΑΤΙΣΜΟΣ in 1 Corinthians 4.6," *NTS* 40 (1994): 143–49. Hall argues in favor of Chrysostom's view: there
were groups of dissident anonymous teachers at Corinth but not related to the leaders mentioned in 1.12, who are a fiction; Paul was transforming the attack on them
on to himself and Apollos. Chrysostom was not so far out there; it was just the idea
of tension between Paul and Cephas that his church dismissed as incredible, but this
seems all too believable today.
[12]B. Fiore, "'Covert Allusion' in 1 Corinthians 1–4," *CBQ* 47 (1985): 85–102,
here 89.
[13]J. S. Vos, "Der ΜΕΤΑΣΧΗΜΑΤΙΣΜΟΣ in 1 Kor 4,6," *ZNW* 86 (1995):
154–72.

exception to Hall's generalization, but the overall context in chs. 1–4, as well as the Pauline parallels, requires "transformed" at 4.6.

The apostle has written as if the issue were between him and Apollos, and his motive for so doing was in part related to the content of the gospel, "that you may learn by us the principle, Not beyond what is written" (we will consider this revealing clause in ch. 4 below). But there is a secondary motive too: "so that you will not be puffed up for the one against the other." The contrasted phrases, ὁ εἷς . . . ὁ ἕτερος, always refer to two parties. "A creditor had two debtors: ὁ εἷς owed him fifty dinars, ὁ δὲ ἕτερος five hundred" (Luke 7.41); "No worker can serve two masters: for either he will hate τὸν ἕνα and love τὸν ἕτερον" (Luke 16.13); "Two men went up to the temple to pray, ὁ εἷς a Pharisee and ὁ ἕτερος a publican" (Luke 18.10); "Paul, realizing that τὸ ἓν μέρος were of Sadducees, τὸ δὲ ἕτερον of Pharisees . . ." (Acts 23.6). Here, then, there are two leaderships, and Paul is trying to stop their supporters being "puffed up for the one against the other." He does not want anyone to be puffed up for him, of course, but the real danger is the Petrines. They were in a position to depreciate Paul and Apollos as not having been sent by the Lord (in the obvious sense of in his lifetime); they belonged to the true church, whose foundation stone was Cephas, as the Lord gave him the name.

The same point comes out in 4.7: "For who is it that distinguishes you?" The Petrines appeal to a person ("who"), Cephas, as setting them apart from other, lesser breeds, and they "boast" (καυχᾶσαι) about him. But actually they are in the same position as every other Christian—they "received" the gospel as the whole church had, so a little humility and gratitude would be appropriate. In fact, many of them, as 4.8–13 testifies, have gone over the top, and in 4.19 they "are puffed up" as if Paul were not coming.

Who is being referred to in the shadowy discussion of 1.10–4.7 is a crucial question, and it creates the first major exegetical division. Broadly, four positions are in contention: (i) The opposition might be the party of Cephas. This was Baur's proposal, and it is defended by Barrett in his 1971 commentary and other writings.[14] I have followed this position above. (ii) They might be the party of Apollos. This also has a long history, and it is supported by Fee.[15] (iii) They might be extremist followers of Paul himself. This was suggested persuasively by Lütgert in *Freiheitspredikt,* arguing that the "pneumatics" had carried to the point of antinomianism Paul's preaching of freedom from the law; they claimed to belong to Christ. (iv) They

---

[14]C. K. Barrett, *A Commentary on the First Epistle to the Corinthians* (2d ed.; BNTC; London: Black, 1971).

[15]Fee, *First Corinthians.* For a list of supporters of Apollos as the opposition leader, see Sellin, "Hauptprobleme," *ANRW* 25.4:3014–15 n. 381; they include R. Bultmann, E. Käsemann, H. Köster, B. A. Pearson, R. A. Horsley, and Sellin himself.

might be wisdom enthusiasts without personal loyalties. This is the position of Wolfgang Schrage.[16]

A few comments may be made on these points:

(i) Baur thought that Peter and James were the more moderate leaders of a Judaizing movement and that their followers pressed the circumcision issue and other matters in Galatia, while a less radical group was active in the Corinthian mission. Many critics, including Lütgert, have objected that there is no sign at all in the Corinthian letters of a pressure to Judaize and that the attitude to circumcision is amazingly relaxed (I,7.18–20). This criticism is not, in fact, justified and will be reviewed in ch. 4 below.

(ii) Apollos has been an attractive candidate as leader of the Corinthian opposition for several reasons. First, Luke says he came from Alexandria (Acts 18.24), and Alexandria was the birthplace of the Wisdom of Solomon and the home of Philo, another Jew learned in the Scriptures and with a great enthusiasm for Wisdom, σοφία.[17] Paul says that Greeks seek wisdom (I,1.22), so a link is at hand between Apollos in 1.12 and the debate over wisdom in 1.17–2.13. Second, Apollos is said by Luke to have been λόγιος, usually translated "eloquent" (Acts 18.24). In a revealing passage in II,10.10, Paul mentions his adversaries' view that his speech (λόγος) was contemptible. We have, then, a plausible contrast between the rhetorical power of Apollos and the stumbling speeches of Paul. Finally, Fee finds confirmation in the long Paul-Apollos passage in I,3.4–4.7: Paul is representing his relations with Apollos as if they were fellow laborers on God's farm and temple, but in fact they were rivals in the eyes of their followers. Fee correctly insists that ὁ εἷς . . . ὁ ἕτερος implies only two parties (Paul's and Apollos's, in his view), and he saves his theory by rendering μετεσχημάτισα "I applied," a rendering also given by the NRSV and other theory-serving versions.

Apollos is, however, excluded by other considerations in addition to μετεσχημάτισα. In I,16.12 Paul says that he often encouraged Apollos to visit Corinth but that it was not God's will for him to come yet.[18] Not only does this show that the two missionaries were in regular and intimate contact; more important still, it shows that Paul had every confidence that their gospel was the same. If I may draw a parallel with a lesser issue, I am fortunate enough to count as my friends two of the leading British advocates of the Q hypothesis. But I would be extremely cautious of ever encouraging ei-

---

[16]Schrage, *Der erste Brief.*

[17]R. A. Horsley, in a series of articles and in *I Corinthians* (ANTC; Nashville: Abingdon, 1998), especially urges a connection with Philo's use of σοφία. But it should be noted that (i) while wisdom is the center of discussion in I,1.17–2.16, it disappears from view almost entirely through the rest of the epistle, and (ii) the phrasing in 1 Corinthians, "the wisdom of a word," "words of wisdom" do not suggest appeal to a divine figure, Wisdom.

[18]See above, p. 4 n. 7, and below, p. 31 (Rom 2.18).

ther of them to visit classes to which I have taught a better solution to the Synoptic Problem. Paul's willingness to encourage (even to beseech) Apollos to visit Corinth shows that they were on the same side of the fence. There is similar force to Luke's account in Acts 18. Luke was looking back on a church that he knew quite well and telling the story of Paul's successful mission there. He knew whether Paul and Apollos were colleagues, and he carefully hides any tensions between them by passing over them in silence; if he says that Apollos continued Paul's mission, then it was so.

The points about Alexandria and about Apollos's eloquence are weak. Many other Jews lived in Alexandria besides Philo, and the wisdom gospel in fact refers to something quite different (see ch. 4 below). The word λόγιος may mean "learned" as well as "eloquent," and in any case, if Paul's addresses were pathetic, many speakers might put him in the shade, not only Apollos.

(iii–iv) Both Lütgert and Schrage present good cases for getting away from the other two leaders named in 1.12 (i.e., Cephas and Apollos): Lütgert aligning the practices of the pneumatics with Paul's own objections to the law, Schrage emphasizing the repeated ἕκαστος (3.5, 8, 10, 13 [2x]). But the same four arguments count against both proposals:

(a) First Corinthians 4.6 says clearly that Paul's representation of the Corinthian rivalries had been in terms of himself and Apollos but that this was a "transforming" of the reality. His aim in doing this had been to put a stop to people being puffed up "for the one against the other." It is thus evident that there are two real factions in the church, of which one is Paul's and the other is not Apollos's. This excludes a general rivalrous spirit as the enemy, and it excludes a concentration on the wisdom or other doctrine as the sole issue. Paul is thinking of loyalty to one of two leaderships.

(b) The competing leaderships cannot be Paul's and Christ's because 3.21 says, "Let no one boast in men," and the point of claiming to be "of Christ" was that one got away from human beings and belonged to a divine figure. Critics often underestimate the force of Paul's καυχᾶσθαι, φυσιοῦσθαι, referring to such comments as "I belong to Paul" in 1.12 as examples of "boasting." Again a lowly modern analogy may be of assistance. Across Europe today, and perhaps the world, young people support their local soccer club. The closest thing in Birmingham, England, to "I belong to Paul" is "I support [Aston] Villa," the main Birmingham team, although others may say, "I support [Birmingham] City," another team, which loses every week. Now, no one could say that such supporters "boasted" of Villa or City (still less that they were "puffed up" on its account). But two of my grandsons do boast (and are slightly puffed up) in their support for Manchester United, the leading national team, which occasionally wins a game in Europe. We are looking for a second focus of loyalty in Corinth besides Paul and Apollos,

someone who could evoke boasting and being puffed up in his supporters
(3.21; 4.6, 7, 19), who was viewed as more than a mere διάκονος through
whom they came to faith (3.5), more than a ὑπηρέτης and οἰκονόμος of
God's mysteries (4.1), but distinguished from the lesser missionaries (4.7).
There is only one candidate who fulfills all these demands: Cephas.

(c) A similar conclusion follows from the verses on baptism in 1.13–17. The
mention of the four "parties" in 1.12 leads on immediately to discussion of
the surprising question, "Who baptized you?" which sounds very close to
4.7, "Who distinguishes you?" Paul is quick to push aside any claim that his
baptism was at all special, and it is difficult to think of anyone else whose
name might make his baptism particularly desirable, with one exception—
Cephas. The Petrine leaders were in a position to say, "If you were baptized
by us, you really are members of the apostolic church, founded by Christ,
with Peter as its accredited leader [and perhaps its foundation stone]." This
was a sacrament that penetrated where other baptisms could not follow.

(d) This would also be in line with the lapse into anonymity in 3.10–17. First
Corinthians 4.6 makes it clear that Paul saw himself and Apollos as proper
colleagues preaching the same gospel. Thus, the watering/building passage
in 3.5–12 was meant straightforwardly: Paul had laid the foundation, and
Apollos had built on it with durable materials and would receive his reward.
But the ἄλλος, the τίς who builds rubbish on the foundation must, then, be
the leader of a third faction, referred to in 4.6 as ὑπὲρ τοῦ ἑνός, in the name
of neither Paul nor Apollos. The obvious candidate again is Cephas.

We may ask why sensible and honest critics such as Fee and Schrage
would have missed so simple a solution, and the question is particularly
acute over μετεσχημάτισα, for which there are four Pauline parallels for the
meaning "transform" and no parallel in all Greek literature for their rendering, "apply a figure, metaphor," and so forth. The reason is evident: they are
convinced that Baur was wrong. It cannot be Cephas, because that would
imply a Judaizing movement as in Galatians, of which there is no sign in
1 Corinthians. The apparent difference between these two epistles on the
law is a problem to which I turn in ch. 4 below; but we may note that both
Fee and Schrage find difficulty with the other, and crucial, clause in 4.6,
"that you may learn by us the principle, Not beyond what is written." Hans
Conzelmann's comments on 4.6 are a tribute to his honesty: "The phrase τὸ
μὴ ὑπὲρ ἃ γέγραπται is unintelligible. Those who do not decide to delete it
as a gloss do not get beyond guesswork. . . . The second ἵνα-clause . . . is likewise difficult to fathom."[19] Those who do not decide to delete the parts of
the NT text that they find problematic may be glad to find an alternative
exegesis.

---

[19]H. Conzelmann, *1 Corinthians* (trans. J. W. Leitch; ed. G. W. MacRae;
Hermeneia; Philadelphia: Fortress, 1975), 86.

I,9.1-12. It is only incidentally that Paul returns to the sore subject of his opponents in I,9. Chapter 8 has been concerned with the issue of idol meat, and he urges those with "knowledge" to forgo any rights they have lest they cause a fellow believer to stumble. Paul himself is an apostle with the freedom to do many things (9.1), including eating and drinking at the church's expense (9.4), but he does not make use of this privilege (9.13, 15). As soon as he begins to expound this apt example, however, the annoying thought occurs to him that some members of the Corinthian church dispute his having this right at all, since he is not (to them) a proper apostle.

This is fretting, for, "if to others I am not an apostle, at least I am to you [having founded your church]." This then leads into a "defense against those who examine me [ἀνακρίνουσιν, as at 4.3]." Of course, Paul has the right to live at the charge of the local Christian community and, for that matter, the right to take a Christian wife around with him at church expense. Soldiers and farm workers do not expect to pay for their own food, and the Bible establishes the same principle even for oxen treading out the corn. Paul has sown spiritual seed at Corinth, and it is a small return to ask for his physical needs free.

Who, then, are "those who examine me"? We have a series of hints. Paul uses the first person plural in 9.4-6—ἔχομεν three times—and the third time he specifies, "I and Barnabas." As Barnabas has had no part in the Corinthian mission so far as we know, his inclusion is surprising. The reason is suggested by the contrast in 9.5 with those who do take their wives on mission with them: "the other apostles and the brothers of the Lord and Cephas." These are the leaders of the Jewish mission: the other apostles (other than "us"); Jesus' brothers, James and Jude and so on, in Jerusalem; and (above all) Cephas. The thought goes back to the scene in Gal 2.1-10, when Paul and Barnabas went up to Jerusalem and parleyed with James and Cephas and John. They were accepted then as apostles, as having the ἀποστολή of the uncircumcision entrusted to them by God—"they gave me and Barnabas the right hand of fellowship." Barnabas is in Paul's mind from the first ἔχομεν in 9.4, on the subject of their expenses, but this leads on to the more questionable (and perhaps resented) Jerusalem claim that wives were included, too, for Paul and Barnabas were the only well-known bachelors. Paul concedes this claim without hesitation but demands the lesser, personal, expense as his privilege if he wishes to use it.

There is a second surprise in the mention of Cephas at the end of 9.5, for he was already included surely in "the other apostles." We have the same locution, curiously, at Mark 16.7: "Go tell his disciples and Peter." Peter certainly was one of "the disciples," but he is mentioned specifically because of his disgrace in Mark 14. The force of the wording is, "and especially Peter," and so it is here. Paul's critics have been saying, "All apostles have the right to have their living expenses paid, and Jesus' brothers, too. When Peter goes around Palestine, he doesn't expect to have to do a day's fishing to pay for his supper. They pay for Mrs. Peter, too, and the other missionary wives. You notice the difference with this Paul." Such a background, in line with the tensions of 1.10–4.7, gives good sense to "and Cephas."

Paul ends his "defense" by saying, "If others share in the claim on you (τῆς ὑμῶν ἐξουσίας μετέχουσιν), do not we more?" (9.12). The "others" must be included in the "other apostles" referred to in 9.5, but they seem to be actually, currently, drawing on the Corinthian fund; they would not, then, be the Jerusalem grandees. Paul spoke of Andronicus and Junia as apostles (Rom 16.7) and of the opposition leaders in II,10–12 as false apostles, so it is likely that the predecessors of the latter group were accepted as apostles at the time of 1 Corinthians. Their criticisms of Paul, such as in 4.1–5, and their association with Cephas in 9.5 make it likely that they are the leaders of the Cephas party.

Schrage reads ch. 9 as a straight example of the renunciation of rights for the furtherance of the gospel; he sees little polemic in 9.3–12 and nothing significant in the mention of Cephas at 9.5.[20] This seems improbable in face of the echo of 4.3 and the strong arguments for a Paul-Cephas rivalry in 1.10–4.7, and it does take Paul a long time to get from his apostolic rights in 9.4 to his renunciation of them in 9.13, 15. Even Fee, who thinks the opposition are disciples of Apollos, takes the mention of Cephas to be emphatic at 9.5 and to imply a contrast with him.[21]

I,10.1–13; 11.17–34. With 10.1–13 Paul returns to exaggerated valuations of baptism, and these recall the discussion of 1.13–17 even if we cannot be certain that the people involved are the same. He wants to stress that baptism does not work magically, *ex opere operato,* so that a Christian is saved no matter how much idolatry he or she has committed: "For I do not want you to be ignorant, brothers, that all our fathers were under the cloud, and they all passed through the sea, and they were all baptized to Moses in the cloud and the sea . . . but with most of them God was not well pleased" (10.1–5). Large numbers of those who experienced the "baptism to Moses" of Exod 14 later perished in the wilderness; their baptism was not an automatic passport to heaven. "So let him who thinks he is standing take heed lest he fall" (10.12). The Christians who so confidently eat idol meat should not suppose that they can get away with it by virtue of having been baptized.

The superstitious view of baptism is extended to the Eucharist. "They all ate of the same spiritual food [the manna], and they all drank the same spiritual drink [the water from the rock]," but the same plagues, serpents, and destroying angels killed them nonetheless. "These things occurred as examples for us" (10.6): we are not to suppose that our spiritual food and drink, the bread and wine of the Eucharist, will protect us if we sin.

---

[20]Schrage, *Der erster Brief,* 2:278–306.
[21]Fee, *First Corinthians,* 404.

The eucharistic scandals of 11.17–34 increase our suspicion that this false theology of the sacraments is in line with the false stress on baptism in 1.13–17. For here again Paul "hears" of σχίσματα in church (as in 1.10), and the attitude he finds so scandalous is one that claims to be "eating the Lord's Supper," but in fact it is nothing of the kind (11.20). Petrine converts think they are the only real Christians because they alone have the apostolic baptism. Some of them are well-to-do people, and they and their hangers-on arrive in good time and set about consuming the common table of food and wine ("For each goes ahead with his own supper"). This is not the κυριακὸν δεῖπνον but rather τὸ ἴδιον δεῖπνον. The result is greed and drunkenness on the one side, and no food for the indigent latecomers on the other. The former "despise God's church and put the poor to shame." Paul goes on to remind them that the Eucharist was a serious institution in recollection of the Lord's death, and each celebration looks forward "until he comes" in judgment. Unworthy participation, with neglect of poor fellow Christians, involves "eating and drinking judgment" to oneself.

I,15.1–11. When Paul arrives at the issue of resurrection, he appeals to Peter and James for support. He had "received" the church's core creed at his conversion, and Jesus' resurrection had been part of it, testified by a whole series of Jerusalem eyewitnesses: Cephas, the Twelve, five hundred brothers, James, all the apostles. In this matter at least, their message and Paul's had been the same: "So whether I or they, so we proclaim, and so you believed."

Paul has to live with a double bind. He cannot deny the authority of Jerusalem, which prudently uses the name of Cephas, even though James may often be the man behind the man behind the gun. So Paul uses it when he can, as in I,15.1–11, bolstering his position on a physical resurrection, and he depreciates it ("God accepts no man's face," Gal 2.6) when he cannot use it. On the other hand, he cannot allow Petrine supporters to undermine his own apostolic authority; hence the constant return to this cardinal issue in the two letters.

I,16.12. "Now about (περὶ δέ) our brother Apollos" suggests that, like other περὶ δέ openings (7.1, 25; 8.1; 12.1), the issue had been raised either in the Corinthians' letter or by word of mouth. With tensions so high in the church and the Petrine missionaries carrying so much before them, the only hope might seem to be a visit from the two founding apostles. This explains the constant references to intended forthcoming visits by Paul himself (I,4.19; 16.5–9; II,1.15–2.4; 12.14–13.4). Paul put pressure on (πολλὰ παρεκάλεσα) Apollos to go, along with "those of Chloe"; Paul and Apollos were "brothers," fellow workers for God, building on the same foundation, and Apollos could do much to stem the Petrine tide. But as with Paul at 4.19, Apollos was not free at present. It was "not [God's] will that he come now," but he would when he was free. No doubt a wide door for effective work was open to him as to Paul (16.9).

The Hebrew רָצוֹן on its own is used commonly in rabbinic literature for the will of God,[22] often in the phrases יְהִי רָצוֹן or יְהִי רָצוֹן לְפָנֶיךָ. Paul puts it into direct Greek as (τὸ) θέλημα both here and at Rom 2.18; cf. also Ign. *Eph.* 20.1; Ign. *Rom.* 1.1. Moving around from one mission field to another was a serious business (II,1.15–22), not to be undertaken without clear signs from heaven. Paul intends to visit Corinth soon ἐὰν ὁ κύριος θελήσῃ/ἐπιτρέψῃ (I,4.19/16.7). θέλημα is a common word in the NT, always with a genitive where human will is involved. If it were Apollos's will in this case (as in NRSV, Fee, etc.), the Greek required would be [τὸ] θέλημα αὐτοῦ. Cf. also Matt 18.14, οὐκ ἔστιν θέλημα ἔμπροσθεν τοῦ πατρὸς ὑμῶν.

---

[22]M. Jastrow, *A Dictionary of the Targumim, Talmud Babli, Yerushalmi, and the Midrashic Literature* (New York: Judaica, 1975), s.v.; G. Schrenk, "Θέλημα," *TDNT* 3:52–62.

⤳ 3 ⤶

CEPHAS IN 2 CORINTHIANS

THE NAMES Cephas and Peter do not occur in the Second Letter, but we seem to encounter a series of indications that emissaries of the Jerusalem apostolate lie behind the text.

THE EVIDENCE OF 2 CORINTHIANS

II,2.14–4.6. Opposition to Paul has hardened between 1 and 2 Corinthians, and the identity of his critics often seems obscure, but with II,3.1–6 comes a flicker of light. Describing God's triumphal procession (2.14–17), Paul comments, "Who is sufficient (ἱκανός) for these things?" (2.16). His mind moves at once to οἱ πολλοί, so different from himself, who water down (καπηλεύοντες) the gospel (2.17), certain people (τινές) who have come to Corinth with letters of commendation. These people have been accorded undue weight in Paul's view (3.1–3). The mention of the letters, and of the emissaries bearing them, was apparently triggered by the word ἱκανός, which Paul returns to with apostolic sarcasm in 3.4–6. The emissaries have confidence (πεποίθησιν) in their position and claim to be "sufficient" in some sense. Paul sees this word as a threat and adopts the same policy as in I,2.6 and elsewhere, of moving the discussion on to a more spiritual plane. "Not that we are sufficient of ourselves to claim anything as of ourselves, but our sufficiency is from God, who has made us sufficient (ἱκάνωσεν) as ministers of a new διαθήκη." These emissaries have only human sufficiency where Paul has divine sufficiency; theirs is a covenant of the letter, his of the Spirit; their ἱκανότης is from one another (ἀφ᾽ ἑαυτῶν, ἐξ ἑαυτῶν), like certain ones who commend themselves and measure themselves by one another in II,10.12.

What, then, lies behind the claim to be ἱκανοί? The word is used both before and after the reference to the letters in 3.1–3 and should be connected with them. Both adjective and verb are used in the papyri as legal terms meaning "authorized, to authorize": "I am writing this to you so that you may be authorized" (γέγραφά σοι ἵνα ἱκανὸς γένῃ); "so that if an account is required, you have been authorized until my arrival" (ἱκανωθῆναί σε) (P.Tebt. 1.37/20, MM 302b). So the letters of II,3.1–3 were not merely commendatory letters (συστατικῶν) as Paul depreciates them; they were authorizing letters, making their bearers plenipotentiaries. They gave them authority to act as might be necessary: λογίσασθαί τι, to give considered opinions—in other words, to make rulings for the church. It would be easiest to see such letters as coming from Jerusalem; this would certainly give their bearers confidence of a different kind from that which Paul enjoyed.

Paul says that God authorized "us" as διάκονοι of a new διαθήκη.[1] The overtone of both words is polemical. In II,11.23 he asks rhetorically, "Are they διάκονοι of Christ?" Part of the newcomers' claim, then, is that they are διάκονοι. The word had a wide use in ancient business for an agent; thus, the newcomers claim to be Christ's agents, authorized to act in his name. But Paul claims himself to be such an agent and to be administering a "new covenant"—the echo of Jer 31.31 rings clear. The newcomers are hanging on to the old covenant, with its dead letter. We are reminded inevitably of the "Judaizers" of Galatians, who came to insist on "the works of the law" as the means to justification; Paul preached justification "in Christ." The two theologies were like two διαθῆκαι, theirs corresponding to Mount Sinai and the present Jerusalem, and Paul's to the Jerusalem that is above (Gal 4.25–26).

Commentators give a rather unsatisfying account of the ἱκανός passage. Barrett follows Dieter Georgi in understanding the opponents as "priding themselves on their self-sufficiency," although he dissents from the suggestion that they saw themselves as θεῖοι ἄνδρες.[2] But if they only said that they were sufficient, we have no link with the letters in 3.1–3. Georgi and Hans Windisch find the transition at 2.16 abrupt, and indeed there are then further abrupt transitions at 3.4 and 3.7.[3] Abrupt transitions (and partition theories) are a sign that the critic has lost the thread of Paul's thought. The θλῖψις in ch. 1 and the troubles occasioning the "tearful letter" in ch. 2 are both consequences of the Petrine countermission (see ch. 16 below, pp. 233–35). It is the threat posed by these Jerusalem emissaries with their letters of authorization that is never far from Paul's mind as he writes.

---

[1] For διάκονος as a go-between or agent, see J. N. Collins, *Diakonia: Reinterpreting the Ancient Sources* (Oxford: Oxford University Press, 1990), 73–191; M. E. Thrall, *The Second Epistle to the Corinthians* (1 vol. to date; ICC; Edinburgh: T&T Clark, 1994–), 1:231.

[2] C. K. Barrett, *A Commentary on the Second Epistle to the Corinthians* (BNTC; London: Black, 1973), 102–3; D. Georgi, *Die Gegner des Paulus im 2. Korintherbrief* (WMANT 11; Neukirchen-Vluyn: Neukirchener Verlag, 1964), 220–25 (ET: *The Opponents of Paul in Second Corinthians* [Philadelphia: Fortress, 1986], 229–63).

[3] H. Windisch, *Der zweite Korintherbrief* (9th ed.; KEK; Göttingen: Vandenhoeck & Ruprecht, 1924), 108.

Victor Furnish is impressed by the use of ὁ ἱκανός for God on five occasions in the LXX and by Philo's use of the word for God; Paul would, then, be influenced by such thinking in Hellenistic Judaism, and we should have no need of opponents' claims to be sufficient.[4] Margaret Thrall is gently skeptical of this, while bypassing the case for a sustained reference to the opposition. But Furnish's view would then divorce the ἱκανός verses from their context on the letters of commendation and from the echoes (συνιστανόντων, ἑαυτοῖς ἑαυτούς, ἑαυτοὺς ἑαυτοῖς) in 10.12. Bultmann correctly sees these expressions as signs of Paul's opponents and renders λογίσασθαι with "make judgments, evaluate."[5]

II,5.11–16. The troubles and anxieties of II,1–2 were aggravated by the presence in Corinth of the emissaries of 3.1–6 with their letters of authorization, but the apostle is not going to be discouraged: οὐκ ἐγκακοῦμεν [4.1] . . . διὸ οὐκ ἐγκακοῦμεν [4.16] . . . θαρροῦντες οὖν πάντοτε [5.6]. Having dealt briefly with some of the points at issue, the law (3.7–4.6) and the resurrection (5.1–10), he returns to his relations with Corinth at 5.11. It is in awe of the Lord, before whom he must stand on judgment day (5.10), that he is trying to persuade them.

Paul is not trying to commend himself again (5.12), as people had been saying at 3.1, but to give them "an opportunity for boasting (καυχήματος) on our behalf, for you to have against those who boast of the surface (τοὺς ἐν προσώπῳ καυχωμένους) and not of the heart. For if we have been beside ourselves, it is to God; if we are rational (σωφρονοῦμεν), it is for you." Christ died and rose for us, "so from now on we know no one after the flesh (κατὰ σάρκα); if we have even known Christ after the flesh, yet now we know him so no more." Christ died to reconcile us to God, and Paul's rational persuading is the exercise of his calling as God's ambassador reconciling Christians.

The boasting theme takes us back to those who "boasted of men" in I,3.21, boasted of the mission that had converted them as something special (I,4.7), and were puffed up for the one leader, Cephas, against the other, Paul (I,4.6). Here the boasting is ἐν προσώπῳ, which recalls Gal 2.6, where the Jerusalem leaders claimed to be something, though "God does not accept man's πρόσωπον."[6] It is Paul's standard defense against Petrine claims. The Cephas party leaders said, "Jesus gave Cephas authority over the

---

[4]V. P. Furnish, *II Corinthians: A New Translation with Introduction and Commentary* (AB 32A; New York: Doubleday, 1984), 196–97.

[5]R. Bultmann, *The Second Letter to the Corinthians* (trans. R. A. Harrisville; Minneapolis: Augsburg, 1985), 75. To Baur (*Paul,* 281), it was plain that the letters must come from Jerusalem.

[6]Bultmann, *Second Letter,* 149, notes that the πρόσωπον/καρδία contrast goes back to the OT (1 Kgdms 16.7) and that Paul has used it before at 1 Thess 2.17.

church, and Cephas [and his Jerusalem colleagues] have given us authority to see that their policies are carried out in Corinth." Paul replies, "This is mere boasting in something merely superficial; I am just as much an apostle as they are. What matters is the Spirit, the quality of Christian life, 'the heart,' and 'I hope too' that my 'sincerity, as one sent from God and standing in his presence' [2.17], 'is well known to your consciences.' This will enable you to do a bit of counterboasting [5.12]."

The force of the individual sentences following can be understood only out of the larger context. Paul is going to offer a justification (συνιστάντες, II,6.4) of his ministry in II,6.4–10: it is a ministry built on the pattern of Christ's life, "dying, and behold, we live" (6.9; cf. 4.11, "always being given over to death through Jesus"; 11.23, "in deaths often"). All he can do is argue the case rationally (and eloquently), and the opposition naturally object to this as a game at which Paul can outplay them. They therefore accuse him of "persuading men" (ἀνθρώπους πείθομεν, 5.11). The same objection is in evidence at Gal 1.10: "For am I now 'persuading men' (ἀνθρώπους πείθω) or God? Or am I 'seeking to please men'? If I were still trying to please men, I should not have been a servant of Christ."

Paul first counters this by appeal to his sincerity, a life open alike to God and to his converts: "we do 'persuade men,' but we have made ourselves open to God (θεῷ δὲ πεφανερώμεθα), and I hope open to your consciences too." He is not commending himself but giving them a chance for a counterboast against the Petrines. He justifies this (γάρ) with 5.13: "For if we have been beside ourselves, it is to God; if we are sober, it is for you." The second clause follows the thrust of the paragraph. Objection has been made to Paul's reasoning arguments, his "persuading men"; the opposition showed their spiritual power not by human argument but by the Spirit in tongues and visions and signs. "I can go into ecstasy too," replies the apostle, "but when I do, it is not to show off to the church, but a private matter between me and God," as in I,14.2. But what matters is the building up of the church, and for this, rational normalcy is needed. εἴτε σωφρονοῦμεν, ὑμῖν is a concise form of the long appeal in I,14 for edification through the mind.

Naturally the Petrine missionaries argue too, and Paul now preempts their position. There are two rational approaches in the field, his and theirs. His depends on the majestic facts of the death and resurrection of Christ for humankind (5.14–15), and this requires a ministry of dying and yet living such as his own has been (6.4–10). It is not that he chose such a ministry; it was Christ's love for him that constrained him (5.14). Once matters have been raised to this pitch (ὥστε), knowledge we may have had on the earthly level (κατὰ σάρκα) is irrelevant. "If we [Christians] have even known Christ on the earthly level," that is all finished now (5.16). All talk about what Jesus said to Peter and who got chosen as an apostle in the Lord's lifetime is passé: "so if anyone is in Christ," there is a totally new, Gen 1 situation. "Old things" that took place in Galilee in the 20s "are passed away; lo, they have become new" (5.17).

Paul is indeed a wise master builder most of the time; he wants a united church, and he is not going to leave the discussion as an argument between two opposing positions. Once more he moves on to the higher ground: the matter is not about persuading or about rationality versus ecstasy; it is about "reconciliation." All these things come from God, "who reconciled us to himself and gave us the ministry of reconciliation" (5.18). The subtle apostle leaves the *us* ambiguous: the first *us* means Christians; the second in fact refers to Paul alone. But "reconciling" means that everyone is going to be a winner, preserving what is central in their belief. "God was in Christ reconciling the world to himself," and he has set ἐν ἡμῖν "the word of reconciliation" (5.19). So, as God's humble ambassador, Paul begs them, "Be reconciled to God." Who could resist so spiritual an appeal? It is just that the terms of reconciliation are the Pauline theology.

The passage is acknowledged to be among the most difficult in the NT, and any exegesis of it must be justified by its ability to follow a thread of argument that makes sense of the whole. Many scholars have correctly seen the force of individual phrases and sentences, but I have not found any, even Barrett, who has fully grasped the force of the apparently wandering text. Baur saw correctly that those who "knew Christ according to the flesh" were the Petrines.[7]

Bultmann noted that "persuading men" was an accusation by the Judaizers in Gal 1.10 and was likely to be the same here. Paul does not use πείθειν elsewhere but more friendly verbs, such as παρακαλεῖν. Furnish accepts this but is distracted by Hans-Dieter Betz's array of Greco-Roman evidence into seeing the accusation as the use of rhetoric. Thrall similarly thinks the criticism was of "unscrupulous" techniques. But Paul does not go on to insist on his simplicity ("not in persuasive words of human wisdom") but on his sobriety (σωφρονοῦμεν) and lack of public ecstatic experience (εἴτε . . . ἐξέστημεν, θεῷ). His opponents objected to his use of rational argument appealing to the mind instead of more impressive χαρίσματα. The link of II,5.13 with the charge ἀνθρώπους πείθομεν is made by Walter Schmithals, with the proper stress on rationality as the issue; his view that the opposition were gnostics has caused many of his insights to be undervalued.[8]

---

[7]Baur, *Paul*, 272–73.

[8]Bultmann, *Second Letter*, 148; Furnish, *II Corinthians*, 306; Thrall, *Second Epistle*, 1:402; W. Schmithals, *Die Gnose in Korinth: Eine Untersuchung zu den Korintherbriefen* (FRLANT 2.48; Göttingen: Vandenhoeck & Ruprecht, 1956), 153–58 (ET: *Gnosticism in Corinth: An Investigation of the Letters to the Corinthians* [Nashville: Abingdon, 1971], 153–58).

The connection of "boasting" ἐν προσώπῳ with Gal 2 is also made by Bultmann and by Windisch and is accepted by Barrett as a likely link with the presumption of the Jerusalem leadership. Barrett is less confident about taking 5.16–17 as a reference to Peter's knowledge of the human Jesus, which is maintained by Hans Lietzmann.[9] But "knowing Christ" κατὰ σάρκα is close to Rom 9.5, ἐξ ὧν ὁ Χριστὸς τὸ κατὰ σάρκα. The last two words are an adverbial phrase in both texts, and in II,5.16 they modify ἐγνώκαμεν: "if on the human level we have even known Christ." Paul does not mean (as has been occasionally and implausibly suggested) that he himself knew Christ in the 20s: the *we* is the Christian community, as in 1 John 1.1–4—the ἡμεῖς of II,5.16 corresponds with the εἴ τις ἐν Χριστῷ in 5.17. The εἰ καί indicates that only some of the Christian community have received this privilege—in fact, only Peter and any other surviving apostles in Jerusalem are meant. Again this exegesis commends itself because it follows Ariadne's thread through the labyrinth: those who claimed "to have known Christ after the flesh" are the same people who "boast in the surface" at 5.12 and object to Paul's "sober persuasion" (5.11, 13), that is, the Petrines. I do not think the apostle would have felt uncomfortable about the pejorative overtones of κατὰ σάρκα.

It is the lack of any clear development of thought that undercuts many suggestions. Thrall denies a link with the troublemakers of II,10–12 and connects 5.11–21 back to 3.1–18, which she sees as concerning non-Christian Jews boasting of the Mosaic covenant. But the letters of commendation were to (and from!) the church, and 5.18–20 is pressing for reconciliation in the church. She confesses that her exegesis of 5.16 makes problematic connections with 5.14–15 and 5.17.[10]

II,10.1–12.13.   With ch. 10 Paul takes up the pen (αὐτὸς δὲ ἐγὼ Παῦλος) and returns to the fight. He had been accused of planning κατὰ σάρκα in 1.17, and in 10.2 there are "certain people" who reckon that he walks κατὰ σάρκα. But this time the indirect allusions to the "certain people" that we have had hitherto are replaced with a full two and a half chapters of altercation. We learn the following things about them:

(i) They are Jewish and pride themselves on so being. "Are they Hebrews? So am I. Are they Israelites? So am I. Are they the seed of Abraham? So am I. Are they ministers of Christ?" (II,11.22–23). These phrases carry echoes from other contexts in the Pauline Epistles. In Rom 9.6–7 Paul explains

---

[9]Windisch, *Der zweite Korintherbrief,* 178; Barrett, *Second Epistle,* 166, 172; H. Lietzmann, *An die Korinther I, II* (5th ed.; supplemented by W. G. Kümmel; HNT 9; Tübingen: Mohr, 1969), 125.
[10]Thrall, *Second Epistle,* 1:405, 419.

that not all who are from Israel are the real Israel, nor are all the seed of Abraham his children, and we have the same argument set out more fully (and aggressively) in Gal 3–4. It is widely thought that the II,11 text represents the viva voce claims of Paul's opponents, and it is likely that such language was a regular element in a power struggle. The opposition might say, "Most of you are Gentiles and have not been brought up to know the finer points of God's law. We are Hebrews."

The rhetoric reaches its climax with "Are they ministers (διάκονοι) of Christ?" and this also raises echoes. In II,3.1–6 the emissaries with their letters provoked Paul to say that God "authorized us as διάκονοι of a new covenant" (3.6), and he repeatedly speaks of his διακονία in 3.7–11; 5.18; 6.3; and so forth. The discussion in II,3 also turned on Jewish issues—the two covenants, stone and human hearts, Moses and Paul—and this encourages us to think that the same Jewish emissaries, with the same Jewish background, lie behind both passages. Further, we have similar language in I,3.3–4.6. Paul and Apollos, on to whom the apostle has transformed the matter (4.6), are only "διάκονοι through whom you believed" (3.5). Paul wants all missionaries to be regarded as servants (ὑπηρέτας) of Christ, and it could be that the new noun has been chosen for irenic reasons.

"Hebrews," "Israelites," and "the seed of Abraham" are all laudatory versions of the term *Jews,* the first stressing racial purity, the other two stressing theological significance. Barrett thinks that Palestinian provenance is suggested, but this is too ambitious; he himself cites the Corinthian inscription "Synagogue of the Hebrews."

διάκονοι Χριστοῦ is likely to be related to II,10.7, "if anyone has confidence in himself Χριστοῦ εἶναι," and to I,1.12, ἐγὼ δὲ Χριστοῦ. Just as Paul responds in II,10.7, "so also are we," in the same way he retorts in II,11.23, "I am more."

(ii) The opposition justify their claims by appeal to human authority: "For we do not dare to classify or compare ourselves to certain of those who commend themselves; but they are without understanding, measuring themselves by one another and comparing themselves to each other (ἐν ἑαυτοῖς ἑαυτοὺς μετροῦντες καὶ συγκρίνοντες ἑαυτοὺς ἑαυτοῖς)." Again the language recalls II,3.1–6 with its συνιστάνειν, ἀφ᾽ ἑαυτῶν, ἐξ ἑαυτῶν and raises the question of what precise measuring and comparing are in mind. In II,3.1–6 the probability seemed to be that the letters of authorization were from an authority higher than Paul, namely, Jerusalem; the same seems likely here. They said, "We have been sent by [Cephas and] James in Jerusalem; they are the head of the church, and we carry their imprimatur. So what we tell you has more authority than this Paul fellow, who is a loose cannon." By contrast, Paul began his letter, "Paul, an apostle of Christ Jesus" (II,1.1), and still more clearly, and disputatiously, in Gal 1.1. He always makes for the high ground because he cannot compete on the low ground.

(iii) The opposition have a different form of Christianity from Paul's: "For if the new arrival (ὁ ἐρχόμενος) proclaims another Jesus, whom we did not proclaim, or you receive a different spirit that you did not receive, or a different gospel that you did not accept, you put up with it splendidly!" (II,11.4). The phrase εὐαγγέλιον ἕτερον recalls Gal 1.6–9, where Paul expresses astonishment that his converts are so soon turning to ἕτερον εὐαγγέλιον, the law-based pseudogospel of the Judaizers. Furthermore, the πνεῦμα ἕτερον recalls Gal 3.1–5, where the apostle demands, "Did you receive the Spirit by doing the works of the law?" Pauline converts received the Spirit at their baptism, and many of the Corinthians certainly had a different idea of the Spirit from Paul's (I,12). The interesting stress on "another Jesus" will need a more detailed discussion in ch. 14 below.

The incoming missionaries have succeeded in cowing the church, for Paul repeatedly uses the verb ἀνέχεσθε, "you submit." This would cohere well with their being authorized by the mother church in Jerusalem, but it does not tell us in what exactly their "different gospel" consisted. A hint is offered in II,11.20: "For you submit if someone enslaves you (καταδουλοῖ), if someone devours you, if someone gets hold of you, if someone domineers, if someone hits you across the face." The verb καταδουλοῦν is very strong and recurs at Gal 2.4, when the Judaizing visitors at Antioch "spied out our freedom that we have in Christ Jesus, that they might enslave us (καταδουλώσουσιν)." Here the meaning is plain: the visitors were suspicious of Paul's lax ways and wished to insist on the full observance of torah. The same image recurs in Gal 4.9, where Paul says the Galatians want to go into slavery (δουλεύειν) to the στοιχεῖα. Combined with other echoes of Galatians noted above, this must raise the hypothesis that we have Judaizers here also, in some form: the emissaries of II,3 were concerned with the glory of Moses and his covenant in letters on stone.

Jerome Murphy-O'Connor accepts the incoming missionaries as Judaizers, while seeing the Corinthian community itself as pneumatics, "Spirit-people";[11] but so monolithic a picture of the church at Corinth is unlikely. Both epistles are full of evidence that "the Corinthian community" was divided, and the Judaizing differs from that in Galatians.

Understanding how the visiting missionary "hit you across the face" and how this came to be submitted to is problematic. It would be abnormal in any modern church for a leader, however arrogant, to hit fellow worshipers; if any leader did, they might be expected to respond in kind. This leads to the thought that the hitting is in some way institutionalized. The synagogue had sanctions for the deviant, including beating, as Paul himself testifies in the same context (II,11.24). Perhaps the face slapping was a mild form

---

[11]J. Murphy-O'Connor, *The Theology of the Second Letter to the Corinthians* (New Testament Theology; Cambridge: Cambridge University Press, 1991).

of a similar discipline and so accepted without demur. Paul comments ironically, "I say to my shame that we have been weak!" (II,11.21). The opposition had repeatedly accused him of "weakness"; he had not the strength of character to insist on church discipline, as they did.

(iv) The opposition leaders spoke of themselves as "apostles." The new arrival of II,11.4 with his different gospel draws a sarcastic comment: "For I reckon that I am in no way behind the superapostles (τῶν ὑπερλίαν ἀποστόλων, 11.5)"; the same phrase recurs in 12.11. In 11.12–15 they "want an opportunity to be recognized as our equals in what they boast about. For such boasters are false apostles, deceitful workers, transforming themselves into apostles of Christ. And no wonder! For Satan himself transforms himself into an angel of light. So it is no great thing if his servants also transform themselves into servants of righteousness." There is no question that the opposition leaders spoke of themselves as apostles; and this confirms the understanding of ἱκανοί, etc., given above. Their letters gave them authorization to act as apostles, i.e., to take the Achaean churches over. The clause in 11.20 εἴ τις κατεσθίει probably implies that they also took the apostolic privilege of having the church pay for their food.

The title they use for themselves is significant. There had been emissaries from Jerusalem to Antioch, both the false brethren of Gal 2.4 and the "certain from James" of Gal 2.12, but neither group is called ἀπόστολοι. Someone has started a pro-Cephas party in Corinth before I,1.12, but the word *apostle* is not used for such a missionary. Throughout the NT the term is reserved for the church's principate, either the Twelve or an extended version of the Twelve to include Paul and Barnabas, Jesus' brothers, and one or two others (perhaps a little flatteringly for Andronicus and Junia). To be an apostle is to wield the church's authority, and someone has sent these newcomers to wield authority as apostles to Achaia; II,11.1–21 certainly portrays them as acting authoritatively. It is difficult to see them as being authorized by any other source than Jerusalem, and they would have needed letters of authorization.

Barrett distinguishes the ψευδαπόστολοι of 11.12–23, who are the local missionaries, from the ὑπερλίαν ἀπόστολοι of 11.5 and 12.11, whom he takes to be the Jerusalem leadership.[12] While this would be possible, the context of 11.5 is against it: 11.4 has spoken of ὁ ἐρχόμενος, the senior local missionary, and there has been no reference, even indirectly, to the Jerusalem pillars.

(v) There is a formidable amount of "boasting" in these chapters, and in much of it the opposition are clearly measuring themselves against Paul and

---

[12]Barrett, *Second Epistle*, 277–79.

comparing themselves to his disadvantage. The matters at issue are these: he is of unimpressive presence (10.1–2, 10); he walks according to the flesh (10.2–3); he is a poor speaker (10.10; 11.6); he has overextended his mission (10.14); he did not claim apostle's rights of subsistence (11.7–11; 12.13); he was weak in imposing church discipline (11.21) and, in general, apostolic dignity (11.23–33); he was not strong in visions and revelations (12.1–10) or in miracles (12.12).

A mirror image thus emerges of the opposition leadership and their boasting. They were confident, impressive people, fluent speakers, well able to control the church and to insist on their standards being observed (if necessary, with physical sanctions). While Paul's mission was a ramshackle affair, inadequately staffed, forever changing its plans and disappointing its converts, they came from the metropolitan church with a clear assignment that they could fulfill. They expected to be paid for by the local church, and were. They were charismatics who had revelations during worship and had on occasion been ravished to heaven for a vision of the throne. They had performed a number of miracles, as apostles should. The more we read Paul's angry response, the less surprised we are at their success: they held every card in the pack but one. The only thing they lacked was Paul's warmhearted affection for his churches, and in the last resort, affection is the only thing that counts.

THE PETRINE MISSION AT CORINTH, 54–56

Paul left Corinth in the autumn of 51, and most critics date 1 Corinthians to early in 54. The letter makes no mention of visiting missionaries; those of Cephas are members of the church. But the strong and clear criticisms to which Paul responds in I,1–4; 9.1–12 have not appeared endogenously. Representatives of the Jerusalem church have visited, and they have been effective. Some passage of time was needed for them to have settled and imparted their message, so perhaps they came in 53. This would leave space for Apollos's mission in 52.

The Petrines made an impression by two things that they said. First, Cephas was in a different league from Paul and Apollos; he was a proper apostle, commissioned by the Lord, as they were not. He was the head of the apostolic church. Those who were not baptized with the apostolic baptism were not proper Christians (I,1.13–17). The Petrines boasted of men (3.21); they refused to treat Paul as a servant of Christ but examined him (4.1–5); they were puffed up for the one leader, Cephas, against the other, Paul (4.6); they thought they were distinguished by the apostle from whom they received the gospel (4.7). Second, they asked unpleasant questions about why Paul had not asked to be paid for while he was in Corinth. Clearly, he was not a true apostle, or he would have had his expenses covered, like the other apostles and the brothers of the Lord and, above all, Cephas (I,9.5).

There is an interval of a year or so between the two Corinthian letters, and the interval includes Paul's unhappy visit to the city and his reproachful letter, now lost. It may well be that the man who insulted Paul (ὁ ἀδικήσας) was a Petrine convert, but we do not know.

Second Corinthians concerns a different situation from that of 1 Corinthians because there is now an official Jerusalem mission in the church, and the tension is much higher. We do best to interpret events in the light of an analogy with those at Antioch. In Gal 2.4 there had appeared in the Antiochene church "false brethren secretly introduced, who had slipped in to spy out our freedom that we have in Christ Jesus." That is, the Jerusalem leaders had sent two members of the church to see what was going on at Antioch. They were not so secret about it because they made public objection to the church's laxity over food and other laws. "To these ones," Paul says, "we submitted not for a moment" (Gal 2.5), and Luke says that Paul and Barnabas had no small dissension and debate with them (Acts 15.2). Having received a report from these emissaries and a visit from Paul and Barnabas, the pillars sent a more formal mission to Antioch, led by Peter himself (Gal 2.11), later reinforced by "certain ones from James." The latter was a man of principle and resolution, and he insisted that the church be run properly.

It looks as if the same pattern of Jerusalem initiatives was followed at Corinth. Someone (perhaps Silas, who suddenly disappears from Acts in the middle of the Corinthian mission) told the Jerusalem leaders that more insubordination was brewing in Achaia, so they dispatched two competent churchmen to see what was happening and stop it. These good people stayed for some months and changed the atmosphere. A number of the Corinthian Christians saw the point: Paul did not have the same authority as Cephas, and one did not want to take any risks by having the wrong baptism. The fact that he had paid his own bills certainly was suspicious. So, whereas Paul submitted to the first Antiochene visitors not for a moment and had no small dissension with them, seeing them off the property with a few well-chosen words, his loyal disciples—Stephanas and others—lacked the confidence and character to make a public stand. This explains the parties of I,1.12 and throughout the letter.

The successful Petrines returned to Jerusalem in the autumn of 53 and reported to the leadership. "Well done," said the latter, "but we have scotch'd the snake, not kill'd it. What we need is a proper mission, with a group of experienced missionaries. We will write them letters of authorization, and they will be the metropolitan church's apostles; they can run the church there and make things so hot that this menace, Paul, will not want to show his face there again." We thus have a new situation late in 54. Whereas the first Petrines acted as plain believers putting the true perspective over to the misguided Corinthians and could be passed over in silence in 1 Corinthians, now a second and much more formidable mission had come. They came with authorizing letters from Jerusalem and styled themselves apostles. They saw themselves as in charge at Corinth.

The fundamental points these men made were the same as those leveled against Paul by their predecessors. He was not properly authorized (II,3.4–6); he had not known Jesus in the flesh (5.16) and had not been called by him (5.12); he was not to be classed as an apostle, as they were (11.5; 12.11). This was demonstrated by his failure to ask the church to pay for him, as all apostles were entitled to (11.7–11; 12.13). But they say many more nasty things about him, to which I will return shortly.

One further item needs to be clarified before 2 Corinthians can be understood. Paul has recently recovered from a severe trial (θλῖψις), in which he thought he would die: "I do not want you to be ignorant, brothers, of our affliction that befell us in Asia, for we were laid utterly low beyond our strength, so that we despaired of life itself; but we ourselves have had the sentence of death in our hearts" (1.8–9). Paul expresses himself ambiguously. Interpreters have thought he meant depression, sickness, persecution by enemies, or imprisonment. But the most likely affliction to have befallen him is his ousting from his mission's capital city, Ephesus, by a Jerusalem countermission. Three lines of evidence point to this conclusion.

First, writing perhaps fifty years later, the writer of 2 Timothy says, "You know this, that all in Asia deserted me, including Phygelus and Hermogenes" (2 Tim 1.15). We do not know if the writer was familiar with 2 Corinthians, but whether he was or not, he knew a tradition that Paul's Asian mission suffered a major setback at the hands of a non-Pauline movement. If he knew 2 Corinthians, he is interpreting II,1.8–9 in the light of this tradition. ἐν τῇ Ἀσίᾳ in both texts is significant. It was not only in Ephesus, according to 2 Timothy, but in the penumbra of smaller Christian communities that Paul found himself persona non grata. Similarly, Paul's "affliction" took place not in Ephesus, where a single trial might have brought on a crisis—a bout of malaria or a thrashing in the synagogue—but "in Asia." When Paul fought with wild beasts, it was in a single location, "in Ephesus" (I,15.32).

Second, Acts 19.21–21.15 describes Paul's last journey to Jerusalem, beginning from Ephesus and making a long excursion through Macedonia to Achaia (19.21; 20.1–2); the route is the same as that evidenced in 2 Corinthians and Romans. There is a long and confused account of a riot in the Ephesian theater (19.23–40), which purports to explain why Paul left the city (20.1), and from 20.3 the party sets out from "Hellas," that is, Corinth. They are taking the great collection up to Jerusalem (unmentioned until 24.17), and Luke is one of their number ("we," 20.5 onward). Paul goes by land from Troas to Assos, where he rejoins the party on the ship (20.13–14). The vessel calls at Mitylene and Samos but misses Ephesus: "For Paul had decided to sail past Ephesus so that he might not have to spend time in Asia; for he was in haste if it were possible for him to be in Jerusalem for the day of Pentecost" (20.16).

Luke is transparently hiding something. Has Paul bought the ship, that he can decide whether it calls at Ephesus or not? He is in such a hurry that he cannot waste time in Ephesus, but there is time to go ashore at Miletus, send a deputation back to Ephesus, collect a party of elders, and have them come down to Miletus for his final testament. All this must have taken a week. It is difficult to escape the impression that the churches in the Ephesus district had "deserted" Paul and given their loyalty to his opponents. Only "the elders of the church" were Pauline loyalists. This was "the affliction that befell us in Asia."

Third, the year 54 was a catastrophe for Paul. He had lost control of his base church at Antioch with Peter's disastrous visit in 49 and had adopted a new strategy of traveling farther and farther from Jerusalem, to Galatia, to Macedonia and Achaia, finally to Asia. At first the new policy was crowned with success: a string of devoted churches sprang up in all four areas. But then came the counterattack. Judaizers canvassed his Galatian churches demanding circumcision. Petrine missionaries had sufficiently upset things at Corinth that he felt obliged to pay a pastoral visit, and during this he was insulted and not supported by the church. He wrote a bitter letter of reproach (the tearful letter) and had no idea how it had been received. There were "many adversaries" at Ephesus (I,16.9). It would be surprising if the Jerusalem pillars did not include Asia in their countermission and if their representatives were not among these adversaries. The countermission might well have been successful here, too.

Paul's language in II,1.8 would fit such a scenario. He had just witnessed the apparent collapse of a lifetime's endeavor, the loss of province after province of his far-flung mission, backed by the experience of personal rejection by many of his converts, of whom Phygelus and Hermogenes may stand as symbolic names, old supporters no longer faithful. Small wonder if such a trauma, θλῖψις, brought on a physical and mental breakdown so that he was looking death in the eye. Such catastrophes are not surmounted in a fortnight either: "for since we came to Macedonia, our flesh has had no respite, but being in everything afflicted—battles without, fears within" (II,7.5). The θλῖψις goes on in Macedonia, too: the influence of the Jerusalem pillars is felt in Philippi (cf. Phil 3.2–21) as well as at Corinth and Ephesus. The pressures are telling still on Paul's marvelous physical constitution (σάρξ). The "battles without" might well be disputations in church with offensive Jewish-Christian emissaries. The "fears within" can hardly be anything else. Paul was not afraid of hardship or whipping or death itself; he saw such things as a sharing in the passion of Christ. What he feared was the corruption of his churches: "I fear lest your minds be corrupted from the simplicity that is toward Christ" (II,11.3), "I fear that when I come I may find you not as I wish. . . . I fear that there may be quarreling. . . . I fear that my God may humble me before you" (II,12.20–21).

Thrall correctly dismisses illness as a likely candidate for Paul's θλῖψις.[13] The affliction is seen as in line with τὰ παθήματα τοῦ Χριστοῦ, not as a trouble that might happen to just anyone; moreover, there is no linguistic link with the "thorn in the flesh" of 12.7, as is sometimes claimed. Besides, if Paul had been very ill, we would expect him to stay on and be nursed in Asia, not starting a new mission in Troas. Nor is it easy to identify a near-fatal disease that just goes away; Paul is soon pursuing his demanding apostolic travels once more and has seven more years of life in him until martyrdom.

Thrall is more impressed with a possible reference to recent severe persecution, mentioning the Ephesian riot of Acts 19 and the supposed imprisonment at Ephesus implied in Philippians. But the former is so confused and the latter so speculative that there can be no confidence in such a proposal. She dismisses "extreme depression" arising from the Corinthians' behavior as not life-threatening. But Paul had more reasons for depression than Corinth, and repeated trauma is often followed by physical as well as mental breakdown.

A text that may be relevant is I,15.31–32: "I die every day. . . . If on the human level (κατὰ ἄνθρωπον) I fought with wild beasts at Ephesus, what would it profit me? If the dead are not raised, let us eat and drink." "I die every day" sounds like II,11.23, "in deaths often." Paul's daily round includes days without food and nights without sleep, beatings by Jewish and Roman authorities, shipwreck and stoning, perils of robbers and of false brethren, the care of all the churches. Ignatius uses θηριομαχεῖν metaphorically, of his military escort (Ign. *Rom.* 5.1, no doubt in imitation of Paul), and it is widely agreed that Paul could not have fought any literal bears or lions. So to whom might he refer as θηρία? He calls his Jewish-Christian rivals "dogs" in Phil 3.2, and Luke represents him as speaking of them as "ravening wolves" in Acts 20.29. What wore him down most was the disputations with Petrine countermissionaries, as we find throughout 2 Corinthians. He has been "fighting with" these "wild beasts at Ephesus," these "many adversaries," for months before he wrote 1 Corinthians. If all this has been done κατὰ ἄνθρωπον, as it would be in a secular community (as in I,3.3), and there were no resurrection to look forward to, what would be the point?[14] Chapter 16 of this book sets out a fuller scenario for the history of Paul's Corinthian mission, and Appendix 1 examines the integrity of 2 Corinthians.

---

[13]Thrall, *Second Epistle,* 1:114–17.
[14]This exegesis is close to that of Fee, *First Corinthians,* 770–72, but he does not specify who the adversaries are.

⟡ 4 ⟡

WISDOM AND TORAH IN 1 CORINTHIANS 1

NOT MANY wise according to the flesh, not many powerful in the universities of the twentieth century, have accepted the force of the arguments for a consistent Petrine opposition through both Corinthian letters. The thesis is a nineteenth-century idea, effectively criticized by Lütgert in 1908. Even the thin red line of the faithful, Adolf Schlatter, Ernst Käsemann, and Barrett, wavers a little in the face of Lütgert's hard pounding. Both Schlatter and Käsemann cite his comment, "The main proof that [the opposition] are not nomists lies in the fact that Paul himself never says this of them."[1] The opponents were Petrines, I would argue, but not the kind of Petrine we meet in Galatians, nomists; they are not trying to impose the law on Pauline converts or have them circumcised. Most scholars have declined the Petrine option because they have seen this problem coming round the mountain: if the opposition are so unlike the Jewish Christians of Galatians and Romans, should we not try some other solution to the parties conundrum?

Paul gives a few verses (I,1.10–16) to the parties and their loyalty to those who baptized them before launching out into a long manifesto-like statement, contrasting his own gospel of the cross with the preaching of the opposition, variously spoken of as σοφία (1.17), ἡ σοφία τοῦ κόσμου (1.20), πειθοὶ σοφίας λόγοι (2.4), σοφία ἀνθρώπων (2.5), and διδακτοὶ ἀνθρωπίνης σοφίας λόγοι (2.13). It thus becomes clear that the opposition's message is centered on "wisdom" and "word(s)," but these are two common Greek words, and it is by no means clear at first glance what is the reality that lies behind them.

It is sometimes thought that Paul's contrast is between his own gospel of substance and an opposition that could speak with cleverness of speech, that is, the much admired skills of a Hellenistic orator.[2] Or it could be that

---

[1]Lütgert, *Freiheitspredikt*, 49; A. Schlatter, *Die Korinthische Theologie* (BFCT 18.2; Gütersloh: Bertelsmann, 1914); E. Käsemann, "Die Legitimität des Apostels," *ZNW* 41 (1942): 33–71; repr. as an independent booklet (Darmstadt: Wissenschaftliche Buchgesellschaft, 1956), 17/40.

[2]So, for example, D. Litfin, *St. Paul's Theology of Proclamation: 1 Corinthians 1–4 and Greco-Roman Rhetoric* (SNTSMS 79; Cambridge: Cambridge University Press,

there is something of this but that wisdom had more than one meaning, and the opposition's activity involved some preaching of wisdom. Conzelmann and Barrett take this line, speaking of (proto-)Gnosticism.[3] Munck and Fee see some Greek philosophizing behind the wisdom,[4] while R. A. Horsley and J. A. Davis turn rather to Philo and Jewish Hellenism.[5] Stronger lines have been advanced by Ulrich Wilckens, who sees a *sophia* Christology behind the passage, and Schmithals, who similarly sees quite a developed Gnosticism at work. Schrage views wisdom as a threat to the Pauline gospel, an alternative way of salvation, even though we may not be able to identify it.[6]

I shall argue in this chapter that σοφία was a term widely used in the Jewish Diaspora for the Jewish way of life, the torah, and that λόγος (= דבר) was a particular ruling by a Jewish sage (חכם). The argument is in three steps: first, consideration of a parallel passage in Romans, in which Paul contrasts his gospel with human religious aspirations, both Jewish and Gentile; second, a brief outline of the use by Greek-speaking Jews of *wisdom* as a term for the practice of their religion; and third, an exegesis of the relevant passage in the first chapter of the First Letter. Chapter 5, below, will discuss other texts in 1 Corinthians that treat of wisdom and torah, and ch. 6 will inquire into the state of the question in the Second Letter.

1 CORINTHIANS 1.17–2.5 AND ROMANS

Paul wrote 1 Corinthians in 54, and Romans perhaps eighteen months later. Both letters start off with a statement of Paul's gospel, and both contrast it with something different:

εὐαγγελίζεσθαι, οὐκ ἐν σοφίᾳ λόγου, ἵνα μὴ κενωθῇ ὁ σταυρὸς τοῦ Χριστοῦ (I,1.17)

εἰ γὰρ οἱ ἐκ νόμου κληρονόμοι, κεκένωται ἡ πίστις (Rom 4.14)

1994); similarly, R. B. Hays, *First Corinthians* (Interpretation; Louisville: John Knox, 1997), 24.

[3]Conzelmann, *1 Corinthians,* 37; Barrett, *First Epistle,* 49.

[4]Munck, *Paul and Salvation,* 135–67; Fee, *First Corinthians,* 64–66.

[5]Horsley has written many articles on 1 Corinthians, in which the theme of a heavenly *sophia* reverenced in Corinth is a *Leitmotif;* cf. esp. "Wisdom of a Word and Words of Wisdom at Corinth," *CBQ* 39 (1977): 224–39; the idea is pervasive in his *1 Corinthians.* J. A. Davis, *Wisdom and Spirit: An Investigation of 1 Corinthians 1:18–3:20 against the Background of Jewish Sapiential Traditions in the Greco-Roman Period* (Lanham, Md.: University Press of America, 1984).

[6]U. Wilckens, *Weisheit und Torheit: Eine exegetisch-religionsgeschichtliche Untersuchung zu 1 Kor 1 und 2* (BHT 26; Tübingen: Mohr, 1959); "σοφία, κτλ," *TDNT* 7:465–528; Schmithals, *Die Gnose;* Schrage, *Der erste Brief,* 1:158–61.

In 1 Corinthians the contrast is between the gospel and "wisdom of a word," while in Romans it is between the promise (the gospel) and the law. In both cases there is the threat that the message of salvation may be "made void" (κενοῦσθαι). Perhaps God might have ordained otherwise, that wisdom/the law should have been the means of salvation, but he has actually brought us justification by the cross of Christ/faith, and he is not going to allow these to be made void.

Ὁ λόγος γὰρ ὁ τοῦ σταυροῦ τοῖς μὲν ἀπολλυμένοις μωρία ἐστίν, τοῖς δὲ σῳζομένοις ἡμῖν δύναμις θεοῦ ἐστιν (I,1.18)

Οὐ γὰρ ἐπαισχύνομαι τὸ εὐαγγέλιον, δύναμις γὰρ θεοῦ ἐστιν εἰς σωτηρίαν παντὶ τῷ πιστεύοντι (Rom 1.16)

Here is the positive statement, put similarly in the two letters. The word of the cross/the gospel is the power of God, and it brings salvation to us who are being saved/to everyone who believes.

I,1.21 also specifies, σῶσαι τοὺς πιστεύοντας.

οὐχὶ ἐμώρανεν ὁ θεὸς τὴν σοφίαν τοῦ κόσμου (I,1.20b)

φάσκοντες εἶναι σοφοὶ ἐμωράνθησαν (Rom 1.22)

In Rom 1 God made known to human beings what was knowable about him, but they changed the glory of the imperishable God into the likeness of an image of corruptible humanity and of animals. There is a verbal echo of Ps 106 (LXX 105).20, which shows that Paul has in mind Jewish as well as Gentile corruptions of religion as revealed by God: ἠλλάξαντο τὴν δόξαν αὐτῶν ἐν ὁμοιώματι μόσχου referred to the golden calf. James Dunn mentions a number of other texts (Deut 4.16–18; Gen 1–3; Wis 14; etc.) that seem to lie behind the passage.[7] Paul attributes these corruptions of true faith to human claims to be wise, φάσκοντες εἶναι σοφοί, and says that they were rendered foolish, ἐμωράνθησαν. This is the same vocabulary that we have more fully in I,1.18–27. In both cases the σοφία consists in trying to substitute something worked up by human cleverness for the simple if paradoxical way of salvation provided by God. Romans 1.21 says, "They were reduced to vanity ἐν τοῖς διαλογισμοῖς αὐτῶν, and their senseless (ἀσύνετος) heart was darkened." The attack is on all human religion in Rom 1—in good Barthian manner—both Jewish and heathen: "The wrath of God is revealed from heaven against all impiety and unrighteousness of

---

[7]J. D. G. Dunn, *Romans* (2 vols.; WBC 38A–38B; Dallas: Word, 1988), 1:51–73.

men" (1.18). Jews have committed idolatry as well as pagans, and the self-righteous Jew of Rom 2, judging fellow humans, is therefore inexcusable.

Ἰουδαίοις μὲν σκάνδαλον ἔθνεσιν δὲ μωρίαν (I,1.23)

Ἰουδαίῳ τε πρῶτον καὶ Ἕλληνι (Rom 1.16)

Paul never forgot that the gospel was to be proclaimed to his fellow Jews as well as to the Gentile world and that it presented special difficulties for the Jews because of claims for their historic religion. This made the cross a stumbling block to them (a theme worked out in much more detail in Rom 9–11).

τὰ ἐξουθενημένα ἐξελέξατο ὁ θεός, τὰ μὴ ὄντα, ἵνα τὰ ὄντα καταργήσῃ (I,1.28)

θεοῦ τοῦ ζῳοποιοῦντος τοὺς νεκροὺς καὶ καλοῦντος τὰ μὴ ὄντα ὡς ὄντα (Rom 4.17)

In I,1 the contrast is between the wise, powerful, and wellborn according to the flesh and the foolish, weak, and despised, the "nonexistent." The latter are the Corinthian Christians, mostly of no very exalted background. It seems natural to understand the former as the more wealthy, influential church members, although we shall need to be cautious over this. In Rom 4 the contrast is between the Jewish people, as the seed of Abraham, and the Christians, as the sons of promise, born from many nations. It is they who are called "as nonexistent into existence."

ὅπως μὴ καυχήσηται πᾶσα σὰρξ ἐνώπιον τοῦ θεοῦ . . . ἐν Χριστῷ Ἰησοῦ, ὃς ἐγενήθη σοφία ἡμῖν ἀπὸ θεοῦ, δικαιοσύνη τέ . . . (I,1.29)

οὐ δικαιωθήσεται πᾶσα σὰρξ ἐνώπιον αὐτοῦ . . . δικαιοσύνη θεοῦ πεφανέρωται . . . Ποῦ οὖν ἡ καύχησις: ἐξεκλείσθη. (Rom 3.20, 21, 27)

In 1 Corinthians God has called a new community, the nonexistent, into being so as to abolish all privilege. There can be no boasting now, because the word of the cross has established a new basis for salvation. This new basis is in Christ, "who has become for us" wisdom, justification, redemption, and so on. Paul's liking for "Christ became for us . . ." with an abstract (II,5, 21; cf. Eph 2.14) is here motivated by the contrast with standard religion. Pre-Christian religion, especially the Jewish religion with its Sinai covenant, saw itself as in possession of the keys of justification, sanctification, and redemption, and as Paul so often bemoans, this led its leaders, especially Jewish leaders, into boasting. There is now no place for such boasting, because Christ "has become for us" all these key elements in salvation.

The picture is closely parallel in Romans. All religious claims have been shown in Rom 1–2 to be folly, and 3.9–18 returns to the conclusion that both Jews and Greeks are all under sin; this then leads into the paragraph cited above. But 2.17–28 is a full-blooded (and largely unfair) attack on the Jewish religion, opening, "But if you call yourself a Jew and repose in the law and boast in God . . ." (2.17). There is no doubt that Paul saw the principal boasters as Jews. All that is over now: "But now apart from the law God's justification has been demonstrated" through faith in Jesus Christ (3.21–22). So this is the end of boasting; it is excluded.

It would perhaps be hasty to assume that Paul has exactly the same target in mind in the two letters, but the common vocabulary is suggestive. Romans, the fuller exposition, makes it clear that the gospel of the cross is in opposition to all human religions, especially Judaism with its tendency to boast. First Corinthians seems to move in the same direction. The most noticeable difference is the much greater stress on σοφία in the latter, and there must be some explanation for this. Romans 1.22 does contain a hint of the same theme, perhaps carried over from the earlier letter.

WISDOM AND WORDS OF WISDOM IN JUDAISM

"Greeks seek wisdom," says the apostle (I,1.22), and so did a good many other people in the ancient world, including the Jews. Already before the exile, a stock of wise words was being built up that was to issue in our book of Proverbs; these were associated with Solomon, whose wisdom was famed. Such wisdom was at first secular: proverbs were recipes for success in life, ways to become wealthy, to live long, to marry sensibly, to make one's way at court. But in so religious a community as Israel, such worldly wisdom needed a pious front, and it was soon insisted, "The fear of the Lord is the beginning of wisdom" (Prov 1.7). Wisdom becomes a kind of majestic panacea, like education in the modern world, but with a higher respect for Religious Education. Impressive poems are written in its (her) praise, as in Job 28, where it is felt she might solve the riddle of the saint's sufferings. Wisdom is personified in Prov 1.20–33 and 9, and in Prov 8 she is seen as God's first creation and God's master worker in all the making of the universe. A further personification of Wisdom, this time with a more nationalist vocation, is to be found in the Wisdom of Solomon.

In the theological climate of postbiblical Judaism, wisdom was increasingly assimilated to religion. For Ben Sira, the Sophia Creatrix of Prov 8 has become Sophia Legislatrix, God's surrogate, synonymous with God's torah. He writes in the name of torah:

> Then the Creator of all things gave me a commandment;
> And he that created me made my tabernacle to rest,
> And said, Let thy tabernacle be in Jacob,
> And thine inheritance in Israel. . . .
> In the beloved city likewise he gave me rest;
> And in Jerusalem was my authority. . . .
> He that obeyeth me shall not be ashamed;
> And they that work in me shall not do amiss.
> All these things are the book of the covenant of the Most High God,
> Even the law which Moses commanded us for a heritage unto the assemblies
> of Jacob. (Sir 24.8, 11, 22–23, RV)

Wisdom has taken up residence in the temple on Zion, and her counsels are coterminous with the law of Moses.

Perhaps a century later (Eissfeldt dates Baruch 100–50 BCE), we find the same identification in Bar. 3.9–4.3:

> Hear, O Israel, the commandments of life; give ear to understand wisdom. How happened it, O Israel, that thou art in thine enemies' land . . . ? Thou hast forsaken the fountain of wisdom. . . . [God] hath found out all the way of knowledge, and hath given it unto Jacob his servant, and unto Israel that is beloved of him. . . . This is the book of the commandments of God, and the law that endureth for ever. (Bar. 3.9–10, 12, 36; 4.1, RV)

The equivalence of wisdom with torah is very widespread in the age of the NT, and it is common in Philo, Josephus, and the rabbis.[8] Philo presents a compendium of Greek ideas, but always with a Jewish veneer, and such a combination marks his treatment of wisdom. This is both the Stoic ἐπιστήμη θείων τε καὶ ἀνθρωπίνων (*Congr.* 79) and the Platonic ideal of wisdom, for which there is a human ἔρως. However, such a Platonic ideal fades into the Jewish God, and wisdom is also the way to union with him—that is, by obedience to torah. Abraham is the prototype of the wise man, and *De migratione Abrahami* describes his journeyings as an allegory. He leaves Haran with "the release from all earthly strivings" (*Migr.* 32) and sets out on "the royal way" of σοφία, whose goal is the ἱερὸς λόγος (28, 30). Ultimately there awaits the wise men ἡ τοῦ φιλοδώρου θεοῦ σύνοδος, which for Philo involves some mystical union. But σοφία is not only the goal of the journey; it is also the guide and the way to such union, τελεία ὁδὸς ἡ πρὸς θεόν (*Deus* 142–43; cf. *Migr.* 175)—in other words, obedience to the law.

Josephus similarly aligns wisdom with the law and with those who interpret it. Jews "said they would gladly accept death rather than dare to transgress the wisdom of the laws (τὴν σοφίαν τῶν νόμων)" (*A.J.* 18.59). God is said "himself to have begotten the laws and given them to us" (*A.J.* 4.319, probably a reference to the begetting of Wisdom in Prov 8.25). Wisdom on

---

[8]Wilckens, *TDNT* 7:465–528, esp. 500–507.

the highest level is restricted to Jewish sages. Joseph had τὴν φρόνησιν καὶ τὴν σοφίαν (*A.J.* 2.87); Solomon's σοφία καὶ σύνεσις became evident centuries later when a spell he devised drove out a demon (8.49); Ezra undertook κατὰ τὴν σοφίαν τοῦ θεοῦ to set up judges who understood the law (11.129). But above all, the scribes were wise, having the authority ἐξηγεῖσθαι σοφίαν νόμων τῶν Μωυσέως (18.82). Jews did not favor speakers with many languages or those who decked out their talk with smooth rhetoric, but ascribed wisdom solely to those who understood τὰ νόμιμα clearly and were able to interpret the sense of the holy writings (20.264).

Philo and Josephus are interesting figures in that they testify to the outreach of Judaism in a way that other authors do not. Ben Sira and Baruch are for Jewish consumption only; the new stress on wisdom as a counterpart to the Torah shows the effectiveness of hellenization. Wisdom in some broad sense has made Greece the basis of civilization through Alexander's empire, and these authors want to include it as a special Jewish wisdom. Philo and Josephus are more confident. Moses knew all about philosophy hundreds of years before Plato, and the only real wisdom is a Jewish possession, the wisdom of God in the Torah and the wisdom of those who interpret it. σοφία is a more attractive label for the Jewish way of life than νόμος; it is something elevated and virtuous, with an aura of respect and success, rather than a set of regulations under threat of judgment.

No code of law can be of practical use to a community without a body of qualified interpretation, and Israel dealt with the problem in part by the fiction that God gave Moses two codes on Sinai, the one written, the other oral. But in practice, scribes and other learned men sat on Moses' seat and made decisions about mint and anise and cumin (Matt 23.2, 23). These decisions were called דברים, words; in Greek, ῥήματα or λόγοι.

Ben Sira contrasts the skilled workman, who also has his wisdom, with him "that hath applied his soul, And meditated in the law of the Most High; He will seek to the wisdom of all the ancients, And will be occupied with prophecies. . . . If the great Lord will, he shall be filled with the spirit of understanding: He shall pour forth his words of wisdom (ῥήματα σοφίας αὐτοῦ), And in prayer give thanks unto the Lord" (Sir 39.1, 6). These words of wisdom are not casual pearls in conversation. They are rulings given "on the seat of the judge," "declar[ing] instruction and judgment," interpretations of parables and proverbs, as he serves among great men and leads public worship (38.31–39.11). Ben Sira thinks this sort of man is very important.

The word λόγος is often used in the NT to mean a saying. Matthew summarizes the Sermon on the Mount with, "So everyone who hears these words (τοὺς λόγους τούτους) and does them," and he ends the Sermon with, "And it came to pass when Jesus completed these words" (Matt 7.24, 28; cf. 19.1; 26.1). The λόγοι are not individual words but sayings, rulings, the commands given by a teacher, in this case the Son of God; the law is still valid, down to the least commandment, but more than this is required to enter the kingdom (5.17–20). Naturally, every religious movement had its own authoritative set of "words," and *1 En.* 99.10 specifies, "Blessed are all those who accept the words of wisdom and understand them [Greek, 'learn them'], and follow the paths of the Most High." The "words of wisdom" are the Enoch community's interpretation of tradition, and they show the way to God.

All communities with scriptures feel a hesitation over the degree of authority given to interpretations of the original. Fourth Maccabees 1.17, aligning Judaism with Stoicism, brings the two together: "This wisdom, I assume, is the culture that we acquire from the law." In practice it is impossible to draw a line between the biblical precept and the application of it. Consequently, σοφία is not just "the book of the covenant of the Most High God, the law which Moses commanded" (Sir 24.23), but this law interpreted by the words of wisdom poured forth by Ben Sira and his colleagues. Rabbinic Judaism distinguishes the דברי תורה from the דברי סופרים, the words of the scribes, but in daily life it was the scribal rulings that counted. The Mishnah speaks of currently mooted halakic interpretations as דברי חכמים, the words of the wise, the sages.[9]

It remained a question how far the term תורה should be allowed to stretch, and we have a discussion in *b. Qidd.* 49b: "What is meant by torah? The exegesis (מדרש) of the Torah." The word is not to be limited to the biblical text but includes its exposition by the learned. But this opens a gate perilously wide: who is competent to make this exposition? The answer is given: "One who can be asked a matter of wisdom (דבר חכמה) in any place, and he can answer it." A ruling on a tricky point is called a "word/matter of wisdom," and to be regarded as competent in expounding Torah, one would need to be able to cite such words of wisdom about any passage in Scripture and to give the correct answer. If such stringent tests were applied in modern universities, few would qualify to be lecturers in theology departments.

WORDS OF WISDOM IN 1 CORINTHIANS 1–4

Consistent meaning is available for I,1–4 only on such an understanding. Wisdom meant Jewish culture, torah in the broad sense, the whole halakic system; and words of wisdom are the דברי חכמה, the rulings made by the Palestinian sages. It is this threat that fills the canvas in 1 Corinthians. Judaism is also important in Romans, but there the argument is broadened to include pagan religions.

---

[9] *m. Neg.* 9.3; 11.7.

The Issue. This gives a convincing context to I,1.17: "Christ sent me not to baptize but to evangelize, οὐκ ἐν σοφίᾳ λόγου, lest the cross of Christ be made void." Verses 10–16 have revealed the presence of parties in Corinth, of which the most worrying is that "of Cephas," with claims that only those baptized by Cephas men are real members of the apostolic church. Paul shrugs off such claims: he was sent to evangelize, not to baptize. The substance of Paul's proclamation comes out in the next verse, ὁ λόγος τοῦ σταυροῦ; employment of the word λόγος implies a contrast with the σοφία λόγου. This is no facile contrast (as in Josephus, *A.J.* 20.264 above) between Paul's substantial message and the rhetorical cleverness of the opposition. The σοφία λόγου is a threat to the word of the cross and poses the possibility that the cross of Christ might be made void.

The Petrines do not talk just about Peter as a true apostle and the significance of apostolic baptism; they have a "proclamation," too, which Paul does his best to depreciate by calling it "the wisdom of a ruling." They said, "God has sent us salvation, as your missionary Paul correctly said. But what he has suppressed is that God has set out the basis of salvation in the torah. Here we have the divine wisdom: it is partly given us in Scripture, as you know, but partly also in the interpretations made by the learned over the years. These are God's commands, and we have all got to keep them. The trouble with Paul is that he does not tell you that you have to keep them. He is a deceiver and a lawbreaker."

It is no surprise that Paul found this position alarming; it threatened to make void the cross of Christ in exactly the same way as he says in Rom 4.14: "If it is the adherents of the law who are to be heirs, then faith has been made void (κεκένωται)." The Petrines not only spoke of their own system as divine wisdom; they also naturally depreciated Paul's extraordinary message as μωρία, *stupidity:* "the word of the cross is stupidity to those who are perishing" (I,1.18). We have a similar reproach in II,4.3: "But if our gospel is veiled (κεκαλυμμένον), it is veiled in those who are perishing." The Pauline gospel was in fact formidably implausible, and it is easy to understand the Petrines saying it was veiled and stupid. Judged from either a Jewish or a Greek background, it was highly paradoxical.[10] Paul's rhetorical gift included the ability to make paradox sound like profound religious mystery: "Has God not made the world's wisdom stupid? Since in God's wisdom the world did not know God through wisdom, God pleased to save believers by the stupidity of the proclamation. . . . For God's stupidity is wiser than men, and God's weakness is stronger than men" (I,1.20–25). The centuries echo with attempts to expound these paradoxes.

---

[10]Schrage, *Der erste Brief,* 1:186–87, cites Justin, *Dial.* 32, 89, for instances of Jewish scandal at the cross, and Cicero, *Rab. Post.* 5.16, and the Alexamenos caricature (in the imperial palace on the Palatine in Rome) for Gentile responses.

Paul's defeat at Antioch had convinced him that there could be no truce with Jerusalem theology. The Petrines' divine wisdom would make the church a submovement within Judaism, and it would wreck the Gentile mission. God, however, had authorized the Gentile mission and had commissioned Paul to lead it, and the word of the cross was the core of God's action in Christ and the essence of the proclamation.[11] The Petrines were therefore wrong, and damnably wrong: they were enemies of the cross of Christ. Like other people of vision with their backs to the wall, Paul saw the issue in eschatological black and white. The entire discussion in I,1–4 is about the situation within the Corinthian church; it is not about people who might be converted. "The word of the cross is stupidity to those who are perishing"— that is, to the Petrines, whose eternal salvation is in peril as they try to frustrate God's mission—"but to us who are being saved," those who have accepted the Pauline preaching, "it is the power of God." Paul saw this issue consistently as a matter of salvation. In Phil 3, in a comparatively serene moment, he can speak of his opponents as dogs, enemies of the cross of Christ, whose end is destruction, whose god is their belly, whose glory is in their pudenda (3.2, 18–19). Earlier, in 2 Thess 2.10–11, they "are perishing because they refused to love the truth and so be saved. For this reason God sends them a powerful delusion." Paul returns to the same issue, in nearly the same words as in I,1.18, in II,2.15; 4.3 (see ch. 6, below).

Most critics take σοφία λόγου and the associated phrases as at least in part references to speaking technique; cf. NRSV's "eloquent wisdom . . . lofty words or wisdom." Litfin has strongly urged this interpretation.[12] He shows how highly the Greek audiences from the Sophists through to Paul's day valued speaking ability; they were fascinated by those who could "make the worse case appear the better" and prized a talent that enabled one to win cases at law and to sway opinion on public issues. Dio Chrysostom preserves for us a speech of a Sophist called Favorinus, whose skills were so valued at Corinth in the early second century that a statue was erected to him.[13] The words λόγος, "eloquence," and σοφία, "cleverness, ability," are used to describe these gifts. Paul himself admits that his opponents said that his λόγος was contemptible (II,10.10). Hence, according to Litfin, the major distinction discussed in I,1–4 is between Paul's word of the cross, which is God's wisdom, and the wisdom of the world, the ability to make black seem white, which was in the hands of the opposition and was winning threatening support.

The case is attractive prima facie but is a misreading, for the following reasons:

---

[11]For this structuring of Paul's thought, see E. P. Sanders, *Paul* (New York: Oxford University Press, 1991).

[12]Litfin, *St. Paul's Theology.*

[13]Ibid., 144.

(i) Paul had the word of the cross to proclaim, and his opponents must have been proclaiming something that was not the word of the cross, which they thought μωρία. It would be difficult to think that he went on for more than a chapter attacking merely the form of their message and never said a word about its substance. Litfin allows that σοφία may contain some reference to the content of the preaching,[14] but it is not likely to be subsumed under language whose main thrust is, according to him, the form.

(ii) Paul's opponents did indeed say that his λόγος was contemptible (II,10.10), but the charge does not worry him much. "Let such a man reckon that as we are τῷ λόγῳ in letters when absent, so are we when present in action" (10.11); "Even if I am ἰδιώτης τῷ λόγῳ, yet I am not in knowledge" (II,11.6). When the issue is clear, he does not ramble on with vacuous antitheses but speaks with confidence.

(iii) Paul is a considerable rhetorician himself, well able to handle anaphora and other techniques: ποῦ σοφός; ποῦ γραμματεύς; ποῦ συζητητὴς τοῦ αἰῶνος τούτου; (I,1.20, cf. 26). It is implausible to suggest that Paul could only use them on paper.

(iv) Litfin draws a picture of large crowds of Corinthians listening to orators on the βῆμα.[15] But the impression we have is that most members of the Corinthian church were not well-to-do and would have had to spend the day earning their living. Public meetings were for the leisured.

(v) The word used for a public speaker was ῥήτωρ, but Paul makes no reference to such persons in 1.20; on the contrary, the people mentioned are classes of learned Jews (see the next section).

The Opponents.   The authorities behind the opposition are Jewish authorities. Paul has accepted the Petrines' formulation of the contrast between the two proclamations: they preach wisdom and the "words" that formulate it, while his word of the cross is stupidity (1.17–18). That is all right, "for it is written, 'I will destroy the wisdom of the wise, and the understanding of the understanding will I set at naught.' " Paul has Isaiah on his side. He then turns on the authorities behind this wisdom: "Where is the σοφός? Where is the γραμματεύς? Where is the συζητητὴς of this age? Has God not made the world's wisdom stupidity?" Schlatter was the first to see that these were *Jewish* authorities. Before the age of rabbis, the senior interpreter of halakah was the חכם, the wise man, σοφός. The main duty of practical application fell on the less learned but competent סופר, of whom there would be at least one in most Jewish communities. The חכמים וסופרים were a common pair in rabbinic writing, and we find them represented in the first-century church

---

[14]Ibid., 173.
[15]Ibid., 143.

also; in Matt 23.34 Jesus says, "Therefore behold I am sending to you prophets and σοφοὺς καὶ γραμματεῖς." Prophets are something special, found now in the church as in olden times in Israel, but the church has its own wise men and scribes, no less than Judaism. They are in the vanguard of the mission and include important people such as Matthew.

Many traditions claimed their own σοφοί, but γραμματεῖς were a different matter. For the Greeks a γραμματεύς was a secretary; an exalted member of this class is the town clerk at Ephesus (Acts 19.35). The name is not given to learned authorities in Greek writing as it is in Jewish material and as it is found repeatedly in Gospel contexts, where the scribes are regularly experts in the law; indeed, Luke prefers νομικός to γραμματεύς as less misleading for his Greek audience.

The third expert is a συζητητής, a word found elsewhere only in Ign. *Eph.* 18.1, where it echoes our present text. Schlatter suggests that it was a rendering for the Hebrew דרשׁן, a third category of learned Jew who "sought out" (דרשׁ) the meaning of Scripture, especially in a בית־המדרשׁ. We have seen above the discussion on the meaning of torah in *b. Qidd.* 49b, where it was held to include exegesis (מדרשׁ). ζητεῖν, "to seek," would be the natural Greek root with which to translate דרשׁ, but since the exegesis was a communal exercise, worked out in discussion, συζητεῖν would be a preferred form, and συζητητής would be a noun to represent דרשׁן. Paul adds the pejorative "of this age": Judaism and its wisdom belong to this age; the word of the cross is the gospel of the age to come, which has dawned with the coming of Christ.

Schlatter makes the proposal, almost en passant, and it has been taken up by comparatively few critics.[16] K. Müller cites a Jewish text, *b. Ber.* 43b, which, in the Codex Monachensis, refers to all three categories of the learned. Schrage himself says that the relation of the names to individual groups remains uncertain; in any case, Paul does not have the Jews in mind for all three. Either the wise were Greek, the scribes Jews, and the disputers both, or, more likely, the σοφός is an echo of the σοφία being attacked, with a Jewish scribe and a Gentile disputer as two instances. Schrage ignores the widespread coupling of חכמים and סופרים in Jewish sources, and of σοφοὺς καὶ γραμματεῖς in Matthew. M. Lautenschlager cites the use of ζητητής for a philosopher in Plato and sees the συ(ν)- as a sign of corporate discussion; the decisive argument against a background in דרשׁן is that this would make all three experts Jewish![17]

---

[16]A. Schlatter, *Die korinthische Theologie* (BFCT 18.2; Gütersloh: Bertelsmann, 1914), 84–85. The critics are listed in Schrage, *Der erste Brief,* 1:176 n. 434.

[17]K. Müller, "1 Kor 1,18–25. Die eschatologisch-kritische Funktion der Verkündigung des Kreuzes," *BZ* 10 (1966): 246–72; Schrage, *Der erste Brief,* 1.142–48; M. Lautenschlager, "Abschied vom Disputierter: Eine Exegese von συζητητής— 1 Kor 1,20," *ZNW* 83 (1992): 276–85.

Jews and Greeks. Under God's provident wisdom, the world did not come to knowledge of God by wisdom; Paul now divides the world into his basic dichotomy, Jews and "Greeks," that is, Gentiles: "For both Jews require signs and Greeks seek wisdom, but we proclaim Christ crucified, a scandal to Jews and stupidity to Gentiles, but to the elect themselves, Jews and Greeks, Christ the power of God and the wisdom of God." Paul is not contrasting a united church ("the elect themselves") with the unbelieving outsiders, Jewish and otherwise. His concern is the divided Corinthian community (1.10–17), and it is to them that the present argument is addressed.[18] "The elect themselves" are the Pauline Christians who accept his "word of the cross, Christ crucified." But there are also within the community those with other criteria; note the present tenses, αἰτοῦσιν, ζητοῦσιν.[19]

For Paul the sign of the Spirit included, in part, its gifts, of which glossolalia was a widespread and obvious example, but far more significant were its fruits—it was the love and joy and peace that fructified in his churches that incontrovertibly declared the presence of the Spirit. To the Petrines, however, this was a secondary matter: they brought a miracle-working Spirit. Its χαρίσματα were first "words of wisdom" and of knowledge, but then faith, bringing with it healings, workings of miracles, and other marvels (I,12.8–10). Paul downplays the miracles and healings, first by placing the gifts in descending order in 12.27–28, with apostleship, prophecy, and teaching ahead of them, and then by showing love as a still more excellent way (12.31–13.13).

But in II,10–12 it becomes clear that the Petrine missionaries "require signs" (I,1.22) as evidence of true apostleship. Second Corinthians 12.1–10 is a response to the requirement that Paul should have had visions and revelations; 12.11–12 is a response to the demand that he show τὰ σημεῖα τοῦ ἀποστόλου. Here Paul was on weak ground, for he was not a great miracle worker, and he deftly changes the meaning of the words: the signs of an apostle were indeed wrought among the Corinthians ἐν πάσῃ ὑπομονῇ. It was his sufferings "in all endurance" that constituted the signs of a true apostle; they were signs and wonders and miracles to the faithful. In the same way, at 6.4 he can say that he commends himself as a minister of God ἐν ὑπομονῇ πολλῇ in his afflictions. The Petrines "required signs," and no doubt other Jewish members of the church followed their lead; Paul could indeed offer signs, but they were the signs of his weakness. We may think that he had in fact done occasional marvels, such as Luke describes at Lystra (Acts 14.8–10), Philippi (Acts 16.16–18), or (as it was supposed) Troas (Acts 20.9–12). But Luke mentions no miracle at Corinth, and Paul cannot get away with such generalizations here.

---

[18]Schrage, *Der erste Brief,* 1.182: "Die Kritik des Paulus primär Kritik an die Korinthern ist."

[19]Ibid.

The Gentile members at Corinth did not know that apostles were supposed to be great miracle workers, but they were impressed by the comprehensive system of halakah on offer by the Petrine delegates, the σοφία with
its λόγοι, about which we hear so much in I,1–4. Greeks were famous as the
inventors of philosophy, a quest for wisdom of all kinds, both practical and
moral. Judaism made a considerable appeal to the Greek world by present-
ing itself as a purveyor of the supreme wisdom. We see this not only from
the use of the word by Philo, Josephus, and other Jewish authors (see above,
pp. 53–57), but also from the well-known attraction felt by a broad spectrum
of Gentiles for the monotheism and high moral aspirations of Judaism.
Hence Paul's depression at finding that Greeks "seek wisdom" (I,1.22) and
fall for the version on offer by the Petrines at Corinth.

As throughout the entire epistle, then, the issue in 1.22 is intraecclesial.
"Jews require signs" that Paul has little record in performing, "and Greeks
seek wisdom," of which an impressive form is on offer in the Jerusalem halakah. Paul's response, as so often, is a paradox: "to us, the [Pauline] elect,
Jews and Greeks," the proclamation is of "Christ, the power of God and the
wisdom of God."

"Jews require signs" is often understood to mean "if they are to accept
Jesus as Messiah." So argues Barrett, citing Mark 8.11 and parallels, where
Jews ask Jesus for a sign, and Num 14.11, 22, where they do the same of
God in the desert. Müller quotes some Jewish texts in support of this, for
example, *y. Ber.* 3b, "If he cannot show you a seal and a sign of confirmation,
you should not believe him" (cited by Schrage). This, however, is implausible on several grounds.[20] (i) No Christian Jew would be likely to
ask for a sign for believing in Jesus, since there was an obvious and universally accepted sign, the resurrection; if any non-Christian Jew were to require such a sign, Paul would presumably have cited the resurrection to him
or her. (ii) In the many contexts in which Jews oppose Paul in Acts, it is
never said that they required a sign; rather, they seem to dispute whether
Paul's preaching fits with prophecy (Acts 13.45; 17.3–5) and to object
that he does not insist on fulfillment of the law (Acts 15.1, cf. Galatians).
(iii) Signs were widely agreed to be unreliable evidence of messiahship
(Deut 13.1–3; Mark 13.22; 2 Thess 2.9; Rev 13.13–14).[21] (iv) Signs were
by no means valued only by Jews; Gentiles are equally impressed by Barnabas and Paul's healing at Lystra and take them to be divine (Acts
14.11–18). (v) There is no evidence of Paul's familiarity with the Gospel tradition of Jews demanding signs; rather, the Pharisees' requirement may be

---

[20]Barrett, *First Epistle,* 54; K. Müller, "1 Kor 1,18–25"; Schrage, *Der erste
Brief,* 1.183.
[21]Cf. Schrage, *Der erste Brief,* 1.183 n. 484.

seen as a reading back into the Gospel of demands by Jewish Christians from Paul and his followers.[22]

There is equal trouble over "Greeks seek wisdom." This has often been taken to mean that Greeks were more interested in, say, Platonism, Stoicism, or Sophist teachings than in the cross.[23] But as Barrett says, this is not particularly in mind here, since no rebuttal of such teachings or echo of them appears elsewhere in the epistle.[24] Barrett and Conzelmann identify Gnosticism as Paul's target, and at least the word γνῶσις is common in the epistle; both scholars are using the word in a loose sense, without implying a division in the Godhead, as is found in full-blown Gnosticism. On the other hand, I,12.8 draws a distinction between λόγος σοφίας and λόγος γνώσεως, and Gnosticism had Jewish, rather than Greek, roots.

A more promising line is proposed by Horsley and Davis, with appeal to Hellenistic Jewish treatment of wisdom, especially in Philo.[25] But it is difficult to tie Paul's language exclusively to Philo or even to Jewish wisdom teaching. σοφία is a general term for human religious aspiration apart from revelation, and Paul says it is turned to stupidity, just as he states in Rom 1.22. The particular form of such wisdom that constitutes a threat at Corinth is Christian Judaism; the Greek members of the church (some of them perhaps formerly attended the synagogue) seek such wisdom, with its clarities and certainties, rather than the means of salvation that God has given, the word of the cross. Horsley sees a hidden agenda throughout the First Letter: where Paul was preaching Christ, his opponents were proclaiming divine wisdom. But while this might be possible for I,1–4, wisdom virtually disappears from the text thereafter.

Boasting. First Corinthians 1.26–31 presents a contrast between the grandiose claims of the opposition and the humble reality of the Corinthian church membership. We are not dealing with a dispute in Paul's imagination but with words cited from his opponents. They based their proclamation on the rulings of the σοφοί and said that Paul's gospel was μωρία. He can say with bitter irony in 4.10, "We are μωροί for Christ's sake, but you are sensible; we are ἀσθενεῖς but you are ἰσχυροί." They despised Paul's gospel not only because they thought it stupidity but also for its feebleness. He did not teach his converts to observe the entire Jewish way of life, torah, while they insisted on the full observance, for they were serious about their religion,

[22]M. D. Goulder, "A Pauline in a Jacobite Church," in *The Four Gospels 1992: Festschrift F. Neirynck* (3 vols.; Leuven: Leuven University Press/Peeters, 1992), 2.859–76.
[23]E.g., Munck, *Paul and Salvation,* 148–54; Fee, *First Epistle,* 74–75.
[24]Barrett, *First Epistle,* 55.
[25]Horsley, "Wisdom"; from his *1 Corinthians,* esp. 47–55; Davis, *Wisdom and Spirit.*

ἰσχυροί. Indeed, their interpretation of "The Lord our God is one" (8.4) was so much vaunted as strong that Paul can ask rhetorically, "Are we stronger than [the Lord]?" (10.22). His converts are despised as weak because they are offended at the sight of an idol being treated as a thing without significance (8.7), and Paul himself is weak in discipline (II,11.19–21).

Again the apostle turns the opposition's claims with a paradox. With God the world's wisdom, the sage, the scribe, and the exegete are nowhere. "For look at those called among you [τὴν κλῆσιν ἡμῶν], brothers, that not many wise after the flesh, not many powerful, not many wellborn [are to be found]." κλῆσιν, σοφοί, δυνατοί take up Christ as God's δύναμιν and σοφίαν τοῖς κλητοῖς from 1.24. "But God chose the stupid things of the world to put the sages to shame"; it is the simple Pauline converts with their "stupid" beliefs who are the elect, not the Jerusalem smart alecks. "God chose the weak of the world to put the strong to shame"; they may call themselves strong, with their whole-hog devotion to torah, and look down on us as weak, but they will hang their heads on judgment day. "God chose the unborn of the world and the despised, the nonexistent, to confound the existent, that no flesh should boast before God." The rhetorical ἀγενῆ contrast with the εὐγενεῖς of 1.26 and are glossed with τὰ μὴ ὄντα. We have the same phrase, τὰ μὴ ὄντα, in Rom 4.17, where the Gentile Christians have been called from nonexistence into existence as children of Abraham; inheritance from the law would have nullified (κεκένωται) faith and invalidated (κατήργηται) the gospel (Rom 4.14).

The combination σοφοί/ἰσχυρός awakens an echo in Paul's comprehensive memory of the LXX text. Jeremiah 9.23–24 runs, "Let not ὁ σοφὸς boast in his σοφίᾳ, and let not ὁ ἰσχυρὸς boast in his ἰσχύι, and let not the rich boast in his riches, but ἐν τούτῳ καυχάσθω ὁ καυχώμενος, in understanding and knowing that I am Κύριος."[26] This is a passage like Isa 29.14, handmade for confounding Jewish claims to offer a σοφία guaranteed by σοφοί, and it draws Paul's mind into the abhorrence for "boasting" that is to be such a feature of his writing—boasting in human leaders (I,3.21), in some distinguishing person ("For who distinguishes you?" I,4.7), in outward appearance (II,5.12), in all manner of fleshly claims (II,10–12), in Jewish privilege (Rom 2.17 and passim). The comparison with Rom 1–4, set out above, shows the direction in which the argument is tending. All human religiosity ends in boasting, and all boasting is folly because human beings have noth-

---

[26]Schrage, *Der erste Brief,* 1:205–6, considers the similar wording of 1 Sam 2.10 as an alternative source for the citation in I,1.31, but as he concedes himself, the triple exposition in vv. 26–28 makes the use of Jer 9 clear. Barrett, *First Epistle,* 51, 61, supports a theory of H. St. John Thackeray that Paul was quoting from a sermon he had written for the ninth of Ab, for which Jer 8.13–9.24 was said to be the haphtarah. But there is no evidence for such a reading at this early date, and the passage fits the present context well. Also, Paul uses the same text again in II,10.17.

ing of which to boast: salvation is a gift of God through the cross. So God chose the world's have-nots to confound the haves "that no flesh should boast before God." But the particular people who are talking about wise men and scribes, and words of wisdom, at Corinth are Petrines appealing to nomistic Judaism; they boast about Peter, and they boast about being wise and strong.

It was "the wise" who brought Jer 9 to mind, and Jeremiah's mention of "the strong" was a bonus, since Paul was much more concerned with the πνευματικοί who claimed to be strong than with the δυνατοί. For the third clause, he declines to include Jeremiah's "rich"; he has no wish to embarrass his better-off converts, in whose houses the church is meeting (Rom 16.23: Gaius). He contrasts the εὐγενεῖς with the rhetorical ἀγενῆ, who are then explained as "the despised."[27]

The same tendency to gloss general expressions with Jewish concepts is evidenced in I,1.30. All Christians come from God in Christ Jesus, "who became wisdom for us"; all these claims to wisdom made by the religions have been turned to stupidity, but Christ has become wisdom for us. Just as God made Christ to be sin for us (II,5.21), so here we become masters of a divine wisdom (I,2.6), communicated to us in the word of the cross. But this general concept of wisdom, which was claimed by other religions besides Judaism, is then expounded as "righteousness and sanctification and re-demption." These are all Jewish ideas, and the contrast with Judaism is again made plain by the fuller explanation in Rom 3: "By works of the law *shall no flesh* be made righteous *before God,* for through the law is awareness of sin. But now apart from law a *righteousness of God* has been manifested . . . being made righteous freely by his grace through the *redemption* that is *in Christ Jesus. . . .* Where then is *boasting?"* (Rom 3.20–27). The same succession of phrases in I,1.26–31 shows that the wisdom Paul has in his sights is a wisdom of works of the law. Sanctification is a further Jewish concept transformed by Christianity. Jews taught, "You shall be holy, for I the Lord your God am holy" (Lev 19.2), but Christians were "made holy, sanctified" (ἡγιάσθητε, I,6.11) by baptism. This citation of Jer 9.23 recurs in II,10.17 with reference to the self-commending Jewish-Christian pseudoapostles. The parallel texts all show the same anti-Petrine tendency.[28]

---

[27]Schrage, *Der erste Brief,* 1:210–11, stresses the theological point as a creation ex nihilo, but the language points to the Abraham story (cf. Rom 4.17) rather than Gen 1, and Schrage misses the overtone of Gentile people being called into exis-tence at the expense of the "existent" Jewish authorities.

[28]Paul has made the same minimal adjustment to Jeremiah in both citations, interpreting ἐν τούτῳ as ἐν κυρίῳ; we may think this entirely justifiable in view of the κύριος following, on Christian presuppositions.

～ 5 ～

WISDOM AND TORAH IN
1 CORINTHIANS 2–16

THE CONTRAST between the word of wisdom and the word of the cross is
sharpened and clarified in the chapters of 1 Corinthians following, especially in the phrase "Not beyond what is written" (4.6), which has seemed so
obscure. Paul returns to his main theme with ch. 2 and pursues it with somewhat wandering feet into ch. 4. He is setting out a series of contrasts between
his gospel and the wisdom of the opposition. He began with:

> not in the wisdom of a word . . . the word of the cross (1.17)

Now we have:

> I came not in the excellence of word or wisdom . . . Jesus Christ and
> him crucified (2.1–2)

> not in the persuasiveness of wisdom, but in a demonstration of the
> Spirit and power (2.4)

> that your faith might be not in the wisdom of men but in the power of
> God (2.5)

> not in taught words of human wisdom, but in those taught of the Spirit
> (2.13)

> Not beyond what is written (4.6)

Paul's meaning is obscured by two features. First, he is speaking to a
context familiar to his readers but concealed from us, so that we have to
infer the force of his repeated antitheses. But then he is also being intention-
ally obscure because he does not wish to be confrontational. Despite his dis-
like of words of wisdom, he is prepared to allow that the Corinthians are
"enriched in every word" (1.5) and that the first gift of the Spirit is a word of
wisdom (12.8). So we have to peer through a double mist, and it is only gradually that the fog clears.

Clarity dawns at 4.6, when Paul takes off the mask of evenhanded fatherliness and explains what he has been up to: "I have transformed these things, brothers, on to myself and Apollos for your sake, that you may learn through us the [principle], Not beyond what is written, that you be not puffed up each for the one against the other." As mentioned above, μετασχηματίζειν always means "transform" in Paul (II,11.13–15; Phil 3.21) and is never found meaning "apply" or "turn into a metaphor" (ch. 2, p. 24). Paul has been speaking as if the crucial tensions (ταῦτα, all the issues that have been discussed so far) were between his converts and Apollos's, with the talk of planting, watering, building, and so on. He has done this δι' ὑμᾶς, "for your sake," for pastoral reasons, because he is trying to hold the church together and not drive out the Petrine converts (still less any waverers). But the real tensions have been with the Petrines. Apollos was merely watering the Pauline seed; it was "someone else" who has been building on Paul's foundation with quite dubious material.

Paul gives the reasons for this move in two ἵνα clauses, which correspond to the structure of the letter so far. Two topics have been handled: the wisdom issue, which has taken most of 1.18–2.16, and the parties issue, which occupied 1.10–17 and 3.1–4.5. But it is clear that the two are aspects of the same problem. The wisdom side is resumed in 3.18–20, for example, and is followed by "So let no one boast in men," Paul, Apollos, Cephas, and so on. In the same way, Paul has had two things in mind in cleverly transposing the issue on to himself and Apollos. He has been concerned, as I argued above, "that you be not puffed up, each for the one against the other"; he does not appreciate people boasting that Peter is a real apostle and Paul is not. But he is also concerned with the substantive issue, about wisdom, which now takes a surprising form: "that you may learn through us the [principle], Not beyond what is written."

This principle, which has caused so much trouble to interpreters, is (as Paul says it is) the key to understanding the whole argument so far. The "words of wisdom" that Paul forswore in 1.17; 2.1, 13 were the words of wisdom that Ben Sira poured forth (Sir 39.6), the דברי חכמה of the rabbis. Wisdom was the whole culture of Judaism, as is said in 4 Macc 1.17. The authorities to whom the Petrines appealed were the sages and scribes and debaters of this age, the חכמים, סופרים, and דרשנים in Jerusalem. The whole system of λόγοι, rulings, constituted the halakah by which normal Jews lived. In 2.13 Paul calls this "taught words of human wisdom," and he contrasts this with the much simplified way of life that he and Apollos taught, "Not beyond what is written"—the Bible and the Bible only.

This uncomplicated solution does justice to all the language used. The word γέγραπται is the standard Pauline form for reference to Scripture (1.19, 31; 2.9; 3.19, etc.). ὑπέρ implies going further than Scripture requires, as is done in the interpretations of the sages. These rulings (λόγοι) were made by the learned and had to be taught (διδακτοί) by scribes and other informed persons (2.13). They were a key part of Jewish σοφία and were regarded by its establishment as the oral torah, on a virtual par with the written Torah; but to a skeptic like Paul, it was merely human (ἀνθρωπίνη) wisdom. Such an understanding thus fits with a familiar distinction in Jewish lore and follows a contrast drawn by Paul himself between 2.13 and 4.6b.

There is a further significant point about 2.13. The phrasing in 1.26–31 showed that Paul was not merely using Jer 9.23 as an isolated oracle to cite in 1.31; he was also drawing on the context, with its three categories of potential boasters, including the σοφός and the ἰσχυρός. We may notice the same feature in 2.13. In 1.19 Paul cited Isa 29.14, "I will destroy the wisdom of the wise, and the understanding of the understanding will I [set at naught]." The previous verse in Isaiah, 29.13, says, "This people approaches me, with their lips they honor me, but their heart is far from me; and in vain do they reverence me, teaching commandments and teachings of men (διδάσκοντες ἐντάλματα ἀνθρώπων καὶ διδασκαλίας)." This text was to become the flagship of Pauline defense against the claims of the traditions of the elders. It was used in Col 2.22 and in Titus 1.14 and is put in full into Jesus' mouth in Mark 7.6–7. Every Pauline knew that the oral halakah had been condemned by God centuries before, and I,2.13 is our first evidence of its presence in the background, οὐκ ἐν διδακτοῖς ἀνθρωπίνης σοφίας λόγοις.

It may be asked how so simple a solution has not been noticed before; the answer will be partly that this is very different from what Paul says about the law elsewhere. But Paul knew, like Jonathan Swift, the eighteenth-century divine, that to change your mind is but to be wiser today than you were yesterday; he often changes his mind, especially about the law. The line he takes in 1 Cor 1–4, however, is substantially that which appears unstated behind the narrative of Gal 2.1–14: The "false brothers" came to spy out Pauline "freedom in Christ Jesus"; that is, they "saw" what they viewed as law-breaking and objected. When Peter came down, at first he "ate" with the Gentiles, but later withdrew. The most easily imagined situation is that the church was meeting for supper in the home of a Gentile, who has supplied meat bought in the market. The false brothers would be scandalized because it did not come from a kosher butcher, and goodness knows how it had been cooked. But both Paul and Peter (for a while) were not too upset by this. Animals had their throats slit in the market, so there was no question of consuming blood, which would have been unthinkable to both of them. But Leviticus does not mention kosher butchers or having two sets of cooking pots, one for meat, one for milk. That is "taught words of human wisdom." Paul and Apollos insisted on the biblical commandments but would have no elaborations on them—"Not beyond what is written."

The context of 2.13 confirms this: "But we did not receive the spirit of the world but the Spirit which is from God, that we may know the things bestowed on us by God, which we speak not in taught words of human wisdom but in those taught of the Spirit, interpreting spiritual things in spiritual teaching. But the natural (ψυχικός) man does not receive the things of the Spirit of God, for they are stupidity to him" (2.12–14). Paul is rounding off the discussion begun in 1.18. "The spirit of the world" is that imbibed by the Jewish sages, scribes, and debaters of this world in 1.20. "The things bestowed (χαρισθέντα) on us by God" are our salvation, our being made righteous, holy, and redeemed, for they are things that "we speak." Halakah rulings do not come into it: we "interpret (συγκρίνοντες) spiritual things in spiritual teaching"[1]—that is, we preach the simple message of the cross, with suitable ethical corollaries. Petrines claim to be πνευματικοί, but in fact they are only ψυχικοί (if not σαρκικοί): the cross is "stupidity" to them.

First Corinthians shows what Paul means. His proclamation had been the cross and the resurrection (I,1.18–2.5; 15.1–11), but the acceptance of this message entails a change of life. In part, this can be read straight out of the Bible. Deuteronomy 23.1 ("A man shall not marry his father's wife, thereby uncovering his father's skirt" [NRSV 22.30, mg.]) tells you that you may not sleep with your father's wife, but even Gentiles know this, and it is not necessary to cite it (I,5.1), although it is worth citing the nearby Deut 22.24, "Purge the wicked man from among you." Similarly, the idol-meat question may be settled on general grounds from Deut 32.17, "They sacrificed to demons and not God," to which Paul appeals in I,10.20. On such points he is not going beyond what is written. But ethical casuistry such as we find in the Mishnah is virtually absent from Paul. When Scripture does not settle a matter, he normally appeals to love as the supreme fruit of "the Spirit." This tells you what to do when your weak brother or sister is watching you go into a pagan temple or when some people come in late for the Eucharist supper.

First Corinthians 4.6b has been something of an aporia. Conzelmann says, "The phrase is unintelligible. Those who do not decide (with Baljon [a nineteenth-century Dutch critic]) to delete it as a gloss do not get beyond guesswork."[2] Fee says, "Here is a case where the apostle and his readers were on a wavelength that will probably be forever beyond our ability to pick up."[3] Schlatter, however, was less despairing and made the text the key to his interpretation of *die korinthische Theologie*. He accepted Lütgert's view of the Christ party as the charismatics who were Paul's anxiety and

---

[1]συγκρίνειν in the LXX normally means "to interpret" (Schrage, *Der erste Brief,* 1.261), as in Gen 40 for the interpreting of dreams, or in Dan 5 of the writing on the wall. πνευματικοῖς should be taken to have λόγοις understood, following the second διδακτοῖς: "interpreting spiritual things in [words] taught of the spirit." Schrage prefers "testing," with the parallel I,12.10 in view, but this introduces a new theme here and weakens the continuity.

[2]Conzelmann, *1 Corinthians,* 86.

[3]Fee, *First Epistle,* 169.

supposed that their slogan πάντα ἔξεστιν meant that one was free to go beyond Scripture with whores, idol meat, and so on. But this seems to require a
Pauline response of "Not against Scripture," rather than beyond it.

Morna Hooker takes the reference to be to the Scriptures cited in chs.
1–3, especially those in 3.19–20; but as Barrett says, "It is not easy to see
how one could go *beyond* the quotations in question." In particular, 4.6 seems
to refer to biblical requirements, but 3.19–20 is about God's knowledge and
apprehension of the wise. Ross Wagner accordingly takes the reference to
be to the requirement about boasting in 1.31, but 1.31 is a long way before
4.6, which gives the impression of being a more general principle. Supposed
echoes of Jer 9.23/1 Kgdms 2.10 in ch. 4 (φρόνιμος, ἰσχυρός, ἀσθενής) are
better taken as part of the current vocabulary of controversy.[4]

Welborn despairs of giving to ἃ γέγραπται the meaning *Scripture;* he
suggests a proverbial saying requiring two sides to a dispute to abide by a
written judgment of arbitration.[5] But one cannot easily envisage a formal ar-
biter in the Corinthian church, still less a written judgment, and the proverbial saying is a speculation.

FIRST CORINTHIANS 2.1–5

The antitheses of 2.1–5 then fall into place. "And I, when I came to you, did
not come in the excellence of a word or of wisdom," unlike the Petrines,
who came with their sparklingly inferred rulings and their trumpeted
halakic wisdom.[6] Paul came "proclaiming the mystery of God," and he "determined to know nothing among you but Jesus Christ, and him crucified."
This was a risky decision because many people, like the Petrines, would find
such a message implausible and think it "stupidity." Accordingly, Paul was
nervous when he stood up in the synagogue[7] to deliver his announcement:
"I was with you in weakness, and in fear and much trembling." Visiting
preachers would normally be semiqualified travelers, as is implied in Acts
13.15; they would be expected to be in contact with discussions of exegesis

---

[4]M. D. Hooker, "'Beyond the Things Which Are Written': An Examination of
I Cor. IV.6," *NTS* 10 (1963/4): 127–32; Barrett, *First Epistle,* 107; J. R. Wagner, "'Not
beyond the Things Which Are Written': A Call to Boast Only in the Lord," *NTS* 44
(1998): 279–87.

[5]L. L. Welborn, "A Conciliatory Principle in 1 Cor.4:6," *NovT* 29 (1987):
320–46.

[6]ὑπεροχή means "(pre-)eminence" and is used here ironically by Paul.
The similar καθ' ὑπεροχὴν δοκοῦντας, "preeminent in reputation," appears in
1 Clem. 57.2.

[7]Paul's use of καταγγέλλειν and κήρυγμα seems to confirm the Lukan picture
of his publicly addressing an assembly (Acts 18.4–6); nor is it easy to see him "in fear
and much trembling" as he talked to passersby and customers at his trade, as is supposed by Sanders, *Paul,* and other skeptics of Acts.

in Palestine and able to present an argued case for some points of halakah, as Paul shows himself able in Gal 3. His bare and paradoxical message was thus likely to be a disappointment.

However, Paul won over enough converts to make the foundation of a flourishing church: "my word and my proclamation were not in the persuasiveness of wisdom, but in demonstration of the Spirit and of power." Normal preachers, including the Petrines, would argue their points by inference from related scriptural texts, ἐν πειθοῖ σοφίας. The πειθ– root is pejorative; Paul was accused of persuading people (ἀνθρώπους πείθω) in Gal 1.10, and he justifies doing so (ἀνθρώπους πείθομεν) in II,5.11. There are always votes to be won by appealing to the "simple" against smart-aleck intellectuals. He spoke with his accustomed passion and the edifying result was "a demonstration of the Spirit and of [divine] power." In this way their faith did not rest "on the wisdom of men," the oral torah, but "on the power of God."

The readings in 2.4 vary considerably. ℵ* B D 33 have ἐν πειθοῖς σοφίας λόγοις (with minor errors), while 𝔓⁴⁶ itᶠᵍ have ἐν πειθοῖ[ς] σοφίας, with a cloud of more complex wordings. Schrage argues that λόγοις has been introduced in reminiscence of 2.13, with a final ς on πειθοῖ (an unusual [Attic] form of noun, but found in Philo and Josephus) turning it into an otherwise unknown adjective.[8] The difference does not greatly affect the interpretation.

Most interpreters continue to see some elements of a contrast between Paul's plain speaking and his opponents' gifts of rhetoric. On this unreal antithesis, see pp. 56–57, above. The real contrast is made plain by 2.13 and 4.6: rhetoric and eloquence have nothing to do with the discussion, which is about substance.

THE PARALLEL DISCUSSION IN COLOSSIANS

Opinion is divided over whether Paul wrote Colossians,[9] but even if it is deutero-Pauline, it is usually thought to be early deutero-Pauline[10] and was probably written within a decade of 1 Corinthians. The discussion in Colossians is in several ways similar to I,1–4. First, σοφία is a significant concept. Paul has been praying continually "that you may be filled with the knowledge of his will ἐν πάσῃ σοφίᾳ καὶ συνέσει πνευματικῇ" (Col 1.9).

---

[8]Schrage, *Der erste Brief,* 1.231–32.

[9]W. Schenk, "Der Kolosserbrief in der neueren Forschung," *ANRW* 25.4: 3327–64.

[10]P. Pokorný, *Colossians: A Commentary* (trans. S. Schatzmann; Peabody, Mass.: Hendrickson, 1991), 4, cites Käsemann: "If authentic, as late as possible on account of the style; if unauthentic, as early as possible" (E. Käsemann, "Kolosserbrief," *RGG* 3:1728).

He proclaims Christ, "warning every man and teaching every man ἐν πάσῃ σοφίᾳ" (1.28). Christ is the mystery of God "in whom are hidden all the treasures τῆς σοφίας καὶ γνώσεως" (2.3). Jewish-style purity rulings "have indeed λόγον σοφίας in self-imposed piety, ascesis, and disciplining of the body, but they have no value in checking the flesh" (2.23). We may note also 2.8: "Let no man take you captive διὰ τῆς φιλοσοφίας and vain deceit."

At first glance, there is a difference of perspective from 1 Corinthians; but we are warned to caution about such differences by Paul's apparent acceptance of λόγος and γνῶσις in I,1.5, "I give thanks . . . for you are enriched ἐν παντὶ λόγῳ καὶ πάσῃ γνώσει," and by his appropriating σοφία in I,2.6, "But we do speak σοφίαν among the perfect, but a σοφίαν not of this age." Such caution seems confirmed by Col 2.8: the Colossian converts are in peril from countermissionaries who may take them captive with vain and deceitful aspirations to σοφία. Such missionaries advocate wisdom, and Paul (or "Paul") is doing his best to trump their ace. He himself teaches everyone in all wisdom; he prays for them to be filled with all spiritual wisdom and understanding (not the other kind); all the treasures of wisdom and knowledge are in fact hidden in Christ. Whereas in 1 Corinthians he spent twenty verses attacking his opponents' wisdom with ironic paradoxes, now, as a more experienced polemicist, he limits himself to adapting their language to his own use.

Second, there is no question about the content of the opponents' wisdom in Colossians: "In [Christ] are hidden all the treasures of wisdom and knowledge. I am saying this that no one may deceive you ἐν πιθανολογίᾳ" (2.3–4). "See that no one takes you captive through philosophy and vain deceit κατὰ τὴν παράδοσιν τῶν ἀνθρώπων" (v. 8). "Let no one judge you over food and drink, or in respect of a festival or new moon or Sabbath" (v. 16). "Why as if you were living in the world do you subject yourselves to dogmas—do not handle, do not taste, do not touch—all of which are destined to perish with use κατὰ τὰ ἐντάλματα καὶ διδασκαλίας τῶν ἀνθρώπων?" (vv. 20–22). It is these practices that have a λόγον σοφίας (v. 23).

The wisdom of the countermission is Jewish Christianity. It prescribes what one is to do about food and drink and about the Jewish calendar. It can tell you in detail what you may not touch or taste. In other words, it prescribes kashruth, with a full treatment of halakah. This is twice said to rest on human tradition (vv. 8, 22), and again there is a reference to Isa 29.13, διδάσκοντες ἐντάλματα ἀνθρώπων καὶ διδασκαλίας, the same text that underlies I,2.13. Colossians 2.23 concedes that such practices offer a λόγον σοφίας, a front of wisdom,[11] so implying that wisdom was what was claimed for them by their proponents. But interestingly, 2.4 warns against being

---

[11]λόγον is used here in a different, though equally pejorative, sense from that in 1 Cor 1.17–2.5; NRSV translates, "an appearance of wisdom." Paul may well be exploiting an ambiguity in the opposition's slogan.

gulled ἐν πιθανολογίᾳ; this draws us back to I,2.4, where Paul's proclamation was not ἐν πειθοῖ σοφίας. Jewish oral torah was always presented as an argument, a rational persuasion by combining two or more scriptural texts, following certain prescribed middot.

There is more going on in Colossae than the advocacy of "normative Judaism" in Christianized form, as we shall see in ch. 7, below. But the essentially Jewish nature of the wisdom on offer there is transparent and confirms the picture of a Jewish-Christian wisdom behind I,1–4. It also confirms the practical response that Paul gave to the problem of the Jewish torah in Colossae. Colossians 2.20–22 is a specific exemplification of the principle laid down in I,4.6, τὸ μὴ ὑπὲρ ἃ γέγραπται. Paul and Apollos taught, "The Bible and the Bible only—no rulings of wisdom." The Colossian countermission laid down regulations (δόγματα), "Do not handle, do not taste, do not touch"—these are just the kind of "taught words of human wisdom" that Paul refused in Corinth (I,2.13), and he rejects them here, too.

PAUL AND THE LAW

Paul's treatment of the law follows this prescription generally, both in 1 Corinthians and in other letters, although he is driven in 2 Corinthians to take a more radical line. He cites the Bible freely as authoritative throughout the First Letter: "For it is written in the law of Moses, 'Thou shalt not muzzle the ox that treads the corn' [Deut 25.4]" (9.9); "It is written in the law that, 'By men of a strange tongue . . .' " (14.21) (although here "the law" is Isa 28.11–12 [cf. Deut 28.49]); women are to be subject "as also the law says" (14.34). But appeal is often made to biblical texts without their citation, as in 11.2–16.

Paul shows himself surprisingly relaxed over the law in I,7.19 ("Circumcision is nothing, and uncircumcision is nothing; but [what matters is] keeping the commands of God") and indeed also in Rom 14, which makes it voluntary whether Christians keep both food laws and "days," that is, Sabbath and other Jewish feasts. This is less problematic than it sounds. There is no text in Scripture that specifically requires Gentiles to be circumcised. Genesis 17 laid circumcision on Abraham and his descendants, and Exod 12.49 required it if slaves and aliens were to eat Passover. In the early church, there were clearly two views on the topic. Jerusalem missionaries could tell Paul's Galatian converts that it was necessary, but Paul could reply, "It is not laid down in the Bible; the rule is, Not beyond what is written."

I have noted above (pp. 3–5) the way the food laws first brought the torah issue to a head at Antioch. Here, too, I,4.6 covers the question. Paul would not consider for a moment authorizing pork or blood offal or strangled birds for an agape. These things were forbidden in Leviticus; it was the detailed kashruth rulings that one could ignore. The Roman church was divided between those who were happy to ignore them and the Jewish-type

Christians who did not feel comfortable with this and restricted themselves
to vegetables. One would have expected Paul to have run into trouble from
early on over Sabbath, because this *was* written and in fact was the fourth
commandment. But he would have dealt with it in the same way that Matthew permits lifting a sheep out of a pit on Sabbath (Matt 12.11). That is, he
would not have produced a legalistic argument, a λόγος σοφίας; instead—
what comes to much the same thing—he would have appealed to "the
Spirit," with love as the fulfillment of the law (I,2.13b; Rom 13.8–10). If you
require a Gentile to keep Sabbath, he will lose his job and his family will
starve; this cannot be τήρησις ἐντολῶν θεοῦ.

The principle set out in I,4.6 resolves the trickier problem of 9.19–23,
especially vv. 20–21, "And I became to the Jews as a Jew that I might win
the Jews, to those under torah as under torah, though I myself am not under
torah; to those without torah [I became] as without torah, though I am not
without God's torah but under the law of Christ, that I might win those without torah." The repeated intrusion of the Hebrew word makes the rendering
inelegant but enables us to retain a term covering both written and oral
commandments. *Torah* means both, whereas *the law* commonly means the
written text. Being a Jew meant living by the whole complex of the rulings of
the sages (ὑπὸ νόμον), and Paul says that when he was among Jews, he
would abide by the halakah. This would involve him in rituals of cleansing,
restrictions of diet, and so forth, and might be undertaken on his visits to
Palestine, but he did not regard himself as "under torah," obliged to observe
all these rules. In his Gentile archdiocese he lived without regard to any rulings of the wise, like his potential converts. He was not, of course, ἄνομος
θεοῦ, for he naturally observed all God's commandments as written; but
more generally, he was ἔννομος Χριστοῦ—he lived by the law of love.

E. P. Sanders has discussed Paul's response to the problem of the law
more than once.[12] He properly insists that Paul drew no distinction between
ritual and moral law; the distinction was, rather, between laws on serving
God and those on one's neighbor. Christians should observe both, although
Paul was reluctant to cite the Pentateuch to this end. He took Lev 19.18 to be
the cardinal principle of love and invoked it in fact to cover both "tables" of
the Decalogue. Sanders misses the force of I,4.6 (and does not ascribe
Colossians to Paul), so some nuances escape him, but his discussion is
illuminating.

Finally, the distinction between what is written (ἃ γέγραπται) and the
torah, the νόμος that is "beyond" it, resolves that long-standing problem,
I,15.56: "The sting of death is sin, and the power of sin is the law."

Paul has an A-B-A′ mentality: he starts many a topic and allows himself
to be diverted, but returns faithfully to the point in the end. This can be seen

---

[12]There is a short and clear account in Sanders, *Paul,* 84–100.

in his letters, including 1 Corinthians. For all that the casual reader feels that he is flitting from topic to topic, the letter has in fact an ordered structure:

> I,1–4. Parties as a threat to the church; the word of the cross as the true gospel, not the wisdom of halakah rulings;

> I,5–7. πορνεία as a moral peril, whether by a church member taking his father's wife, by the dangerous slogan "Anything goes," or by unreal asceticism, which will end in the same;

> I,8–10. εἰδωλόθυτα as a second moral peril: they should not be eaten even if idols do not exist, for the weak believer's sake, just as Paul forgoes his apostolic rights; tables of demons must be shunned, as Israel should have shunned idolatry of old;

> I,11–16. Cliques as a threat to the church at the Eucharist; the ordering of worship (11.2–16; 12–14); the true gospel of cross and resurrection, which is now in dispute (ch. 15); personalia.

Such a structure was in some sense given. πορνεία and idolatry were the two standard temptations for Gentiles, as Jews thought, and they had been the subject of Paul's agreement with the pillars, according to Acts 15.29; 21.25. They therefore form the core of the letter, and Paul prefaces his own informed comments (chs. 5–6) to the discussion of sexual matters raised in the Corinthians' letter (ch. 7). But these moral questions arise only because of a deeper malaise: the church's division on issues of loyalty and doctrine. Hence the "envelope" of chs. 1–4, 11–16. Paul thanks God that the church is enriched in every word and in all knowledge (1.5), gifts that head the list in ch. 12. He laments the divisions and quarrels (1.10–12), which reemerge in disorder at the church supper with women behaving badly, greed and drunkenness, the abuse of tongues, and general disedification (chs. 11–14). Personal notes about Stephanas and Apollos reappear in ch. 16, and there is more about Timothy and Paul's planned visit (4.17–21; 16.5–11).

The central doctrinal issue in chs. 1–4 was the substance of the gospel: was it the word of the cross that brought salvation, or was it the torah, the law with its penumbra of rulings of the sages, the taught words of human wisdom? Paul has defended the former: God decided to save believers by the stupidity of the κήρυγμα, he proclaims (κηρύσσομεν) Christ crucified, his κήρυγμα was in demonstration of the Spirit. He is not going to let this central topic lapse in a welter of practical trivia (chs. 11–14). So, having almost completed his responses to the Corinthians' letter (περὶ δέ, 7.1, 25; 8.1; 12.1; 16.1), he breaks off from their agenda and returns to his own in ch. 15. This was the εὐαγγέλιον that he had proclaimed to them, and the other apostles proclaimed it also (κηρύσσομεν, κήρυγμα), that Christ died for our

sins, was buried, and was raised the third day. First Corinthians forms a majestic *inclusio,* with ch. 15 resuming and completing the statement of the
κήρυγμα in chs. 1–2.

In 1.17–2.16 the word of the cross was contrasted with the halakah as
the means to salvation, and with the talk of σοφία went an unreal fantasy
that the kingdom of God had come already for the πνευματικοί (4.8–20).
Paul's resumption of the central κήρυγμα issue in ch. 15 moves on to the
theme of resurrection to counter this unreality. We are not spiritual people
already reigning; flesh and blood cannot inherit the kingdom of God. We
shall bear the image of the second, spiritual man, Christ, when he comes
from heaven, being transformed into new, spiritual bodies ourselves. The
Corinthian pneumatics have forgotten about Christ's physical resurrection,
which is the guarantee that our own will be physical also.

Paul expounds his understanding of the resurrection at the fullest
length of any topic in the epistle, more than fifty verses. It is only at the
end that we begin to realize that the denial of a resurrection from the
dead (15.12) with physical bodies (v. 35) is associated with claims to be
πνευματικοί already (vv. 44–49), in the kingdom of God (v. 50), as in
4.8–20. Having delivered the coup de grâce with his citation of Hos 13.14
and reached a climax of eloquence (15.54–55), he cannot resist putting the
knife in the torah spirituality that was the opposition's basic creed: "the sting
[of Scripture's θάνατος] is sin, and the power of sin is the law." Paul's readers knew that this was a resumption of his assault on the σοφία system of
1.17–2.16; νόμος is the Greek for *torah,* including the λόγοι σοφίας that
make the OT prescriptions into a practicable way of life. Perhaps some of
them had heard him expound the argument of Rom 7 during his first mission to the city, but to those who had not, the words may have come as a bit
of a surprise, as they have to most modern commentators.

Critics continue to wrestle with the riddle. F. W. Horn follows the suggestion of Straatman in 1863: a disciple of Paul has glossed in the verse to as-
similate the argument to Rom 7. H. Hollander and J. Holleman observe that
Cynic preachers associate degeneracy (i.e., sin and death) with the provisions of law; Paul sympathizes with them rather than with Philo, who
thought torah observance was salvific. T. Söding is closer to my exegesis. He
notes that the Adam/Christ typology of I,15.20–22, 42–49 is associated with
the Jewish law in Rom 7. The power of sin is contrasted with the power of
God in the σοφία discussion of I,1–2, and σοφία is associated with νόμος.[13]

---

[13]F. W. Horn, "1 Kor 15,56: Ein exegetische Stachel," *ZNW* 82 (1991):
88–105; H. W. Hollander and J. Holleman, "The Relationship of Death, Sin, and
Law in 1 Cor 15:56," *NovT* 35 (1993): 270–91; T. Söding, " 'Die Kraft der Sünde ist
das Gesetz'—1 Kor 15:56: Anmerkungen zum Hintergrund und der Pointe einer
gesetzkritischen Sentenz des Apostels Paulus," *ZNW* 83 (1992): 74–84.

↘ 6 ↙

THE OLD COVENANT

THE SEMIOFFICIAL Petrine emissaries of 1 Corinthians commended their teachings as words of wisdom; Paul saw them as a menace and treated them seriously. But although only a year separated the two Corinthian letters, it was a year full of shocks, and in 2 Corinthians he treats their teachings still more seriously. The summer visit to Corinth in 54 had been a disaster; a letter from his Galatian churches showed that an aggressive countermission was on the point of introducing circumcision there, and his flagship churches in and around Ephesus had turned against him. It is small wonder that in 2 Corinthians he was anxious to deal with the issue.

There is a faint echo of the old language in II,1.12, where Paul protests that his actions had all been in godly sincerity and not ἐν σοφίᾳ σαρκικῇ, but the proper discussion is in 2.14–4.6, where a different vocabulary is used because the new, official emissaries, the so-called apostles, are making a higher claim. All commentaries note the sharp change of topic that begins with 2.14, and many have supposed a different letter to begin there. But a simple explanation, in line with the manuscript tradition, would be that Paul wants to be done with his personal introduction and to get down to the main point in question. Just as the observance of torah, λόγοι σοφίας, was the first topic of 1 Corinthians (I,1.17–2.14), so the observance of torah, the glorious Mosaic covenant, is the first topic in 2 Corinthians (II,3.7–4.6). In both letters the substantive issue is entwined with charges on both sides of false claims to apostleship.

THE OLD COVENANT IN II,2.14–4.6

This is a difficult section because Paul is engaging closely with reported comments by his opponents, and these we have to infer from our one-sided text. Most of the inferences, however, may be made with some confidence; see the following short list of the Petrines' claims as they appear. We are helped by the fact that (as so often) Paul returns to his point of departure: 4.1–6 is in part a recapitulation of 2.17–3.6.

First, the Petrines carried letters of authorization from Jerusalem, naming them as apostles to the Corinthian church; they denied that Paul had any apostolic authorization (3.1–6, cf. pp. 35–36, above). He was forever, therefore, commending himself ("Are we beginning to commend ourselves again?" 3.1; 4.2).

Second, Paul was a mountebank who distorted the word of God (περιπατοῦντες ἐν πανουργίᾳ καὶ δολοῦντες τὸν λόγον τοῦ θεοῦ). Not only does Paul deny that he has been behaving so in 4.2; he returns, somewhat ironically, to the charge in 12.16: "All right, I did not burden you, but being a mountebank I trapped you dishonestly (ὑπάρχων πανοῦργος δόλῳ ὑμᾶς ἔλαβον)!" Their assertion that he misrepresented (δολοῦντες) the Christian message is balanced by Paul's equally forthright statement that they watered down (καπηλεύοντες)[1] the word of God (2.17).

Third, Paul's message was unintelligible: "And even if our gospel is veiled (κεκαλυμμένον), it is veiled in those who are perishing" (4.3). He is not likely to have conceded voluntarily that his gospel was obscure, and the opening εἰ δὲ καί does not in fact concede it.

Fourth, the Mosaic covenant was the way to life. Paul did believe in the Mosaic law (I,4.6!); it was holy and just and good (Rom 7.12) and is not overthrown by faith (Rom 3.31). But it was not the way of life—that was what the gospel was. He therefore introduces the notion that "the letter kills" (II,3.6), that the law is "the ministry of death" (3.7), "the ministry of condemnation" (3.9), "the old covenant" (3.14). The same doctrine of the law as the bearer of death is set out more fully in Rom 7.4–11; Paul drew the idea from the Adam story.

Finally, Moses had received the law on Sinai from the כבוד, the δόξα (3.7–11), the glory of God, which not only guaranteed its divine authority but even transformed Moses himself, whose face was infused with the same glory (3.10, 13). We may attribute this claim to the Petrines because, again, Paul does his best to diminish it: the glory of Moses' face was nothing compared to that in the face of Christ and was losing its force (3.10, 18; 4.6).

Less generally inferred, but still probable, is a second claim about the δόξα. It was an accepted part of the visionary tradition in Judaism that the adept might be carried into the presence of the divine glory, visible on the *merkabah,* and that he would then be transformed himself and would participate in this glory. The sudden stress on this having happened to Moses suggests that a similar claim was made by the new "apostles": *they* had been privileged to see the glory and had been transformed, and should accordingly be treated with supernormal respect. We seem to catch an echo of this in 4.5, "for we preach not ourselves but Jesus Christ as Lord," and where Paul presents himself as a mere "slave" of the church "through Jesus." Simi-

---

[1]Thrall, *Second Epistle,* 1:212–15, hesitates over authority for this translation but comes down in its favor, with a hint of financial dubiety.

larly in 3.18: "But we all with uncovered face beholding as in a reflector the Glory of the Lord are transformed into the same image from glory to glory." The "apostles" made these arrogant claims for themselves alone, but they are actually true—in a rather different sense—for the whole community, ἡμεῖς δὲ πάντες. Paul's ἡμεῖς πάντες is intendedly ambiguous: he means all Pauline Christians and indeed the whole church if they will join him.

If such a claim underlies the passage, it makes an important difference to the exegesis of the entire letter and can do with some further support. This is available from the prologue to the Fourth Gospel, where Jewish Christians draw on the same passage of Scripture, Exod 34, for the same purpose and John rebuts it with an argument close to Paul's. John 1.14 declares, "The Word became flesh and tabernacled among us, and we beheld his glory, glory as of the only-begotten of the Father, full of grace and truth." This is the glory that Moses saw in Exod 33–34, when the Lord proclaimed the name of God as "abounding in grace and truth" (34.6),[2] and that later filled the tabernacle (Exod 40) and tabernacled in Israel.[3] John 1.16 adds, "We have all (ἡμεῖς πάντες) received of his fullness, and grace upon grace." This grace is distributed to the whole church, which advances from glory to glory, and is not a privilege for the elite. A third point is made in John 1.17: "The law was given through Moses; grace and truth came through Jesus Christ." The divine gift did not come through the old covenant, the ministry of death, but through Jesus Christ. Finally, 1.18 concludes, "No one has ever seen God; the only-begotten God who is in the bosom of the Father, he has declared him." All claims to divine visions are fraudulent; what is given us is the illumination of the knowledge of the glory of God in the face of Jesus Christ.[4]

Commentaries on II,2.14–4.6 are normally rich in discussing the verbal links with, and differences from, Exodus, Jeremiah, and Ezekiel, but leave the reader unclear as to why the epistle is moving in this direction. Windisch famously isolated 3.7–18 as a "midrash" on Exod 34, an insertion of an earlier piece of writing ("eine literarische Einlage") into the Pauline context. He used *midrash* to mean exegesis, but his view of the section as an

---

[2]LXX differs from John with πολυέλεος καὶ ἀληθινός, but R. E. Brown, *The Gospel according to John* (2 vols.; AB 29–29A; Garden City, N.Y.: Doubleday, 1966–1970), 1:14, notes that John is not faithful to the LXX and that χάρις is a good translation of חסד.

[3]Ibid., 1:33; B. Lindars, *The Gospel of John* (London: Oliphant, 1972), 93; C. K. Barrett, *The Gospel according to St. John* (2d ed.; Philadelphia: Westminster, 1978), 165; and R. Schnackenburg, *The Gospel according to St. John* (3 vols.; trans. K. Smyth; New York: Herder & Herder, 1968–1982), 1.269–70, all refer John's ἐσκήνωσεν to God making Israel his σκηνή (Sir 24.8–10) and to God's taking up his dwelling (שכן) in temple and people (Exod 24.16; 25.8; 29.46; 40.35; Num 9.18).

[4]Petrine claims to divine visions will again engage us in ch. 7, below. In the meantime, we have enough confirmation of such a background to attempt here a more three-dimensional exegesis than is usual.

attack by a Christian on Judaism made its relevance obscure. Windisch is partly followed by Thrall. Others, such as Furnish, accept that the passage involves polemic but do not attempt a presentation of the opposition's case; however, caution then results in a wooden and unsatisfying exposition.

Joseph Fitzmyer contents himself with an analysis dependent on the association of certain key words—*letters, glory, veil,* and so forth—but the result of such an approach is inevitably to lose the thrust of meaning in the verbal maelstrom. Rhetorical analyses are similarly perilous; among the best is that of Jan Lambrecht, with its persuasive series of A-B-A' units, but it is stronger on structure than on line of thought. Other critics take risks. Murphy-O'Connor posits a double opposition, the Judaizers and the Spirit people, and has Paul attack the one and placate the other by turns, but the passage is more naturally read as against a single opposition.[5]

The most lively picture of the background to the passage is offered by Michael Theobald, who sees its thrust to be polemical throughout, with contemporary Christians in Corinth claiming to have been transformed by visions of the divine glory (as in the fifth point above).[6] The section thus belongs in its context and is about the struggle between Pauline and Jewish Christians, not about Christianity and Judaism. It is relatively unimportant that Theobald hypothesizes a written tradition from which we can derive key phrases and that he accepts an independent letter fragment, 2.14–7.4. His boldness deserves a warmer response than it has had; it has been accepted by Lambrecht but by few others.[7]

II,2.14–17; 4.1–5.   Paul began his letter with a personal introduction—a salutation, a thanksgiving, an account of his recent trials, an explanation for his delayed visit, a recommendation of kindness for the man who had offended him, an expression of relief and happiness. One cannot go on like this forever, and with 2.14 he bends his steps toward the primary trouble spot outstanding, the οἱ πολλοί of 2.17 who are watering down (καπηλεύοντες) the divine message, the so-called apostles with their letters of authorization from Jerusalem (pp. 35–36, above). The first issue that must be argued out is their wrongheaded claim that salvation is through the Sinai law, whose glory they are trumpeting. Their "different gospel" (11.5) no longer limits itself to assertions of "wisdom" but is offering an impressive appeal to the Exodus story, with pretensions to similar experiences of glory for the "apostles" themselves. So it is not so surprising if we find a sharp turn in Paul's thought.

[5] J. A. Fitzmyer, "Glory Reflected on the Face of Christ: 2 Cor 3:7–4:6," *TS* 42 (1981): 630–46; J. Lambrecht, "Structure and Line of Thought in 2 Cor 2,14–4,6," *Bib* 64 (1983): 344–80; Murphy-O'Connor, *Theology,* 35–41.
[6] M. Theobald, *Die überströmende Gnade: Studien zu einem paulinischen Motivfeld* (FB 22; Würzburg: Echter, 1982), 167–239.
[7] Lambrecht, "Structure," 372–80.

Paul's recovery from the Asian disaster provides the bridge into the new topic: "But thanks be to God who always leads us in triumph in Christ and displays the scent of his knowledge through us in every place" (2.14). The success of the mission in town after town (ἐν παντὶ τόπῳ)— Troas, Philippi, Thessalonica, and Corinth, too, now that Titus has brought better news—makes him think of a Roman triumphal procession: God is the victorious general, and the Christians are his conquered prisoners. Objects following θριαμβεύειν are elsewhere always the conquered, and Paul likes to speak of himself paradoxically as "the prisoner of Christ" (Phlm 1) or his slave. Such processions were religious in character, ascending to the temple of Jupiter in Rome, and it is likely that they were normally accompanied by censing priests, as we hear of the triumph of Scipio Africanus (Appian, *Hist. rom.* 8.66), or of the reception of Antoninus at Alexandria (Herodian, *Hist.* 4.8.8), or of the bridal procession in the Song of Songs.[8] ὀσμή and εὐωδία are terms derived originally from the smell of sacrificed animals (Lev 1.9, 13, 17; 2.12; etc.) but had come to be used of the scent of flowers: "As cinnamon and aspalathus I [Wisdom] have given a scent of perfumes (ἀρωμάτων ὀσμήν), and as choice myrrh I spread abroad a pleasant odor (εὐωδίαν) . . . as the fume of frankincense in the tabernacle" (Sir 24.15). The association of temple incense with the two nouns is especially relevant. Paul is spreading abroad "the scent of the knowledge of God" as the missionary procession advances: "we are the scent of Christ to God" (II,2.15), as the Roman thurifer spreads incense to the glory of Jupiter.

Scott J. Hafemann's account of Roman triumphal procedures shows beyond question that the object of θριαμβεύειν is always the conquered, never the victorious army.[9] He exaggerates, however, the "executions" at the end of the march. Josephus mentions seven hundred tall, handsome young Jews who were selected for Titus's triumph (*B.J.* 6.417–419), but they are not massacred; in *B.J.* 7.153–155 Simon son of Gioras alone is put to death (to public ovation). Josephus, who enjoys relating the tragic loss of life by his compatriots, would not have omitted the slaughter of the seven hundred had it taken place. Similarly, Appian does not suggest that it was the custom to kill all the prisoners in a triumph: Pompey was singular only in not killing *any* of them (12.12.116–117). Hafemann's insistence on the death symbolism of ὀσμή/εὐωδία is also exaggerated, and his exegesis of Sir 24.15 is perverse.[10]

---

[8]"Who is this coming up from the wilderness like a column of smoke, perfumed with myrrh and frankincense, with all the fragrant powders of the merchant? Look, it is the litter of Solomon!" (Song 3.6–7).

[9]S. J. Hafemann, *Suffering and the Spirit* (WUNT 2.19; Tübingen: Mohr, 1986), 18–39.

[10]Ibid., 41–51.

The same group seems to be at risk in II,4.3–4: "And even if our gospel is veiled, it is veiled in those who are perishing, among whom the god of this age has blinded the minds of the faithless lest they behold the illumination of the gospel of the glory of Christ." It is the new missionaries who have put Paul's gospel down as κεκαλυμμένον (along with some other offensive suggestions in 4.1–2), and Paul responds with a somewhat feeble riposte: it is veiled to them because they are blind. As in 2 Thess 2.10–12, the blindness is imputed to superhuman agencies who are deliberately deluding them so that they should not (εἰς τὸ μή) see the light. Here it is God's temporary usurper, Satan, the god of this age, who is frustrating their vision of Christ's glory, and it will later turn out that he has also sent these people (II,11.14–15). According to 11.15, their "end will be according to their deeds," that is, ἀπώλεια. They are spoken of here as τῶν ἀπίστων, an expression that in the NT sometimes means non-Christians and sometimes faithless Christians.

To Paul, as to John and other later followers, the true gospel was a matter of life and death, spiritual as well as physical. The word of the cross was the wisdom of God and brought salvation to those who believed; the law was fine in its way, but it could not save you. The corollary of this clear distinction was that there were two religions: Pauline Christianity, whose gospel was the cross and the resurrection, and Judaism, whose gospel was the law. Some Jerusalem "Christians" were in fact still Jews, including the Corinth "apostles"; nor was it only Paul who saw things in this way—James and Peter probably saw the Christian movement as a messianist sect of Judaism, hoping to take over the whole.

A further corollary of this black-and-white thinking is that the countermissionaries are deceivers, obstructing the preaching of the true gospel and seducing the simple into error. Such counterpreaching was not a forgivable lapse; it was damnable, and Paul consistently says so. In 2 Thess 2.10–12 he writes of those who proclaim that the Day of the Lord has come (2.2): "they refused to love the truth and so be saved. For this reason God sends them a powerful delusion so as to believe a lie, so that all who have not believed the truth but took pleasure in unrighteousness might be damned (κριθῶσιν)."[11] In Phil 3.18–19 the Jewish-Christian "dogs" are enemies of the cross of Christ, and their end is destruction (ἀπώλεια), eternal death. Similarly, in our own epistles, it is said of Petrine missionaries, "If anyone destroys the temple of God, him will God destroy" (I,3.17), and, "whose end will be according to their deeds" (II,11.15).

---

[11]I have defended Pauline authorship of 2 Thessalonians in M. D. Goulder, "Silas in Thessalonica," *JSNT* 48 (1992): 87–106. Those who think the letter to be inauthentic may accept the evidence of Phil 3.18–19 and see 2 Thessalonians as a development of the same dogmatic intolerance in the next generation.

The ἀπολ- root is used by Paul three further times, each in the form τοῖς ἀπολλυμένοις, for those who reject his gospel: once in I,1.18 and twice in our present passage, II,2.15 and 4.3. In I,1.18 the meaning is open; the phrase might mean those outside the church who do not accept the preaching or those within who label the Pauline gospel stupidity. In II,2.15 the image of the triumph makes it plain that it is the "many who water down the word of God" who are perishing. God is leading a triumphal procession of his prisoners (the church), and the procession is censed, in part with "the odor of life to life" (for the Pauline Christians) and in part with the "odor of death to death" (for the false apostles). It was only prisoners marching in a Roman triumph who ended the day executed, not those watching, and some (like the Paulines) might have their lives spared.

ἄπιστος is used regularly in 1 Corinthians (eleven times, in four contexts) to mean *pagan,* and it appears once in the Pastorals in the same sense (1 Tim 5.8). Elsewhere it means faithless Christians/Israel (Matt 17.17 par. Mark 9.19 par. Luke 9.41, "O faithless generation"; Luke 12.46, "put him with the faithless," in contrast with the faithful steward of 12.41; John 20.27, "Be not faithless but believing (ἄπιστος . . . πιστός)"; Titus 1.15, "to the corrupted and faithless nothing is pure," in contrast with pure [Pauline] Christians; Rev 21.8, "But as for the cowardly, the faithless," in contrast with those who conquer). There are three uses in 2 Corinthians (4.4; 6.14, 15), in the last of which ἄπιστος is again contrasted with πιστός, a term never used to mean a Christian.[12]

Paul frequently ascribes the failures of God's people to predestination. According to Romans, God laid a stone of stumbling for Israel (9.33); he gave them a sluggish spirit and eyes that would not see (11.8) and darkened their eyes (11.9). Paul never uses such language for those outside the elect community. It is best, therefore, to take all three references to τοῖς ἀπολλυμένοις in Corinthians as intending Paul's Petrine opponents. It is they who speak of God's wisdom as stupidity, they who water down the word of God and will end the divine triumph in death, they who speak of Paul's gospel as veiled because Satan has blinded their minds. Like other saints, Paul had endless patience with outsiders, but when it was with counter-missionaries who should know better, he felt all the sympathy of Stalin for the Trotskyists.

II,3.1–6. "Are we beginning to commend ourselves again? Or do we need as some do letters of commendation to you or from you?" Paul had heard of a repeated attack: "We are apostles to the Corinthian church, with letters of authorization from the Jerusalem leaders. This Paul has no such authority, and all he can do is commend himself, with his 'I was here first' [I,4.15], his

---

[12]See Goulder, "2 Cor. 6:14–7:1," 47–57; and p. 228, below.

supposed visions [I,9.1; 15.8], and his marvelous speaking with tongues [I,14.18]." The reference to his sincerity in 2.17 would invite the same jibe, and Paul takes the offensive.

First, he depreciates the new missionaries' authority. They had letters authorizing them (ἱκανότης, ἱκάνωσεν, 3.5–6, pp. 33–35), but Paul speaks of their letters as merely συστατικῶν ἐπιστολῶν, commendatory letters, requesting a favor from the recipient.[13] Such letters might in turn be written by the Corinthian community to its daughter churches at Cenchreae or Nicopolis, commending the Jerusalem missionaries, but the papers they brought from Palestine would not have been couched in such humble terms.

Second, Paul adroitly takes the high, spiritual ground, adapting his opponents' claims, as he does so often. Did they proclaim wisdom? "But we do speak wisdom among the perfect, but it is . . . a wisdom of God" (I,2.6–7). Do they carry letters? "You are our letter, inscribed on your hearts, known and read by all men."[14] Everyone in Corinth can be aware of the transformed lives of its church members and can read such a letter as Paul has inscribed on them; the rhetorical twist flatters, challenges, and edifies, and the reader is left feeling that the discussion has moved on to a higher plane.

The apostle is even subtler. His opponents have come proclaiming salvation through the law, which God gave to Moses in Exod 31.18 in the form of two πλάκας λιθίνας γεγραμμένας τῷ δακτύλῳ τοῦ θεοῦ. But Ezekiel was to prophesy that God would give Israel a heart of flesh to replace their old stony heart (ἀφελῶ τὴν καρδίαν τὴν λιθίνην ἐκ τῆς σαρκὸς ὑμῶν καὶ δώσω ὑμῖν καρδίαν σαρκίνην, Ezek 36.26, cf. 11.19). Paul is already playing on this contrast: the law was written in stone for stony hearts, the gospel is written (ἐγγεγραμμένη) on the hearts of the Corinthian Christians. This becomes clear in 3.3: "[as you] display that you are a letter of Christ, administered by us, inscribed not with ink but with the spirit of the living God, not on stone tables but on tables of hearts of flesh." The πλαξίν makes clear the reference to Sinai, the combination λιθίναις/καρδίαις σαρκίναις shows the influence of Ezekiel. The law was a hard thing, for the hardhearted; the gospel is the saving word of God, implanted in human hearts at

---

[13]Thrall, *Second Epistle,* 1:217–22, argues, against a Jerusalem background, that such letters should have been more than συστατικαί if they were to convey the apostolic authority evident in chs. 10–13. But she misses the force of ἱκανοῦν, -ότης and underestimates Pauline guile.

[14]There is variation in the textual tradition here: ἡμῶν 𝔓⁴⁶ A B C D etc.; ὑμῶν ℵ 33 *pc.* The context seems to require the minority ὑμῶν. It is the Christian lives of the Corinthian church members that are known and read by all people, displaying that they are a letter of Christ, and Paul has just shown how careful he needs to be about commending himself. The variant ἡμῶν could have been introduced from a scribe's familiarity with II,7.3, ἐν ταῖς καρδίαις ἡμῶν, or from the similarity of sounds; so Bultmann, *Second Letter,* 71, Barrett, *Second Epistle,* 96 n. 3, and hesitantly Thrall, *Second Epistle,* 1:223–24.

the end of this age, as God promised. This is depreciation of high quality, the state of the art.

In 3.4–6 Paul combines defense with further attack: "But such confidence have we through Christ toward God; not that we are ἱκανοί of ourselves to make any judgments as of ourselves, but our ἱκανότης is from God, who also ἱκάνωσεν us as ministers of a new covenant." He does not have any letters from Jerusalem, but he has unshakable confidence in his position, which stems from his call by Christ on the Damascus road; so his authorization (ἱκανότης, pp. 33–35) is from God direct, who has authorized him (ἱκάνωσεν) as minister of the "new covenant," which Jeremiah prophesied would replace the old Sinai covenant. These new missionaries may wave their letters that purport to give them authority to lay down halakah (λογίσασθαι) about this and that. Paul does not rely on human authorization (ἀφ' ἑαυτῶν, ἐξ ἑαυτῶν; cf. II,10.12); he was given his commission as apostle to the Gentiles directly by Christ. He is not speaking rubbish; the reality of his vocation was his fundamental conviction.

II,3.7–11. Paul's problem is that he must concede the glory of the Sinai dispensation because it is in Exodus, whereas he has no basis for claiming such glory for his own ministry. His solution is to depreciate Sinai further and to make inferences to the glory of the gospel by the Jewish technique of קל־וחומר. The Sinai covenant, "the ministry of death engraved in letters on stones," as he puts it so appreciatively, was indeed instituted "in glory," just as the new missionaries claim. It is true that "the children of Israel could not gaze on Moses' face because of the glory of his face, which was being brought to nothing." But how much "more," then, "will the ministry of the Spirit be in glory!" The Sinai covenant was "the ministry of death"—Adam was given the commandment, and it brought him to death (Rom 7.4–11); it was "in letters engraved on stones" and could never achieve what a law written in the heart could do. Moses' glory was only a temporary thing, "being brought to nothing." καταργουμένην should not be translated "fading"; it is a passive, and Paul intends it so—*God* was bringing it to nothing, as God is bringing the whole Exodus covenant (3.11). In 3.9 Sinai is spoken of as "the ministry of condemnation," contrasted with the gospel as "the ministry of righteousness," and in 3.11 "that which is being brought to nothing" is set against "that which abides." In 3.10 "that which has been glorified"—Moses' face in Exod 34.35—"has not been glorified" at all "in respect of [this contrast] [ἐν τούτῳ τῷ μέρει], because of the overwhelming glory" of the Spirit. Romans 8.4–11 expounds more fully the same opposition between law and Spirit.

II,3.12–13. It may be doubted whether this sally would have carried much conviction with Corinthian doubters, so the apostle renews the attack, with increasing unfairness. He teaches "with complete openness (πολλῇ

παρρησίᾳ), and not as Moses put a veil over his face, so that the sons of Israel should not gaze on the end of that which was being brought to nothing."
The Exodus story says that the shining of the skin on Moses' face caused the
Israelites to fear coming near him (Exod 34.31), that he told them the divine
law unveiled (34.32), and that thereafter he put a veil on his face, which he
removed when speaking with God (34.33–35). There is no suggestion in the
text, nor in any Jewish exegetical tradition, that the glory was fading or that
Moses was trying to hide anything from the people. This is simply Paul's
eisegesis, his further attempt to denigrate Sinai. Moses, he says, put the veil
on to stop (πρὸς τὸ μή) the Israelites seeing how temporary his glory was.
The introduction of the veil (κάλυμμα) theme arises from the new missionaries' slur on Paul, that his gospel was "veiled" (κεκαλυμμένον, 4.3); he is determined to hoist them with their own petard.

II,3.14–18.   A veil already suggests a barrier, and Paul was exploiting this in
v. 13: with "such a hope [of glory in the Spirit] we use complete openness,
and not as Moses." Paul certainly did say openly what he thought God had
given him to say, but then, so did Moses; there was no veil when Moses delivered the law in Exod 34.32. But the image is too good to miss, and the
apostle turns it to new account in the following verses. "But their minds were
hardened," despite (ἀλλά) the glory attending Sinai; he has in mind passages
such as Isa 6.9–10 and uses the same verb, ἐπωρώθη(σαν), at Rom 11.7. "For
to this day the same veil remains at the reading of the old covenant, not
being lifted, because in Christ it is being brought to nothing." Paul sees "the
same veil" as a barrier of understanding: it symbolized the failure of the
Sinai covenant to bring salvation, and the barrier remains "to this day"
when the torah "is read," whether in synagogue or in church. Paul expects
the Corinthians not to be ignorant of many matters of which they could
hardly have known without some liturgical reading, and the new Jewish-
Christian leadership will surely have insisted on such.

The Sinai covenant is now spoken of as "the old covenant," in contrast
to the new covenant promised in LXX Jer 38.31, with the suggestion of its ob-
solescence. Paul's thought is compressed to the point of obscurity. The reading of the Torah is the centerpiece of his opponents' message and, as such,
constitutes a barrier to salvation, a veil. But the thought then arises, Why
continue reading it? The answer is, It does no harm and is useful for ethical
guidance and other matters; but in Christ it is replaced by the gospel. "But"
unfortunately it does do some harm: "till today, whenever Moses is read, a
veil lies on their heart," and Jews and Jewish Christians alike still think the
torah the way to salvation.

"But when he turns to the Lord, the veil is taken away"; that is, now
and again one of "them" (αὐτῶν, v. 15) turns to the Pauline gospel, and then
the veil is removed and that person sees the divine truth. Paul is adapting
Exod 34.34, which says of Moses, ἡνίκα δ' ἂν εἰσεπορεύετο ἔναντι κυρίου

λαλεῖν αὐτῷ, περιηρεῖτο τὸ κάλυμμα; in Exod 34.31 the congregation turned to (ἐπεστράφησαν πρός) Moses. It was Paul's experience that Jews did turn to the Lord in ones and twos; there were Jews in the Corinthian church (I,7.18), and he hoped to win more (I,9.20). But the big rush would not come till the end (Rom 11.7–36). The word κύριος in Exodus means Yahweh, of course, but Paul often uses it of Christ as well as of God. Here, however, he clears up the ambiguity: "But the Lord is the Spirit." In the earlier verses of the chapter, he was contrasting the ministry of the letter with the ministry of the Spirit (3.3, 6, 8), so he prefers *the Spirit* to *Christ.* He treats Christ and the Spirit as virtually the same in Rom 8.9–11: "the Spirit of God dwells in you . . . Christ is in you . . . the Spirit of him who raised Jesus from the dead dwells in you."

As so often with Paul, the background to a passage becomes clear at its end. "And where the Spirit of the Lord is comes freedom." The issue is the same as that Paul debated at greater length and with greater passion in Gal 4. There the law exercised a kind of slavery over those under it, but with baptism we received the Spirit of God's Son and so freedom. Freedom, ἐλευθερία, was freedom from the angelic "elements" who administered the law, and Paul could end, "For freedom has Christ set us free: stand firm, therefore, and do not submit again to a yoke of slavery." The Jerusalem "apostles" have come glorifying the old covenant, but it is a ministry of condemnation; righteousness and freedom lie in the word of the cross alone.

But there is a reason for the new missionaries' appeal to the "glory" of the Sinai covenant and to its transformation of Moses' face, which have been such a feature of the discussion. Second Corinthians 12.1 shows that Paul was criticized for spiritual inadequacy in that he did not have visions of God (pp. 108–10), and the same issue underlies the present chapter. The new leaders claim to have had visions of the כבוד, the δόξα, the glory of God.[15] They have been ravished (ἁρπαγέντα, II,12.2–3) to the presence of the *merkabah;* and they, like Moses, have been transformed into the shining reflection of that glory.[16] It is this claim that has led to all the discussion about δόξα in 3.7–11 and about the veil in 3.12–18 and that now concludes

---

[15]See C. C. Rowland, *The Open Heaven: A Study of Apocalyptic in Judaism and Early Christianity* (London: SPCK, 1982), 94–96, 280–81; C. R. A. Morray-Jones, "Transformational Mysticism in the Apocalyptic-Merkabah Tradition," *JJS* 43 (1992): 1–31; A. F. Segal, *Paul the Convert: The Apostolate and Apostasy of Saul the Pharisee* (New Haven: Yale University Press, 1990), 34–71; J. D. Tabor, *Things Unutterable: Paul's Ascent to Paradise in Its Graeco-Roman, Judaic, and Early Christian Contexts* (SJud.; Lanham, Md.: University Press of America, 1986), 9–19; M. Barker, *The Great Angel: A Study of Israel's Second God* (London: SPCK, 1992).

[16]See pp. 76–78 above. Morray-Jones, "Transformational Mysticism," gives examples of transformation by vision from the apocalypses, Qumran, and Philo: Enoch, Adam, Moses, Melchizedek, the righteous. Often their bodies are turned to

with a spiritualized counterclaim: "But we all with unveiled face, beholding as in a reflector the glory of the Lord, are transformed into the same likeness from glory to glory, as from the Lord the Spirit."

The new missionaries claimed to have seen the glory and to have been physically glorified as they beheld it, "but we all," every (Pauline) Christian, have "beheld" in a different way the divine glory; Moses had a veil over his face, but we have our vision of Christ "with unveiled face." They boast of a face-to-face vision of the glory—not indeed of the very God, which would kill them, but of God's image; "We behold [as] in a reflector the glory of the Lord," that is, Christ.[17] In II,4.4 Paul will speak of "the gospel of the glory of Christ," and in II,4.6 of "the glory of God in the face of Jesus Christ." In the back of his mind is Num 12.8: "I will speak to [Moses] mouth to mouth, ἐν εἴδει καὶ οὐ δι' αἰνιγμάτων, καὶ τὴν δόξαν κυρίου εἶδεν." This leads him to write in I,13.12, "For now we see δι' ἐσόπτρου ἐν αἰνίγματι, τότε δὲ πρόσωπον πρὸς πρόσωπον." We do have a vision of God's glory here, in Christ, but it is an indirect vision as via a reflector of polished bronze, with all its distortions; the full vision will be hereafter. As Paul used ἔσοπτρον in I,13.12, so he uses κατοπτριζόμενοι now—our vision is still indirect.[18]

Jewish mystical tradition stressed the transformation of the adept from his vision of the glory: he would be glorified by the experience and turned marvelously into the likeness of the image of God.[19] And so, says Paul, are "we all transformed into the same Image from glory to glory." Our glory is not the visible kind the others talk about but a transformation of the character, worked through suffering,[20] and we advance daily from one level of such glory to another. We are being transformed into the image of God, spo-

---

fire, which might not happen to the ordinary adept, but only the transfiguration of Moses' face is in Scripture, in the passage from Exod 34 under discussion. He notes the presence, in II,3.18, of key *merkabah* vision language: εἰκών, κατοπτρίζεσθαι, μεταμορφοῦσθαι.

[17]κατοπτρίζεσθαι is most usually rendered "behold as in a mirror," although alternatives are "reflect" and "behold" (the mirror idea having faded). Evidence for the latter is late, and it would be peculiar for Paul to use so rare a word (here only in his writings) without its metaphorical force. There is no evidence for "reflect" in the versions and disputable evidence in the Fathers. See the full discussion in Thrall, *Second Epistle,* 1:290–92. Lambrecht (Bieringer and Lambrecht, *Studies,* 299 n. 15) cites as recent defenders of "reflect" some eminent names—Dunn, Hooker, C. F. D. Moule, W. C. van Unnik.

[18]Thrall, *Second Epistle,* 1:293, points to the differences of context with I,13.12 and prefers a link with Wis 7.26, which certainly may not be denied.

[19]So *2 En.* 22.10; *3 En.* 9–15; Philo, *Mos.* 1.155–158. For the equivalence of *image* and *glory,* see J. Lambrecht, "Transformation in 2 Cor 3,18," in R. Bieringer and J. Lambrecht, *Studies on 2 Corinthians* (BETL 112; Leuven: Leuven University Press/Peeters, 1994), 295–307.

[20]See II,4.7–15 on Paul's sufferings; cf. I,4.10, ὑμεῖς ἔνδοξοι, ἡμεῖς δὲ ἄτιμοι.

ken of in Gen 1.26, and this image is Christ (cf. II,4.4, "the illumination of
the gospel of the glory of Christ, who is the Image of God"). Such transformation is the work of "the Lord the Spirit," who brings forth fruit of love,
joy, and peace in our hearts and impressive gifts besides.[21]

II,4.1–6. Paul rounds off the discussion by returning to the altercations of
2.15–3.6, in part fending off his rivals' attacks (pp. 81–83) and in part offering his own riposte. Verses 1–2 of ch. 4 are a reprise of 3.12, "So having such
hope we use complete openness"; "Therefore having this ministry, as we
have received mercy, we do not default, but have forsworn the hidden
things of shame." The uses of ἔχοντες in both passages and the parallel
οὖν/διὰ τοῦτο suggest that the same contrast is in mind. The trouble with
telling people about your visions and about your face being transformed
with divine glory is that your face looks very much as it did yesterday and
the experience seems always to be a private one. Hence Paul's challenge.
Everything he says is πολλῇ παρρησίᾳ; their claims are always of private
events, τὰ κρυπτά, which he glosses naughtily as τῆς αἰσχύνης, "of disgrace."[22] He has had his own experience, when he received the divine
mercy (ἠλεήθημεν) on the way to Damascus (cf. II,12.7), which he has been
quite open about. He does not default (οὐκ ἐγκακοῦμεν)[23] on the commission he then received, either by failing to keep his promised visits (1.17–22;
12.14–18), by embezzlement (πανοῦργος δόλῳ, 12.16), or by failing to present the gospel with which he has been entrusted (δολοῦντες τὸν λόγον τοῦ
θεοῦ). On the contrary, he "commends himself to everyone's conscience before God by the demonstration (φανερώσει) of the truth." He is quite open
about everything.

Verses 3–4 offer a counter to charges that Paul's gospel is "veiled,"
that is, obscure; he makes the tu quoque that it is only "veiled among
the perishing," whom Satan has blinded.[24] But with v. 5 he returns to the
offensive: "For we do not proclaim ourselves but Jesus Christ as Lord,
and ourselves your slaves through Jesus." How different are the new

---

[21]A variety of translations have been proposed for ἀπὸ κυρίου πνεύματος
(Thrall, *Second Epistle,* 1:287, prefers the one given here). But the logic behind it
seems clear: for Paul what matters is the transformation of the heart in love.

[22]It is a problem to know when Paul is defending and when he is attacking.
Thrall, *Second Epistle,* 1:300–301, suggests that Paul took a resolve at his call
(ἀπειπάμεθα) to be straightforward. But this seems unlikely, and μηδὲ δολοῦντες
τὸν λόγον τοῦ θεοῦ sounds very much like οὐ . . . ὡς οἱ πολλοὶ καπηλεύοντες τὸν
λόγον τοῦ θεοῦ (2.17).

[23]BAGD gives the translations "become weary, tired," and "lose heart, despair," but these renderings are not given at all in LSJ, which gives "behave re-
missly." The latter is justified by Thrall, *Second Epistle,* 1:299, and gives good sense
here and in 4.16 as well as some other Pauline passages.

[24]Paul does not mind using θεός of other gods (I,8.6b; Phil 3.19), although this
is rare; Murphy-O'Connor, *Theology,* 42, prefers "Beliar" to "Satan."

missionaries![25] They proclaim themselves with their marvelous visions and their transformation into glory, and in consequence of such claimed experiences, they lord it over the church (11.18–21). Whereas Paul is the δοῦλος of the Corinthians, his rivals enslave them (καταδουλοῖ, 11.20); it sounds as if they regard themselves, not Jesus Christ, as lords of the church.

Paul opens his final sentence, v. 6, with a puzzling stress: "because it is God who said, 'Out of darkness light shall shine,' who shone in our hearts for the illumination of the knowledge of the glory of God in the face of Jesus Christ."[26] The ὅτι must be a link back to the previous discussion, and several features warn us that Paul is picking up elements of his rivals' claims.[27] "It is God who said" implies a contrast with someone else saying it. *Knowledge,* γνῶσις, is a major feature of the Petrines' vocabulary (see ch. 7, below). "The glory of God" has been the centerpiece of their message in the foregoing discussion. The long catena of genitives is itself a sign that Paul is glossing the opposition's creed: they claimed "the illumination of the knowledge of the δόξα."[28] He explains this as "the glory of God" and adds what he believes himself, that this glory is to be seen "in the face of Jesus Christ."

If Paul is taking up so much of the opposition's language, we may think it proper to explain the whole of v. 6 on this basis. Paul proclaims himself "your slave through Jesus," in contrast to his rivals' arrogance, "because" (ὅτι) it is God, not they, who summoned light out of darkness. What God said in Gen 1.3 was γενηθήτω φῶς, and it has been a problem why Paul cites the text in the form Ἐκ σκότους φῶς λάμψει.[29] We may suppose that here, too, we have his rivals' words. Perhaps as the adept closed his eyes and "went down" to the Chariot, he hypnotized himself with the words "Out of darkness light shall shine," or perhaps he instructed aspirants to hope for such an experience with these words. We would then have some explana-

---

[25]Others see this as defensive: perhaps Paul was attacked for talking too much about his great experience (Furnish, *II Corinthians,* 249). But we do not hear much about the Damascus road in the Epistles.

[26]Thrall, *Second Epistle,* 1:314 n. 862, claims the syntax is awkward and justifies the RSV and the JB in rendering, "the God who said Out of darkness shall light shine, is the one who shone." This certainly is awkward, not to say forced, Greek (*pace* Barrett, *Second Epistle,* 127); it is more natural to supply ἐστίν after θεός. Furnish, *II Corinthians,* 224, avoids the awkwardness by treating ὅς as an anacoluthon.

[27]Furnish, *II Corinthians,* 223, is sympathetic to Plummer's suggestion that the "God" of light in 4.6 is contrasted with "the god of this age" of darkness in 4.4, but this would seem to require ἀλλά.

[28]M. D. Goulder, "The Visionaries of Laodicea," *JSNT* 43 (1991): 15–39, here 19–20.

[29]The phrase φῶς λάμψει comes in Isa 9.1, without ἐκ σκότους, but the emphatic ὁ θεὸς ὁ εἰπών shows clearly that Genesis is in mind. When Jewish mystics ascended (as we would say) for the vision of the divine Chariot (following Ezekiel), they often used the verb יֹרֵד, "to descend"—hence perhaps the reference to darkness. Cf. I,2.10, τὰ βάθη τοῦ θεοῦ.

tion for the implied contrast "it is God who said" (ὁ θεὸς ὁ εἰπών), for the linking "because," and for the future λάμψει where we would have expected a subjunctive and the Genesis form. The adept is not in a position to command *Fiat lux,* "Let there be light," but he is in a position to prophesy and may adapt Gen 1.3 to Isa 9.1. φωτισμός similarly is not a Pauline word; it is likely that it was part of the new missionaries' message, which Paul is aligning with his own theology.[30]

CONCLUSION

The countermission to Corinth came from Jerusalem, and it had the same fundamental concern there as it had in Galatia: the torah, written in the Pentateuch and expounded by the sages, was the word of God and the essential basis of salvation. For centuries Jews had commended their way of life in the Diaspora as a divine "wisdom" rather than as a law; it was more attractive to see Jewish ways as the road to success, long life, and peace of mind than as a set of regulations whose infraction might involve punishment. Thus, when the first Petrine emissaries reached Corinth in 53, they spoke of the torah as wisdom and of the specific rulings of the sages as "words of wisdom," a phrase going back to Ben Sira and used in the Talmud. They did not begin by requiring circumcision. It was not clear that the law required Gentiles to be circumcised, and Diaspora synagogues in general accepted a penumbra of uncircumcised Gentile attenders, God-fearers; also, common sense might suggest that it was not the easiest place to start.

Paul knew that this was the fundamental battle he had to fight, and he opens 1 Corinthians with four chapters dealing with it. It is interwoven with the authority question, so the discussion moves back and forth between the claims of Cephas's followers and the issue of wisdom. The followers of Apollos also have their place, but this is as a smoke screen to prevent the letter becoming a confrontation between Paul and the Petrines. Paul defends the line "The Bible and the Bible only." The oral torah, the traditions of the sages, are "taught words of human wisdom"; Paul and Apollos have kept to the principle "Not beyond what is written." This leads him on to deal rather fiercely with the man who has married his father's wife, with other sexual issues (I,5–7), and with the worship of idols (10.1–22). πορνεία and idolatry were the two cardinal Gentile sins, and he needed to show that he was firm about these. He could afford to be relaxed about circumcision

---

[30]The suggestion is, of course, speculative, but with such a verse all exegetes must speculate. Thrall, *Second Epistle,* 1:316–18, invokes a supposed Pauline account of the apostle's christophany, in which he used the word λάμπειν, which later reappears in Luke's telling of the story in Acts 26.13 (actually λαμπρότητα, περιλάμψαν) but was omitted in Acts 9.22, where φῶς occurs.

(7.18–19). But the law was not the means of salvation; this belonged to "the word of the cross" alone. The law might be useful for moral guidance, but in the end the negative attitude surfaces that we find developed in Romans: "the power of sin is the law" (I,15.56).

In 54 came a second, official delegation from Jerusalem, with letters authorizing the leaders as apostles. They cut out the talk of wisdom as too weak a line. God had given Israel a "covenant" through Moses. Wisdom is a quality to which it would be prudent to aspire, but a covenant is by divine command and mandatory. The stakes are now higher: the church must choose between obedience to the Mosaic covenant (and the Jerusalem "apostles") and destruction. Furthermore, much stress is laid on the "glory" of the Sinai covenant. It is a set of laws given with all the splendor of the glory of God, described in Exod 33–34, and actually, physically reflected in the faces of the new leadership, just as it was in the face of Moses of old. But for all their exaltation of the torah, the new missionaries do not press the circumcision issue, as their colleagues did in Galatia: get the principle accepted first, and the rest will fall into place in due course.

So the gloves are off, and Paul does not pull his punches, developing the negative line on the law as he had done in Galatians and would do in Romans. The highly prized Sinai covenant was "the old covenant," of which the prophets had been so critical. Jeremiah had said it would be replaced by a new covenant written on the people's hearts; it was a covenant engraved in letters on stone, and Ezekiel had said God would take away Israel's heart of stone and give it a heart of flesh. The letter killed; it was a dispensation of death, of condemnation, in process of abolition. The thought follows the line of Gal 3.23–5.1. Before faith came, we were imprisoned and guarded under the law, our "disciplinarian" (παιδαγωγός, NRSV); heirs, as long as they are minors, are no better than slaves (Gal 3.23–24; 4.1–2). The law has been replaced by the Spirit, "and where the Spirit of the Lord is, there is freedom."

What has happened, then, to Paul's famous principle, "Not beyond what is written," of I,4.6? It has not been forgotten, but the central topic has moved on. In 1 Corinthians Paul was concerned to defend both his gospel and his pastoral practice; he had to explain why he did not insist on kosher butchers. In 2 Corinthians pastoral practice is secondary: II,3 is solely about the inadequacies of the Sinai covenant, for all its vaunted glory; it is nothing compared to the glory of the permanent, new covenant of the Spirit, which alone brings life and righteousness.

Of course, the law is holy and just and good, and is not overthrown but upheld as a guide to moral life (Rom 3.27; 7.12). Paul often cites it—Lev 26.12 and Isa 52.11, for example, at II,6.16–18, or Deut 19.15 at II,13.1. It just so happens that no issue from the traditions of the sages comes up in the epistle, so much of which is given to Paul's apostolic authority. But when Judaizers put on the pressure at Colossae, he (or his alter ego soon after) could still say, "Why do you submit to regulations (δογματίζεσθε), Do not handle, do not taste, do not touch?" (Col 2.20–21). So, in outline, Baur was right, and his many critics mistaken, even Käsemann and Schlatter. The opposition in Corinth is substantially the same as that in Galatia, and the issue of the law is as crucial in the Corinthian letters as elsewhere in the Paulines, mutatis mutandis.

◥ 7 ◤

KNOWLEDGE AND VISION

1 CORINTHIANS

THE CHALLENGE of halakic wisdom fills Paul's mind in the opening two chapters of I Corinthians, and λόγος σοφίας, a ruling of wisdom, is the first of the gifts of the Spirit in 12.8. But we are soon aware that there is a second and even more dangerous charisma, γνῶσις, "knowledge." This alarming gift seems capable of justifying any behavior—πάντα ἔξεστιν (6.12; 10.23)—including idolatry (ch. 8) and sexual license (chs. 5–7). λόγος γνώσεως, "a word of knowledge," holds second place in the list of gifts at 12.8. It would certainly be helpful if we were able to clarify this gift and see what gave its possessors their confidence. Paul refers to it, usually obliquely, five times in the First Epistle: in the thanksgiving at 1.5, on the lack of knowledge by the rulers at 2.6–10, on the eating of idol meat in ch. 8, in the list of gifts at 12.4–11, and, in particular, in contrast to love in chs. 13–14. There are also a number of references in 2 Corinthians; these will occupy us later in this chapter.

1,1.4–8. "I give thanks to my God always for you because of the grace of God that has been given to you in Christ Jesus, for in every way you have been enriched in him, in every ruling (λόγῳ) and in all knowledge, even as the testimony to Christ has been confirmed in you, so that you do not come short in any spiritual gift . . ." As is his custom, Paul opens with a thanksgiving to God that touches tactfully on the topics he means to handle in the letter. Here apostolic tact is to the fore. χαρίσματα, "spiritual gifts," are a major cause of dissension in the church (chs. 12–14); the two that cause the most trouble, and that come first on the Corinthians' list, are λόγος σοφίας and λόγος γνώσεως (12.8). These gifts give rise to boasting, which Paul deplores, and to claims that their possessors are "enriched" (ἐπλουτήσατε, 4.8). But the wise master builder knows better than to set off with divisive reproaches. He can use such language himself if he wishes (2.6; II,11.6), but the best move is certainly to begin with compliments and encouragement. The χαρίσματα are a guarantee (ἐβεβαιώθη) of the "testimony to Christ" that the Corinthians had received in his preaching, and they "come short" (ὑστερεῖσθαι) in none of them. With such gentle phrases does he hope to still the fears and dissensions of his community.

It is normal to translate ἐν παντὶ λόγῳ as "in all speech" or a similar phrase, but as I have argued in ch. 4 above, the context of 1.17–2.16 is about "rulings of wisdom," "the excellence of a ruling or of wisdom," "taught rulings of human wisdom," that is, the halakah taught by the *hakham* (חכם), the *sopher* (סופר), and the *darshan* (דרשן). λόγος should therefore be understood here as a "ruling" (דבר). λόγος is a common word of wide meaning, and another context would give another sense. In II,11.6 Paul concedes that he is an amateur "in speech," τῷ λόγῳ, but not "in knowledge," τῇ γνώσει; the context of II,10.10 shows that the discussion is about Paul's speaking powers.

The context here, with its stress on the proclamation of the cross, similarly settles the translation of τὸ μαρτύριον τοῦ Χριστοῦ: the genitive is objective, Paul's "testimony to Christ."[1]

It is a mistake to see Paul's approach here as ironic.[2] Paul can be sarcastic, as in I,4.8–10, but here he is trying to establish common ground and to be as irenic as possible. There is all this talk about rulings of wisdom and about knowledge, and wisdom and knowledge are indeed charisms given to the church by the grace of God. Paul, then, is being totally genuine in thanking God for these gifts, which he allows also in 12.8. It is only that he and his followers have the real wisdom, God's wisdom, the word of the cross (2.6), and they also have the true knowledge (II,8.7; 10.5; 11.6). Unfortunately, some members of the church have a spurious wisdom and a scandalous misunderstanding of knowledge, but there is no need to mention these things in a thanksgiving. Sometimes the phrase *captatio benevolentiae* (a courting of the reader's favor) is used of 1.5, but this, too, is rather misleading. Paul sees himself as father of the Corinthian church, able to use a metaphorical cane, if necessary, and quite capable of imposing the discipline of shunning (5.9) or excommunication (5.5). It is not in his character to butter up his churches with insincerities.

I,2.6–10. Wisdom and knowledge are soon seen to be interconnected:

> Yet among the perfect we do speak wisdom, though it is not a wisdom of this age, or of the rulers of this age, who are being brought to naught; but we speak God's wisdom in a mystery, which has been hidden, which God foreordained before the ages for our glory; which none of the rulers of this age knew, for if they had known they would not have crucified the Lord of glory. But as it is written,

---

[1] So Barrett, *First Epistle*, 38. Cf. 15.15, ἐμαρτυρήσαμεν.
[2] Hays, *First Corinthians*, 18.

> What eye saw not and ear heard not,
> And came not up on to the heart of man,
> What God prepared for them that love him;

But God revealed these things to us through the Spirit; for the Spirit searches all things, even the depths of God.

It is at first sight surprising that, in the middle of a discussion of wisdom, we should find two references to knowing (ἔγνωκεν, ἔγνωσαν). But we did have a reference to the two topics in the thanksgiving (1.5), and they come together again in 12.8, so perhaps the combination is natural; the Petrines might have appealed to both wisdom and knowledge. This time, for all its obscurity, we begin to see what the vaunted knowledge is.

The Petrines' gospel is in part the wisdom of rulings. Their converts know they must keep torah—that is, torah as expounded by the sages and scribes of Jerusalem. But Paul has a higher wisdom, God's wisdom. He is in the happy position of holding all the trumps and is able to take every trick. Do they have letters of commendation? He has a better one, the Corinthian church, a letter of Christ written with the Spirit. Do they have spiritual gifts? He can show them a still more excellent way, that of love. Paul has bid a grand slam, and he means to make it. But as in 1.5, he knows how to give a subtle echo of his opponents' language. They claimed to be τέλειοι, "perfect," a word widely used for religious pundits of the time. In controversy with similar Jewish-Christian missionaries at Philippi, Paul says, "Not that I have already attained, or have already been perfected (τετελείωμαι)" (Phil 3.12), and he takes up the word again there: "So as many as are τέλειοι let us think so" (3.15). The truly mature, "perfect" Christians are the Paulines: "we speak wisdom among the perfect." Only a clever ambivalence leaves the reference fuzzy; any fringers who come to see things Paul's way may count themselves as included.

τέλειος, a term used by Greek philosophers and Stoics, was taken up and used extensively by Philo: Abraham, Moses, and Aaron were perfect men, as is any true observer of torah. The LXX uses it both literally, for sacrifices, and metaphorically—for example, "perfect in heart"—and we similarly hear of the "perfect (תמים) of way" at Qumran. Paul is nervous when his opponents overuse a word, but Matthew is happy to commend it (Matt 5.48; 19.21).[3]

A problem with 2.6 is "the rulers of this age"; these ἄρχοντες are now widely thought to be human rulers, and it is not obvious why they and their lack of knowledge should have been drawn into the discussion. We have to concede that the whole passage is polemical if we are to make sense of it.

---

[3]Cf. G. Delling, "τέλειος," *TDNT* 8:67–79.

Opposition leaders have been claiming to possess a wisdom that will make a person perfect, that will transform a person from being ψυχικός to being πνευματικός. They also appealed to a knowledge (8.1–13), and Paul's repetitive use of words for knowing suggests that he is countering this appeal (2.8–16):

> which none of the rulers of this age knew (ἔγνωκεν)
> for if they had known (ἔγνωσαν)
> for what human knows (οἶδεν) the things of a human
> so also no one knows (ἔγνωκεν) the things of God
> that we may know (εἰδῶμεν) the things of God bestowed on us
> and [the psychic] cannot know them (γνῶναι)
> for who has known (ἔγνω) the mind of the Lord?

Paul is staking out a countercase for knowledge as a perquisite of his mission, not theirs. The repeated τῶν ἀρχόντων τοῦ αἰῶνος τούτου (2.6, 8) is also self-evidently polemical, as is the phrase "who are being brought to naught" (2.6).

Earlier commentators, including Barrett and Conzelmann, took the ἄρχοντες to be demonic; they were partly influenced by Col 2.15 (τὰς ἀρχὰς καὶ τὰς ἐξουσίας), where such powers are also associated with the crucifixion; Eph 2.2 (τὸν ἄρχοντα τῆς ἐξουσίας τοῦ ἀέρος); and other parallels. But opposition to this position has been rising.[4] This has been partly on linguistic grounds: ἄρχοντες in the plural is never used of demonic powers either in the NT or in Jewish sources. It is never said that the powers killed Christ; rather, Col 2.15 says that the cross was their undoing. The phrases "of this age" and "which are being brought to naught" are used in I,1–2 of humans. But above all, Paul has inserted into the LXX citation in 2.9 the word ἀνθρώπου, which was not in Isaiah; it is human limitation that is at issue. Schrage has it both ways: the rulers are earthly tools of heavenly powers.[5]

So much countering enables us to offer a plausible outline of the opposition's message. They did not merely proclaim the torah, requiring adherence to the divine wisdom revealed on Sinai and expounded on Moses' seat at Jerusalem. They also claimed a knowledge of the deep things of God that had come to leading Jews, men who claimed to have had visions and heard divine words in secret. This spurious knowledge has led to serious moral

---

[4]G. Miller, "ΑΡΧΟΝΤΩΝ ΤΟΥ ΑΙΩΝΟΣ ΤΟΥΤΟΥ—A New Look at 1 Corinthians 2:6–8," *JBL* 91 (1972): 522–28; W. Carr, "The Rulers of This Age—I Corinthians II.6–8," *NTS* 23 (1976): 20–35; Fee, *First Epistle,* 103–4; Horsley, *I Corinthians,* 58.

[5]Schrage, *Der erste Brief,* 1:253–54.

scandal at Corinth and needs to be attacked in principle from the start. And so, as soon as Paul has done battle with the falsely called "wisdom," he turns his guns on the pretended knowledge.

The leading classes of Jewish authorities were mentioned in 1.20—the sage, the scribe, the inquirer "of this age." What they had to offer was "the wisdom of the world." There were not many such sages or people of power and position in the Corinthian church (1.26), and God meant to "bring" such people "to naught" through the foolish things "of the world" (1.28). The reappearance of these phrases in 2.6–10 suggests that the same people are in mind there. Paul knows, of course, that the crucifixion was ordered by a Roman governor and carried out under Roman law, but he assigns the major responsibility to "the Jews who killed the Lord Jesus" (1 Thess 2.15). It was this Jewish religious leadership that had handed Jesus over. Where, then, can be the sense in appealing to their claims of dispensing wisdom and of knowledge of the depths of God? Paul uses the word ἄρχοντες for accuracy, because it is the Sanhedrin who gave the orders; but then the Sanhedrin was seventy-one strong and overlapped with the senior exegetes. They gave authority to what the exegetes and holy men decided; as Matthew puts it, "the scribes and Pharisees sit on Moses' seat" (Matt 23.2).

Paul does not mind trumping some other aces while he is about it. We already had a hint of the opposition's claim to deliver a "mystery" in 2.1: "And I, brothers, when I came to you, did not come proclaiming the mystery of God according to the excellence of a ruling or of wisdom." The point becomes plain in 13.2: "And if I have prophecy, and understand all the mysteries and all knowledge . . ." They have "knowledge," and it is knowledge of divine secrets, "mysteries," which they can divulge—very surprising secrets, too—and which are "hidden" from psychic people. The marvelous thing about knowledge of this kind is that it gives its possessor a halo of "glory." When Moses spoke with God on Sinai, his face reflected the divine glory, and anyone who descends into the divine presence will have the same experience. Already reigning in the kingdom of God, they have become glorified, ἔνδοξοι (4.10), and the claim to glorification will become a central issue in II,3.7–4.6.

Paul cannot let such pretensions pass. No, he has "God's wisdom," and it is indeed ἐν μυστηρίῳ, the "mystery" of the cross. It is in fact "hidden" still from those whose vision is blinded by their hard-heartedness (II,4.4), although God has revealed it to us now through the Spirit (I,2.10)—"us" being the church, including everyone in the Corinthian community who is willing to see the light. The wise pastor constantly leaves the gate open to the lingering. The opposition are right in a way: God did "foreordain" the whole thing "before the ages for our glory." As Paul will expound the point more fully in the Second Epistle, we all, not just the inner clique, with unveiled face behold the glory of the Lord and are transformed into the same image from glory to glory (II,3.18). Only it is a real moral glory, not some pretension to a physical radiance like Moses'.

Claims to knowledge by Jewish religious pundits are self-evidently ill grounded. They handed Jesus over to Pilate and so have primary responsibility for "crucifying the Lord of glory," and they had no "knowledge" then of what they were doing. How, then, are they to be trusted now with their so-called mysteries and knowledge? Paul rubs in the salt by using a title for Jesus that we know from its regular use in *1 Enoch* (22.14; 25.3, 7; 27.3, 4; 63.2), which repeatedly speaks of God as "the Lord of Glory," an especially apt title in an apocalypse, where Enoch is being elevated to the highest heaven, in which he will see the glory of God on God's throne. We cannot tell if the Corinthian opposition used the phrase themselves, but so much else in the paragraph echoes their claims that we must think it possible.

"Knowledge," then, was regarded by the Corinthian opposition as the private revelation of secrets that produced glorification in the knower; it was associated with masters of such knowledge in Jerusalem, "rulers of this age." It is not until 2.9 that we obtain an insight into how such knowledge was obtained. There Paul writes, "But as it is written," and as this is his almost invariable formula for citing Scripture, we may take it that he has the OT in mind, not the *Apocalypse of Elijah* (Origen) or an unknown apocryphon (Schrage).[6] Paul, like other NT authors, feels free to combine and adapt Scriptures (I,15.45; II,6.16–18; Eph 4.7; 5.14; Luke 4.18; Matt 27.9–10), and it is sensible to assume that he has done the same here.

Schrage indicates that the closest texts are Isa 64.3 and 52.15, but neither is close enough to be a citation; Paul cites Isa 52.15 accurately in Rom 15.21, so a lapse of memory is unlikely.[7] Schrage, however, does not consider whether Paul might have adapted Scripture to his purposes, and the opening formula indeed settles the question—this is from the Bible.

The closest text overall is LXX Isa 64.3:

ἀπὸ τοῦ αἰῶνος οὐκ ἠκούσαμεν οὐδὲ οἱ ὀφθαλμοὶ ἡμῶν εἶδον θεὸν πλὴν σοῦ καὶ τὰ ἔργα σου, ἃ ποιήσεις τοῖς ὑπομένουσιν ἔλεον.

Paul's first and third lines follow this in structure and wording:

Ἃ ὀφθαλμὸς οὐκ εἶδεν καὶ οὖς οὐκ ἤκουσεν . . .

ἃ ἡτοίμασεν ὁ θεὸς τοῖς ἀγαπῶσιν αὐτόν.

The phrasing of this last line is different from Isa 64.3, but the structure (ἃ–verb–[ὁ θεός]–τοῖς–dative plural participle) is the same. Paul's wording

---

[6]Ibid., 1:245–46.
[7]Ibid.

is a more christianized form of Isaiah: Christians have already received God's mercy in the incarnation and the Spirit (I,2.12, τὰ ὑπὸ τοῦ θεοῦ χαρισθέντα ἡμῖν). Paul therefore substitutes his own preferred phrase, "those who love him," which he also uses in Rom 8.28 (cf. Sir 1.10). He puts "God prepared" for the unsuitable future ποιήσεις, in line with the preordination (προώρισεν) of 2.7. Isaiah 65 was a favorite chapter of the apostle, and 65.16 closes,

κανὶ οὐκ ἀναβήσεται αὐτῶν ἐπὶ τὴν καρδίαν.

He slightly adapts this to give weight to his opening line:

καὶ ἐπὶ καρδίαν ἀνθρώπου οὐκ ἀνέβη.

This now brings us to the real problem of 2.9, which is not where the citation comes from but why it was felt to be relevant and why the wording has been adapted. The answer is likely to be, like so much else in the chapter, from the polemical context. The claimed knowledge derived from experience of visions. Opposition leaders claimed to have had visions of the Lord of Glory, like Enoch and Moses, and they criticized Paul for not having had such visions (II,12.1). They could rely on a long history of such experiences in Jewish tradition, back to Ezekiel, Isaiah, and Moses in Exod 19; 24; Num 12. On the other hand, there was the equally venerable tradition that no one could see God and live (Exod 33–34), and Paul draws on this for his strong negation. As Scripture (virtually) puts it, "Eye has not seen nor ear heard, and it has not come up into the heart of man."

The immediate anxiety is the content of such visions—the knowledge, for example, that anything is permissible, that one may eat idol meat in a pagan temple and have sexual license. It is "things that," in fact, "ear has not heard." But what gives the authority to such knowledge is the claimed vision itself: "what," in fact, "eye has not seen." Isaiah 64.3 does not quite give the sense Paul requires; it said, "From eternity we have not heard, nor have our eyes seen any God but you, and your works that you will do for those who wait upon your mercy." It thus becomes clear why Paul has amended the citation. He has cut out the offending central words, which accept the vision of Israel's God, and substituted the harmless clause from Isa 65.16, which then confirms the denial of any such possibility. It is entirely plausible that his opponents made use of the Isa 64 text, which would justify their claims both to the vision of God and to God's revelation of divine counsels. But even if they did not, Paul has grossly distorted the meaning of the original, just as he does at I,15.45 (and 15.55). He knows the LXX like the back of his hand, and the Corinthians are mostly ill-instructed Gentiles, without a copy of it; he can get away with massaging the text and feels it is his duty so to do—the truth of the gospel is at stake.

Such a context is confirmed by 2.10. Divine secrets are not vouchsafed through visions, with accompanying words from an angel ("what ear has heard"); they are "revealed" by God "to us through the Spirit; for the Spirit searches all things, even the depths of God." Jewish mystics spoke of their ecstasies as "descending" (ירד), and Paul can speak of the βάθος of God's riches and wisdom and knowledge in Rom 11.33, and of βάθος absolutely as a divine power in Rom 8.39. But more relevant is probably Rev 2.24, where those who have not followed the false prophetess Jezebel are described as "those who have not known the deep things (τὰ βαθέα) of Satan." It is likely that the disapproved Thyatirans are "Nicolaitans" who have adopted policies of partial assimilation and have justified these by appeal to visions of the depths of God; these claims are then travestied by the seer as visions of the deep things of Satan.[8] The term is commonly exploited in gnostic circles; Hippolytus says, "They called themselves Gnostics, saying that they alone had knowledge of τὰ βάθη" (*Haer.* 5.6.4: cf. 6.30.7; Irenaeus, *Haer.* 1.21.2; Tertullian, *Val.* 1; *Acts Thom.* 143).[9]

The hints thus gleaned from I,2.6–10 at last provide us with a plausible picture of what was going on at Corinth. The opposition is "of Cephas," Jewish Christians and their followers, who proclaim two ways to salvation, wisdom and knowledge. Wisdom is the Jewish way of life, obedience to the laws of Moses as expounded by the sages, scribes, and expositors of Jerusalem. Knowledge comes from direct vision of God (and perhaps other revelations) and is mediated by visionaries who are members of the community. A different word is in use because a quite different method is involved, and the messages resulting are known by different phrases, λόγοι σοφίας and λόγοι γνώσεως (12.8). Paul dislikes the wisdom gospel because it is the antithesis of his own gospel of the cross; it has the full support of the Jerusalem pillars and is a primary threat to his mission, as was to appear in Galatia and Asia. Hence he attacks it first, in 1.17–2.5. But pastorally far more damaging was the local visionary movement because there was no ethical control over it. With the Bible, you knew where you were; no one was going to offer an interpretation permitting idolatry or fornication. But with "knowledge" there was no control. If the visionary heard the angel say, "Anything is all right," what was to stop a mass exit to the brothel? And so most of 1 Corinthians is a response to the purveyors of knowledge rather than of wisdom, which is hardly mentioned again.

Such a context commends itself by two further considerations: the use of γνῶσις in broader society, especially in Judaism, and the constant negative comments on visionary claims throughout the NT. Knowledge is felt to

---

[8]H. Räisänen, "The Nicolaitans: Apoc. 2; Acta 6," *ANRW* 26.2:1602–44, here 1617, with a list of supporting commentators.

[9]See H. Schlier, "βάθος," *TDNT* 1:517–18.

be basically a kind of seeing in Greek (ιδ–) and is classically a function of scientific or philosophical thinking. By the turn of the era, however, a more gnostic treatment of the term had come in, as may be instanced in the Hermetic writings, dated by W. Scott to 100 B.C.E.–100 C.E. in their developing form.[10] Bultmann (citing *Corp. herm.* 1.30; 10.4–6; 13.13ff.) writes of them, "γνῶσις . . . is a χάρισμα which is given by God to man. It is thus radically distinguished from rational thought; it is illumination. God is inaccessible to man as such. . . . But he knows men, i.e., the pious, and reveals Himself to them. . . . Such γνῶσις is ecstatic or mystical vision, and to this extent knowing is still understood as a kind of seeing." Bultmann goes on to speak of such knowledge as bringing salvation through hearing the word and of its being maintained by ascesis, both matters of concern at Corinth.[11]

In the OT, knowledge is primarily knowledge of God, in a related way, and implies acknowledgment (Hos 4.1; 6.6; Isa 11.2, 9; Prov 1.7; 9.10; etc.). Such knowledge is available to all through torah, but it is mediated through privileged prophetic figures who have access to the divine counsel or through divine truths that they "see." Moses is unique; God spoke to him face to face. But this was only a more direct form of prophetic vision: "When there are prophets among you, I the LORD make myself known to them in visions" (Num 12.6, NRSV). The rise of apocalyptic emphasized the revelation of heavenly secrets in such visions. Daniel saw a series of striking images that communicated to him God's will and intentions as רזין, μυστήρια.

Daniel was acceptable, for he championed traditional Jewish piety against a Syrian oppressor and his collaborationist allies, but the visionary movement was not always so dependable, and in principle it was uncontrollable. It posed the same threat that the Spirit posed to ecclesiastical establishments in the seventeenth century, and the rabbis did their best to rein it in after the death of Akiba ben Joseph. Mishnah *Hag.* 2.1 forbids the exposition of Ezek 1, the classic account of the vision of the *merkabah,* to anyone but a sage "who understands of his own knowledge." A double guarantee is required. The expositor must be a חכם in his own right, an accepted member of the elite of those learned in torah. And he must also have experience as a visionary himself; such experience is spoken of as "his own knowledge."

We meet such knowledge ("falsely so-called," 1 Tim 6.20) in our NT Pastorals, in 1 Timothy, where it is associated with strong denials of human vision of God.[12] The King of kings "alone has immortality and dwells in un-

---

[10]W. Scott, ed., *Hermetica: The Ancient Greek and Latin Writings Which Contain Religious or Philosophical Teachings Ascribed to Hermes Trismegistus* (4 vols.; Oxford: Clarendon, 1924–1936), 1:5–6.

[11]R. Bultmann, "γινώσκω, κτλ," *TDNT* 1:689–719, here 694.

[12]M. D. Goulder, "The Pastor's Wolves," *NovT* 38 (1996): 242–56.

approachable light, whom no man has seen or can see" (1 Tim 6.16). Anyone else would die in his presence; the light is so bright that no one could approach him; no human ever has seen him—even Moses saw only his back view—or can see him. "Now to the King of the aeons, imperishable, invisible, the only God be honor and glory" (1 Tim 1.17). All those negatives, and the two uses of μόνος, suggest that another gospel is being contested. Someone is claiming to have γνῶσις, to have had visions of God and to have seen God's glory, or God's image, or some such thing.

The same contention over knowing God and seeing him pervades the Johannine writings: "Whoever [really] knows God listens to us . . . everyone who loves is born of God and knows God. Whoever does not love does not know God. . . . No one has ever seen God; if we love one another, God lives in us. . . . we have seen and do testify that the Father has sent the Son. . . . So we have known and believe the love that God has for us" (1 John 4.6–16). False claims of having seen God and of knowing God circulate, but there have never been any direct visions of God—we have seen God's revelation, Jesus, and God is known only by those who show love. Similarly in the Gospel: "The law was given through Moses; grace and truth came through Jesus Christ. No one has ever seen God" (John 1.17–18); "No one has ever ascended into heaven except the one who descended from heaven, the Son of Man" (3.13); "not that anyone has seen the Father but he who is with the Father; he has seen the Father" (6.46). The further repeated denials confirm the picture of 1 John: there are no visions of God. What is available is discipleship to Jesus: "whoever has seen me has seen the Father" (14.9).

Claims to heavenly visions were not new at the end of the century. We find them already in Colossians. Jewish Christians who made judgments about food and Sabbath (Col 2.16) tried to disqualify other church members, "insisting on ascesis and veneration of angels, dwelling on the things that they have seen" (2.18). Paul stresses, per contra, that Christ is the image of the invisible God, the beginning (1.15–18). No one can see God; God is invisible. And as for accounts of people seeing an archangel, spoken of as beginning or image (Gen 1.1, 26), that is none other than Jesus Christ. Such controversies go back to Paul's own days, as becomes clear in II,12.1–5.[13]

Commentators do not usually draw a distinction between *wisdom* and *knowledge*. Horsley, for example, is able to cite numerous passages from Philo that give the same meaning to the two terms. But this leaves us without an account of how knowledge came to be linked to vision, or why the terms "wisdom" and "knowledge" are distinguished in I,12.8, or why they sometimes issued in ascetic demands (ch. 7) and sometimes in antinomianism (chs. 5–6, 8–10). And we have more evidence to consider.

---

[13]M. D. Goulder, "Vision and Knowledge," *JSNT* 56 (1994): 51–69.

I,8.1–4. The practical perils of knowledge become evident in the discussion of idol food, the eating of which is justified by γνῶσις. Such knowledge leads to the maxim πάντα ἔξεστιν (10.23), and the same slogan is used to legitimate loose sexual morals in 6.12. These topics will be dealt with in succeeding chapters, but we should notice now an alarming feature of this γνῶσις: it is apparently a Jewish-Christian form of knowledge. This comes through in two details. First, 8.4 reads, "We know . . . that there is no God but one [οὐδεὶς θεὸς εἰ μὴ εἷς]"; this is sufficiently close to Deut 6.4, "The LORD our God, the LORD is one," a text familiar enough from its use in the Shema to make it unlikely that it stems from any alternative source. The words are a standard proclamation of Jewish monotheism in defiance of other religions. But I,8.7 also implies a Jewish origin: "but not all have knowledge; some from being accustomed till now to the idol, eat [the food] as sacrificed to an idol." The "weak" (8.9) person who does this is clearly a recent convert from paganism, and this suggests that the "strong" (10.22) person is a Jewish Christian (see pp. 267–69).

But how are we to account for two groups of Jewish Christians at Corinth, the one insisting on the wisdom of the halakah and the other with these heterodox ideas? Judaism was not monolithic, and among its many varieties it included a majority that was conservative and nomistic, and a minority movement that was innovative and mystical. In a charismatic movement such as the early Jerusalem church, the innovative element was naturally to the fore. Old men dreamed dreams and young men saw visions, and the Spirit was poured on women as well as men. It was inevitable that those who had visions came up with messages from heaven that were a surprise to more traditional members. This is what Paul says happened at Corinth: "For to one is given through the Spirit a word of wisdom, and to another (ἄλλῳ) a word of knowledge according to the same Spirit" (12.8). The follower of σοφία could tell you what you should not touch or taste; the visionary, with a word of knowledge, might reveal that idol food was quite all right, since there were no other gods but God.

I,13. Paul, the tactful pastor, allows that both these practices are inspired by the Spirit, even though his real feelings about wisdom were apparent in chs. 1–2 and about knowledge in chs. 8 and 10. In large measure, the discussion in chs. 12–14 is about the conduct of the church service—is it to be dominated by unrestrained glossolalia, or should more rational appeals ("prophecy") have priority? Chapter 13, however, gradually reveals that the major threat for Paul is not tongues but knowledge.

At first he contrasts love with a series of gifts: tongues ("the tongues of humans and of angels"), prophecy, knowledge ("all mysteries and all knowledge"), miracle-working faith ("all faith so as to move mountains"), ascesis ("giving away all my possessions, giving my body over [to God]") (13.1–3). But from 13.8 the field narrows. Whereas love never fails, prophecy will be brought to naught, tongues will cease, and knowledge will be brought to naught. Perhaps the faith and miracles and the self-giving were consequent effects of the knowledge, for the πίστις of 13.13 is not associated with miracles but with perseverance, and we hear of miracles and of self-devotion no more.

Paul thinks prophecy is among the highest of the gifts of the Spirit (14.1), but he depreciates both it and knowledge in comparison with love. They are inferior because they are partial ("for we know in part, and we prophesy in part") and are therefore temporary ("but when the perfect is come . . ."). It will not be long until the Lord comes, and then we shall see how limited our knowing and our prophesying have been. But also, like the early phases of human development, they are immature, infantile: they are "childish things," which are put away when we reach adulthood.

By 13.12 it is only knowledge that is left in the ring: "For now we see via a reflector dimly (ἐν αἰνίγματι), but then face to face: now I know (γινώσκω) in part, but then I shall really know (ἐπιγνώσομαι) just as I am really known (ἐπεγνώσθην)." Paul's mind has gone to Num 12.6–8: "If there be a prophet of you to the Lord, I will make myself known (γνωσθήσομαι) to him in a vision and I will speak to him in sleep. Not so my servant Moses . . . I will speak to him mouth to mouth, visibly and not in riddles (ἐν εἴδει καὶ οὐ δι᾽ αἰνιγμάτων)." Paul is aligning the Christian's perfect knowledge of God at the παρουσία with the full, direct vision vouchsafed to Moses. Our present limited knowledge is like that of the OT prophet, in riddles ("dimly," ἐν αἰνίγματι, I,13.12), whereas then we shall be face to face—a little more diffident than the Pentateuch's "mouth to mouth." But the reference makes clear the link in Paul's mind between prophecy (προφητεία), knowledge (γνῶσις), and vision (ὅραμα). Those who claimed knowledge at Corinth did so through their visions, which, among other things, enabled them to make prophecies. Paul belittles this by saying that it is δι᾽ ἐσόπτρου, via a piece of polished bronze that served in place of our glass and mercury but gave no clear image. Our knowledge is a kind of dim seeing (βλέπομεν). The full vision awaits us at Christ's coming, when all present pretensions to knowledge will be put in perspective.

Thus, the γνῶσις that underlies so much of the First Letter, and so menacingly, takes on a clearer and more familiar form. It is a Jewish-Christian kind of knowledge (8.4, 7), but it is distinct from Jewish-Christian wisdom (12.8). Just as mainstream Judaism had its exegetes of Scripture and its mystical visionaries, so did the early Church. Jewish-Christian adepts knew the deep things of God (2.10), saw the glory (13.12), and were transformed by it (4.10); they returned to earth with a personal knowledge that overbore long tradition. Eating idol food was no longer to be thought of as idolatry (chs. 8, 10), and some people even thought that anything was permitted (6.12; 10.23).

2 Corinthians

Paul was critical of Petrine claims to wisdom and to knowledge, but he was far from resigning these key terms to opposition use. He had God's wisdom, and we have seen that in I,2 he repeatedly challenges claims to a monopoly of knowledge. In the Second Letter, he quietly appropriates the word for his own theology and fights a difficult battle to maintain his authority as a mystic.

γνῶσις appears six times in 2 Corinthians. Once, in 8.7, it rings a little hollow, echoing the old flattery of I,1.5; 12.8: "but as you excel in every-thing, in faith and in word and in knowledge and in all enthusiasm." Paul was genuinely delighted by the Corinthians' newfound loyalty and zeal on his behalf. But the echo of I,1.5, ἐν παντὶ λόγῳ καὶ πάσῃ γνώσει, raises the suspicion of a little pastoral oil.

But more usually Paul means business. For example, in II,11.6 he writes, "But even if I am an amateur in speaking, I am not in knowledge, but in everything giving revelations in all matters to you." Carping at his speaking talents was trivial; he had what mattered, knowledge, and with this he was able to reveal (φανερώσαντες) everything to them. He stresses the complete-ness of his revelation: ἐν παντί, ἐν πᾶσιν. Similarly, in 6.6 he follows the catalogue of his trials with a list of his virtues: "in pureness, in knowledge, in long-suffering. . . ." Moral qualities are interspersed with revelatory gifts: his mission was marked not only by pureness, long-suffering, kindness, and love, but also by knowledge, by the word of truth, and by the power of God. All of this came from "the Holy Spirit" and was either its fruits or its gifts.

Petrine visionaries spoke of knowledge in the absolute (I,8.1–2, 7). Paul more commonly specifies its object, making clear that true knowledge is knowledge "of Christ" or "of God." So in II,2.14 God "leads us in triumph in Christ and makes known (φανεροῦντι) through us in every place the scent of his knowledge." In city after city the divine progress advances, with the church as its members, God's prisoners, spreading clouds of sweet in-cense as they go; and this sweet incense is the knowledge of God, or perhaps of Christ. This is the only knowledge that matters. The little section that be-gins with 2.14 ends with 4.6: God "shone in our hearts to enlighten us with the knowledge of the glory of God in the face of Jesus Christ." The long chain of genitives suggests that Paul is glossing Petrine claims to a knowl-edge of divine glory, no doubt through mystical vision. But our true enlight-enment comes only from "the face of Jesus Christ." God may have made himself known to Moses in Exod 33–34; Num 12.8, but now "we all" (II,3.18) have seen the face of Jesus Christ and are being transformed by the knowledge of the true glory of God there revealed.

With ch. 10 comes Paul's full onslaught on Petrine pretensions. In 10.4–6 he speaks of the powerful arms that he wields, "demolishing arguments and every bastion raised against the knowledge of God." The new apostles had attacked him, but he wrests the initiative from them in a massive counteroffensive. He has "armaments with divine power to the overthrow of strongholds"—he is thinking of battering rams and the testudo. His attackers' sophistries are described as πᾶν ὕψωμα, raised defensive positions, "bastions," which are also "proud resistance to the knowledge of God." Once more Paul turns the tables by taking over the opposition's claims. They have no real knowledge of God; this has been given to the Paulines alone.

II,12.1–10. Paul can speak of his knowledge of God and of Christ, but he is aware that he has a weak flank. It was commonly assumed that, from Ezekiel's time on, holy Jews had had visions of the divine throne, and Paul has never had such an experience. It was natural, therefore, that his opponents should stress this "weakness" among many others; if they had had such visions and been transformed by them (I,4.10; II,3.7–18), surely their authority far transcended his. So their sniping at Paul's weaknesses reaches a climax in II,12. He lacks presence and oratory (10.7–11); his mission has exceeded his power of sustaining it (10.12–18); he is not a proper apostle (11.1–6); he never claimed his expenses as an apostle (11.7–15); he did not require a full discipline (11.16–21); he lacked dignity and was forever in trouble (11.22–33); and, finally, he had been granted no vision (12.1–10) and had performed few miracles (12.12).

The chapter begins, "I have to boast; it is not helpful, but I will come to visions and revelations of the Lord (ὀπτασίας καὶ ἀποκαλύψεις κυρίου)." The new apostles boast about their visions of the Lord (II,3) and point the finger at Paul; what can he do but put up a defense, futile as this will be? The context shows that ὀπτασίαι and ἀποκαλύψεις are not the same thing. In an ὀπτασία one was ravished away to the third heaven, or to Paradise, for a "vision" of the *merkabah*. Paul knows a man in Christ, no doubt a Pauline Christian, who has had such an experience, but he forcefully contrasts him with himself: "on behalf of such a man I will boast, but on my own behalf I will not boast, except of my 'weaknesses' " (12.5). Paul himself has never had such a vision.

An ἀποκάλυψις is something different: it is a revelation on earth, perhaps in the form of a christophany (I,9.1; 15.8) or perhaps in a clear conviction that things were so and not otherwise, but essentially it involves some communication, something being revealed. In Gal 1.12 Paul received the gospel "by revelation of Jesus Christ." In Gal 1.16 God "was pleased to reveal his Son in me so that I might proclaim him among the Gentiles," presumably a reference to Paul's call to the Gentile mission on the Damascus road. In Gal 2.2 he "went up by revelation" to see the pillars in Jerusalem; we may think that, as we would say, he saw the writing on the wall. The revelation was that the false brethren would report to the apostles and he would find his mission interdicted if he did not take swift action. Paul had had many such revelations (II,12.7), but they were all down here, and the ones he mentions in particular all involve a communication from heaven. Only his friend had been carried up to the throne, and he had received no message there that he was to communicate.

Such definition of the language is not universal, but we have echoes of it elsewhere. The visions in the book of Daniel are normally described as ὁράσεις, but when Daniel sees the divine "man" in Dan 10, the LXX translator uses the word ὀπτασία (10.1, 7, 8, 16). For Ezekiel's vision of the glory in Ezek 1.1, Aquila, Symmachus ben Joseph, and Theodotion all render it with ὀπτασία, and the same word is used of God's appearing in Mal 3.2 and in Sir 43.16. In Acts 26.16 Luke says that Jesus appeared (ὤφθη) to Paul, and in 26.20 this is described as an ὀπτασία; Luke uses the same word of Gabriel's appearance to Zechariah in Luke 1.22. In all these instances, the vision takes place on earth. The author is more impressed by the visionary element than the message, and ὀπτασία seems to be preferred for visions of God, Christ, or angelic figures.

A distinction between a vision and a revelation is clear in the Shepherd of Hermas. The so-called *Vision* section describes five experiences of Hermas. The first four are spoken of as ὁράσεις and take place in the open air as the Spirit takes him and carries him away into remote country. Sometimes he sees heaven opened (Herm. *Vis.* 1.2). He sees revelatory persons, such as the old lady, or phenomena, such as the tower. But the fifth experience is spoken of as an ἀποκάλυψις, and it consists of a communication from the Shepherd indoors. The distinction is not the same as Paul's, since Hermas never leaves the ground, but there clearly is a distinction—he has had four visions and one revelation.

In the face of this distinction, it is likely that the new apostles merely said, "And he has never had an ὀπτασία." Paul had written before to the Corinthians, "Have I not seen Jesus our Lord?" (I,9.1), and his free use of ἀποκάλυψις elsewhere suggests that he made no secret of his revelations. It would therefore have been pointless for his opponents to bring ἀποκαλύψεις into the discussion. Paul has himself bracketed the two together because revelations are his strong point, and he can use them as a counter to his lack of visions while at the same time making a great show of not doing so. He will boast only of his weaknesses.

Almost all commentators, from Irenaeus on, have taken the "man in Christ" to be Paul himself. The reason is that II,12.7 makes clear reference to the apostle's "excess of revelations," and, to people without a strong mystical background, visions and revelations are the same thing.[14] But this then

---

[14]Lambrecht, *Second Corinthians,* 200: "a kind of hendiadys."

leaves two insoluble problems: (i) Why does Paul say, "I know a man in Christ," if he is speaking of himself? He never does this elsewhere, nor is any ancient parallel adduced from any other author. (ii) The idea seems to be ruled out by the plain denial of 12.5: "On behalf of such a man I will boast, but on my own behalf I will not boast."

A variety of rather lame responses is on offer to counter these objections:

(i) Paul is unwilling to claim charismatic experiences to support his apostleship and distances himself from them.[15] This is a surprising argument. When Corinthian charismatics overvalued speaking with tongues, Paul does not distance himself but firmly thanks God that he speaks in tongues more than them all (I,14.18). When revelations were mentioned, he has had so many that God had to give him the thorn in the flesh lest he get above himself (II,12.7). When divine power was needed to proclaim the gospel, he labored more abundantly than all the apostles—not he but the grace of God that was with him (I,15.10). Of course, he does not regard any of these charisms as a base for his apostleship, but he does not mendaciously attribute them to third parties.

(ii) It was a convention to praise others rather than oneself; rhetoric demanded modesty.[16] Appeal is made to Plutarch, *De laude* 10, and to Quintilian, *Inst.* 11.1–21. But in addition to the problem of showing that Paul was familiar with such a tradition, the texts cited do not provide a parallel. Plutarch advises that we praise ourselves indirectly, by praising others with whom we are associated (as Antony might praise Caesar). Quintilian says that Cicero used to boast by citing complimentary remarks by other people. There is no suggestion of gaining credit by telling an autobiographical anecdote as of another person.

(iii) Paul sees two men within himself, the natural man and the spiritual man.[17] Thus Paul says, "So then it is no longer I who do it, but sin that dwells in me" (Rom 7.17, cf. 7.20), and, "It is no longer I who live, but Christ lives in me" (Gal 2.20). Likewise, Paul mentions our outer person and our inner person in II,4.16. The point is, however, quite different from that in II,12. In Romans and Galatians Paul is treating the familiar paradox of grace and sin

---

[15]Käsemann, "Legitimität," 67/60; Georgi, *Opponents,* 298 n. 4; Furnish, *II Corinthians,* 543–44; Lambrecht, *Second Corinthians,* 200–201; Bultmann, *Second Letter,* 219–20: "As it were to an observer . . . an alien."

[16]H.-D. Betz, *Der Apostel Paulus und die sokratische Tradition* (BHT 45; Tübingen: Mohr, 1972), 95; A. T. Lincoln, " 'Paul the Visionary': The Setting and Significance of the Rapture to Paradise in II Cor. XII.1–10," *NTS* 25 (1979): 204–20; Segal, *Paul the Convert,* 36.

[17]Lietzmann, *An die Korinther,* 153; Barrett, *Second Epistle,* 307.

in conflict with the human will: he wishes to do good, but sin overbears him; he achieves good beyond his power through grace. The human heart is up against otherworldly forces. And II,4.16 merely contrasts the failing body with the determined spirit. But in II,12 the supposed split is between Paul the Christian with his series of revelations and a somehow different Paul the Christian with his moment of vision. It is not explained how the divisions in other passages are relevant.

(iv) The vision of the glory transformed the visionary into a new person; the "man in Christ" is Paul's transformed self.[18] Baruch, for example, can say, "And having come to myself, I gave glory to God" (*3 Bar.* 17.3). But visionaries normally recount their experiences in the first person, without a new personality taking over after the vision; they may now participate in the divine glory, but the "I" is still "I" before, during, and after the vision.

II,12.2–4. "I know a man in Christ who, fourteen years ago (whether in the body I know not, or out of the body I know not; God knows), such a man was ravished to the third heaven. And I know such a man (whether in the body or apart from the body I know not; God knows), that he was ravished to Paradise and heard unutterable utterances, which a man may not speak." Paul's defense is weak indeed. He has never had a throne vision himself; he knows only one man in his movement who has, and that was fourteen years ago, about 41, when he was in Antioch. But his purpose in mentioning the incident is not without his usual subtlety. Two things are basically wrong with the whole topic.

The first is that the topic leads to unspiritual boasting, and this takes the form of grandiose and unreal descriptions of what is supposed to have happened. Some of these visionaries think that as πνευματικοί they have left their bodies behind and have been "ravished" (ἁρπαγέντα, ἡρπάγη) "apart from the body" to heaven. Others insist that the angels carried them away body and all, like Ezekiel by his hair. Some of them speak familiarly of the "third heaven," others of "Paradise." Paul's repetitions, and his "I know not; God knows," betray his impatience with the whole business. His pesky tone recalls Gal 2.6: "But from those who claimed to be something—whatever they were makes no difference to me: God does not show partiality."

It is probable that in early centuries the simpler three-heaven image preceded the more elaborate seven heavens of later mystical speculation.[19] The three-heaven scheme is implied in *T. Levi* 3.4 and underlies Enoch's vi-

---

[18]C. R. A. Morray-Jones, "Paradise Revisited—2 Cor. 12.1–12: The Jewish Mystical Background of Paul's Apostolate," *HTR* 86 (1993): 177–217, 265–92.

[19]For this paragraph I am indebted to the persuasive discussion of Morray-Jones, ibid.

sion in *1 En.* 14.8–25. Just as Solomon's temple consisted of a holy walled area within which stood the temple building, and behind that the holy of holies, so are there three heavens that form God's temple: the world that Enoch lives in with its heaven, then the dangerous building that he enters, and finally the divine presence. Solomon's temple was decorated with golden fruits, and so behind the veil in the heavenly temple there is a paradise. It was to this garden that Aqiba and three other mystics came in the famous story (*t. Ḥag.* 2.1; *y. Ḥag.* 77b; *b. Ḥag.* 14b–15b; *Song Rab.* 1.28). In its earliest form, the others were nameless, and only Aqiba survived the vision because of his good deeds. Paul and his opponents seem to be familiar with this early form of the tradition: the divine glory is in the third heaven, also called Paradise, and holy people can be transported there and return intact. It is not surprising that both sides boast about such an experience.

The second thing wrong with these claims is that they purport to bring messages from heaven that will affect church life. Once this is allowed to pass, it will be the complete end of Paul's authority. If Christ could say to the seer, "You have some [in Pergamum] who hold to the teaching of Balaam" (Rev 2.14), and could speak of Jezebel and the Nicolaitans, no doubt other seers could tell how they had seen the throne and him who sat on it, and could call excommunication on those who defied the law of God. In Col 2.18 Paul (or his disciple) gives similar warning against those who insist on ascesis and on the angels' worship of God and take their stand on what they have seen. Such experiences enable them to "disqualify" (i.e., expel) other Christians and to dogmatize, "Do not handle, do not taste, do not touch."

The mystical movement presented the same problem for the rabbis, who resolved it by a variety of measures: limiting the public reading of Ezekiel's throne vision,[20] prescribing that its exposition be done only by the learned and only to one pupil, and regulating what might be communicated.[21] In particular, it became accepted that one might retell what the angels sang in praise of God, the קדושה and its elaborations, but not what they said.[22] Angelic messages might easily contravene torah and so cause confusion. We have the same threat latent in II,12.4. Paul's friend heard ἄρρητα ῥήματα, ἃ οὐκ ἐξὸν ἀνθρώπῳ λαλῆσαι; note the insistent double negative, "unutterable utterances that it is not permitted for a human to speak." Of course, Paul's friend, as a decent and humble Christian, never breathed a word. Would that this were true of the new apostles, who were only too

---

[20] *m. Meg.* 4.10; but Rabbi Judah permitted it, and it is not forbidden in the Tosefta.

[21] *b. Ḥag.* 2.1; Gen 1, where the secrets of creation were thought to be hidden, might be communicated to two pupils. Cf. Rowland, *The Open Heaven*, 275–77.

[22] P. Schäfer, "New Testament and Hekhalot Literature: The Journey into Heaven in Paul and in Merkavah Mysticism," *JJS* 35 (1984): 19–35, here 23.

pleased to take their stand on what they had seen and pontificate on what might be touched or eaten!

The visionary movement was to cast a long shadow over the Pauline churches, which soon felt compelled to deny the possibility of the vision of God. A number of insistent negatives on such claims are instanced above from the Johannine writings and the Pastorals (p. 101). In the meantime, we may pause once more to admire Paul's lightness of foot. His adversaries have him in a corner: it is agreed that God vouchsafes visions to his saints—how is it then that they have visions and he does not? But the wily master player wrong-foots them every time. (i) Boasting of such matters is unspiritual and unproductive. (ii) Pauline Christians do sometimes find themselves "ravished" to the throne. (iii) Squabbles about whether the visionary is taken up "in the body or without" are vain speculation; only God knows. (iv) Anyone who has heard the secrets of heaven should know that they are "unutterable" mysteries and are not to be blurted out. (v) Paul does take a proper pride in such a person, who saw so much and said nothing. (vi) Paul has never been taken to heaven himself, but he has had so many revelations that he had to be kept in his place. (vii) Far be it from him to boast about such marvels; he will boast only of his weaknesses. Game, set, and match to the apostle. See Appendix 2 for a further discussion of spiritual acts of power.

∿ 8 ∾

LIBERTINES?

THE PETRINES' "knowledge" showed itself in two main areas, sex and idolatry, the two central bogies for orthodox Jews. This was an androcentric society, and the problems over sex, and women more generally, were varied. They included a crisis over a man's concubinage with his dead father's second wife, the pressure for sexual abstinence in a number of forms, the behavior of women in worship, and the standard lapses from accepted norms.

It is over sex that every reader of the Corinthian letters faces a dilemma. In I,5–6 the opposition appear to be libertines; they not only connive at the incest in ch. 5 but also seem to justify sexual promiscuity at large with their "Anything is permissible" in 6.12–20. When we turn to ch. 7, however, we find them behaving as ascetics: they seem not only to abstain from sex themselves but also to require the same standard from other people—husbands are not to sleep with their own wives, the unmarried are to stay celibate, married couples are to divorce. This presents the reader with a paradox: Paul's opposition were libertines and ascetics at the same time.

Three avenues of escape seem possible in face of this impasse: the libertine interpretation of chs. 5–6 might be wrong; the ascetic interpretation of ch. 7 might be wrong; or some reconciliation might be possible. The last option is normally adopted, but in the face of the glaringly apparent contradiction in the contiguous passages 6.12–20 and 7.1–11, which is often glossed over rather quickly and sometimes ignored.[1] Barrett, for instance, contents himself by saying, "We know that developed Gnosticism in the second century moved sometimes in the direction of asceticism, sometimes in that of libertinism. The disparagement of the material could already have led to the moral indifferentism of 'All things are permitted me'—nothing done in the body really matters, and therefore anything may be done." The same line is taken by Schrage: "Eine entscheidende, überall und auch in Korinth zugrundeliegende Voraussetzung sowohl des Libertinismus wie auch der

---

[1]This is especially the case with articles, e.g., B. Rosner, "Temple Prostitution in 1 Corinthians 6:12–20," *NovT* 40 (1998): 336–51. But Fee, *First Epistle,* 249–357, hardly mentions the problem in a discussion of a hundred pages.

Askese, ist ein negatives σῶμα-Verständnis das denn auch gerade in 6,12ff. frontal angegriffen und zurückgewiesen wird."[2] Schrage lists a number of patristic passages in which the followers of Basilides[3] and Carpocrates and other gnostic groups are said to have acted as they pleased.[4]

Such an explanation sounds persuasive at first hearing, but it raises the suspicion of being too easy, and it is soon seen to be a cul-de-sac. Barrett and Schrage suppose that the same group of gnosticizing pneumatics lies behind both approaches, and this is supported by the text. At no point does Paul suggest that there is more than one opposition group involved. The people who maintain that "Anything is permissible" in 10.23 base themselves on their γνῶσις (8.1–4), and Paul's final word in 7.40, "I think that I too have the Spirit of God," implies that his opponents make the same claim. But surely the same people cannot simultaneously maintain that sexual acts are immaterial ("Like drinking a glass of water," as Lenin put it) and that celibacy is the rule for all.

A modern parallel may help to make the point clear. The charismatic movement is, as a whole, admirably conservative on sexual morals—not ascetic but at least intolerant of deviance. As often happens with movements of the Spirit, however, there may be an overreaching for the spiritual, and such happened in the early 1990s in Sheffield, England. An innovative pastor introduced a "Nine O'clock [P.M.] Service" with beat music and strobic lighting, and sex sessions in the vestry. No doubt some religious front was provided to the people taking part in the last, but there was a blatant contradiction between the evangelical purity professed by the movement generally and the libertinism being practiced. Inevitably, the immorality became known, and a scandal followed in which the pastor was expelled. One cannot have two obviously contradictory moral standards practiced by the same person; the term for that is hypocrisy. The same must surely have been the case for any gnosticizing pneumatics at Corinth. We have only to imagine ourselves expounding the doctrine of the valuelessness of the body to see how difficult we would find it to draw two conclusions: (i) you may do what you please sexually, and also (ii) there is to be no more sexual activity at all.[5]

---

[2]Barrett, *First Epistle,* 44–45; Schrage, *Der erste Brief,* 2:15.

[3]"[Basilides] holds . . . the practice of every kind of lust a matter of perfect indifference" (Irenaeus, *Haer.* 1.24.5).

[4]Schrage, *Der erste Brief,* 2:54–56, returning to the topic, notes that 7.1 represents the opposite pole to the libertinism of the previous verses. He is able to provide better evidence of gnostic ascesis, but his reconciliation of the two poles remains the same, a radical devaluing of the bodily.

[5]A modern parallel is the Waco, Texas, sect in which David Koresh simultaneously required sexual abstinence from others and enjoyed license himself. But this could only be achieved in a closed community with a single dominant leader—a very different situation from the open and divided community in Corinth.

The reconciliation theory is not, of course, tied to the Barrett-Schrage hypothesis of a single opposition. There might be two groups, or two wings of the same group. Thus Conzelmann speaks of "discussion between the libertinist and the ascetic persuasions within the community," and Hays thinks of some church members sleeping with prostitutes while others were ascetics—perhaps the standards expected by the latter were too high for the former and drove them to it.[6] But we have to remember that any "discussion" would have had a rather dogmatic tone to it ("Sex is fleshly, and Christians should be spiritual"; "I acted in the name of the Lord Jesus—anything is permissible") and that those who slept with prostitutes (according to Hays) justified their doing so. But the Sheffield parallel shows the difficulty of the two positions existing side by side in the same community. Furthermore, the form of the correspondence seems to rule out any discussion hypothesis. The church has written to Paul asking what he thinks about the ascetic demand to give sex up altogether. If there were two abnormal views of sex on offer, we would have expected their letter to have said, "Some of our leaders say we should give up sex, and others say any sexual union is all right. What do you think?" Furthermore, Paul himself would surely have exploited the difference. We might have expected him to say, "How can you condone whoredom and at the same time submit to demands for celibacy?"[7]

The alleged parallels for a libertine Gnosticism are also weak. It is easy to find allegations by orthodox theologians that their gnostic enemies were immoral, but there is no hint of such looseness in the Nag Hammadi documents. K. Rudolph comments, "Thus far no libertine writings have appeared even among the plentiful Nag Hammadi texts. The witnesses for the libertine tendency are restricted to the Church Fathers." Rudolph cites considerable evidence for gnostic ascesis from the gnostics' own writings. There is no hint of loose sexual morals. Indeed, such looseness would run counter to the general attitude to sex among gnostics.[8] Women were suspect, and it was sometimes thought that they would need to become male if they were to be saved (*Gos. Thom.* 114); but fundamentally, sex was the enemy—it led to conception and so to the endless extension of the world of darkness.[9] We need not think that the Fathers were lying over sex scandals in gnostic

---

[6]Conzelmann, *1 Corinthians,* 115; Hays, *First Corinthians,* 115–18.

[7]Horsley, *I Corinthians,* 94, suggests a slightly different form of the reconciliation theory: Paul was merely warning the church against fornication in 6.12–20—nobody had done it as yet, but he saw it coming. The discussion, however, includes a series of Corinthian slogans (four, according to Horsley) justifying πορνεία, and three times Paul opens a sentence with the withering "[Or] do you not know?" Rosner, "Temple Prostitution," 337–38, is right to insist that something scandalous has happened.

[8]K. Rudolph, *Gnosis: The Nature and History of Gnosticism* (trans. R. McL. Wilson; San Francisco: Harper & Row, 1983), 254, 257.

[9]Ibid., 270–72; cf. 88–113 and *Corp. herm.* 1.18, "*eros* is the cause of death."

groups; most groups include some members who are led into temptation, and the Fathers just were happy to believe the worst.

The other two possible solutions to the dilemma have found few champions. Schmithals thought his gnostics to be straightforward libertines, and he contended that I,7 was misunderstood as ascetic. It was Paul, speaking in the Spirit, who thought widows should not remarry (7.39), so probably the gnostics thought they should. Their letter's query was prompted by Paul's hard line on whoredom: If they should not sleep with a whore, ought this to be extended to all sexual activity?[10] But Schmithals's exposition has found little support (see also ch. 9, below).

The third possibility, that the pneumatics were ascetic only, has occasionally been defended, but with idiosyncratic arguments. J. H. Bernard took this option in 1907 but supposed that the incestuous man's father was still alive and was pursuing him through the secular courts (6.1–11).[11] R. Kempthorne took 6.12–20 to be an extension of the argument of ch. 5 but saw σῶμα as referring throughout to the body of Christ.[12] More recently W. Deming has proposed a solution similar to Bernard's: the church was divided over the man and his stepmother, and hard-liners took the issue to court and lost; the stepmother was selling her services to the "brother," so indignation was high in the community.[13] I agree with these scholars in thinking that 6.12–20 resumes the topic of sexual misconduct from ch. 5, but I would advance this thesis on different grounds: vv. 12–20 have been misread. The opposition were ascetics; their policy was what underlies ch. 7. They condoned the incest of ch. 5, no doubt because the man was an important member of the church. They did not defend whoredom. They were not libertines.

JUSTIFYING πορνεία (I,4.18–5.5)

But some of you puffed yourselves up as if I were not coming. But I will come to you soon, if the Lord wills, and will get to know not the talk of the puffed up but their power; for the kingdom of God does not consist of talk but of power. What do you want? Am I to come to you with a cane or in love and the spirit of meekness? It is actually reported that there is whoredom among you, and such whoredom as does not

[10]Schmithals, *Die Gnose*, 194–201, esp. 198.
[11]J. H. Bernard, "The Connexion between the Fifth and Sixth Chapters of I Corinthians," *Expositor* 7.3 (1907): 433–43.
[12]R. Kempthorne, "Incest and the Body of Christ: A Study of I Corinthians VI.12–20," *NTS* 14 (1968): 568–74.
[13]W. Deming, "The Unity of 1 Corinthians 5–6," *JBL* 115 (1992): 289–312. The proposal is properly criticized by Rosner, "Temple Prostitution," 338–40: the reconstruction is fanciful, especially that the stepmother should be paid.

even occur among pagans, so that a man is living with his father's wife! And are you puffed up? And did you not rather go into mourning, so that he who has done this thing should have been removed from among you? For I, absent in body but present in spirit, have already pronounced judgment as if present on the man who has behaved so in the name of the Lord Jesus: when you and my spirit are gathered together, with the power of the Lord Jesus, [the verdict is] to hand such a man over to Satan for the destruction of the flesh, that his spirit may be saved on the Day of the Lord. (I,4.18–5.5)

Many commentators draw a line at 4.21: the first four chapters cover the divisions in the Corinthian church and the problem of wisdom; then, in chs. 5–6, there is an abrupt move to the scandals of which Paul has heard orally. But Fee and Schrage are right to point to elements of continuity in the argument.[14] In particular, there are verbal echoes: ἐφυσιώθησαν (4.18), πεφυσιωμένων (4.19), πεφυσιωμένοι (5.2); καυχᾶσαι (4.7), καύχημα (5.6). Paul's threat of the "cane" is a semijocular reference to his intention to administer discipline; he could not do this to people prating about wisdom or claiming to be reigning in the kingdom of God, but it certainly could apply to the moral failures of chs. 5–6. Especially significant is the repeated contrast of "talk"/"power." He "will get to know not the talk of the puffed up but their power"; the kingdom of God "does not consist of talk but of power." The sinner has claimed to act "in the name of the Lord Jesus," but we will have condemned him "with the power of our Lord Jesus," and he will fall ill and perhaps die.

The syntax of the phrase "in the name of the Lord Jesus" is a long-standing problem. Does it modify κέκρικα, "I have pronounced judgment in the name of the Lord Jesus," or συναχθέντων ὑμῶν, "when you are gathered in the name of the Lord Jesus," or κατεργασάμενον, "him who has acted so in the name of the Lord Jesus"? Current opinion (Schrage, Hays, Horsley) favors the last as the most natural reading of the order of words and as suitable for a pneumatic/libertine, but Barrett accepts the older link with συναχθέντων, and Fee that with κέκρικα. The close similarity of the "name" and the "power" phrases, however, and their echo of the λόγος/δύναμις contrast in 4.19–20 seem to confirm that Schrage is correct.[15]

For once, the situation is clear in outline. No word is spoken of discipline on the woman, so she is not a Christian. Paul is doing his best to

---

[14]Fee, *First Epistle,* 194–95; Schrage, *Der erste Brief,* 1:368,

[15]J. Murphy-O'Connor effectively proposes this argument in a well-known article, "I Corinthians, V, 3–5," *RB* 84 (1977): 239–45. It is sometimes suggested that Paul has slightly adapted the man's words, that the man actually said, "I am acting in the name of Christ" (1.12; 12.3), but the Pauline version makes it the more obviously scandalous.

maximize the scandal, and he would rub it in further if the father were still alive. Since it was forbidden under Roman law to marry one's dead father's wife, the man has probably taken the woman as a concubine.[16] A century before, one Sassia had married her son-in-law at Larinum, provoking the artificial indignation of Cicero. Paul speaks as if such events were unheard of, but perhaps he had not read *Pro Cluentio.*

English has some problems in rendering πορνεία. We need a word that will have the same root for translating πόρνη, so *immorality* is unhelpful (besides lacking color); no money is passing hands, so *fornication* and *prostitution* are not involved. I have fallen back on *whoredom, whore,* which have the advantage of being used to express an aggressive attitude to sexual deviance, without the necessary suggestion of payment. πορνεία is used in this way in 5.1 (twice), and πόρνος in 5.11; and πόρνη is used frequently in an extended and noncommercial sense, the great whore, in Revelation.

What makes the case so particularly scandalous is that the church has not merely tolerated it but justified it: "And are you puffed up?" The transgressor has not merely broken a reiterated law of God (Lev 18.8; Deut 23.1; 27.20); he has claimed to be doing so "in the name of the Lord Jesus," and he could not have dared speak such blasphemy without the support of other members of the community, who have just shown themselves to be "puffed up" by other unrealities in 4.8–10. One might have expected them to do without food and washing and marital relations, to "go into mourning," in prayer; if they did, the miscreant "might be removed from among" them under force of community pressure. The church's first concern must be the purity of the church.

Paul was later accused of being too weak to apply proper discipline in the church (II,10.6; 11.21), but he could hardly be more firm in the present instance; that indeed could scarcely suit him better in his fight with the pneumatics. While they (ὑμεῖς, 5.2) puff themselves up, he (ἐγώ) in Ephesus has "passed judgment" on the man. The scene is reminiscent of the courts of justice in Soviet Russia. The commissar has spoken from the party office, and the case is finished. Paul is not waiting to hear counterarguments; his spirit is at the meeting the church is to hold in his absence, and he is taking the chair. He has already declared the verdict. All they have to do is rubber-stamp it and carry it out, and they will have "the power of our Lord Jesus" behind them.

The sentence is "deliverance to Satan." The idea goes back to Job 1.12; 2.6, where God puts Job in the power of Satan to despoil him of his goods and family and of his health. Here it is the health only that is to be affected: the man is to be handed over "for the destruction of the flesh." Paul makes a similar comment in 11.30–31, where many of those who are weak or ill are

---

[16]C. S. de Vos, "Stepmothers, Concubines, and the Case of Πορνεία in 1 Corinthians 5," *NTS* 44 (1998): 104–14.

suffering the consequences of their abuse of the Eucharist and some have even died because of this. None of these cases is quite the same as Job's. Job was a good man, and he was handed over to Satan to test his goodness. No formal action was taken by the Corinthian church for its members' failure to examine themselves properly at the Eucharist. Paul clearly has something similar in mind in the present passage, although now there is to be some liturgical action to expel the man from the community of grace. What is expected is that he will fall ill (εἰς ὄλεθρον τῆς σαρκός) or conceivably even die, but the kindly pastor knows that this will be for his eternal good, "that the spirit may be saved on the Day of the Lord." We may contrast this with 1 Tim 1.20, where, similarly, Hymenaeus and Alexander have been "handed over to Satan" that they may be taught not to blaspheme. The "teaching" there is punishment (παιδευθῶσιν), and there is no evident concern for their ultimate salvation.[17]

Paul has now, in principle, settled the disciplinary problem and turns his mind to the more important issue of the church's purity: such sin is like leaven and, if tolerated, will corrupt the whole lump. The man must be expelled. Paul has scriptural authority for this: Deut 23.1 forbade a man's taking "his father's wife," and in the next chapter, in Deut 24.7 (cf. 22.24), the community is commanded to "purge the evil from among you" (cf. I,5.13). In his "previous letter," Paul had in fact dealt with the issue of those who went whoring and had required the same discipline of shunning (5.9). The citation of Deut 24.7 recapitulates the deliverance to Satan in I,5.5 and the command to purge out the old leaven in 5.7, and it brings the issue of practical action to an effective close.

πορνεία UNJUSTIFIABLE (I,6.12–20)

First Corinthians 6.1–11 brings in a new issue, the pursuit of legal claims before non-Christian courts. On the first scandal, 5.12 says, "For what concern is it of mine to judge those outside [the church]? Do you not judge those within? God will judge those outside." This then leads naturally to the allied topic of litigating before unbelievers. There is no indication that this action is being justified by any "knowledge." It is just convenient to Paul to have a series of scandals with which to reproach the church and to lampoon their puffed-up claims to being spiritual. By 6.9, however, his mind is wandering back to the sexual issue: "Do not be deceived—neither whorers nor idolaters nor adulterers nor sodomites nor homosexuals . . ." He can lay it on

---

[17]J. T. South, "A Critique of the 'Curse/Death' Interpretation of 1 Corinthians 5.1–8," *NTS* 39 (1993): 539–61, is correct that exclusion rather than death is in Paul's mind, but it is not believable that he is thinking of the destruction of the lusts of the flesh.

thick, implying that the whole gamut of iniquity is either practiced in the Corinthian church or soon may be, and it is sexual sins that head the list, as πόρνος did in 5.11.

The problem is 6.12–20, which is generally agreed to be difficult to follow. It is clear that Paul is citing catch phrases used by his opponents and then demolishing them, and there are some persuasive suggestions on how to see which is which. But the subject of the paragraph is not made plain and is generally misunderstood. We may accept the following punctuation of 6.12–17:

> "Anything is lawful for me"—but not everything is beneficial. "Anything is lawful for me"—but I will not be dominated by anything. "Food is for the stomach and the stomach for food, and God will bring both to nothing"—the body is not for whoredom but for the Lord, and the Lord for the body, and God both raised the Lord and will raise us up through his Spirit. Do you not know that your bodies are limbs of Christ? Am I then to take the limbs of Christ and make them limbs of a whore? Never! Do you not know that the man who is united with the whore is one body [with her]? For it says, "The two shall become one flesh." But he who is united with the Lord is one Spirit [with him].

The tag cited twice in 6.12—"Anything is lawful for me"—appears again in 10.23, where it is part of the knowledge enabling one to eat idol meat. But here the context is about "whoredom" (6.13c, 18), "a whore" (6.15b), "the whore" (6.16a). This has led to the widespread conclusion that the opponents' knowledge justified the use of prostitutes on the basis that "anything is lawful" and that they were therefore libertines. This fitted well with earlier commentaries' descriptions of Corinth as a sink of sexual vice (Κορινθιάζεσθαι) with sailors, a temple of Aphrodite, and Strabo's thousand cult prostitutes. But this colorful picture of the opponents is difficult to support for several reasons.

First, when Paul has a scandal on his hands, he makes the issue plain in order to shame those responsible:

> It has been reported to me by Chloe's people that there are quarrels among you. . . . Each of you says, "I belong to Paul. . . ." (1.11–12)

> Already you are sated! Already you have become rich! Already, without us, you have begun to reign! (4.8)

> It is actually reported that there is whoredom among you. (5.1)

> When any of you has a case against another, how dare you take it to court before the unrighteous? (6.1)

So by your knowledge those weak believers for whom Christ died are destroyed. (8.11)

Any woman who prays or prophesies with her head uncovered disgraces her head. (11.5)

When you come together it is not [really] to eat the Lord's Supper . . . each goes ahead with his own supper, and one goes hungry, and another becomes drunk. (11.20–21)

How can some of you say there is no resurrection of the dead? (15.12)

The first thing to strike the reader of 6.12–20 is the absence of any clear context. We might have expected something like this: "I am astonished that some among you are uniting yourselves with whores and are also claiming to do this in the name of the Lord. For it is said, 'Anything is lawful.' " Surely, if Paul heard that his converts were whoring, he would hit the roof, as he does in II,12.21, and the first reaction of indignation would be to specify the scandal. If the context is prostitution, why is he strongly condemning this as blasphemy?

Second, when Paul is faced with a scandal, he does what he can to discipline the sinner; if he cannot, he threatens supernatural sanctions. Since the opposition have been puffed up over their leadership and have had pretensions to reigning in the kingdom of God, Paul promises to come, perhaps with a cane, and find out their power (4.18–21). The man with his father's wife is to be delivered to Satan for the destruction of the flesh (5.3–5) and, in the meantime, is to be shunned (5.11). The litigants in secular courts will not inherit the kingdom (6.9–10). Those who dine in an idol temple sin against Christ (8.12) and may die, like the idolaters in the wilderness (10.6–11). He threatens with having her hair shorn the bareheaded woman who prays and prophesies (11.6), and those who defile the Eucharist with greed and drunkenness may expect sickness and death, if not divine judgment (11.27–32).

Action against the sexual transgressor was Paul's first disciplinary measure. He had written in the "previous letter" that anyone found whoring should be shunned—not, of course, anyone at all, but only any Christian man (5.9). And now the same discipline (5.13) is to be applied to the man (described as a πόρνος) with his father's wife, the secular litigant (πλεονέκτης, ἅρπαξ), any idolater (cf. ch. 8), reviler (λοίδορος; cf. 4.12, λοιδορούμενοι), or drunk person (μέθυσος; cf. 11.21, μεθύει). Paul intends to apply discipline to the πόρνος but wants only to sound menacing over the rest; he cannot have half the church shunning the other half.

It is likewise in the Second Epistle. In II,6.14–7.1 Paul demands that the faithful stop their yoking with alien faithless Christians, who are unrighteous (ἀνομία) and idolatrous (εἰδώλων); they are to come out from among

them and purge themselves from all defilement.[18] In 12.20–21 Paul promises to come and discipline those who have quarreled and also "many of
those who sinned before and have not repented of their uncleanness and
whoredom and licentiousness." Whoring had been a problem from the beginning of the Corinthian church and would extend beyond the confines of
our four letters.[19] The remarkable thing is that there is no mention of any
discipline in I,6.12–20. The absence of any hint of apostolic punishment
raises problems for the libertine interpretation.

Third, much has been written in recent years on Paul's rhetoric; one
repeated rhetorical strategy we certainly find is the A-B-A' pattern. Paul
opens the letter with the church's divisions (1.10–17) but moves on to the
substantive issue underlying them in 1.17b–2.16, only to return to relations
between himself, Apollos, and "another"/Cephas in 3.1–4.7. The idol-meat
issue is discussed in chs. 8–10, with an excursus on giving up one's rights in
ch. 9. Other instances will spring to mind. The opening of 6.12–21 suggests
that we have the same structure in chs. 5–6. Chapter 5 has dealt with the
practical issues raised by the incest: the man is to be expelled and shunned,
and the church purged of corruption. But the underlying issue has not yet
been dealt with: the man claimed to be "acting in the name of the Lord
Jesus," and this cannot be allowed to pass without comment. So Paul returns
to the battle in 6.12.

The man maintained that he was "acting in the name of the Lord
Jesus" because under the new dispensation, "Anything was permissible."
The opposition's slogan provides the specific justification for what anyone
else would have thought impermissible. The lack of any linking particle
shows that 6.12 does not follow on from 6.11. In the same way, 4.1, οὕτως
ἡμᾶς λογιζέσθω ἄνθρωπος, lacks a connecting particle and resumes the
topic of the pneumatics' attitude to Paul from 3.21a: "So let no one boast of
men." But with or without a particle, Paul is liable to return to an earlier thesis without warning, as he does in 10.1. He cites the tag twice in 6.12, only to
rebut it twice. Even if things are permissible, this does not mean they are
profitable. Even if things are permissible, I do not want to get myself in the
power of anyone/anything. ἐξουσιασθήσομαι is a kind of play on ἔξεστιν.
τινός might mean "anything" (out of the πάντα), but the ὑπό makes "any-

---

[18]Goulder, "2 Cor. 6:14–7:1."

[19]The πορνεία reproved in the letter previous to 1 Corinthians and that threatened in II,12.21 are distinct from the case in I,6.12–20 in that there is no suggestion
that anyone justified the former. It is clear that the incest had come as news to Paul
(5.1) and was unconnected with the cases in the "previous letter." Those who
"sinned before" and had defied Paul at his second visit (II,13.2; cf. 12.21) are accused of sexual faults, but the arrogance (φυσιώσεις), etc., seem to be a different
issue in II,12.20. Fornication was very widespread in ancient cities (1 Thess 4.3–7;
I,7.2).

one" also likely: the man has put himself in the power of his concubine, as will be argued in 6.16.

It appears that the tag of 6.12 did not originally have anything to do with sexual relations. In 10.23 it is cited again in the generalized form πάντα ἔξεστιν and in the context of idol meat: anything is permissible for the knowledgeable because idol gods do not exist. Here, 6.13 gives the same context: "Food is for the stomach and the stomach for food, and God will bring both to nothing." The πάντα ἔξεστιν tag belonged in the discussion about idol meat, and it was a rather reasonable inference from the entirely reasonable premise that there is only one God (8.1–6). The incestuous man has applied this apparently universal tag to his own situation, adding μοί: "Anything is permissible for me." It sounds accordingly as if it applied to all ethical questions, including πορνεία (or stealing or murder)—something it was never intended to do. In 6.14 Paul cites the basis for it in the idol-meat discussion and so shows that it has been torn out of context and exploited for the man's advantage.

Paul continues his rebuttal with some effective ripostes. "Food is for the stomach and the stomach for food" is answered with "But the body is not for whoredom but for the Lord, and the Lord for the body." Paul agreed with the opposition about the one God (8.6) and, with strict reservations, thought one could eat meat (in private, if unobserved, if not told it had been sacrificed) without coming to any harm (10.25–30). He even extended the principle to meat at church suppers (Gal 2.11–14). But what may be allowed in eating cannot by any means be applied to sex. There it is not the stomach that is involved but the body.[20] Sex involves a special dimension (6.15–19). The Christian has consecrated his or her body to Christ, and any relation of whoredom is unthinkable. Paul adds "and the Lord for the body" as a rhetorical flourish. πορνεία here bridges the specific to the general: the man's relation with his concubine was whoredom (5.1 [2x]), but the principle applies to sexual laxity at large.

The opposition were pneumatics for whom the flesh was on a lower level than the spirit. They were already πνευματικοί, enriched, reigning, glorified. To them food and the stomach into which it goes are on the fleshly level, which "God will bring to nothing"; what matters is the spirit, and it is this that will survive death. But this attitude will not do for Paul, who responds, "and God both raised the Lord Jesus and will raise us up by his power." Jesus was raised physically (ch. 15), and we will be raised physically, too,

---

[20]A long tradition understands Paul's use of σῶμα to represent not just the physical but the whole person; so R. Bultmann, *Theology of the New Testament* (2 vols.; trans. K. Grobel; New York: Scribner, 1951–1955), 1:194–95; J. A. T. Robinson, *The Body* (SBT 1.5; London: SCM, 1952). This has been strongly disputed, however, by R. H. Gundry, *SOMA in Biblical Theology* (SNTSMS; Cambridge: Cambridge University Press, 1970).

with a transformed body. So God has already shown his deep concern for the body, our physical as well as our spiritual being, and what we have done with our bodies will be important (II,5.10), above all, what we have done sexually.

The special position of sexual acts is set out in the following verses. Paul regards it as self-evident and underscores this with a triple "[Or] do you not know?" (6.15, 16, 19). "Your bodies are limbs of Christ: am I then to take the limbs of Christ and make them limbs of a whore?" Again πόρνη serves a double purpose. It is an abusive term for the concubine in the case under discussion (like πορνεία in 5.1 or πόρνος in 5.11) and also a general term for sexual misconduct, an ever-present temptation in the tolerant ancient-city culture (5.9; II,12.21). The presence of the incest case in Paul's mind is clear from the article in 6.16: "Do you not know that he who unites himself to the whore (τῇ πόρνῃ) is one body?" Which whore? Paul means the concubine, and ὁ κολλώμενος means the man who has her.

Underlying the argument is Gen 2.24: "The two shall become one flesh." The words were intended to refer to marital union, but Paul takes them to cover all sexual union and to see sex as forming a permanent meta-physical unity: copulation creates an indissoluble new combined σῶμα, a single σάρξ, into which it is unthinkable (μὴ γένοιτο) that the members of Christ could be fused. On the contrary, "he who unites himself to the Lord is one spirit." Paul could have said "one body" (12.12–27), but he wants as strong a contrast as possible with the fleshly union under discussion. He has slightly amended the LXX προσκολληθήσεται to κολλώμενος, retaining the notion of joining without the sexual limitation.[21]

Characteristically, Paul now closes the topic by making it more general and by lifting the eyes to a higher, divine level. "Flee whoredom" of all kinds, he says, just as he will say, "Flee from idolatry" (10.14)—whoredom and idolatry, the two great perils for a Gentile Christian. "Every [other] sin that a man does is outside the body, but the man who goes whoring is sinning against his own body." Paul would not think that gluttony or drunkenness or suicide were exceptions to this: people take in excessive food or alcohol, or slit their wrists, from ἐκτὸς τοῦ σώματος. There may be many sins of thought (διαλογισμοὶ πονηροί, Matt 15.19), but the only sin that a man can "do" (ποιήσῃ, I,6.18) from within the body is πορνεία, for, as Gen 2.24 makes clear, the sexual sinner unites himself for eternity in one flesh with the whore. Nor is it just the woman who is debauched (ποιεῖ αὐτὴν μοιχευθῆναι, Matt 5.32); the whorer "is sinning against his own body," which can never break free from her. He has put himself in her power (6.12; 7.4).

[21]B. N. Fisk, "ΠΟΡΝΕΥΕΙΝ As Body Violation: The Unique Nature of Sexual Sin in 1 Corinthians 6.18," *NTS* 42 (1996): 540–58, agrees in taking the verse as Pauline, not a slogan of the opposition. His exegesis is close to mine.

A good menacing warning is a fine note to end the discussion, but Paul can rise above that and appeal to the aspiration that has, in the long run, given his Christianity the victory. "Do you not know that your body is a temple of the Holy Spirit, which you have from God?" Indeed we did know this: we had something like it (about the whole church, actually) in 3.16, and it is a thought that will serve more powerfully than any threat to keep the young believer from the brothel. "You are not your own, for you were bought for a price." Slave and slave owner alike, we have all been bought into God's household at the price of the cross. The man of God who can produce such a theology needs no more to persuade us to "glorify God in our bodies."

The text leaves us, then, with a plausible scenario. Paul's opponents are people of high principle, ascetics, who have given up sex altogether as a practice of the flesh and who are pressing others to abstain from marital relations, to remain celibate if unmarried and to divorce if not (7.1–11). They are Jewish Christians working on the basis that there is one God (8.4) and risking the salvation of their Gentile fellow believers, who have been until recently accustomed to idol worship (8.7). So their sexual asceticism is a deviation from normal Judaism and may be related to visionary techniques (2.9; 13.12; II,12.1–5).[22] This deviation is, however, a mild one compared with their attitude to idol meat, which is justified by a logical inference from classical Jewish monotheism (8.1–4). No doubt, this surprising development is a consequence of the group's membership. It includes wealthy or influential people whose social and commercial position depends on attending dinners, some of them held in pagan temples (8.10).

It is likely that the incestuous man in ch. 5 is in the same category. It is easy to exercise discipline when a church member is socially weak, and it is easy to overlook the peccadilloes of those who contribute generously to church funds or open their homes for church meetings. Nor need the case have seemed so scandalous as Paul makes it out. In the first century, men often died in their forties, women in their thirties.[23] Perhaps the now dead father had taken a second wife in her teens a few years before he died.[24] Often such young widows could not return to their former homes and might stay on. Coeval with the heir and still in the bloom of youth, she might well attract his affection, as Abishag attracted Adonijah's, and what went on at night might be veiled from prurient speculation. With time the concubinage became known and winked at, and when criticism was finally voiced, he

---

[22]Goulder, "Vision and Knowledge."

[23]Deming, "Unity," 294 n. 16, gives a good list of references for ancient life spans according to gender and for consequently differentiated ages of marriage.

[24]Under the early principate, girls were routinely married at fourteen; P. Brown, *The Body and Society: Men, Women, and Sexual Renunciation in Early Christianity* (Boston: Faber & Faber, 1988), 6.

could appeal to the principle "Anything is permissible," now established for the idol-meat question. He had been acting "in the name of the Lord Jesus" and could say defiantly, "Anything is permissible for me."

Such brazenness would place his ascetic friends in a severe dilemma, and we cannot tell how they responded. Two possible policies are suggested by later church practice. One might be this: "It is a passing infatuation; he'll get over it in a month or two if we leave him alone. Hush it up so far as we can." Another could be this: "The torah says יקח לא, and this means, 'He shall not marry.' The words do not apply to concubines." The casuistic skills of Catholic exegetes have found many an inconvenient marriage to be annullable. Often an heir may have slept with his father's slave girls without a thought,[25] and the concubinage is scandalous only when Paul's theology makes it so. We may, then, accuse his pneumatic opponents of respecting persons and of inconsistency, procrastination, and dishonesty; but not of gnostisizing Libertinism.

---

[25]Ibid., 23.

⤳ 9 ⤵

WOMEN AND ASCESIS

IT IS now generally allowed that Paul's opponents in I,7 were sexual ascetics. The church had written to him querying the suggested principle "It is good for a man not to touch a woman" (7.1).[1] He approves in part, wishing that all men were [continent] like himself (v. 7), but he knows that they are not, that Satan will tempt them because of their lack of control (v. 5) and that there will be "fornications" (v. 2). So it is best for couples to maintain sexual relations: "let each have his own wife and each her own husband" should be understood sexually, as is shown by vv. 3–4. "Do not deprive one another" of marital pleasure, says the apostle, making exception only "for a short period by mutual consent, for prayer"; after this they "should again be together" (v. 5).[2] The pressures are clear. Some people are saying, "Christians should give up sex for good." Behind this, no doubt, lies their belief that they are πνευματικοί and have risen above things of the σάρξ, that they have begun reigning in the kingdom of God, and that other Christians need to be exhorted to rise to a higher spirituality.

The same leverage may be felt behind Paul's counsel to widows and the unmarried (τοῖς ἀγάμοις, widowers, bachelors, and spinsters):[3] "It is good for them if they remain" so, "like me too; but if they have not self-control, let them marry" (vv. 8–9). Passions are strong, and marriage is a better solution than repression. He is countering an unrealistic, ultraspiritual pressure group who want no more marriages in the church and for whom sex is only for the σαρκικοί.

---

[1]Schrage, *Der erste Brief,* 2:53–54, gives reasons for ascribing v. 1b to the Corinthians' letter (esp. the use of ἀνθρώπῳ for ἀνδρί, which Paul uses regularly in the following verses). Hays, *First Corinthians,* 113–14, suggests that the Corinthians have taken over and developed Paul's own attitude to sex, but Schrage discounts this. Their asceticism stems from a wide assertion of the "spiritual" in a form alien to him.

[2]Jewish tradition provided for sexual abstinence for periods of prayer (*T. Naph.* 8.8; *m. Taʿan.* 1.6).

[3]Schrage, *Der erste Brief,* 1:93–94, takes ἄγαμοι to include both those not yet married (cf. 7.32) and those no longer married (cf. 7.11). The policies advocated by Paul are the same as those set out more fully for engaged couples in 7.25–38.

More surprisingly, the ascetics not merely disapprove marriage but even press Christian couples to divorce. "But the married I enjoin, indeed not I but the Lord, that a wife part not from her husband . . . and that a husband divorce not his wife" (vv. 10–11). The λέγω of vv. 8, 12 is now replaced by the stronger παραγγέλλω, and (a notable rarity) a saying of Jesus is produced to settle the question. But even this does not really settle it, because Paul goes on to provide for the alternative: "but if she does actually part . . ." Things have moved a long way. Once it is accepted that sex is a temptation of the flesh, what is the sense of a young couple going to bed together? They are bound to end up falling. The only sensible thing is for them to live apart, and one couple at least has taken this step, let Jesus say what he might. No doubt he was laying down the law for people with more worldly concerns, but this is a spiritual motive, and the Spirit is our guide. Well, Paul agrees with this (v. 40) and is prepared to allow the present case provided the woman does not end up by marrying someone else.

In vv. 10–11 Paul uses χωρίζεσθαι (twice) of the woman and ἀφιέναι of the man, but with unconverted partners in vv. 12–16, he uses ἀφιέναι of both man and woman and χωρίζεσθαι of the pagan husband. Hence, it is usually taken that there is no distinction between the two terms. But the suggestion of reconciliation (v. 11) makes one think that no irretrievable step has been taken, and often those whose concerns are spiritual are less concerned about the legal. The Gospels use ἀπολύειν for *divorce*.

If the Petrines pressed Christian couples to live apart, how much more would they have urged Christians with unbelieving partners to do the same. The apostle fears for the unnecessary breakup of happy homes and tells such church members to stick by their unconverted spouses (vv. 12–13). He supports this with the thin religious pretext that the believing partner sanctifies the unbelieving (vv. 14–15), and (more plausibly) may convert them (v. 16). Being sanctified has no cash value for the nonbeliever; he or she is not saved by the relationship with a Christian spouse. The idea stems from the uniqueness of sexual union that Paul expounded in 6.16–18: as Gen 2.24 said, it establishes a couple as one flesh, either a holy body or an unholy one, and Paul will not allow that a regular union with one Christian partner is other than holy. The Petrines may (and very likely did) assert the opposite.

Paul returns to the issue of the unmarried in 7.25, with the most common form of the problem, περὶ δὲ τῶν παρθένων, about (engaged, cf. 7:27 δέδεσαι) girlfriends.[4] The discussion continues to the end of the chapter and covers fiancés (vv. 39–40) as well as fiancées (vv. 25–38); it thus is an extension of the problem considered in vv. 8–9, the ἄγαμοι and χῆραι. This time,

---

[4]BAGD cites a secular use of τὴν ἑαυτοῦ παρθένον meaning "his sweetheart," but we lack any parallel for "fiancée," which is required by the context here—the man is "bound" (δέδεσαι, 7.27). In a Jewish-thinking community, the girl would only become ἡ παρθένος αὐτοῦ at betrothal.

unfortunately, he "has no command of the Lord" but, as in v. 12, is in a position to supply a ruling "as one granted mercy by the Lord to be reliable," commissioned as apostle on the Damascus road. The rule is, as in vv. 8–9, that "it is good for a man to remain as he is," that is, not to marry; but if the couple are keen to go ahead and marry, they have not sinned (vv. 26, 28). The only difference in situation from vv. 8–9 is that in ancient times girlfriends had a firmer arrangement than modern couples, with a proper betrothal: "Are you bound to a woman" by such a contract? "Do not seek a release. Have you been released? Do not seek a woman" (v. 27). Once again we sense the ascetics' pressure. We would never have thought that a man was sinning by marrying his fiancée, and vice versa, nor would Paul be denying it, unless someone were saying, "Sex is fleshly, so marriage is just licensed sin."

The apostle is a liberal intellectually, but his instinct is with the ascetics, and he offers two rather weak reasons for his conclusion, "So he who marries his girlfriend does well, and he who does not marry her does better" (v. 38). One is "the impending" ἀνάγκη (v. 26), the "tribulation in the flesh" that is to come in the end time, now that "the time is short" (vv. 28–29). Perhaps he has in mind the trials of pregnant and suckling women in that time of terror (Mark 13.17), but he does not say so, and he knows that some power is holding back the coming crisis (2 Thess 2.6–7). We come closer to his real motivation when he speaks of married Christians caring for each other while unmarried ones can devote their care to the Lord ἀπερισπάστως (7.32–35). He knew from his own missionary experience the advantage enjoyed by unmarried people like himself and Barnabas, and perhaps contrasted this with the limitations imposed on Peter and others by the need to travel *en famille* (9.5). But he also knew full well the value of a Christian family like those of Priscilla and Aquila, Philemon and Apphia, and the hosts in whose houses all his churches met.

Many commentators take ἐνεστῶσαν ἀνάγκην as "present necessity"; Schrage compares 10.11, "on whom the ends of the ages have come."[5] Hays takes the phrase to mean "the present necessity to evangelize," comparing 9.16, but this still leaves 7.28: "[the married] shall have tribulation in the flesh."[6] But there is no sign of any persecution or tribulation at Corinth to justify "present necessity," and 2 Thess 2.2 speaks of the idea that the Day of the Lord ἐνέστηκεν as a deceit. That chapter sets out a program of coming troubles not yet begun, and the problems of expectant and nursing mothers in Mark 13.17 are also in the future, after the abomination. Indeed, "the short time" of 7.29 implies that the necessity is only "impending."[7]

---

[5]Schrage, *Der erste Brief,* 2:157.

[6]Hays, *First Corinthians,* 129.

[7]Cf. M. D. Goulder, "The Phasing of the Future," in *Texts and Contexts: Biblical Texts in Their Textual and Situational Contexts* (ed. T. Fornberg and D. Hellholm; Boston: Scandinavian University Press, 1995), 391–408.

The element of antisex pressure again becomes evident in 7.36–38: "If anyone thinks he is not behaving properly with his girlfriend, if he is very passionate and it has to be, let him do as he pleases; he does not sin; let them marry." There is the wagging finger behind the screen again: "Sex is sinful." "But he who has taken a stand steadfastly in his heart, not under necessity, but has control over his own will, and has taken this decision in his own heart to keep her as his girlfriend, will do well." The trouble is that often a young chap has not taken any steadfast stand but has acted under intense pressure (ἀνάγκη); he does not have control over his own will at all and has not taken any decision in his own heart.[8] Insistent propaganda by ascetic hard-liners—revelations in worship, prophecies, praises of virginity, criticism of the pregnant, private counseling, prayer meetings—soon deprive the intending bridegroom of his freedom. The piling up of clauses requiring independence, and the repeated ἴδιος, show which way the wind is blowing. A man's decision for a permanent Platonic relationship is frequently not made when he is in control of "his own will," "in his own heart": and thus the native hue of resolution is sickli'd o'er with the pale cast of thought, and enterprises of great pith and moment with such demands their currents turn awry, and lose the name of action.

Paul's evenhandedness is suspended in this paragraph because the initiative does not lie with the fiancée whether to turn the betrothal into a marriage. But it is only temporarily suspended. Schrage suggests that the "woman" who "is bound" (δέδεται, v. 39) is a betrothed girl (cf. δέδεσαι, v. 27) whose fiancé dies.[9] This is rather convincing and saves the vacuity that otherwise attaches to the verse: everyone knows, or did then, that a married woman is bound while her husband is alive. "If [the betrothed girl's] man falls asleep [in death], she is free to marry whom she will—only in the Lord." So the final two verses are not about widows at all (χῆραι are not in the text), and Paul's discussion remains evenhanded to the end.[10]

LADIES FIRST

So much may be felt to be uncontroversial: the Petrines were ascetics; they had given sex up themselves and pressed other Christians to do the

---

[8]Barrett, *First Epistle,* 184, and Schrage, *Der erste Brief,* 2:201–2, understand the ἀνάγκη to be the man's sex drive, which would contrast happily with ὑπέρακμος in 7.36. But this gives no force to the repeated ἴδιος, and Fee, *First Epistle,* 353, is persuasive in relating the accumulated conditions to the general context of ascetic pressures.

[9]Schrage, *Der erste Brief,* 2:205.

[10]H. Chadwick, " 'All Things to All Men' (1 Cor. ix.22)," *NTS* 1 (1954/5): 261–75, presents a picture of Paul as a wily trimmer of his sails to the wind, a consummate controversialist. I agree in admiring the apostle's forensic powers, while feeling his sincerity in every line.

same. A second feature, however, has been claimed as significant in recent years, though less widely accepted: the apparent prominence of women in the discussion.

Fee again expounds this well, and it is accepted by Horsley and Hays. Its fullest advocate has been Antoinette Clark Wire, not without some well-based feminist feeling.[11]

In general, Paul seems to fall into line as part of the androcentric ancient worldview, even if he is on the liberal end of it. He thinks the husband is the head of the wife (11.3); she was created for the sake of the man (v. 9), his image (v. 7). If she prays in public, it should be with a hood over her face; otherwise, she can have her hair cut off (vv. 5–6). Women should be silent in church and ask their husbands at home if they do not understand (14.34–35). They should be subject to their husbands as the law says (14.34). This is the kind of approach that has led some to speak of Christianity as irremediably patriarchal.

But I,7 is apparently a happier passage for Christian feminists. Throughout the chapter, the woman is treated on a parity with the man. Each man is to have sex with his own wife, each woman with her own husband; the husband is to render to his wife her conjugal due, and the wife to her husband; she no longer has control over her body, nor he of his—they are not to deprive one another. The wife may not part from her husband, nor the husband divorce his wife, and the same is said of both partners in mixed marriages; if the pagan partner does dissolve the marriage, the brother or the sister is not bound. When the discussion moves on to betrothed couples, it is the same: the man is told, "If you marry, you have not sinned," and if the girlfriend marries, she has not sinned. The married man cares for the things of the world, how to please his wife, and the woman how to please her husband; the unmarried man cares for the Lord's affairs, and the woman likewise. The betrothed man may marry if he is passionate about it or—better—remain celibate if it is really his own decision. If he dies, his girlfriend may marry whom she wants or—better—stay as she is.

This somewhat surprising evenhandedness is underlined by two passages where the woman is taken first: "The woman does not have control over her own body but the man; and similarly the man" (v. 4); we may be in doubt if this is significant, for perhaps Paul is forming a chiastic exposition of v. 3. But there is no doubt over vv. 10–11: "that the wife should not part from her husband—and if she does part, let her remain unmarried, or else be reconciled with her husband—and that the husband should not divorce the wife." Here the concern is with the woman's initiative, and the man's is relegated to an appendix. It seems clear that at least one woman has separated

---

[11]A. C. Wire, *The Corinthian Women Prophets: A Reconstruction through Paul's Rhetoric* (Minneapolis: Fortress, 1990).

from her husband (whether officially divorced is unclear).[12] Her motivation is so strong that she has felt it suitable to defy a prohibition by Jesus himself that Paul knows and could hardly have failed to pass on in an eighteen-month mission; she also has sufficient support in the community that the apostle does not feel that he can simply order her back on pain of excommunication.

It is difficult to resist the cumulative force of these features of the discussion. Paul's sudden evenhandedness has not arisen from a burst of repentance at his male chauvinism. As ch. 7's heading indicates, he is responding to an inquiry from the church, and the inquiry is about pressures for sexual asceticism, partly led by women. The proposed principle, "It is good for a man not to touch [sleep with] a woman," is neutral between the sexes; it means, "Abstinence in marriage is the Christian policy." But Paul knows that the sex drive is stronger among men. In 1 Thess 4.4–5 he wants each Christian man to have his own partner (σκεῦος), not in the passion of lust like the Gentiles; he does not trouble to mention the women's needs there. But here he has to mention the women every time. "The woman does not have control of her own body, but the man" looks like a response to some alarming feminist claim, "Why should we put up with sexual demands from our husbands? Women, too, would like to live the spiritual life. Our bodies are under our ἐξουσία; why should we be treated as things of the flesh?" The use of the term σκεῦος might not unreasonably be resented. Such aspirations may find an echo in modern feminist hearts, but the apostle has outmaneuvered them. The wife has control of "her husband's body," but he has control of hers.

Wire argues that the Corinthian women prophets claimed, "A woman has control over her own body," and that there were some women in each of the groups mentioned by Paul who took this line in order to give themselves to prayer.[13] She is properly suspicious of Paul's sudden evenhandedness. Just as it was considerably easier to circumcise a man than to uncircumcise him (7.18), so the higher male sex drive would ensure that sexual relations often continued because the man desired them even when the women did not. The apparent evenhandedness is in fact subtly slanted, according to Wire. Paul appeals to the threat of "fornications," that is, to male needs, without regard to women's aspirations. And so, in the end, he is part of the oppressive male hegemony, treating women as a means to men's spiritual well-being.[14] The discussion leaves the defender of St. Paul feeling rather uncomfortable.

---

[12]ἐὰν δὲ καὶ χωρισθῇ (v. 11) might refer to a future possibility but could also be used for a present reality, and it is hardly believable that Paul would make provision for a possible future transgression of a dominical interdict.

[13]Wire, *Corinthian Women Prophets,* 81–82.

[14]Ibid., 114.

It is the same issue over the breakup of Christian marriages. Perhaps the Lord was concerned with divorces for incompatibility or burning the dinner or losing one's looks, but now the aim of a Christian woman must be to be holy, to be spiritual, and one cannot do this if one shares a bed each night with an amorous husband. The Lord did not have such a situation in mind, and the Spirit commands purity and abstinence from fleshly lusts. So the woman has left her husband and is living the holy life; she has no intention of either remarriage or reconciliation.

WOMEN IN WORSHIP

The call for sexual abstinence seems repeatedly to be rooted in the feeling that sex is fleshly and therefore sinful, but I,7 does not offer a wider context to explain this conviction. We may have a hint in 7.5: "except by agreement for a time, that you may devote yourselves to prayer (ἵνα σχολάσητε τῇ προσευχῇ)." The ascetics, it is suggested, wanted to give up sexual relations so that they could pray. It is difficult to think that they wanted to pray all night, so that there was no leisure for lovemaking, and the objection to sex is that it is fleshly, not that there is no time for it. This, then, leads us on to the further discussion of women's position in I,11 and 14.

The Authenticity of I,14.34–35.   There is a textual problem in that 14.34–35 is displaced to after 14.40 in D F G 88* and five Old Latin MSS, and doubt has arisen whether they were in the autograph, since (i) the tone is much harsher than that adopted by Paul in chs. 7 and 11 and (ii) there seems to be an open contradiction between his concession in 11.5, "every woman praying or prophesying" (cf. 11.13), and the brusque command of 14.34, "Let women keep silence in church." There is, however, a noticeable similarity in the pattern of argument in the two passages.
First Paul appeals to the law:

> For man was not created for woman, but woman for man. (11.9)

> Let them be in subjection, as also the law says. (14.34)

Next he moves on to natural decency:

> Is it proper (πρέπον) for women to be praying to God unveiled? Does not nature herself teach you? (11.13–14)

> For it is disgraceful (αἰσχρόν) for a woman to speak in church. (14.35)

Then there is the suggestion that any disagreement is disputatious:

But if anyone seems to be contentious . . . (11.16)

If anyone seems to be a prophet . . . but if anyone does not recognize this he is not recognized. (14.37–38)

Finally there is an authoritarian statement that the same rule applies in every other church:

We have no such custom, nor do the churches of God. (11.16)

As in all the churches of the saints, let women be silent. (14.33–34)

Or did the word of God go forth from you? Or did it come to you alone? (14.36)

So close a similarity of argument suggests that Paul wrote both passages. The tone is less irenic after the long discussion with the pneumatics, and it may be that we can find a solution to the supposed contradiction with 11.5: 14.33b–38 forms a satisfying *inclusio* with 11.2–16, and it is Paul's normal strategy to deal gently with his problems at first but to be firm and clear when he returns to the topic (I,1.10–17 and 4.6–21; I,8 and 10; II,3 and 10–12).

Fee presents a sustained argument for excising 14.34–35 as an interpolation by a scribe more sympathetic to the approach of the Pastorals (cf. 1 Tim 2.8–15):[15]

First, Johann Bengel, the eighteenth-century theologian, laid down that the text critic should prefer the explanation that most easily accounts for the variants. Here no convincing account is on offer for why some scribes would have transposed 14.34–35 to the end of the chapter, and such transpositions are unexampled. Glosses may, however, creep into the text at more than one place, such as the *pericope adulterae* in John 8 and also in John 21 and Luke 21.

Second, if 14.34–35 is excluded, a much clearer thread of thought emerges: "For God is not a God of disorder but of peace, as in all the churches of the saints. . . . Or did the word of God go forth from you? Or did it come to you alone?" Both the preceding verses and vv. 37–40 are about prophesying, and vv. 34–35 about women are an interruption.

Third, the context is the edification of the church, but here the text turns aside to consider a group of people, women; moreover, whereas in chs. 7 and 11 Paul is scrupulously evenhanded in his treatment of the two sexes, here he appears as a shameless male chauvinist.

---

[15]Fee, *First Epistle,* 699–708.

Fourth, it is unbelievable that in 11.5, 13 Paul would have accepted (even if reluctantly) the principle of women praying and prophesying in church and then issued the staccato prohibition of 14.34.

Finally, elsewhere, when Paul refers to the law, he cites it, but, uniquely, not here—he only says, "as also the law says." In addition, this is the only place where Paul would be citing the law as binding on moral behavior; nor does the law ever say that women should be subject! In view of so much cumulative evidence, we should excise the two verses as not written by Paul and see them as an early gloss, which has taken over the whole tradition, Western (after 14.40), and other (after 14.33). Schrage, Horsley, and Hays follow Fee in this conclusion.

These arguments are not strong, and UBS is fully justified in printing the verses with a B rating, for the following reasons:

First, there is an important difference between the *pericope adulterae* and I,14.34–35 in that the former is missing from ℵ B and many MSS, while I,14.34–35 is present in every manuscript, in one or other position. Nor is it so that there is no parallel transposition: Matt 5.4–5 is, as Fee mentions, found in reverse order in the Western tradition, but this reversal (from poor–mourners–meek to poor–meek–mourners) does not correspond with Luke 6.20–21 (as Fee suggests), where the order is poor–hungry–weeping. Omissions occur mostly from fatigue. Maybe a scribe's eye ran from ἐκκλησίαις in 14.33b to ἐκκλησίᾳ in 14.35b, and (like Fee) he thought the sense ran on naturally. Checking over, he added the missing verses at the end of the chapter, perhaps with an obelus to show where they should have stood.

Second, all modern editions print "As in all the churches of the saints" as the beginning of a new paragraph.[16] This is for a good reason: 14.33a, "For God is not a God of disorder but of peace," is a statement about God and not about life in all the churches. "As in all the churches of the saints" is in place as part of the basis for Paul's decree "let the women be silent in the churches," like the similarly impatient 11.16, "we have no such custom, nor do the churches of God"; and it is well followed up by 14.36, "Or did the word of God go forth from you?" There is, then, no smooth follow-on as Fee would like; v. 36 does not follow on from v. 33b at all: "As in all the churches of the saints or did the word of God . . . ?"

Third, Paul might be just as concerned for the edification of the church if it was at risk from the indiscipline of women members, and their immodesty (as he sees it) would have no balancing failure by the male members.

Fourth, Bengel certainly would not have approved the principle: if we find a contradiction in the text, we should excise it. It might seem better to try to resolve the contradiction in another way—which I shall do.

---

[16]WH, Bover, NA²⁶, BF², ASV, RSV, NEB, Zür, Luth, JB, Segond, NRSV.

Finally, as so much of 14.34–35 echoes 11.2–16, it is likely that "as the law also says" refers to the passage already expounded in 11.8–9, namely, Gen 2.18–23. It is true that these verses do not command the subjection of women, but Paul is arguing that they do, and Gen 3.16, "He shall rule over you," comes very close to it. Most of Paul's contemporaries would have agreed with him on this.[17]

The Common Message of I,11.2–16 and 14.33–37. The interpretation of 11.2–16 is a nest of controversies. It is common to understand the issue to be whether women should pray with hair flowing or tied up in a bun (Schrage, Horsley, Hays); others speak of veils and head caps. J. Murphy-O'Connor takes the issue to be homosexuality.[18] There are wide differences of opinion over the meaning of κεφαλή and over both ἐξουσία and the angels in 11,10. The rise of feminist criticism has made the passage topical, especially in view of the Vatican's appeal to it to deny the priesthood of women.[19]

Once it is accepted that I,11.2–16 and I,14.33–37 is that which left Paul's hand, it is possible to find a resolution of its considerable problems. Women have been praying and prophesying (11.5, προσευχομένη ἢ προφητεύουσα; 14.32, πνεύματα προφητῶν; 14.37, προφήτης . . . ἢ πνευματικός) with their hair down (11.15, γυνὴ δὲ ἐὰν κομᾷ; 11.5, ἀκατακαλύπτῳ τῇ κεφαλῇ; cf. 11.6, 13). To a Jew such as Paul, this was self-evidently scandalous; it was grounds for divorce if a Jewish woman went in public with her hair loose (*m. Ketub.* 7.6). Jewish women went abroad with their faces covered; Susanna was veiled so that her face was invisible (Sus 32), following the example of her ancestress Rebecca, who came veiled to meet her bridegroom (Gen 24.65). Talmudic lore provides in detail how the veiling should be done.[20] If modesty had so to be protected in the street, how much more in worship![21] A picture from the synagogue in Dura-Europos shows the women dressed in the standard ἱμάτιον, with its hood pulled up over the head and covering the upper part of the face.[22] Such hoods could be pulled down to cover the whole face and were pierced with

---

[17]P. W. van der Horst, *Hellenism–Judaism–Christianity: Essays on Their Interaction* (Kampen: Kok Pharos, 1994), 73–95.

[18]J. Murphy-O'Connor, "Sex and Logic in 1 Corinthians 11:2–16," *CBQ* 42 (1980): 482–500; idem, "1 Corinthians 11:2–16 Once Again," *CBQ* 50 (1988): 265–74.

[19]A. Feuillet, "L'homme 'gloire de Dieu' et la femme 'gloire de l'homme': 1 Cor. XI.7ᵇ," *RB* 81 (1974): 161–82; J. P. Meier, "On the Veiling of Hermeneutics: I Cor 11:2–16," *CBQ* 40 (1978): 212–26.

[20]Str-B 3:427–35.

[21]Cf. Tertullian, *Virg.* 13: "As [church virgins] veil their head in presence of the heathens, let them at all events in the church conceal their virginity, which they veil outside the church."

[22]Schrage, *Der erste Brief,* 2:492 n. 19.

two eyeholes. Tertullian (*Virg.* 17) must have received the interpretation of the passage through actual use in churches, and he has no doubt that women should have their faces covered in worship. "Faces" meant down to the neck: "The whole head constitutes the woman [in I,11.2–16]. Its limits and boundaries reach as far as the place where the robe begins . . . in order that the necks too may be encircled [by the hood]." He holds up for admiration Arabian women who make do with a single eyehole.

It is this full covering that Paul thinks suitable: "Judge among yourselves: is it proper for a woman to pray to God not covered down [ἀκατακάλυπτον]?" (11.13).[23] The word is used again of her head in 11.5 and is implied twice in 11.6: "For if a woman is not covered down [κατακαλύπτεται] . . . let her be covered down [κατακαλυπτέσθω]." But as Schrage notes aptly, if she did this, it would make it impossible for her to pray or prophesy in the assembly.[24] Precisely so—this is exactly what Paul wants and what he commands in 14.34: "Let women keep silence in the churches, for it is not permitted to them to speak." So far from there being a contradiction between 11.5 and 14.34, the two passages have the same meaning. The first passage does not concede to women the right to pray and prophesy. Paul says, "Any woman praying or prophesying without her head being covered down shames her head," and it is her *head* that is to be covered down, not her hair. He offers her the two alternatives, equally shameful, of having her hair cut off or being shaved to the skull; if she does not want either of these, let her wear her hood down below her chin (κατακαλυπτέσθω). We would all like Paul to be as nice as we are, but if he is politically incorrect, it is better to say so.

That this is the point at issue is apparent from 11.7: "For a man should not have his head covered (κατακαλύπτεσθαι τὴν κεφαλήν), being the image and glory of God." Paul uses the word *head* here because it is part of his argument, but it is not the scalp and hair that make a man the image of God but his face. Paul in II,3.18 says, "But we all with unveiled face beholding as in a reflector the glory of God, are changed into the same image," and in II,4.6 he says that God has "shone in our hearts to the illumination of the knowledge of the glory of God in the face of Jesus Christ." So a man should not have his face covered, but a woman should.

---

[23]ἀκατακάλυπτος occurs once in the LXX, at Lev 13.45: the luckless leper is to be clad in rags and to "let the hair of his head be ἀκατακάλυπτος [MT פָרוּעַ, 'let loose']" and to have the upper half of his face veiled, and to cry, "Unclean, unclean." He is to look like a scarecrow and to keep ordinary people away. The text does not specify what it means by κατακαλύπτεσθαι τὴν κεφαλήν; nor are we helped by Num 5.18, where the priest ἀποκαλύψει τὴν κεφαλήν of the woman suspected of adultery, so disgracing her (Str-B 3:428–29).

[24]Schrage, *Der erste Brief,* 2:492.

The trouble with practices that are self-evidently scandalous is that it is difficult to explain why they are so, and 11.2–16 is problematic because Paul has to resort to obscure and disreputable argumentation. He starts off with a rather insincere compliment, "I praise you that in everything you remember me." He is about to show that he has heard of a flagrant instance in which the traditions that he passed on to them have been neglected and defied; but at least Chloe's party remembers them, and he can portray this as praiseworthy in contrast to the much worse abuse of the Lord's Supper. He then moves to theological profundities to help him: "But I want you to know," says the uncomfortable expert, "Christ is the head of every man" in the church. Just as Paul uses the temple image in two ways, for the individual Christian and for the church as a whole, so he uses the body image in two ways. In ch. 12 Christ is the body and we its members; here and in Col 2.19, Christ is "the head from whom the whole body, nourished and held together by its ligaments and sinews, grows with a growth that is from God." Ephesians 5.22–24 links the subjection of a wife to her husband as her "head," with Christ being the head of the church, his body. In the same way here, "the husband is the head of his wife" because the woman is fundamentally just the man's rib, as we read in Gen 2.21–23, "and the head of Christ is God." The last statement is a rhetorical flourish, as in 3.23; it is resumed in 11.12, "all things are from God," and reassures the hearer that the status quo is the divine will.

Final Considerations.   Four passages deserve our special attention before we conclude our inquiry into women and ascesis in Corinth: I,11.4, 10, 11–12, and 13–16.

(i) "Any man praying or prophesying κατὰ κεφαλῆς ἔχων disgraces his head" (I,11.4). The meaning of the Greek expression is made clear by a parallel in Plutarch: Scipio ἐβάδιζε κατὰ τῆς κεφαλῆς ἔχων τὸ ἱμάτιον. The Loeb translator renders unhappily, "with his toga covering his head."[25] Scipio had come to inspect Alexandria, and had he done so with his toga over his head, he would have seen nothing, and he would quickly have measured his length in the gutter. As in the Dura-Europos painting (and many other illustrations), he was wearing a ἱμάτιον with its hood drawn down over his face so as to remain anonymous while seeing all through the eyeholes. The Alexandrians soon guessed who he was and cheered when he lifted the hood.

This understanding is confirmed by 11.7, "For a man ought not κατακαλύπτεσθαι τὴν κεφαλήν," which means "have [a hood] down over his face."[26] If he did this, he would be concealing his head, and Christ is his

---

[25]Plutarch, *Moralia,* "Sayings of the Romans" 200F (trans. F. C. Babbitt; 15 vols.; LCL; Cambridge: Harvard University Press, 1927–1969), 3:191.

[26]"A man ought not κατακαλύπτεσθαι τὴν κεφαλήν" cannot mean that he ought to pray bareheaded. Both high priests (Exod 28.4, 37–38) and ordinary priests (Ezek 44.18) ministered in turbans (J. Murphy-O'Connor, "Sex and Logic"; "Once

head (v. 3). The play on two meanings of κεφαλή makes the thought obscure and raises the suspicion that Paul may already have forgotten v. 3. Perhaps he just means that it would be disgraceful (αἰσχρόν), in the social mores of the time, for a man to go veiled, and it is for this reason that he would be disgracing his head. But Paul returns to theology in v. 7: God made man in his image (Gen 1.27); thus he is "God's image and glory," and this is something to be proud of and not concealed. But the same would not apply to the woman. It is true that Gen 1.27 says, "in the image of God created he him; male and female he created them." But it was only the man ("him") who was made in God's image. The way in which God created woman is told in detail in Gen 2.18, 21–24.[27]

This brings us to the point: "But any woman praying or prophesying with her head unhooded disgraces her head, for she is one and the same thing as a woman shaven." This again is explained in 11.7b, "but the woman is the glory of the man." She came "from the man" (v. 8) and "was created for the man" (v. 9), so her function is to serve him, and with her pretty face and attractive hair (v. 15) she is his glory. She should therefore cover her face with a decent hood when she is in mixed company. Otherwise she will be inviting lustful looks and so disgracing her head, that is, her husband. The cutting or shaving of a woman's hair was a means of disgracing her, in use by the Germans in Tacitus's time (*Germ.* 19) and by the French in 1945; no doubt there were occasions of such treatment in Paul's Corinth, for he refers to such a case with the definite article, τῇ ἐξυρημένῃ, and says that it is a disgrace for a woman to have her hair cut off or shaven (11.6b).

Schrage points out that the cutting of women's hair was often a rite of mourning, but it is difficult to think that an injured husband might not be provoked into applying a similar discipline to an erring wife. He suggests that Paul is resorting to rhetorical exaggeration, as at Gal 5.12 over circumcision: if they expose their hair and so disgrace themselves, why not go the whole hog and cut it off?[28]

Again"), and it is entirely possible that the tradition of Jewish men wearing skullcaps at prayer is derived from this (cf. Str-B 3:423–25; Barrett, *First Epistle,* 250). R. E. Osler Jr., "Use, Misuse, and Neglect of Archaeological Evidence in Some Modern Works on 1 Corinthians: 1 Cor. 7:1–5; 8:10; 11:2–16; 12:14–26," *ZNW* 83 (1992): 52–73, gives evidence for the widespread use of male head coverings in contemporary worship.

[27]A late Jewish tradition confirms Paul's exegesis: "Eve was not created in the image of God, but was formed out of Adam," *Tanhuma B Tazria* 10, cited by Jacob Jervell, *Imago Dei: Gen. 1,26f in Spätjudentum, in der Gnosis, und in den paulinischen Briefen* (FRLANT 58; Göttingen: Vandenhoeck & Ruprecht, 1960), 110; Schrage, *Der erste Brief,* 2:509. Jervell (p. 401) cites other texts in which Eve is ignored—*Life of Adam and Eve* 12–17; *Apoc. Mos.* 24.4; *2 En.* 58.3–6.

[28]Schrage, *Der erste Brief,* 2:508.

Some women at Corinth have in fact been praying and prophesying with their hoods thrown back. They must have worn them back while they were eating the supper, and they have simply moved on into the vocal part of the evening without adjustment. Paul had founded the church, and he would have had a few Jewish women like Priscilla, or God-fearers used to synagogue ways, and so have set the tone with "the traditions as I handed them on to you" (11.2). This arrangement suited Jewish ideas of female modesty, but it had the additional advantage that it was impracticable for women to say anything publicly. Paul stresses the immodesty now (αἰσχρόν), and the consequent reduction to silence comes out only in 14.34. In 14.28 he recommends a similar silence where there is no one who can interpret tongues; the glossolalist is then to be silent in church (like the women in 14.34) and "speak to himself and God."

The impossibility of a hooded woman addressing a public meeting is illustrated by an incident recounted by Simeon, bishop of Beit Arshan in the sixth century. Ruma, widow of the martyred saint Arethas, was brought before the persecuting king of Nagran (north of Yemen) in his harem. She took off her veil in order to testify to the women, to general scandal, for she was a young girl, and no man (apart from her husband) had ever seen her face before.[29]

(ii) Woman owes her origin to man, as Genesis says. She is her husband's glory and he is her head, and for this reason (διὰ τοῦτο) she ought to have control (ἐξουσία) over her head. In 7.4 the wife has control over (ἐξουσιάζει) her husband's body, and he of hers, with the right to marital union. Now the wife has a duty rather than a right: her head is her husband, and she ought to keep careful control over it, so that he is not dishonored by her. Paul says this is "because of the angels" (11.10). His mind is still on the scene in Paradise, where, in Jewish lore, Satan seduced Eve,[30] not with the apple only, and the sexual susceptibility of angels is graphically confirmed a few chapters later in Genesis. The peril in which the daughters of men stood in view of angelic lusts was patent from the tale of their seduction in Gen 6.2, which stood almost at the head of the Torah, and had caused the flood.[31] The story was repeated in many intertestamental texts and was developed homiletically in *T. Reu.* 5:

---

[29]R. de Vaux, "Sur le voile des femmes dans l'Orient ancien," *RB* 44 (1935): 397–412.

[30]The tradition is familiar in the Talmud—*b.* ʿ*Abod. Zar.* 22b; *Šabb.* 145b–146a; *Yebam.* 103b (where it is ascribed to Rabbi Johanan)—and may have been current in Paul's time. There are possible echoes in *1 En.* 69.6; *2 En.* 31.6; *Apoc. Ab.* 23. It may underlie Paul's contrast in II,11.2–4 between the church as Christ's pure bride and the "deception" of Eve.

[31]That Gen 6.2 lay behind the reference to "the angels" seemed obvious to Tertullian (*Virg.* 7).

Accordingly, my children, flee from sexual promiscuity, and order your wives and your daughters not to adorn their heads and their appearances so as to deceive men's sound minds. For every woman who schemes in these ways is destined for eternal punishment. For it was thus that they charmed the Watchers, who were before the Flood. As they continued looking at the women, they were filled with desire for them, and perpetrated the act in their minds. Then they were transformed into human males, and while they were cohabiting with their husbands they appeared to them. Since the women's minds were filled with lust for these apparitions, they gave birth to giants. For the Watchers were disclosed to them as being as high as the heavens.[32]

The Gen 6.2 story is retold in *1 En.* 6–7; 19; 69; *2 Bar.* 56.10–12; *Jub.* 4.21–22; 5.1; Josephus, *A.J.* 1.73; but only the author of *Testament of Reuben* puts his imagination to working out the detail, as he does also over Bilhah. The seductive power of women is a constant theme of contemporary Judaism.[33] Genesis 6.2 calls the "Watchers" the sons of God, but the LXX (Codex Alexandrinus) renders this οἱ ἄγγελοι τοῦ θεοῦ. Paul knows of fallible angels, for the church will judge them (I,6.3), and they are part of the persecuting powers in Rom 8.38. Angels were thought of as especially present in worship, whence they would carry human prayers to God.

Fitzmyer notes a number of passages in the Qumran Scrolls stressing that holy angels will accompany the sectaries and forbidding participation by the disabled as unholy.[34] He suggests that the angels are similarly guarantors of order in the church, and this idea is taken up by Horsley and Hays. Schrage points out the absence of any reference to the disabled in I,11 and prefers the traditional interpretation: angels are easily tempted.[35]

(iii) As elsewhere, we find the liberal struggling with the reactionary Paul.[36] He cannot have the church meeting wrecked by scandalous indiscipline, with wild women standing up unhooded, with their hair streaming, and presuming to address the assembled men (11.3–10). But then (πλήν), in Christ there is neither male nor female (Gal 3.28): "neither is the woman without the man, nor the man without the woman, in the Lord. For just as the woman came to existence out of the man, so too the man has his existence through the woman—and everything is from God" (I,11.11–12). Each is dependent on the other. The happy phrase "in the Lord" leads on to the

---

[32]Translated by H. C. Kee (*OTP* 1:784).

[33]Cf. van der Horst, *Hellenism–Judaism–Christianity,* 74–81, who cites some politically very incorrect passages from Ben Sira, Philo, Josephus, and the *Life of Adam and Eve,* and interprets I,11.10 in the light of them.

[34]J. A. Fitzmyer, "A Feature of Qumran Angelology and the Angels of 1 Cor 11:10," *NTS* 4 (1958): 48–58.

[35]Schrage, *Der erste Brief,* 2:516–17.

[36]Cf. Eph 5.21, "Be subject to one another out of reverence for Christ"; 5.24, "Just as the church is subject to Christ, so also wives ought to be, in everything, subject to their husbands."

doctrine of the order of creation. Women are equal to men in the sight of God; it is just that they should be subject to them in ordinary life, in the same way that slaves should work extra hard for Christian masters. Such conclusions are perilously close to double-talk, and feminists will be justified in resenting the smooth "and all is from God." As Dr. Pangloss would observe to Cunégonde in *Candide,* all was for the best in the best of all possible worlds.

(iv) The apostle knows that his theologizing is convincing no one, so he turns to more secular arguments (I,11.13–16), as he will in 14.34–35. Is unhooded praying proper? Judge for yourselves. What does nature teach you? Long hair on a man is a sign of a pansy, but a woman's long hair is her glory. It was given her for a περιβόλαιον, a mantle (Exod 22.25; Deut 22.12) of modesty. Lady Godiva rode through the empty streets of Coventry appareled only in her long hair, and in less brazen times than ours, biblical illustrators screened Eve with carefully draped tresses. This, not public display, is the reason women have long hair. But finally Paul's patience is exhausted: "If anyone seems to be contentious, we have no such custom" as unhooded women speaking in church, "nor do the churches of God."

A Problem Solved?

The issues raised by such women, over sexual abstinence and over participation in worship, occupy about 14 percent of the First Epistle but are never mentioned in the Second. We may think optimistically that the problem went away. In the longer run, common sense will concur with natural appetites to ignore idealist intrusion into family privacy. For the tension over worship, it cannot have been so easy. Until Titus's visit, the Petrines clearly have been gaining ground, and it is unlikely that their women have been shamed into their hoods by the apostle's frail arguments and fading authority. More probably they have persevered, but custom has diminished the scandal. So Paul has heard no more about them, and if he did, he had more serious troubles to think about.

But if Paul's problems resolved themselves with time, we cannot say the same about our own. No evident link has emerged between women's asceticism in I,7 and their barefaced praying and prophesying in I,11. Worse, it had appeared that the Pauline opposition were Petrines, that is, Jewish Christians with a loyalty to Jerusalem; but as is well known, Jews were no ascetics where sex was concerned but, rather, regarded marital union as a duty. It is such questions that must exercise us in another chapter.

10

Sex and God

Billerbeck comments on the ascetic stand taken by Paul's opponents in I,7.2: "This fundamental proposition did not correspond to the ideas of the ancient synagogue."[1] Numerous comments are available from early Jewish writings that promote sexual union as a duty as well as a delight, and no doubt a wise instinct was at work, providing for large families as a bulwark against a hostile environment. The presence of this considerable corpus has driven commentators to speculate on Hellenistic influences behind the Corinthian enthusiasm.

Jewish Backgrounds to Ascesis

There is, however, an exception to the positive Jewish attitude to sexual relations: when one was in close contact with God, they were contraindicated. When David is fleeing from Saul, he asks Ahimelech, the priest at Nob, for five loaves of bread to feed his companions, to which the latter replies, "I have no ordinary bread at hand, only holy bread—provided the young men have kept themselves from women." David reassures him: "Indeed women have been kept from us as always when I go on an expedition; the vessels of the young men are holy even when it is a common journey: how much more today will their vessels be holy?" (1 Sam 21.3–5). One should not have contact with the holy, in this case God's shewbread, unless one's "vessel" was holy—that is, unless one had not slept with a woman.

Similarly, when Israel comes to Mount Sinai in Exod 19, Moses is given strict instructions to make the people holy before the delivery of the torah. For two days they are to wash their clothes and keep well away from the holy mount, for on the third day will come the revelation. Moses passes on the command, ending, "Prepare for the third day: do not go near a woman" (19.15). Abstinence from sex is an important element in preparing for contact with God. In fact, any form of sexual activity, even unconscious

---

[1] Str-B 3:367–68, cited by Barrett, *First Epistle,* 154.

ejaculation in sleep without a woman present, made a man unclean while on campaign (Deut 23.10–11; cf. Lev 15.16–18). He was disqualified for a day from participating in God's holy war.

What went for the people before Sinai would apply the more strongly to Moses himself, and Philo paints in the detail:

> But first [Moses] had to be clean, as in soul so also in body, to have no dealings with any passion, purifying himself from all the calls of mortal nature, food, drink and intercourse with women (τῆς πρὸς γυναῖκας ὁμιλίας). This last he disdained for many a day, almost from the time when, possessed by the Spirit, he entered on his work as a prophet (ἤρξατο προφητεύειν), since he thought it fitting to hold himself always in readiness to receive the oracular messages (τοῖς χρησμοῖς).

Then, after forty days fasting on the mountain,

> he descended with a countenance far more beautiful than when he ascended; nor even could their eyes continue to stand the dazzling brightness that flashed from him like the rays of the sun. (*Mos.* 2.68–70; trans. F. H. Colson, LCL)

We seem to have here a number of echoes of the Corinthian opposition: abstinence from sexual relations, prophesying, the Spirit, glory visible in the face. Perhaps the opposition were not so un-Jewish after all, but were following a prescribed path to a higher holiness, fit for the divine presence.

Philo sees the ascetic practices of the Therapeutae in the same light. He writes of aged virgins in the community in Egypt "who have kept their chastity, not from compulsion . . . but of their own free will, in ardent yearning for wisdom" (*Contempl.* 67). "Wisdom" here means the spiritual life. We may compare the Lukan figure of Anna, eighty-four years of age, living for so many years a widow after her husband's death, devoted to God in prayer and fasting (Luke 2.36–38).

It has often been suggested that there was a similar devotion to divine service in celibacy among the Qumran sectaries. This was indeed asserted by Pliny the Elder and by Josephus, but there is no substantial evidence for it in the Scrolls.[2]

ASCESIS IN I,14

This seems to provide a consistent background to the passages discussed in our last three chapters. The opposition are Petrines, as throughout the letters, with their roots in Jewish spirituality. But it is an apocalyptic, mystical

---

[2]See J. C. VanderKam, *The Dead Sea Scrolls Today* (Grand Rapids: Eerdmans, 1994), 90–91.

spirituality, aspiring to the vision of God and to possession by his Spirit, such as Moses experienced on Sinai. Moses prophesied; he was God's spokesman, delivering his commands, providing insight into the divine character, foreshadowing the will of God for the future. He interceded for Israel; his words of prayer had power to move the Almighty. It is these gifts of prophecy and prayer that are now claimed by the Corinthian and other Christian communities and that make church gatherings a focus of electric excitement.

Prayer was not seen in the early church as the repeating of the Shema or the Eighteen Benedictions; it was the action of the Spirit, expressed in cries and in wordless language. When Christians cried out "Abba," it was the Spirit bearing witness with their spirit that they were children of God (Rom 8.15–16). They did not know how to pray, so the Spirit interceded for them with sighs too deep for words (Rom 8.26). In prayer they spoke in the tongues of humans and of angels (I,13.1); they spoke in tongues to God (14.2), they prayed in a tongue (14.14). Prayer therefore was not a human initiative; it came from God and had the power to move mountains (13.3). How important, then, that we should make ourselves ready at all times, as Moses did, purifying ourselves from all the calls of mortal nature, such as eating and sex! Fasting was too normal a practice to leave a big mark on our traditions, but it would unquestionably have been part of Christian ascesis (Matt 6.16–18). It is not possible to give food up permanently, but one can give up sex permanently, "disdaining" it as did Moses. Hence Paul's comment in I,7.5 that it may be given up temporarily, by agreement, ἵνα σχολάσητε τῇ προσευχῇ.[3] The image in his mind is not of two humble figures kneeling side by side in their nightclothes by the bed; it is of a strong-willed couple repressing their desires night after night so that they may be ready vehicles for a hurricane of the Spirit. Gandhi was not the first great soul to magnify his spiritual power by sexual self-discipline. The reward for such abstinence would be seen the next Saturday evening in voiceless sighing, in unintelligible syllables, and in cataracts of tribal dialect and familiar Greek (ταῖς γλώσσαις τῶν ἀνθρώπων, I,13.1).

Paul is not critical of such aspirations, either the abstinence that prepares the way for them (temporarily, I,7.5; permanently if you have the χάρισμα, 7.7 and throughout the chapter) or their achievement in worship. He has the gift of continence himself and (he alleges, not too plausibly) speaks in tongues more than them all (14.18). Tongues do in fact have a limited edifying effect: "In the law it is written, 'By men of other tongues (ἑτερογλώσσοις) and by the lips of others will I speak to this people; and not even so will they hearken unto me,' says the Lord. So tongues are a sign, not

---

[3]σχολάζειν was losing its sense of "have leisure for" by NT times and means "devote oneself to," as in NRSV.

to the believers but to the unbelievers" (14.21–22). This is explained in the next verse, which is rarely understood: "So if the whole church is gathered together and all are speaking with tongues, and newcomers or unbelievers come in, will they not say that you are inspired (μαίνεσθε)?" Although μαίνεσθαι is used twice elsewhere in the NT, and both times (as here) in the second person of the present tense, to mean "you are mad" (Acts 12.15; 26.24, μαίνη), the verb often has positive connotations. The μάντις was an honored figure whose inspired ravings brought communication from the gods; cf. Heraclitus, frg. 92, Σίβυλλα δὲ μαινομένῳ στόματι. The tongues of the church are, as Isaiah said, a word from God, a sign not for the people of God, who will not listen to them, but for outsiders. When they hear them, they will be impressed. The standard translation here, "you are mad," is an error.

Christians have been "praying and prophesying" (I,11.4–5), and I,14 is given to pressing the priority of the latter as more edifying.[4] The pent-up psyche can more easily find release in uninhibited emotional outpouring without regard to being understood, and often more impressively, too. Paul would like the glossolalia limited to two or three church members, and to silence if there is no interpreter present (14.27–28). He favors prophesying because this is the only path to edification for the believers and to conversion for the outsiders; it is not enough that the latter be merely impressed by the sign of tongues—they need to be driven to their knees in contrition.

Prophecy has two effects. First, it consists of powerful preaching against sin, particularly against the crude sins Paul often lists, and to which Gentiles were especially liable: "If all prophesy, an unbeliever or outsider who enters is reproved by all and called to account by all. After the secrets of the unbeliever's heart are disclosed, that person will bow down before God and worship him, saying, 'God is really among you' " (14.24–25). Perhaps some readers have experienced the guilt-inducing power of an evangelical sermon, accompanied by testimonies and a prayer meeting. But also, for church members, there is the possibility of a "revelation" (14.26, 30). The Revelation (ἀποκάλυψις) of St. John is spoken of as a prophecy, and the revelations at Corinth may have resembled brief sections of that majestic work—warnings to the church to hold fast, visions of the divine throne, anticipations of persecution, of supernatural terrors, and of the punishment of the damned. Sexual delights might seem cheaply sacrificed if such a recompense followed. It is no small thing to be a divine prophet and approved by one's peers as such.

---

[4]For the exegesis of I,14.20–25, I am indebted to Stephen Chester, "The Secrets of the Heart Laid Bare" (paper presented at the British New Testament Conference, Leeds, September 1997). I am grateful to Dr. Chester for permission to use his material; he now thinks "you are inspired" to be too weak a translation.

First Corinthians 14.3 specifies the content of prophecy as οἰκοδομὴν καὶ παράκλησιν καὶ παραμυθίαν. The seven letters of Rev 1–3 might come under παράκλησις, while the rest of the book could give παραμυθία; the whole would bring οἰκοδομή. The seer's prophecy offers a revealing insight into I,14.24–25. A succession of speakers like him would be quickly unnerving: "The Lord says to the angel of the church in Corinth, I know your works. . . . You have some who hold the teaching of Jezebel. . . . She deceives my servants so as to commit whoredom and to eat idol meat." What had before seemed a harmless family party in the Asclepieion, or a lighthearted evening sporting with Amaryllis in the shade, is now publicly confessed (φανερά) in the edifying symbol of self-prostration (πεσὼν ἐπὶ πρόσωπον).

There seems thus to be an Ariadne's thread running through I,7; I,11.2–16; and I,14. The renunciation of sex was seen, as by Philo, as the gate to spiritual power, to effective prayer, to the conviction of sin in the heart of the unconverted, to visions of glory and adumbrations of things to come. Only one feature is still to be explained. The old Jewish sense of the holy as incompatible with sex was limited to men, but now we find the principal pressure is from the women. It is they who are keen to suspend marital relations and must be reminded that their husbands have control over their bodies. It is they who dare to separate from their husbands, even in defiance of a dominical prohibition. It is they who have thrown the claims of decency to the winds, praying barefaced with their hair visible and addressing an assembly of men without shame. Such things were not done in Israel.

Not in contemporary Israel indeed. But in earlier times, before life was organized and the patriarchal monopoly of power could be imposed, Deborah had been honored as a judge, and the Deuteronomic revolution was sanctioned by a prophetess, Huldah (2 Kgs 22.14–20). The church was likewise an organization struggling to survive, and was often indebted to wealthy or talented women: Chloe and Phoebe, the benefactress (προστάτις) of many (Rom 16.1–2), from Achaia; Apphia at Colossae (Phlm 2); and many women named in Rom 16. Total male domination is, in any case, a caricature for first-century urban society. A woman might become a Christian without her husband (I,7.13), and women with money were important figures even in Jesus' day (Luke 8.3), not to speak of Lydia and Damaris. The church needed its women, and in the republic of the Spirit they claimed an equal place with the men. It would not be surprising if in fact they claimed a more than equal place. They did not have education to provide words of wisdom from Scripture, and they were often excluded from decision making by their lack of experience; but when it came to holding the floor with drama and volubility, they could more than hold their own. The length of I,14, forty verses, and the abrasive tone of 14.34–35 assure us that they seized their opportunity with both hands.

The Perseverance of Jewish-Christian Ascesis

Pauline common sense was a sufficient force to stem the requirement of ascesis for all, but possession by the Spirit and the vision of God were widely felt to be noble aspirations and were to have a long history in the church. Second Corinthians has no hint of the problem. No doubt there were still women prophesying and couples practicing sexual abstinence, but we do not hear of their pressing others to share their ideals.

It is not until the 70s C.E. that we catch the echo of ascesis again. Matthew adds to the Markan pericope on divorce this surprising conclusion: "For there are eunuchs who were born so from their mothers' womb, and there are eunuchs who were made so by men, and there are eunuchs who made themselves so for the sake of the kingdom of heaven. He who can manage it, let him manage it" (Matt 19.12). The first two clauses speak of literal eunuchs, which might dispose us to take the third clause in the same way. Origen was a fine exegete, and he understood it so and acted upon it, as did many of his contemporaries.[5] Most modern commentators prefer, however, a metaphorical interpretation, and this would be in line with the discussion in I,7. Both the Petrines and Paul himself opted for permanent sexual abstinence for spiritual reasons: the Petrines because it gave them power in prayer and prophecy, Paul so that he might devote himself to the affairs of the Lord without encumbrance. Both could use the phrase "for the kingdom of heaven [God]," although it would be more natural to the Petrines (I,4.20; 15.50). But the final sentence aligns Matthew with Paul. Such aspiration was not for everyone: Paul says, "each has his own χάρισμα" (7.7); Matthew, ὁ δυνάμενος χωρεῖν χωρείτω.

Matthew is the evangelist most sympathetic to Peter and the Jewish-Christian tradition, and he is followed in this respect by the seer of the book of Revelation. In the 80s the church seemed to the seer to be composed of two great wings, the Jewish and the Gentile churches, and in Rev 14.1–6 he envisions them:

> And I saw, and lo, the Lamb standing on Mount Zion, and with him a hundred and forty and four thousands, having his name and the name of his Father written on their brow. . . . These are they that have not defiled themselves with women, for they are virgins (παρθένοι). These are they that follow the Lamb wherever he goes. These were ransomed from men as a firstfruit to God and to the Lamb, and in their mouth was found no lie; they are blameless. And I saw another angel flying in mid-heaven, having an eternal gospel to proclaim to those dwelling on the earth and to every nation and tribe and tongue and people.

---

[5]The story of the church's renunciation of sex, often with self-castration, is admirably told by Brown, *Body*.

The problem here has been the παρθένοι. It surely cannot be the seer's meaning that only male Christians without sexual experience are among the community of the saved, but attempts to find other meanings for παρθένος have been wrecked on the preceding phrase: "they have not defiled themselves with women." A solution is provided by the broader context. There are two wings of the church. In 14.1–5 the seer beholds the Jewish Christians: they are "standing on Mount Zion," the center of Jewish Christianity, and they number 144,000, like the twelve 12,000s "from every tribe of the sons of Israel" in Rev 7.4–8. All Christians have the name of Christ on their forehead, but these have also "his Father's name" because they were true Jews before they became Christians. They were "redeemed as a firstfruit to God": there was a flourishing Jewish church before any word reached Gentiles in Antioch. Then in 14.6–7 John sees a second "angel, flying in mid-heaven" so as to proclaim his gospel to all humankind. This time the message is not for Jews only but "to every nation and tribe and tongue and people." Those who hear are the Gentile church, and in 14.14–16 they and their Jewish fellow believers are reaped by the one like a Son of Man.

The seer has a high opinion of Jewish Christians: they show a dedication that even Gentile Christians cannot emulate. This dedication is partly expressed generally: "they follow the Lamb wherever he goes," all over the land of Israel, if necessary to martyrdom. But partly their devotion is shown by their sexual abstinence. John himself is celibate and has accepted the dogma that those who sleep with women "defile themselves"; he has accordingly a high regard for those who "are virgins." He sees the whole Jewish-Christian wing of the church as having made this noble sacrifice. Gentile Christendom was a fine thing, but it had never quite gone the whole hog.

There are two other passages in Revelation where John shows his perception of a two-wing church. In 7.4–8 the 144,000 are sealed "from every tribe of the sons of Israel," 12,000 from each tribe, and these are followed, as in 14.6, by "a great multitude, which no one could number, from every nation and all tribes and peoples and tongues."

In 11.1–14 there is a vision of Jerusalem, the holy city that is to be trampled by the Romans for forty-two months (v. 2), the great city that is spiritually called Sodom and Egypt, where the believers' Lord was crucified (v. 8). Two witnesses prophesy there for 1,260 days. They have authority to shut the skies from raining, as Elijah did, and to turn water into blood, as Moses did. When they have finished their testimony, Titus, the Roman beast, will make war on them and kill them, and their bodies will lie in the streets. Christ had two witnesses whose testimony in Jerusalem continued until 70 C.E.: like Moses, who was sent to the people of Israel, and like Elijah, who was sent to the Gentiles (Luke 4.25–26). But Jewish and Hellenistic alike were massacred in the great bloodbath when the city fell.

The same ascesis is evident in the Jewish-Christian movement behind the Pastorals. But whereas the seer admired Jewish Christianity as an equal member with the Gentile mission, the writer of the Pastorals sees it as the enemy. Its leaders occupy themselves with myths and genealogies and desire to be teachers of the law (1 Tim 1.4–6). They pay attention to Jewish myths and commandments; some of these are purity rules, but "to the pure all things are pure" (Titus 1.14–15). Titus is to silence idle talkers, especially those of the circumcision (1.10).

A feature of this Jewish Christianity is its aspiration to have the vision of God, and this the writer of the Pastorals finds particularly misguided and obnoxious. Jesus Christ "dwells in unapproachable light, whom no one of mankind has seen or can see" (1 Tim 6.16). If the writer denies it three times, we may take it that his adversaries are asserting it. The light is ἀπρόσιτον, so no Jewish Christian could have approached it; no human being has ever seen the divine presence, nor is it possible to do so—claims of divine visions thus are lies. First Timothy 1.17 similarly is a doxology "to the King of the Aeons, imperishable, invisible." God is ἀόρατος, so they have not seen him.

Like Moses in Philo, these earnest Christians have been schooling themselves for the *visio Dei;* it has meant giving up marriage. The writer of the Pastorals speaks of them as apostates following deceitful spirits, their consciences being seared with a hot iron, "discouraging marriage" (κωλυόντων γαμεῖν, 1 Tim 4.3); perhaps, as in 1 Cor 7, they discouraged all Christians from sexual relations, or perhaps it was only in the Jewish-Christian community. But the writer has read 1 Corinthians and thus knows what will happen if women are given an inch. Therefore, they are to dress modestly and decently without ornaments and to learn in silence with full submission; he does not permit them to teach or have authority over a man (1 Tim 2.8–12). Women can be saved (they will be glad to hear) through childbearing, provided they continue in modesty (2.15). Regular marital relations and pregnancies will keep them out of charismatic mischief, but they must also dress drably and not say anything. Similarly, younger widows are to marry, have children, and manage their households, not gadding about; moreover, the rules for older widows to draw church benefits are so strict that the expenditure must have been very limited. The writer is a misogynist, and he is against women because they are a powerful force in Jewish Christianity.

The link between sexual abstinence and women's ministry may be traced into the second century. Increasingly the Pauline churches were growing stronger, and male dominance became the norm, often with appeal to Paul's comments in 1 Corinthians and to the Pastorals. But such dominance was not yet universal. The *Acts of Paul* contains a long section sometimes called the "Acts of Paul and Thecla," which, in fact, glorifies a woman, Thecla, from Seleucia. Twice preserved miraculously from martyrdom, Thecla is authorized by Paul to go to Iconium and teach the word of God (*Acts Paul* 41), and she ends the work by enlightening many. However, the leitmotif of the story is the need for celibacy, which is the core of Paul's message and of Thecla's creed. Paul says,

> Blessed are the pure in heart, for they shall see God.
> Blessed are they who have kept their flesh pure, for they shall become a temple of God.
> Blessed are the continent, for to them will God speak. . . .
> Blessed are they who have wives as if they had them not, for they shall inherit God. . . .
> Blessed are the bodies of the virgins, for they shall be well-pleasing to God and shall not lose the reward of their purity. (5–6)

The centrality of continence is unmistakable. The celibate will see God, be God's temple, receive God's revelations, inherit God. The echoes of 1 Corinthians ("temple of God," "have wives as if they had them not") mingle with the Matthean Beatitudes to form a manifesto for virginity that will lead on to the spiritual ministry of a woman: Thecla throws over her affianced, Thamyris, and her repeated deliverances from martyrdom are the sanction of her preaching. Furthermore, there is an eternal "reward of her purity"; she will "inherit God" and "become as his angel"; she will not "see the bitter day of judgment" (*Acts Paul* 6). Continence is the only way: "Otherwise there is no resurrection for you, except you remain chaste and do not defile the flesh, but keep it pure" (12).

The Thecla traditions were familiar to Tertullian and Hippolytus, so they went back well into the second century. The echo of Rev 14.4 in the last text cited (*Acts Paul* 12) and the Matthew-type beatitudes suggest a sympathy with Jewish Christianity. But in other ways there is a more evident affiliation to the tradition of the Petrines of I,7, 11, and 14. Sexual abstinence is not for those who have the gift; it is for all, and without it there is no resurrection. It gives spiritual power: the continent, the pure in heart and flesh, are those who will see God, being carried up to the throne; they are those to whom God will speak. Behind this lies the same drive for spiritual power that was the motive force for Paul's opposition—abstinence in I,7, prophecy in I,11 and 14. But the abstinence is, above all, abstinence for women and leads on to the preaching and teaching of women. Thecla is a woman herself and deprives her betrothed Thamyris of his expected rights, and she is one of many women and virgins who imbibe the doctrine (*Acts Paul* 7). It was women especially who renounced sexual relations in I,7 and women whose unhooded praying and prophesying were such a scandal in I,11.2–16, and who had to be silenced in I,14.34–35. Thecla is just the sort of woman who could reduce Paul to a chauvinist authoritarian in twenty minutes.

The ascetic/feminist strand in Petrine practice was to have a notorious outworking in the Montanist movement in Phrygia, later extended to Africa and Rome. Montanus called his movement the New Prophecy, and he claimed to speak in the name of the παντοκράτωρ, indeed of the Trinity. He delivered oracles that were often interpretations of biblical texts and appealed to the Johannine doctrine of the Paraclete as one who would guide into all truth and reveal things to come. Some of the inspired matter was delivered in strange language. He dissolved marriages, and some of his leading disciples were women, that is, Priscilla and Maximilla, who had divorced their husbands. This was part of an ascetic program that included fasting and vegetarianism. Visions were an important element in the movement's aspirations and in its appeal. Montanus saw the little towns of Pepuza and Tymion as the focus of the new Christian world and named them Jerusalem.

Christine Trevett links the Montanists with the church at Thyatira, not far away in Asia, the subject of a critical letter in Rev 2.18–29 and of related letters in Rev 2–3.[6] The leadership of "the woman Jezebel, who calls herself a prophet, and is teaching and beguiling my servants" (Rev 2.20) is a link with the Montanist women leaders, Priscilla and Maximilla, and later Quintilla. Jezebel's teaching is described as "knowing the deep things of Satan (τὰ βαθέα τοῦ Σατανᾶ)" and is probably the same as "the deep things of God" (τὰ βάθη τοῦ θεοῦ) in I,2.10, known by "descending" into the divine realm in quest of the heavenly vision. She—and also the Nicolaitans of Rev 2.15 at Pergamum—teaches that one may eat food sacrificed to idols, a further echo of 1 Corinthians. At Smyrna and Philadelphia there are opposition Christian groups, "synagogues of Satan who say that they are Jews and are not" (2.9; 3.9). Philadelphia was to be named "the new Jerusalem" (3.12).

It looks, therefore, as if Montanism was an Asian development of the Petrine form of Christianity that we find mirrored in 1 Corinthians. There is a central emphasis on prophecy, and oracles are often delivered in strange, ecstatic language (παρέκστασις, ξενοφωνεῖν, πνευματοφορηθῆναι),[7] as in I,12 and 14. The leadership was, to a large extent, in the hands of women, and the same is implied in I,7; 11.2–16; and 14.34–35. The Montanists felt the need to abstain from sex if one was to be a vehicle for divine revelations, and this was carried as far as divorce, at least by Priscilla and Maximilla; again we have the parallel in I,7, especially 7.10–11. Although there is nothing specifically Jewish-Christian in Pepuza, there are clear Jewish-Christian elements in the Asian churches criticized in Rev 2–3, and these in turn are associated with the Petrines of I,8–10 by their permissive attitude to idol meat.[8]

---

[6]C. Trevett, *Montanism: Gender, Authority, and the New Prophecy* (Cambridge: Cambridge University Press, 1996), provides a full account and discussion of the movement, with Eusebius's anonymous author as a primary source and amplified, with discrimination, from Tertullian, Epiphanius, and other later authors. The connection with Thyatira is expounded on pp. 24, 144; that with Philadelphia on pp. 19–23, 34–38.

[7]Ibid., 86–91.

[8]Trevett, *Montanism,* 142–45, makes the link with Jewish Christianity.

It would not be difficult to pursue the attraction of sexual ascesis on to Tertullian and indeed to modern times, but the aspiration was as common in mainstream as in deviant churches and goes back to Paul himself. Enough evidence is available, in any case, to show that there is no need to go to Hellenistic sources for its origin. The OT knew that contact with women must be forgone if one was to have contact with the divine, at least if one was to receive revelation, and this tradition is expressed clearly by Philo. With the coming of the nascent church, spiritual aspiration is extended to women. Luke speaks of the four virgin daughters of Philip who had the gift of prophecy, and I,7; 11.2–16; and 14 are evidence of the movement among the Petrine women at Corinth. Lifelong abstinence from sex is indicated in Matthew, but, as in I,7.7, only for those who have the gift. Revelation 14.1–6 implies that such lifelong renunciation is the practice of the whole Jewish wing of the church, and the Pastorals are critical of Jewish Christianity, which combines discouragement of marriage with the practice of divine vision. The same practices and aspirations are testified in second-century sources, in the "Acts of Paul and Thecla," and in Montanism, except that in these, women have taken the lead as in Corinth. We have the impression that the Pauline, and later the mainstream, churches were content with sexual ascesis as a means to prophetic inspiration so long as there were men in charge. It was only the ministry of women that stuck in the catholic gorge.

~ 11 ~

IDOL SACRIFICES: I

ALL SUCCESSFUL Diaspora Jews were faced with the problem of assimilation. If you were poor and lived in a Jewish quarter (if there was one) and worked for Jews, you did not have a big problem. However, as soon as you began to make your way, you found yourself doing business with Greeks and other Gentiles, and so mixing with them socially. Jews wanted to be citizens of the Greek cities they lived in, with proper civic rights. They wanted the respect that comes from being educated, and education here meant Homer and Euripides and Plato. They wanted to belong to secular society without giving up their own Jewishness; then as now, this involved compromise.

The most immediate problem was sharing a meal with a Gentile host. If you were being strict, this was impossible. It was likely that any animal had been prayed over before being killed, with prayers offered to some heathen deity, and the same would apply to wine, which was commonly opened with a libation. It was certain that no tithe had been paid on the food, and it was extremely unlikely that it had been bought from a kosher supplier who had followed the correct slaughtering procedure. Simply put, if you were strict, you would never be part of the society you lived in; conversely, if you wanted business success and good relations with your neighbors, and so security, you would have to compromise.

For Jews in Palestine and for most Jews in the Diaspora, eating Gentile food was self-excommunication. According to 4 Macc 5.2, Antiochus Epiphanes had required Jews to eat pork or meat offered to an idol, and those who refused were martyred. The classic text that proved the iniquity of such food was Num 25, where Israel ate the sacrifices of the Moabite gods, referred to as זִבְחֵי מֵתִים, the offerings of the dead, in Ps 106.28. Tosefta *Hullin* 2.18, for instance, says that an animal slaughtered to any deity other than God, or even to the archangel Michael, is meat from the offerings of the dead (cf. Philo, *Mos.* 1.295–305; *Spec.* 1.54–58). The *macellum* (provisions market) at Pompeii was surrounded by altars at which butchers could make at least token offerings to one god or another, and Jews knew there was no safety in eating such meat.[1]

---

[1] Schrage, *Der erste Brief,* 2:216 n. 16; 263 n. 300.

There were Jews, however, who got around these restrictions. Some renounced their Jewishness completely for political or social advantage; others attempted to salve their consciences by allegorizing the cultic texts (Philo, *Migr.* 89–93). John Barclay has collected the evidence for such assimilation.[2] But the clearest evidence for Jewish compromise comes from the NT itself. In Rev 2–3 the seer's opponents are twice spoken of as Nicolaitans (at Ephesus and Pergamum); in Pergamum they hold the teaching of Balaam, to eat food sacrificed to idols (2.14–15). Balaam's oracles appear in Num 23–24 and immediately precede the Baal-Peor incident in Num 25; Num 31.16 interprets the two incidents as being connected; and Irenaeus, *Haer.* 1.26.3, categorizes Nicolaitans as Jewish Christians. The prophetess Jezebel at Thyatira puts forward the same teaching (Rev 2.20), along with "the deep things of Satan," that is, Jewish visionary techniques disapproved by the seer, and the churches at Smyrna and Philadelphia contain members who "say that they are Jews and are not, but are a synagogue of Satan" (2.9; 3.9). The Asian churches, then, seem to be bedeviled by a form of Jewish Christianity that sanctions the eating of idol meat.

The arrival of the Christian missions brought the same problems to Gentile converts, for the food laws were (in outline) in the Bible. Paul's refusal of the web of halakic interpretation, the rulings of the wise, might solve the problem of kosher slaughter, with his "Not beyond what is written," but idolatry was forbidden in the Bible in passage after passage. Furthermore, matters were much more acute for Gentile converts than for Jews. They had associations going back over their whole lives with non-Christian family and friends and professional acquaintances. There were weddings and meals in honor of the dead, club dinners and parties given by friends, and business entertaining. It was impracticable to require these links to be severed overnight. The same difficulty applied to both the factions at Corinth. There were clearly well-to-do Petrines who had been seen dining in a temple restaurant (εἰδωλεῖον), but the Paulines were in exactly the same dilemma. They included the wealthy Gaius and Erastus; Chloe and Phoebe were well placed also, and perhaps others. It is not surprising that the church raised the question περὶ δὲ τῶν εἰδωλοθύτων (I,8.1).

The opposition solved the problem on the basis of agreed γνῶσις: "We all have knowledge." The knowledge looks like Jewish-Christian knowledge, for it takes the form "There is no God but one," which recalls the Shema, "Hear, O Israel: the LORD our God is one" (Deut 6.4). Also, Paul warns the knowledgeable that "some from being accustomed to an idol till

---

[2] J. M. G. Barclay, *Jews in the Mediterranean Diaspora: From Alexander to Trajan (323 BCE–117 CE)* (Edinburgh: T&T Clark, 1996), 103–12, 321–26. There is a similar discussion in P. Borgen, *Early Christianity and Hellenistic Judaism* (Edinburgh: T&T Clark, 1996), 14–32; Borgen shows how difficult it is to be sure whether Jews who assimilated were able to continue seeing themselves as Jews.

now are eating" the meat "as sacrificed to an idol, and their conscience, being weak, is defiled" (I,8.7).[3] The "weak" are Gentile Christians who until recently were idol worshipers, and this suggests that the knowledgeable were Jewish Christians. It is tempting to follow many commentators and to call the γνῶσις group "the strong," even though Paul does not use the word here, but he did say sarcastically to the Petrines in 4.10, "we are weak, ὑμεῖς δὲ ἰσχυροί," and he asks in a similar tone at 10.22, "Are we stronger than [God]?" They had the strength to stand out against tradition in the power of the new revelation and could look down on the Gentile convert who still half-believed in pagan gods.

The Petrine claim to knowledge was hard to fault. All Christians (and Jews) knew that there was "no God but one" and, in consequence, that "there was no idol [god] in the world" (8.4). "For us," including Pauline Christians, "there is one God the Father, from whom is everything and for whom we exist" (8.6a). God is often addressed as Father in Jewish prayers, meaning both Creator and Redeemer, and the statement is rooted in Gen 1. But if there are no other gods, the Petrines concluded, then sacrifice to them is absolutely null and utterly void, and there is no harm in eating the sacrificial meat. Indeed, this meat should be referred to as ἱερόθυτον, not εἰδωλόθυτον; even Paul uses the neutral form when he is not being so polemical (I,10.28). It is just a "temple offering" that the benighted host may think of as dedicated to Isis or Serapis but the enlightened Christian may see as offered really to God (cf. 10.30–31). "Anything is permitted" (10.23) once you have seen this obvious truth. In any case, one cannot come to any harm by "eating at their table and drinking their cup" (10.21). "The meat is for the belly and the belly for the meat, and God will bring both to nothing" (6.13); it cannot do you any harm.

Opinions differ on whether 8.6a was part of the language of Paul's opposition, as is thought by many, or was a traditional Hellenistic Jewish formula.[4] At least the εἷς θεός is standard, but Paul produces similar doxologies elsewhere (Rom 11.36), and so the whole verse is likely to be his own. The references to creation (πατήρ, ἐξ οὗ) are far from irrelevant, as is sometimes said, since Paul will later argue that we may eat anything created by God—"the earth and its fullness are the Lord's" (10.26). Some critics (e.g., Eriksson) attribute 8.6b also to "the Corinthians," but this is mistaken

---

[3]The word συνείδησις presents problems, but I have retained the traditional *conscience* as a translation, and also the adjective *weak,* although *delicate* is sometimes more suitable. One's συνείδησις can be "defiled" (8.7), "built up" to do something wrong (8.10), or "struck," "violated" (τύπτοντες, 8.12), and one can avoid scandalizing behavior διὰ τὴν συνείδησιν, whether one's own or someone else's (10.25, 27, 28). Borgen, *Early Christianity,* 32–38, prefers *consciousness* and is followed by Horsley, but Paul's use is of a nontechnical, everyday word that seems to correspond most closely to our *conscience,* its etymological equivalent.

[4]Schrage, *Der erste Brief,* 2:239–41.

(see below, ch. 13). Conzelmann noted parallels with 8.6a in Marcus Aurelius and other Stoics, but the Jewish context seems determinative. Horsley sees the language as deriving from Philo and thinks of Paul as replacing the Hellenistic σοφία with Christ.[5]

The boldness and simplicity of this solution draws our admiration. Indeed, anyone who has been fortunate enough to be invited to the consecration of a new Hindu idol, and joined in the subsequent banquet, has no doubt silently taken the Petrine line. But we may also be surprised that a Jewish-Christian group should opt for such a solution. If so, the surprise may arise from a lack of awareness of the variety of Jewish responses to the challenge of assimilation, including Jewish-Christian responses (Rev 2–3). There were good old-fashioned hard-liners, such as James, Jesus' brother, who lived in Jerusalem and did not see the problem; there were also bold accommmodaters, such as (we may suppose) Nicolas the proselyte of Antioch or whoever stands behind the Nicolaitans at Pergamum, Ephesus, and elsewhere.

It is perfectly believable that this tension over assimilation split the Jewish Christians at Corinth. No one who put his or her confidence in the wisdom of rulings, derived from Scripture and handed down by the sages, scribes, and debaters of this age, could be happy with what looked like blatant idolatry: what happened to those who ate the offerings of the dead in Num 25? But the bold insouciance of the Petrines in I,8–10 is based not on wisdom but on knowledge, and these two are seen as different gifts in 12.8. Rather, we may see the vaunted knowledge as the child of divine vision and so arising from a second source of authority. Assimilation at Thyatira was advocated by a self-proclaimed prophetess "knowing the deep things of Satan" (Rev 2.20, 24). Words of wisdom were derived by professional exegetes from the Torah; words of knowledge came to the visionary by direct inspiration. Two authorities, two powers in heaven, mean in the end two sets of praxis. Just as the rabbis acted to restrict the visionary movement, so would the Jacobite Petrines have quailed at the excesses of the Nicolaitan Petrines. But at Corinth social pressures favored the latter, and young Gentile converts with no training in Scripture were drawn naturally to the γνῶσις as being at once more exciting and more practical.

The limpid clarity of this logic is irresistible and drives the unhappy apostle on to the bad-tempered defensive. He cannot but agree with most of it. "We know that" there is this common "knowledge" (8.1); "about food offered to idols we know that no idol in the world" has any divinity (8.4). So what is wrong, then? Well, the whole idea of knowledge is wrong. It "puffs up where love builds up. If anyone thinks he knows something, he does not

[5] A. Eriksson, *Tradition As Rhetorical Proof: Pauline Argumentation in 1 Corinthians* (ConBNT 29; Stockholm: Almqvist & Wiksell, 1998), 120–27; Conzelmann, *1 Corinthians,* 144; Horsley, *I Corinthians,* 119.

yet know as he ought to know. But if anyone loves God, he is known by him" (8.2–3).[6] Paul administers his standard snub: what matters is not our knowledge but God's knowledge of us (cf. 13.12, "then I shall know even as also I have been known"; 14.38, εἰ δέ τις ἀγνοεῖ, ἀγνοεῖται; Gal 4.9, "you have come to know God, or rather to be known by him"). He also tends to fall back on the sarcastic use of δοκεῖ when the argument is not going well (I,3.18; 11.16; 14.37; Gal 2.6, 9).

The Petrines' logic may sound impressive, but Paul will not accept idolatry. He inserts a slightly ambiguous clause to distance himself: "although there are so-called gods in heaven or on earth (as there are many gods and many lords), yet to us there is one God." We shall see later that, although Paul believed in one God and accepted that there were no idol gods, yet these many so-called gods had a reality behind them—they were demons. But in the meantime, he attacks the opposition's claims with two quite distinct arguments, as follows.

Rights and Responsibilities

Scandalizing the Weak (I,8.7–13).   The somewhat sour comments on knowledge and love have a real basis in a genuine concern for "the weak brother" (and sister). Paul knows that there are a number of recent Gentile converts in the church who do not "have this knowledge"; they have been used to worshiping idols, and if they eat idol sacrifices, they will think of it as worship, and "their conscience, being weak," will be "defiled" (8.7). The Serapeum at Corinth had its dining facilities looking on to an open courtyard, and here or elsewhere the knowledgeable might be "seen reclining in the εἰδωλείῳ" (8.10a).[7] The sight will encourage ("build up," οἰκοδομη-θήσεται) the fellow Christian's conscience; this believer will eat, and so at best become a hypocrite; at worst he or she may leave the church, believing that such eating is incompatible with Christianity. The argument is not a feeble evasion. Paul deploys the same approach in Rom 14, but with the opposite intention. There the weak are the Jewish Christians with their attach-

---

[6]𝔓[46] omits τι in 8.2 and both τον θεον and υπ αυτου in 8.3, with support from some Fathers in each case and from ℵ* 33 in the last. Horsley defends these omissions, and a better sense is given without τὸν θεόν, as the argument goes on to speak of loving "one's brother." But "he is known" is surprising without "by [God]," and 𝔓[46] may have written an abbreviated version in line with what seemed a better sense. Fee, *First Epistle,* 367–68, thinks that Paul drew in the reference to the loving of God from Deut 6.5.

[7]J. Murphy-O'Connor, *St. Paul's Corinth: Texts and Archaeology* (Good News Studies 6; Wilmington, Del.: Glazier, 1983), 161–64, gives drawings of a number of reconstructions of first-century Corinth, including the temple area of Asclepius (the Serapeum), with three dining rooms leading out to an open courtyard.

ments to food laws and Sabbaths, and Paul urges the mature Gentile Christians to bend to their weakness and respect the old traditions—only so can the unity of the church be preserved. You have to be fair-minded as well as clever if you want a united church.

But Paul is indeed clever as well as fair-minded. The knowledgeable had cited the Shema in the form "There is no God but one" (8.4). They did not, however, accept the Paulines' belief that "Jesus is Lord." κύριος was the LXX term for Yahweh, and when the Paulines cried out their confession of faith during worship, their opponents felt it to be blasphemous, and it drew aggressive countercries of Ἀνάθεμα Ἰησοῦς (12.3; see below, pp. 211–12). With this in mind, Paul introduces the term κύριος, beginning from 8.5. Deuteronomy 10.17 had said, "The LORD your God is God of gods and Lord of lords," so he can say now, "there are many gods and many lords." This enables him to cap the agreed "But to us there is one God the Father from whom is everything and we to him" with a controversial parallel line: "and one Lord Jesus Christ, through whom are all things and we through him" (8.6b). He is not going to fight this issue with one hand tied behind his back. He needs to assert Jesus Christ's eternal lordship, his activity in creation as the image of God through whom the universe was made (Gen 1.27) and through whom we have our redemption. These doctrines are expounded more fully in II,3–4, in Phil 2.6–11, and in Col 1.14–20.

For the Petrines, the word of the cross was stupidity. Jesus was a prophet who had announced the coming of the kingdom of God; his crucifixion was the tragic end to his mission, but it had no more significance than the death of any martyr, say, Isaiah. With the kingdom had come the Spirit with its many gifts, including the all-important γνῶσις: we now know that we can eat what we like (I,6.13; 8.4). But it is not the food that matters. "Food will not commend us to God: if we refuse to eat [such idol sacrifices] we miss nothing, and if we eat [them] we gain nothing" (8.8) because they are not sacraments with religious power of salvation like the Eucharist.[8] But what does matter is one's fellow Christian—Christ died for that person. "Watch that this license of yours [ἐξουσία, cf. ἔξεστιν, 6.12; 10.23] does not become a stumbling block to the weak" (8.9). Fellow believers will see you enjoying your banquet and you will have "destroyed by your knowledge" the brother for whom Christ died."

The Petrines were content to enjoy the transports of the new life of the πνευματικοί. They were not much worried about the halfway Christian ψυχικός. But Paul is the good pastor who cares for his sheep: the salvation

---

[8]Barrett, *First Epistle,* 195, and many commentators take 8.8 as a Corinthian slogan; partly from its similarity to 6.13 and partly from the succeeding ἡ ἐξουσία ὑμῶν (8.9). But Fee, *First Epistle,* 381–84, points to the similarity to Paul's own views—e.g., on the indifference of circumcision (7.19)—and Paul elsewhere cites his opponents' slogans without a connecting δέ.

of the new convert is imperiled by the careless selfishness of the knowledge-able. By such actions they "are sinning against their fellow Christians and as-saulting their consciences, and so sinning against Christ" (8.12). For it was Christ who died for them: this central truth, δι' ὃν Χριστὸς ἀπέθανεν (v. 11), takes up the Pauline creed of v. 6b, εἷς κύριος Ἰησοῦς Χριστός . . . ἡμεῖς δι' αὐτοῦ. We are saved through him and he died for us; the same preposition, διά, does double duty, followed by different cases. So scandal-izing one's fellow believer with idol meat is unthinkable (v. 13).

Giving Up One's Rights (I,9.1–27). Knowledge was a key issue to the Petrines because it told them that everything was permissible. The slogan πάντα ἔξεστιν gave them a lot of ἐξουσία: a woman had ἐξουσία over her own body and could refuse her husband marital rights (7.4); one had the ἐξουσία to eat idol sacrifices (8.9). Once people start clamoring for their rights—the right to abstinence, the right to eat in a pagan temple—an im-passe is at hand. Paul seeks to bypass trouble by his own example.

It is now generally agreed that ch. 9 is an extension of the argument of ch. 8 on claims to ἐξουσία. Paul himself had the ἐξουσία "to eat and drink" at church expense (9.4), "to take round a Christian wife" (v. 5), "not to work" (v. 6), a right that can be established by many arguments—natural, scriptural, and dominical (vv. 7–12). "But we have not made use of this ἐξουσία" (v. 12b); "But I have not made use of any of these rights" (v. 15). The force of this central theme is clear; what obscures its centrality is the in-troductory three verses, 9.1–3, and the somewhat wandering conclusion to the chapter.

Paul wished to argue that just as he had the right to live at church ex-pense but did not use the right, so should the Corinthians not use their right to eat in pagan temples. Unfortunately, he had to rebut criticism on this very point. The visiting missionaries from Jerusalem had themselves claimed to live on church contributions (v. 12, "If others share in this right over you . . .") and had argued that Paul was no true apostle, that otherwise he would have claimed this apostolic right. Hence the indignant opening, "Am I not free [to exercise rights or not as I please]? Am I not an apostle? Have I not seen Jesus our Lord? . . . My defense to those who examine me is this . . ." In the second half of the chapter, Paul returns to his "freedom" (v. 19) "to make the gospel free" (v. 18) and to claim nothing for himself. But he then di-gresses a little into his missionary strategy, "that [he] may by all means save some," and on the physical discipline that this requires.

So the second argument is an extension of the first. Paul has the right as an apostle to have his living paid for by the church, but he gave up this right in the hope of saving as many people as possible. And so should the Corinthians give up their claimed right to eat idol sacrifices for the salvation of their "weak" fellow Christian.

THE TRUE NATURE OF IDOLATRY

The Fate of Idolaters in the Bible (I,10.1–13).   One of the disturbing things about the Petrines was their overconfidence. Paul has already hinted at this at the end of ch. 9: "So run that you may win . . . lest having proclaimed to others I myself become disqualified" (9.24, 27). Chapter 10 then begins, "For I do not wish you to be ignorant, brothers." He then makes a singular exposition of the exodus story: "Our fathers . . . were all baptized into Moses in the cloud and in the sea [of Exod 14], and did all eat the same spiritual food [the manna] and did all drink the same spiritual drink [the water from the rock]; for they all drank from the spiritual rock that followed them, and the rock was Christ." In Jewish sources, we never read of the exodus as "baptism into Moses." This is Paul's own rendition of the story, and it stems from Petrine confidence in the quasi-magical power of the sacraments. The Petrines thought that having the apostolic baptism was the only path to salvation (1.13–17) and that one could behave as one pleased at the Eucharist (11.17–34); the Petrine baptism brought one into the community of the saved, and the sanctified bread and wine kept one saved. Paul ridicules this confidence by recalling a series of episodes in Exodus and Numbers in which Israelites who had gone through the primary experiences of "baptism" and "spiritual food and drink" later came to a bad end—after the golden calf, the refusal to enter the land of Canaan, and the idolatry at Baal-Peor. He piles up the contrasts: "all . . . all . . . all . . ." experienced the OT baptism and spiritual food and drink, but "some of them . . . some of them . . . some of them . . ." subsequently died in various plagues. "So," he concludes, "let him who thinks (ὁ δοκῶν) he stands watch lest he fall."

It is noticeable that Paul has moved on to a new argument. Eating idol meat is not reproved here because it may cause the weak believer to stumble; rather, it constitutes idolatry in itself. This point is expressly made in 10.7: "And do not become idolaters as some of them did; as it is written, 'The people sat down to eat and drink and rose up to play' [Exod 32.6, at Sinai]." In 8.10 this was precisely what the Petrines had been doing: reclining in an idol temple restaurant, eating and drinking! The word *play* was a euphemism for sexual license, which in turn was often an equivalent for idolatry. Furthermore, 10.8 makes reference to the standard Jewish text on idolatry: in Num 25 Israel went whoring with the women of Moab and ate "the offerings of the dead," in consequence of which twenty-four thousand of them died of the plague. Paul says, "Neither let us go whoring, as some of them went whoring, and fell in one day twenty-three thousand." He gives a slightly lower figure, one thousand short, perhaps to keep on the safe side and to avoid the favorable number twenty-four (twice the holy twelve, Rev 4.10). It is not, then, just a matter of the weak believer's conscience; "our fathers," the spiritual ancestors of Jews and Christians alike, committed idolatry by eating food offered to a pagan god, and those who do the same today are idolaters, too, and may expect the same fate.

The Table of Demons (I,10.14–21). Paul pursues another facet of this argument in the following verses, beginning, "So, my beloved, flee from idolatry." Eating idol meat is shown to be idolatry not only from frequent references in Scripture but also from common sense: "I am speaking as to sensible people—judge what I say for yourselves." When you eat or drink consecrated food and wine, you become a "partaker" (κοινωνός) of that mystery. When we Christians bless the cup or break the eucharistic bread, we become partakers in the blood and body of Christ. It is the same with Israel after the flesh: they sacrifice an animal at the Jerusalem altar, and when they eat, they make themselves partakers in their religion.

Now what about this idol meat that some of you have been eating? "What am I saying? That an idol offering is anything, or that an idol is anything?" This is the uncomfortable moment, because Paul has already conceded that there is no idol(-god) in the world (8.4), but he in fact believes that there is a reality behind the idol and its offering—a demonic reality. Idol offerings are being sacrificed to "demons" and not to God (10.20), and those who eat of them make themselves partakers in demonic worship. Paul draws on a text from Deuteronomy to make his point: "They sacrificed to demons, not to God" (Deut 32.17). So, although there is no idol god in the world (I,8.4) and to us there is one God, the Father (8.6), yet at the same time there are many so-called gods and lords (8.5), and these are, as Scripture says, demons. And "you cannot share in the table of the Lord and the table of demons." You Petrines despise the "weak" ex-Gentile Christian and speak of your being strong enough to ignore prayers to pagan gods: "are we moving the Lord to jealousy [Deut 32.22]? Or are we stronger than he?"

Chapters 8–10 present the commentator with an apparent contradiction. In ch. 8 Paul seems to concede that there is nothing wrong with idol food in itself; what is wrong is the failure of those with knowledge to respect the weaker believer's scruples. And a similar line seems to come in 10.23–11.1, where Paul cites a psalm, "The earth is the Lord's and the fullness thereof"—Christians have freedom, limited only by the conscience of others. On the other hand, 10.1–22 seems to take a different line: Israel was frequently punished in the Torah for eating idol food, which was idolatry and thus wrong in itself, and those who indulge in it become partakers in the table of demons.

In face of this problem, a number of solutions have been offered. First, Johannes Weiss suggested that parts of two different letters had been combined.[9] Verses 1–22 had been part of an earlier Pauline letter and had been

---

[9] *Der erste Korintherbrief* (KEK; 9th ed.; Göttingen: Vandenhoeck & Ruprecht, 1910).

inserted into the discussion in the canonical epistle, 8.1–13; 9.19–23; and 10.23–11.1. This seems less appealing today, partly because there is no support for it at all in the manuscript tradition and partly because no explanation is still offered why Paul should hold such very different views, at first so conservative, later so liberal.

Second, Conzelmann holds that Paul vacillates between arguments addressed to two different addressees.[10] Paul addresses 8.1–13 and 10.23–11.1 to the "strong," admonishing them to recognize a limit on their freedom, in the conscience of a "weak" believer; but in 10.1–22 he warns the whole community of the danger of such eating, which is now seen as sacramental— it unites the worshiper with his or her god, and this worship must be exclusive. The difficulty with this position is that there is no hint, in the text, of a change in the group addressed, and, in any case, the theory does nothing to ease the contradiction between the two attitudes to idol food.

Third, a more generally accepted line today entails taking one part of the chapters as Paul's teaching and treating the other as a side issue. Thus, Barrett, Schrage, and Joel Delobel[11] regard 8.1–13 and 10.23–11.1 as Paul's real view and 10.1–22 as a subsidiary section referring only to participation in actual worship in a pagan temple, as opposed to social occasions that might take place in a temple restaurant. Thus Barrett says that "the Christian is always free to eat any food whatever," that a Christian should "avoid feasts in religious temples if these had a markedly religious content," that "it is not the eating of sacrificial food (which Paul permits), but direct participation in idolatry which will separate the Christian from Christ."[12] For this view, Paul is on the side of the "strong."

This solution depends on some glosses ("feasts . . . of markedly religious content," "direct participation in idolatry") that are not in the text. Eating from the table of demons is to Paul a thing of horror, and he does not say anything about special religious ceremonies. He says it is like a Jewish thank-offering: any guest at a Jewish party is sharing in the altar, that is, in the worship of God. One would have thought he meant the same sort of thing about the idol food, regardless of whether one had been present at the offering. Also, Paul was a Jew who had been brought up to believe that all idol food was the offerings of the dead, condemned in Num 25, and he even refers to this incident himself in 10.7. It therefore seems implausible that he would invoke this classic passage without making clear where idolatry began. If Paul is on the side of the strong, he certainly sounds very disagreeable about them in 8.1–13 and 10.22.

---

[10]Conzelmann, *1 Corinthians*, 137.

[11]J. Delobel, "Coherence and Relevance in 1 Cor 8–10," in *The Corinthian Correspondence* (ed. R. Bieringer; BETL 125; Leuven: Leuven University Press, 1996), 177–90.

[12]Barrett, *First Epistle*, 244, 230, 237; Schrage, *Der erste Brief,* 2:380–487.

Fourth, an alternative solution would be to take 8.1–13 and 10.1–22 as Paul's teaching and to treat 10.23–11.1 as the side issue. Thus Fee, followed by W. L. Willis, Horsley, and Hays, sees 8.10 as a significant verse: the Corinthians had written to ask, "May we eat in an εἰδωλεῖον?"[13] Paul offers a series of four arguments, all concluding no. In chs. 8–9 come two arguments about the weaker believer and one's rights; in 10.1–22 idolatry is forbidden at the table of demons, which is also in an εἰδωλεῖον. But 10.23–11.1 takes up the point made in 8.1–6; Horsley calls it "almost an afterthought," "apparently to soften the impact" of the earlier prohibitions.[14] Fee draws in the traditional theological notion of the adiaphoron: God is the creator of everything; food makes no difference with God; an idol is nothing; eat what you please unless someone makes an issue of it.[15]

But similar objections to those against the third solution apply here also. The focus of stress on the εἰδωλεῖον seems to go beyond what is in the text. The discussion in 8.7–13 uses the temple restaurant only as an instance of how the weaker believer can be scandalized, and the impression given is that consciously eating what has been sacrificed makes one a partaker in the worship, whether or not one has been in the temple (10.18).

PRACTICAL GUIDELINES: I,10.23–11.1

The behavior of the Petrines has been scandalous on two grounds. First, they have exalted their so-called knowledge over love and have risked the salvation of weaker believers for whom Christ died (8.1–13), insisting on their rights (ch. 9). Second, despite their sophistry about there being one God, eating idol meat is blatant idolatry, condemned repeatedly in Scripture, and self-evidently participation in idol worship. Few things are so satisfying to the imperiled pastor as the conviction that his critics are idolaters. The only trouble is the question of his own supporters: if idol meat involves idolatry, how are Gaius and Erastus going to do business any more, or attend family weddings, or go to their fathers' funerals?

Paul links the new question on to the old. When Petrines ate idol food, they excused it on the basis that "Everything is permitted." Yes, but "not everything is helpful; not everything builds up" the church. A basic principle is, "Let no one seek his or her own interest, but that of the other." Christians may often have no idea whether what they have bought has been prayed over or where their host obtained the meat and the wine; we are all going to be put in ambiguous situations, and the thing is to exercise what

---

[13]W. L. Willis, *Idol Meat in Corinth: The Pauline Argument in 1 Corinthians 8 and 10* (SBLDS 68; Chico, Calif.: Scholars Press, 1985).

[14]Horsley, *I Corinthians,* 115–16.

[15]Fee, *First Epistle,* 477.

freedom we can, as long as we do not scandalize anyone. "Whatever is sold in the market, eat without asking any questions for conscience' sake, for 'the earth is the Lord's and the fullness thereof.' " If you eat meat that you know has been offered to a pagan god, you are making yourself a partaker in the table of demons. But you are not obliged to ask the butcher any questions. It is reasonable to assume that the meat is not tarnished unless you are told it has been, on the ground that God is the creator of everything.

The same principle operates with a dinner invitation. "If any unbeliever invites you, and you want to go, eat whatever is set before you without asking any questions for conscience' sake. But if anyone says to you, 'This is a temple offering (ἱερόθυτον),' do not eat it for the sake of the man who informed you and conscience—I mean conscience not of you yourself but of the other man." As with the meat from the market, you are free to eat without unnecessary curiosity. But, of course, if you are told that the meat has been on a pagan altar, that is different, and you should at once say, "Thank you for telling me; I had no idea," and put away your plate. This is not because of any feelings of guilt in your own conscience, "for why should my freedom" to eat without asking questions "be judged by someone else's conscience? If I partake with thankfulness, why should I be denounced for that for which I give thanks?" A Christian who follows Paul's line has nothing to be ashamed of.

With the mention of the other person's conscience, we are back in the discussion of 8.7–13. "So whether you eat or whether you drink or whatever you do, do everything to the glory of God." Eating meat, at home or in a friend's house, is done to the glory of God when you are grateful for God's creation, and the apologetic declining of a dish declared to be a temple offering is done equally to God's glory—you are taking care not to scandalize. "Cause no offense either to Jews or Greeks or to the church of God." It has not been clear what sort of person Paul had in mind, who informed him, "This is a temple offering," but it now seems that he has a wide view of possibilities. Jews did not ask questions about market meat; they assumed the worst and would not touch it. Perhaps, then, a Jew will be horrified to see you about to eat "the offerings of the dead," and you will of course put it away, becoming as a Jew to the Jews that you may win the Jews (9.20). But there was no need to take the pessimistic Jewish position; you had freedom to make a more optimistic assumption, and there was no reason for your freedom to be judged by his or her conscience.

Or it could be a Greek—a non-Jew—who suspects you of hypocrisy and wants to embarrass you, or one who thinks you are put in a false position by your ignorance and wants to warn you. Or it could be a weak believer from the church. The faithful apostle can appeal to his own example in life, set out at the end of I,10: "just as I too try to please (ἀρέσκω) everyone in everything, not seeking my own advantage but that of the many, that they may be saved. Be imitators of me, even as I am of Christ."

Paul is genuine twenty-four-carat gold all through, and he deserved to have his teaching accepted.

Here, then, is a plausible solution to a long-standing problem: Paul thought the conscious eating of idol food was wrong both because it offended the weak and because it was idolatry. He thought there was a practical way in which Christians could still take part in social life, including meals, and this was to ask no questions—assume the food is God's creation unless you are told something more. But a modern reader may feel anxious about Paul's integrity. Is the apostle equivocating here?

I do not think so. It is sometimes conjectured that virtually all meat was sacrificed by pagan priests who doubled as butchers, but we do not need to accept that, and it would make nonsense of Paul's argument if this were the case. As long as there was reasonable ground for an open mind, a Christian was entitled to assume the best; only in this way could many Christians continue to combine the life of faith with their family obligations. A similar policy has seemed prudent in modern times. During the Second World War, it was possible in England to buy a pound of butter on the black market for £1 (then = $4), but principled families would not touch it. What, then, if you were invited to a party with hosts whose principles were less clear? It would seem priggish, and possibly offensive, to ask, "Is this dish made with black-market butter?" Rather, you should eat whatever is set before you, asking no questions for conscience' sake; but if some helpful person said, "Isn't this black-market butter a blessing?" this would precipitate an embarrassing crisis. Of course, there was no question of a Christian partaking in the table of demons by unconscious eating of temple offerings. Paul did not believe in an automatic, *ex opere operato,* effect of any sacrament. It was only if you ate consciously of idol food that you were involved with demons.

So, once more, it seems possible to salute Paul as a clear-headed and humane pastor, concerned both to keep his church clean of idolatry and, at the same time, to enable those with pagan contacts—most of his church—to carry on a practicable and principled lifestyle. To live ethically, we need some sensible casuistic thinking.

~ 12 ~

IDOL SACRIFICES: II

IDOL SACRIFICE was an important issue in 1 Corinthians, taking up three chapters, 15 percent of the letter. One might have expected that so divisive a question would have cast its shadow over church life both before and after 1 Corinthians. Indeed, Luke tells us in considerable detail that it was a major issue at the Jerusalem conference of Acts 15 and was resolved in the famous apostolic decree of Acts 15.20, 29. There is a virtual consensus among scholars, however, that the decree bears no relation to 1 Corinthians. As Conzelmann says, "Paul says nothing of the 'apostolic decree' which surely regulates the eating, or rather avoiding of εἰδωλόθυτα. . . . Why not? Because he is unaware of it, since it had not been issued at the time of 1 Corinthians? Or does he ignore it purposely? If so, why?" Conzelmann opts for the first alternative, Barrett for the second.[1]

In the same way, commentators in general go through 2 Corinthians without finding any reference to the issue. An important exception is Fee, with whom I agree in finding that the point underlies the much-disputed passage 6.14–7.1. This chapter will try to swim against two tides and maintain that in 1 Corinthians Paul was being faithful to the decisions of the Jerusalem conference while 2 Corinthians shows, as so often, a development in the struggle between him and his Corinthian opponents. These two passages, Acts 15 and 2 Cor. 6.14–7.1, enable us to set I,8–10 in a larger context.

THE JERUSALEM COUNCIL: TWO VIEWS

Paul's account of the Jerusalem conference is in Gal 2.1–10, and it is designed to show that he does not owe his authority to the Jerusalem leadership. He therefore gives the impression that the pillars tried to force his hand on a series of matters but that he never conceded an inch. They sent false brethren to spy out the freedom Paul advocated, "to whom we did not submit

---

[1]Conzelmann, *1 Corinthians,* 138; C. K. Barrett, *The Acts of the Apostles* (2 vols.; ICC; Edinburgh: T&T Clark, 1994–1998), 2:709–46.

even for an hour" (v. 5). They tried to force Titus to be circumcised, but Paul would have none of that: "even Titus, who was with me, being a Greek, was not compelled to be circumcised" (v. 3). Questions over torah came up, but "the so-called leaders imposed nothing on me" (ἐμοὶ γὰρ οἱ δοκοῦντες οὐδὲν προσανέθεντο). On the contrary, they ended by recognizing the Pauline mission and extending the right hand of fellowship.

Thus does the embattled apostle to the Galatians remember the tense negotiations of six years before, seen through the veil of current attempts to force the same issues in his absence. But we may take a more relaxed view of the conference of 48 C.E. James and Peter heard reports of lawbreaking in the so-called Christian church at Antioch, and naturally they were anxious, if only for their movement's reputation among pious Jews in the metropolis. When Paul and Barnabas arrived to discuss the various teachings they had been propagating ("I expounded to them the gospel that I preach among the Gentiles . . . lest I should run, or have been running, in vain," v. 2), they must have asked for a reassurance that Paul taught observance of torah. In particular, it was well known to all Jews that Gentiles were easily given to the two sins of fornication and idolatry, and it was inevitable that they would ask for a reassurance that these things were clearly forbidden. Paul would have been only too eager to give an answer: of course, they were forbidden— Pauline Christians were taught to aspire to holiness. Any report of πορνεία was taken up with witnesses, and offenders might find themselves shunned (I,5.9; II,12.21; 13.1–2) or even delivered to Satan (I,5.5). Christians in Antioch did not always know if meat had been prayed over at a pagan altar, but if it was known so to be, naturally it was not touched—that would mean partaking in the table of demons.

The particular issue that the pillars had heard about from their emissaries (the "false brethren") was nonkosher meat: they had "spied this out," and later, when Peter came, he was faced with the dilemma whether to join in the meal (Gal 2.12). The host at the Antioch church, then, would have been a Gentile and would have bought the meat in the market. This went against the fundamental Jewish practice of eating kosher meat only and was bound to raise eyebrows. Paul implies that it was indeed discussed at the conference but that he gained the pillars' acquiescence in his practice: "they imposed nothing on me."

The way in which Paul argued his case can only be inferred from other passages, but a likely key is I,4.6: "Not beyond what is written." "What about this meat at your church suppers?" the pillars would have enquired. "You don't eat blood, do you?" "Of course not," he would have replied. "We keep everything in the Bible. But you have to realize that Antioch is not like Jerusalem, and there are many matters of established halakah here that we could not observe. Our host is a good person and wants to cooperate, but we cannot arrange for different cooking for meat and milk. We take the line: if it is not in Scripture, it's not important. But, of course, eating blood would be unthinkable. Actually, this is not a problem at Antioch. I often visit the *macellum,* and you can see the sheep having their throats cut." In some such way might the imperiled apostle to the Gentiles have pleaded for a measure of ἐλευθερία and moved the kindly heart of the not-too-clearheaded Peter.

While Luke's account of the conference contains some marked divergences from Paul's, it is astonishingly close on many points, and there can be little doubt that Acts 15 describes the same events and that the differences can be largely explained by Lukan tendencies—to magnify Paul, to suppress any differences between him and Jerusalem. This is illustrated in the following six examples:

First, the trouble began with a visit of some strict Jerusalem Christians to the church at Antioch: "false brethren secretly introduced who slipped in to spy out our freedom" (Gal 2.4); "And certain men came down from Judea" (Acts 15.1). Although Paul refers to the false brethren in the middle of an account of his Jerusalem visit, he slips into an anacoluthon, and it is more plausible to see the ἐλευθερία as being practiced at Antioch than at some private celebration in Jerusalem.

Second, these men raised the issue of whether Gentile converts were being circumcised: "but even Titus, who was with me, being a Greek, was not compelled to be circumcised" (Gal 2.3); " . . . and taught, 'Unless you are circumcised after the custom of Moses, you cannot be saved' " (Acts 15.1). Paul had taken Titus with him, intending to make him a test case.

Third, there was an unpleasantness over this at Antioch, and Paul refused to give way: "we did not submit to them, even for an hour" (Gal 2.5); "and after Paul and Barnabas had no small dissension and dispute with them" (Acts 15.2).

Fourth, Paul and Barnabas then went up to Jerusalem to settle the matter: "I went up to Jerusalem with Barnabas, taking Titus with me too; I went up by revelation" (Gal 2.1–2); "Paul and Barnabas and some of the others were appointed to go up to Jerusalem to discuss this question with the apostles and elders" (Acts 15.2). Paul's "revelation" probably means no more than "I saw the writing on the wall," but even if he saw an angel in a dream, he still needed to take counsel with Barnabas and other church leaders at Antioch. Luke stresses the united action of the Antioch church and (15.3) their support from other churches on the road south.

Fifth, on arrival Paul and Barnabas held a discussion with the Jerusalem leadership: "I laid before them the gospel that I proclaim among the Gentiles, but privately to the so-called leaders (τοῖς δοκοῦσιν), lest I should be running, or had run, in vain" (Gal 2.2); "when they came to Jerusalem, they were welcomed by the church and the apostles and elders, and they reported all that God had done with them" (Acts 15.4). Luke knows that there were apostles, such as Peter and John, at the meeting and elders, such as James. He makes the atmosphere genial ("welcomed," "all that God had done with them") and amplifies the occasion: there are no longer five people meeting in private; instead, it is a large (and enthusiastic) public meeting. But we may think that Luke's public meeting was not a fiction. The Antioch delegation had to travel for a fortnight each way, and it is not likely that they were sent home quietly after an afternoon's parley. They would have stayed for at least one Sunday and no doubt were welcomed with enthusiasm in view of their missionary success and the approval of the pillars.

Sixth, the principal negotiators were Paul and Barnabas for the Gentile mission, Peter and James for Jerusalem. Paul's ordering, "James and Peter and John" (Gal 2.9), implies the chairmanship of James, who also speaks last and proposes the decree in Acts 15. We may allow that his and Peter's speeches are Lukan compositions. Luke says that the question of observing "the law of Moses" was raised by "certain of the sect of the Pharisees who had believed" (Acts 15.5), whereas Paul says such matters were raised by the pillars themselves. But this is to be explained by Luke's wish to have a united pro-Pauline church. Indeed, both Josephus and Hegesippus imply that James was close to Jewish Pharisees.[2]

If Luke is so close to history in so many details, we should take seriously his report of the terms agreed for the Gentile mission. These seem to be close to what we have concluded above:

No compulsory circumcision (Gal 2.3; Acts 15.19, 29);

No idolatry = eating idol offerings (Acts 15.20, 29);

No loose sex (Acts 15.20, 29);

No eating of blood—that is, of strangled animals (Acts 15.20, 29).

Paul adds that the pillars asked for a collection to be raised from the (wealthy?) Gentile churches for the "poor" Jerusalem and Judean communities (Gal 2.10). Luke does not mention this, partly because it would lower the tone and partly because, when Paul did finally come with the money, it was refused. Luke makes only an oblique reference to the money in Acts 24.17 and transfers the incident to an earlier context (Acts 11.29–30).

Discussion has focused on τοῦ πνικτοῦ/καὶ πνικτῶν in Acts 15.20, 29, since it is difficult to find any reference to strangling in Jewish texts. Philo criticizes those who aspire to novel pleasures and prepare unsacrificeable

---

[2]Josephus, *A.J.* 20.9.1, says that "those in the city who had a reputation for greater fairness, and strict observance of the laws"—probably the Pharisees—protested over James's murder. Hegesippus, in Eusebius, *Hist. eccl.* 2.23.10–16, says that the Pharisees came to James to ask him to speak to the people *against* the messiahship of Jesus.

meat by throttling and strangling the animals (ἄγχοντες καὶ ἀποπνίγοντες, *Spec.* 4.122), thus "entombing within the body the blood which is the essence of the soul, and should be allowed to run freely away." The trouble with kosher butchery is that all the blood is washed out of the system, and with it some of the taste; the gourmets Philo has in view obtain a finer flavor for their dish at the cost of a little "red gravy." But Philo knows they are just eating blood, in defiance of Lev 17. Such practices are, however, clearly rare. Butchers killed sheep and, when necessary, cows by slitting their throats. They may well have strangled hens and geese, but these might be too expensive for church suppers.

Why, then, does Luke write τοῦ πνικτοῦ καὶ τοῦ αἵματος/αἵματος καὶ πνικτῶν in Acts 15.20, 29? Is the doubled expression not superfluous, as Barrett says?[3] It is indeed, and we may think that this is Luke's point. The issue at Antioch had been whether the meat at the agape had to be kosher, and the Jerusalem conference had agreed not to insist on this. Paul had argued that the details of halakah as practiced in Palestine were not possible in a mixed church in Syria, that the aim was to keep the biblical provision in Lev 17 that one should not eat blood. True, the text specified that the animal should be brought to the tent of meeting, but it was universally agreed that this did not mean the temple, especially in the Diaspora. What was stressed was the prevention of idolatry ("so that they may no longer offer their sacrifices to goat-demons," Lev 17.7) and the prohibition of eating blood (17.10–13). Not eating blood was to be taken to mean not eating an animal that had been strangled; kosher butchers and kosher cooking were not insisted on—they were "beyond what is written."

Such a conclusion seems very straightforward; we may ask, then, why it has been neglected by so many scholars. The first reason seems to be the misunderstanding of I,8–10. It has been so widely agreed that I,10.23–11.1 permitted the eating of εἰδωλόθυτα that the Pauline discussion seems either to ignore or to defy the decree. But the argument of our last chapter goes against this accepted exegesis. Paul regards the conscious eating of idol sacrifices as partaking in the table of demons, in just the same way as Luke equates εἰδωλόθυτα (Acts 15.29) with "the pollutions of idols" (τῶν ἀλισγημάτων τῶν εἰδώλων, 15.20).

Once a barrier has been erected between the supposed Pauline teaching and the decree, exegetes are left with an insoluble puzzle over the latter. Barrett sets out four options currently on offer:[4] (i) the decree required the use of Jewish butchers only, since they alone insisted on fully draining away the blood, and such use was a condition of salvation; (ii) the so-called Noachian commandments, which first occur in *Jub.* 7.20, were thought to

---

[3]Barrett, *Acts,* 2:732.
[4]Ibid., 2:733–34.

apply to Gentiles, and of the seven found in later developed lists, four are roughly in line with the decree; (iii) Lev 17–18 contains laws against eating blood and against πορνεία, understood as marrying incestuously; (iv) a number of rabbinic passages list matters for which Jews were expected, if necessary, to die: idolatry, "shedding of blood" (that is, murder), and incest. Barrett himself is dissatisfied with all of these. He thinks the decree contained a mixture of ritual and ethical commands and forbade idolatry, fornication, nonkosher meat, and violence; Paul ignored it because he disagreed over forbidding εἰδωλόθυτα.

A second reason for questioning Paul's knowledge or use of the decree is his failure to refer to it. But this is easily explained. Galatians shows Paul's emphasis on his independence as an apostle: he was called by Jesus Christ and not appointed by humans, and his mission had been accepted by the pillars as on a parity with Peter's. He is not going to tell his Corinthian converts that he is keeping rules laid down by Jerusalem. On the other hand, he structures his First Letter in such a way as to suggest that he has something like the decree in mind. He opens with four chapters on his church's divisions and on the centrality of his gospel of the cross. He then has three chapters on various sexual problems (chs. 5–7), of which the moral is φεύγετε τὴν πορνείαν (6.18). There are then three chapters on idol sacrifices (chs. 8–10), of which the moral is φεύγετε ἀπὸ τῆς εἰδωλολατρίας. Finally, chs. 11–16 return to the divisions in the church and to a statement of his gospel of the resurrection.

What, then, about blood and things strangled? At Antioch the church's host had been a Gentile, and the issue had arisen because the host bought meat in the market. At Corinth we never hear about the problem, and this must mean either that Gaius, the church's host (Rom 16.23), was Jewish or else that he went to a kosher butcher so as not to offend a weaker believer (this time, as in Rom 14, a Jew). So many problems get an airing in the Corinthian letters that it is hardly believable that there was trouble over the meat at the agape without our hearing of it. So Paul does not mention blood and strangling because they were not an issue at Corinth, but he does strongly support the decree's provisions on idol meat and sex. To Luke, however, it is important to stress the limitations agreed at the conference. There had been no insistence on kosher meat. The agreement was not to eat the animal's blood, i.e., a strangled animal. αἷμα and πνικτά are just two ways of expressing the same point: Christians observe Lev. 17, but not the sages' halakah on kashruth.

The inclusion of Acts 15 in the picture enables us to confirm a speculation in our last chapter: there was a difference in the Petrine camp over idol sacrifices. As we should have expected, the Jerusalem authorities were conservative on the question. Jews had reacted against any possibility of eating "pollutions of idols" as "offerings of the dead," and James follows this line, with its long history back into Scripture. He relied on tradition, "the rulings of the sages." But the Jerusalem church was a charismatic society, gifted with revelations and visions, and once away from Jerusalem, with a young church of maybe mostly Gentiles, the charismatic enthusiasm gained the upper hand. Once one realized that there was only one God, one knew that there could be no idol gods, and so came the knowledge, with the authority of revelation, that old taboos were meaningless: Christians could eat what they liked, where they liked. This knowledge was particularly appreciated where church members had family and business commitments that required socializing with nonbelievers over meals.

It is possible, though no more than an attractive speculation, that the rift in Jerusalem went as far as between James and Peter. It has often been suspected that James's primacy over Peter and John was not achieved without some friction, that the list of appearances of the risen Lord in I,15.5–7 masks two parallel, competing lists,[5] and that the account in Gal 2.11–14 reveals an important difference of principle between Peter and James, whose emissaries force him to change ground. Luke attributes the proposal of the decree to James: it was James who insisted that there be no eating of idol sacrifices. But Luke also portrays Peter as a visionary in Acts 10, with a direct knowledge of the revealed will of God, and the insight that is given him is that all food is available to be eaten—what God has cleansed, he is not to call profane. The issue is not identical: it is "unclean" animals, not their blood, that is the point. But the matters are close, and Peter did at first eat nonkosher meat with the Gentiles until James put a stop to it (Gal 2.12). And the Jerusalem party at Corinth who were so keen on knowledge did claim to be "of Cephas." It might well be that Peter thought prayers over meat to a pagan god were an irrelevance while to James they were a horrific scandal.

Ongoing Problems in II,6.14–7.1

The problem of idol sacrifices did not go away. The Second Letter finds the Petrines more deeply dug in than in the First Letter, and they were not likely to have given up so convenient a practice. The controverted passage II,6.14–7.1 recalls the language of I,8–10 and shows the issue at a more developed point, with a sharper remedy required.

In Num 25.3 Israel had "yoked itself to" (צָמַד) the Baal of Peor by eating the sacrifices of the Moabites' gods and sleeping with their women; the phrase "yoked yourselves" is repeated at 25.5. Paul accordingly opens his new charge on the subject, "Do not misyoke yourselves with faithless men" (μὴ γίνεσθε ἑτεροζυγοῦντες ἀπίστοις). In three passages of 1 Corinthians

---

[5]See W. Pratscher, *Der Herrenbruder Jakobus und die Jakobustradition* (FRLANT 139; Göttingen: Vandenhoeck & Ruprecht, 1987), 35–46.

(6.6; 7.12–14; 10.27), ἄπιστοι means *unbelievers,* non-Christians, but in
II,4.4 Paul is speaking of his opponents, the "many" who water down the
word of God and falsify it in their cunning, and he refers to them as the
ἄπιστοι whose minds the god of this world has blinded. The word often carries the meaning *faithless* in the NT (Mark 9.19; Luke 12.46; John 20.27). In
the last two of these texts, it is contrasted, as here (6.15), with πιστός, meaning *faithful*—πιστός never means a Christian in contrast with an unbeliever.
So Paul is reopening the issue of idol sacrifices, which he forbade in I,10, referring to the classic Jewish text of Num 25 in I,10.8. His use of the form
ἑτεροζυγοῦντες also recalls the "misyoking," ἑτερόζυγον (LXX Lev 19.19),
of two animals, whose cross-breeding was forbidden. The difference is that
in I,8–10 those who ate idol sacrifices were merely misguided, preferring
their knowledge to love of the weaker believer and sharing, if they would
think about it, in the table of demons. Now they are "faithless" Christians,
and sterner measures are needed.

There follows a series of five rhetorical questions. "For what partaking
(μετοχή) is there between righteousness and lawlessness? Or what fellowship (κοινωνία) is there of light with darkness? And what agreement does
Christ have with Beliar? Or what share has a faithful person with an unfaithful? Or what agreement has the temple of God with idols?" The echoes of
I,10.14–21 are plain. In Christian worship we all "partake" (μετέχομεν) in
the one bread (I,10.17); one cannot "partake" (μετέχειν) in the table of the
Lord and the table of idols (I,10.21). The cup and the bread are a κοινωνία
in the blood and body of Christ; Israel after the flesh are κοινωνοί in the
altar, and Paul does not want the Corinthians to be κοινωνούς in the table of
demons. The opposition between Christ and Beliar is the same as the opposition between the table of the Lord and the table of demons in I,10.20–21,
and that between the ναὸς θεοῦ and idols echoes the warning to flee idolatry
in I,10.14. Pauline Christians practice OT righteousness, not the lawlessness
of idolatry; as children of light, they have no truck with darkness.

Paul saw the church as the ναὸς θεοῦ in I,3.16, with the Spirit of God
dwelling in it (οἰκεῖ ἐν ὑμῖν). He is looking now in II,6 for a scriptural text
proving God's holy presence among his people, and Lev 26.12 comes to
mind: "I will walk among you, and I will be your God, and you will be my
people." But this lacks any echo of the temple image, so he adapts it, prefac-
ing the words ἐνοικήσω ἐν αὐτοῖς καί; God indwells his community, as in
I,3.16, and so there is the requirement of perfect holiness. This means, just
as in I,5 with the case of incest, the need to purge out the corruption, and the
thought moves on to Isa 52.11: "Depart, depart, go out from there! Touch
no unclean thing; go out from the midst of it, separate yourselves." Again he
slightly adapts: "Therefore go out from the midst of them"—it is the faithless
Petrines from whom separation is necessary, not "it," Babylon. He puts this
and "separate yourselves" first because that is the action needed. He adds
"says the Lord" for the rhythm and for authority, and ends with "And touch

no unclean thing"—no food that they know to have been offered to a pagan god.

The house of God that is also a household of God is a theme with a resonance in 2 Sam 7, where David planned to build God a temple but was made the founder of a human house. There Nathan says, "Thus says the Lord Almighty (παντοκράτωρ) . . . 'I will be to him a father, and he shall be to me a son' " (2 Sam 7.8, 14). Paul closes his citations with a third adaptation: "And I will receive you, and I will be to you a father, and you shall be to me sons and daughters, says the Lord Almighty (παντοκράτωρ)." The εἰσδέξομαι came from Ezek 20.34, and the "sons and daughters" from Isa 43.6. With the high privilege of membership in God's family goes the responsibility of separation from the unholy. Of course, Paul does not want a holy rump that has left the idolatrous majority; despite Isaiah's image, he just wants the idolaters excommunicated.

With 7.1 he then draws the charge to a close: "So having these promises, beloved, let us cleanse ourselves from every defilement of flesh and spirit, making holiness perfect in fear of God." μολυσμοῦ reminds us of the weaker believer of I,8.7 whose conscience was defiled (μολύνεται) by seeing a fellow Christian eating in an εἰδωλεῖον. If we touch idol food, we defile our flesh; if we associate with those who do such things, we defile our spirit. We are God's temple, God's community, God's children, and can be content with nothing short of complete sanctity. Purge out the old leaven; separate yourselves.

The paragraph has been widely suspected of being an insertion into the main text of the epistle, on three grounds: (i) it seems to break the thread of thought with the earlier part of ch. 6 and the remainder of ch. 7; (ii) it has often been interpreted to mean, "Have no dealings with unbelievers," and thus might be a part of the "previous letter," which was thought by the Corinthians to deal with unbelievers; and (iii) the preceding verse, 6.13, closes, "you too, be open," and the next following verse, 7.2, begins, "Make room for us"; with the omission of 6.14–7.1, this would make excellent continuity of thought.

The second and third of these arguments are less weighty than the first. Paul often veers away from his topic, only to resume it after an excursus, as when he leaves the Paul-Apollos-Cephas parties issue in I,1.17 but resumes it in I,3, or when direct discussion of the idol-meat problem is suspended during I,9. The possibility that our verses were originally part of the "previous letter" is merely a speculation.[6] But the first argument is more

---

[6]The proposal is suggestive in another way. In the "previous letter," Paul had used some expression for unfaithful (fornicating) Christians that had seemed to the Corinthians to refer to non-Christians. Surely the word ἄπιστοι is a likely candidate. In 1 Corinthians it means unbelievers, in 2 Corinthians unfaithful Christians.

serious: the apparent absence of a plausible thread of thought is a serious question, to which I proposed an answer in an article in 1994.[7]

Paul is faced with a recurrent problem, attacks on his apostleship, and he tends to deal with them with a syndrome of thought. Behind the parties in I,1.10–17 lay the suggestion that Paul was not a proper apostle like Cephas; the new missionaries with their letters of authority say the same thing in II,3, and it is brought out into the open in II,10–11.

In the face of this, Paul's first move is to claim that he is a proper minister of God:

> Let a man so reckon us as servants of Christ and stewards of the mysteries of God. (I,4.1)

> But in everything commending ourselves as ministers of God . . . (II,6.4)

> I reckon in no way to fall behind the superapostles. . . . Are they ministers of Christ? I am more. (II,11.5, 23)

Second, the difficulty confronting Paul was that Peter, and the Jerusalem missionaries, carried official authorization, lived at church expense, and so forth, while Paul spent his life in undignified scrapes, in trouble with the police, and working his fingers to the bone. He is therefore then driven to a paradoxical glorying in his trials, to show that this is what real apostleship means:

> To this present hour we both hunger and thirst and go naked and are beaten and are homeless and labor, working with our hands; reviled we bless, persecuted we endure, slandered we encourage. (I,4.11–12)

> . . . in persecutions, in necessities, in distresses, in beatings, in imprisonments, in riots, in labors, in sleeplessness, in fasting . . . by glory and dishonor, by slander and popularity. (II,6.4–5, 8)

> . . . with far greater labors, far more imprisonments, with countless floggings, often approaching death. (II,11.23)

In II,12.11 Paul adds, "I have been a fool; you compelled me"; some such glorying in his trials was required in face of the aspersions cast on his apostolicity. The attacks in II,3.1–6 indeed issued in a preliminary recital of his "weaknesses" in 4.7–12, which is then resumed in 6.4.

---

[7]Goulder, "2 Cor. 6:14–7:1."

Third, Paul was a warmhearted man, and he saw his sufferings as having a direct consequence in the strengthening of his churches (II,1.3–11). So each catalogue of his afflictions tends to issue in some expression of affection, as he thinks of himself as a father with his children:

> I do not write this to reproach you, but as counseling my beloved children. For if you have ten thousand tutors in Christ, yet you have not many fathers; for in Christ Jesus through the gospel I begot you. (I,4.14–15)

> Our mouth is opened to you, Corinthians, our heart is widened; you are not narrowed in us, but in your own affections. Make the same response—I speak as to my children—be widened too. (II,6.11–13)

> I seek not yours but you; for children should not save for parents, but parents for children. . . . If I love you the more, am I loved the less? (II,12.14–18)

Others may think all this a rhetorical strategy. But it seems to me the overflowing of genuine emotion, stirred by the memory of so much suffering on the one side and enthusiastic discipleship on the other.

Fourth, Paul has a kind heart, but he is no sentimentalist. Fathers in his day put their foot down and had order in their houses. So the thought of fatherhood leads on naturally to discipline:

> But I will come to you soon, if the Lord wills, and I will find out not the talk of these arrogant people but their power. . . . What do you prefer? Am I to come to you with a cane, or with love in a spirit of gentleness? (I,4.19–21)

> Do not be misyoked with faithless people. . . . come out from them, and be separate from them, says the Lord, and touch nothing unclean. . . . let us cleanse ourselves from every defilement of body and spirit. (II,6.14–7.1)

> This is the third time that I am coming to you: every case will be established at the mouth of two or three witnesses. . . . If I come, I will not spare. . . . So I write this in my absence so that I may not use severely the authority that the Lord gave me for building up and not for pulling down. (II,13.1–10)

Thus, II,6.14–7.1 is far from out of place in the sequence of thought of II,3–7. Paul regularly counters attacks on his apostleship with claims to be a genuine minister of God and one whose afflictions are a testimony to true apostleship. This then leads on to expressions of fatherly affection and thence to demands for discipline. Indeed, the calls for discipline may themselves be part of the Pauline response to his detractors: they thought he was weak and lacked presence and authority (10.10; 11.20–21).

The issue of idol sacrifice, then, runs right through the early history of the Corinthian church. Paul concurred with the Jerusalem pillars in rejecting εἰδωλόθυτα. But whereas they would have followed traditional Jewish scruples and refused any meat or wine that had not come through the kosher system, his converts lived in a world where such a practice would have been social suicide. He therefore forbade any conscious consumption of idol sacrifices and advised a policy of asking no questions. The Jerusalem conference of 48 accepted this compromise, as is implied in Paul's account and stated openly in the decree of Acts 15. The addition of "things strangled" to "blood" is to make clear that throat cutting in the market was normally sufficient; there was no insistence on kosher butchers or cooking.

Paul's compromise solution fell under attack from two opposite quarters. The visits of Peter and later of "certain from James" at Antioch resulted in a revocation of the Jerusalem concord; Paul was forced to have kosher meat at church suppers there, and he made similar arrangements at Corinth, so that the question of meat at the agape never came up. But the Petrine missionaries believed not only in Scripture and the wisdom that interpreted it; they also believed in knowledge, the revealing of new truths in visions or revelations. Here there came a challenge from the opposite angle: if there was one God, then there were no idol gods, and sacrifice to them was meaningless. A Christian might then eat idol sacrifices without harm to himself or herself.

In the First Epistle, Paul was content to dispute this conclusion, first with appeal to the weaker-believers argument, then with the more robust reminder of the fate of idolaters in Scripture and an argument about the table of demons. One must flee from idolatry, but there was no sin if one did not know the food had been tainted. The discussion in I,8.1–11.1 ends with the relaxed counsel to do everything for the glory of God, to give no offense, and to be imitators of the apostle. But things in this respect, as in most others, have become worse by the time of the Second Letter. The new missionaries are more aggressive and more confident, and the eating of idol meat has continued, and in temple restaurants as before. Kid gloves are no longer appropriate; now is the hour of the iron fist. Paul knows there cannot be peace with people of this kind, ἄπιστοι, and having them in the church is a misyoking, ἑτεροζυγεῖν, like the Israelites in Num 25. The only recourse left is excommunication: "come out from among them, and be separated from them, says the Lord."

∽ 13 ∾

"No Resurrection of the Dead"

PAUL FLAGS most of the issues facing him in the thanksgiving of I,1.4–9: his church's enrichment with all knowledge, their falling short in no spiritual gift, and their "awaiting the revelation of our Lord Jesus Christ" (1.7). We are torn between admiration of the saint's diplomatic mastery, on the one hand, and wry smiles at the ironies that will be revealed at our awaiting, on the other. For, of course, he has ambivalent feelings about γνῶσις and χαρίσματα and talk of enrichment, and it turns out that "some" of his churchpeople are not awaiting anything at all (15.12), least of all being judged on the day of our Lord Jesus.

EARLIER HINTS OF THE PROBLEM

The problem that strikes every modern reader is how any Christian could fail to believe in so central an element of the creed as the resurrection of the dead. The atmosphere suggested in 4.8–20 seems to give a broad hint. Church meetings encouraged an unreality in which people spoke of them-selves as "reigning" already (v. 8), and Paul refers to this as "talk" of "the kingdom of God" when what matters is the reality (δύναμις, v. 20). He goes on in ch. 6 to make a number of negative comments about their claims to the kingdom of God: "Or do you not know that the unrighteous will not in-herit the kingdom of God? Do not deceive yourselves: neither whorers nor idolaters . . . shall inherit the kingdom of God" (6.9–10). He returns to this concept in 15.50 in the context of denial of the resurrection: "But this I say, brothers, that flesh and blood cannot inherit the kingdom of God." The τίνες (15.12) supposed that they did not need to think about glories here-after: they had inherited the kingdom of God already.

Paul's sarcasm in 4.8–10 shows some of the absurdities that were cur-rent in such an atmosphere. Petrines (vv. 8–9, p. 74) spoke of themselves as "sated" (κεκορεσμένοι), "enriched," "wise (φρόνιμοι) in Christ," "strong," "glorified" (ἔνδοξοι). They had been transformed from normal human vul-nerability on to a higher level of being, as πνευματικοί. They had their fill of all that was needful, physical and spiritual. They had wisdom from the

Jewish sages to interpret Scripture. They had knowledge through visions and revelations. They had strength on a superhuman level. Their contact with the divine had given them a reflection of the heavenly glory, like Moses at Sinai. We have seen what further unrealities were latent in such a hot-house: a man who felt he could defy the law of incest "in the name of our Lord Jesus Christ"; women who had authority over their own bodies and could deny their husbands; enthusiasts who demanded celibacy for all and divorce for the married; smart alecks who argued that it was all right to eat idol meat; women praying and prophesying without any veil over their faces; greed, drunkenness, and exhibitionism at the Lord's Supper. Those who kidded themselves that this was the kingdom of God already come could hardly have taken an interest in a further kingdom in the future.

The battle line is already visible in I,6.12–14. The Petrines have laid down the principle "Everything is permissible." The slogan had originally been developed in the idol-food context (10.23), and this lies behind its use in 6.12, for in 6.13 it is explained as "Meat for the belly and the belly for meat, but God will bring both to nothing." Food and the belly are things of passing significance, they said; in the course of time we shall die, and God will bring both belly and food to nothing. What then? Why, the spiritual person is already living on a higher level, and the spirit will go marching on. Paul categorically rejects their logic: "But the body is not for whoring but for the Lord, and the Lord for the body. And God both raised the Lord and will raise us out through his power." The opposition has two things wrong. Whoring is in a different category from food because it is a sin against one's own body (6.18). And in any case, their argument does not apply. Death does not see the end of what we have done here; we shall be raised to a new life, just as Christ was.[1]

Paul's Response in I,15

Paul has begun to set out the difference between his gospel—the word of the cross—and that of the Petrines with their words of wisdom. However, there are many distractions, and it is ch. 15 before he has leisure to deal with what threatens to be a major crisis. This is not another περὶ δέ section: he has not been asked about the resurrection; he has just heard that it is being openly denied by some church members, and he feels the need to weigh in with all

---

[1]G. Sellin, *Der Streit um die Auferstehung der Toten* (FRLANT 138; Göttingen: Vandenhoeck & Ruprecht, 1986), 49, thinks there is a discrepancy between 6.14 and ch. 15, the former verse apparently assuming an agreed belief in the resurrection of the dead. But it seems natural to take 6.14 as Paul's riposte to the meat-for-the-belly slogan, just as 6.12 gives two Pauline ripostes to "Everything is permitted." Sellin draws the unhappy inference that 1 Corinthians is not a single letter.

he has. There can be little doubt that these τίνες are Petrines, Jewish Christians. We have already seen their links in 4.8–10 with those who "were puffed up for the one [the Petrine leadership] against the other [that of Paul and Apollos]." The slogan, "Everything is permissible," in 6.12 is associated with Jewish-Christian claims of knowledge in 8.1–7. In 15.42–49 the opposition's theology draws on a sophisticated Jewish exegesis of the two "men" in creation (Gen 1.27; 2.7). In 15.56 Paul brings in a reference to the law, "The power of sin is the law," a theme familiar from other debates with Jewish-Christian opponents and hardly here by accident.[2]

I,15.1–11.   For once Paul feels he has his opposition in a double bind, for he is able to cite their own authorities against them. This was the gospel that he delivered to the Corinthians: Christ's death for our sins and his resurrection. He did not make it up; it was handed on to him at his conversion. The resurrection in particular was a phenomenon to which both wings of the leadership could bear witness: first Cephas and the Twelve, then James and others, and finally Paul himself, who before his conversion had been as worthless as an abortion[3] but was by God's grace elevated to a unique calling—"So whether it was I or they, that is how we proclaim and how you came to faith." Surely he has them in a corner this time: Peter was the first to see the risen Jesus, and James's name was in the list of witnesses. They called themselves "of Cephas" and relied on the authority of James in Jerusalem. The Twelve were on the list, too, and all the apostles; and Paul probably throws in the five hundred brothers and sisters besides. They increase the feeling that the testimony is irrefutable, and the fact that some of them have "fallen asleep" raises the uncomfortable question of death, which is to haunt the discussion.

---

[2]Understanding of I,15 has grown with the realization that there are variant interpretations of Gen 1–2 in Philo. So esp. B. A. Pearson, *The Pneumatikos-Psychikos Terminology in 1 Corinthians* (SBLDS 12; Missoula, Mont.: Scholars Press, 1973); K.-G. Sandelin, *Die Auseinandersetzung mit der Weisheit in 1. Korinther 15* (Åbo, Finland: Åbo Akademi, 1975); R. A. Horsley, " 'How Can Some of You Say That There Is No Resurrection of the Dead?' Spiritual Elitism in Corinth," *NovT* 20 (1978): 203–31. This has recalled the association of Apollos with Alexandria and has led to the speculation that the τίνες of 15.12 are followers of Apollos. But T. H. Tobin, *The Creation of Man: Philo and the History of Interpretation* (CBQMS 14; Washington: Catholic Biblical Association of America, 1983), shows that Philo is the heir to a long tradition, which is not limited to Alexandria, and that in 15.1–11 Paul appeals to an experience shared by him with the leading Petrines.

[3]For the problems of ὡσπερεὶ τῷ ἐκτρώματι, see Fee, *First Epistle*, 732–34. H. W. Hollander and G. E. van der Hout, "The Apostle Paul Calling Himself an Abortion: 1 Cor.15:8 within the Context of 1 Cor.15.8–10," *NovT* 38 (1996): 224–36, provide copious parallels for understanding ἔκτρωμα as something miserable and valueless, e.g., Philo, *Leg.* 1.76. The article τῷ is an inadequate basis for the speculation (BAG, s.v.) that the term was used as an insult to Paul.

I,15.12–19.   The question Paul asks is our question, too: "If Christ is proclaimed, that he has risen from the dead, how do some among you say, 'There is no resurrection of the dead'?" How did they come to move so far from the unanimous testimony of all the authorities in the church? The answer may lie in differences of perceived significance. To Paul, and so to orthodox Christianity, the cross and resurrection are cardinal, but perhaps this is because to Paul Christ is a divine figure. To the Petrines Jesus was a prophet (see below, ch. 14), and it was a standing feature of NT rhetoric that prophets were persecuted and put to death and that God acted on the shedding of their blood. Luke 11.50–51 mentions the blood of all the prophets, down to that of Zechariah in 2 Chron 24, which will be visited on "this generation." But in the Maccabean histories, the death of the martyrs has a more positive effect. The prayer of the seventh son in 2 Macc 7.37–38 has the power to turn God's anger with Israel into mercy, so that Judas's army becomes invincible (8.2–7). In 4 Macc 17.20–22, the effect is spiritual. The death of the Jewish martyrs results in King Antiochus being punished and the country cleansed (καθαρισθῆναι) with "their having become as it were an expiation (ἀντίψυχον) for the nation's sin. And through the blood of those pious ones and the atonement (ἱλαστηρίου) of their death the divine providence saved Israel which before had been laid low." So we might think that the Jerusalem church felt the same way: Jesus had died a martyr's death, and this would act as an expiation for Israel's sins. One might link this with the marvelous and uncovenanted arrival of the Spirit. Insofar as the traditional formula stressed the cross as being "for our sins according to the Scriptures," most suggested texts, such as Isa 53, stand in a context of blessing for Israel, as does 4 Macc 17.20–22, not of bringing personal salvation to each believer.

We tend similarly to see Jesus' resurrection through the Pauline lens, but it may have been more matter-of-fact to Jerusalem Christians. In an hour of crisis in 2 Macc 15, Judas sees in a vision the ex–high priest Onias "praying with outstretched hands for the whole body of the Jews" (15.12); he is accompanied by an even more impressive figure, Jeremiah the prophet of God, who again prays much for the people and who hands Judas a holy golden sword, a gift from God (15.15–16). From a little later, we have traditions of the *Martyrdom and Ascension of Isaiah.* These holy men are all imagined as in heaven, interceding for Israel like Christ in Rom 8.34 or Acts 7.56. Peter and James and the others had seen Jesus alive after his passion, so no doubt he was doing good for us, praying to God with outstretched hands.

It is clear that the experiences of seeing Jesus after his death acted with enormous force on the first Christian community. The accumulated conviction that this was the promised prophet, God's anointed, had not been a delusion; it was a proven fact. Jesus had spoken of the kingdom of God, the closing period of human history, and if he had risen from death, this period had begun. It would have been remarkable if people had not asked, "Is this the beginning of the resurrection of the dead, foretold in Dan 12.2–3?" But after a short period of wondering and hoping, such speculations were seen to have been misguided. That idea was a mistake. There is no resurrection of the dead; what has happened is, rather, the establishment of God's kingdom on earth, as prophesied in Dan 2.44 or 7.9–18. Indeed, they would argue, people who pine for the Lord's return and all that, have failed to understand what God has already done with the kingdom and the Spirit. Daniel 12.2, πολλοὶ τῶν καθευδόντων . . . ἀναστήσονται (LXX; ἐξεγερθήσονται, Theodotion), taken as a prophecy of the general resurrection, was a mare's nest: ἀνάστασις νεκρῶν οὐκ ἔστιν.

G. Barth argues that belief in the resurrection of the dead was not general among Jews until the second century C.E.[4] But the relevance of this claim seems to be countered by Paul's response, which is extended into a series of arguments. First there is a sequence of frontal attacks: (i) "But if there is no resurrection of the dead, neither has Christ risen." This is not a very strong piece of logic because there might be an exception to a general rule. (ii) "And if Christ is not risen, then our proclamation was empty, and your faith too is empty; and we are found to be false witnesses of God, because we witnessed of God that he raised Christ—whom he did not raise if the dead turn out not to be raised." Paul's converts would certainly be unwilling to think that he had been wrong on so central an issue, and Peter and James would be "false witnesses," too. (iii) "For if the dead are not raised, neither has Christ been raised. And if Christ has not been raised, your faith is vain, and you are still in your sins." Since Pauline theology made the resurrection half of its centerpiece, this is an effective argument, even if it applies to the reader only. (iv) "So too those who have fallen asleep in Christ have perished. If in this life alone we have been hoping in Christ, we are of all men most pitiable." The nasty question arises, then, about Christians who have died, including some no doubt at Corinth, relations or friends of surviving Christians. There must be a strong reluctance to think that such dead "saints" have "perished," an ambiguous term full of menace, and no one wants to think that their relatives have kidded themselves in this life and are now rotting or, worse, frying.

Despite its curious word order ("if in this life in Christ we have been hoping alone"), there can be little doubt that Paul regards denial of the resurrection as hope in this life alone; the same presupposition underlies 15.29–32. The Petrines thought that as πνευματικοί they would transcend death, if indeed they ever died (15.26, 54–55). But Paul believed in the

[4]G. Barth, "Zur Frage nach der in ersten Korintherbrief bekämpften Auferstehungsleugnung," *ZNW* 83 (1992): 187–201.

Bible. When you died, you went to sleep in Sheol, and if you were not resurrected, that is where you would stay.

There has been a remarkable controversy over what precisely the τίνες maintained. Three main possibilities are on offer.

(i) There is no resurrection of the dead at all: dead Christians are indeed lost, and only those who survive to the παρουσία will be saved. Such a view was proposed by Albert Schweitzer and was defended by B. Spörlein; it is given a more recent form by Barth.[5]

(ii) There will be no bodily resurrection—no resurrection of corpses (νεκρῶν)—but the spirit will persevere after death for the πνευματικοί. This is the most popular view today, advocated by B. A. Pearson, G. Sellin, A. J. M. Wedderburn, and M. C. de Boer, as well as in the commentaries of Fee, Horsley, and Hays.[6]

(iii) There will be no future resurrection, but the resurrection has happened already, in a spiritual sense. Paul (or an early disciple) seems himself to hint this in Col 3.1, "If you are risen with Christ" (cf. 2.12; Rom 6.4), and it is openly stated as an error in 2 Tim 2.18 to say that the resurrection has taken place already. Such a view is proposed by Schmithals, Bultmann, Käsemann, A. C. Thiselton, and recently by C. M. Tuckett.[7]

None of these options is acceptable in its crude form. For the first option, we have a number of possibilities. The παρουσία goes with the raising of the dead (I,15.45, 47; 1 Thess 4.16, Christian dead first) and with universal judgment (II,5.10), so it is not likely that those who denied the resurrection would expect the παρουσία. Barth argues that I,15.19, "if in this life only we have hoped in Christ," excludes the possibility of even a spiritual survival of death and that the same inference should be drawn from 15.29, "if the dead are not raised at all," and 15.32, "if the dead are not raised, let us eat and drink." But Paul is the heir of the biblical tradition: the human person is a body inbreathed with spirit, and if there is no body, there is no real perseverance of the person. If Christians are not raised, they must be still in Sheol.

---

[5]A. Schweitzer, *The Mysticism of Paul the Apostle* (London: A. & C. Black, 1931), 93–94; B. Spörlein, *Die Leugnung der Auferstehung* (BU 7; Regensburg: Pustet, 1971), 190–91; Barth, "Auferstehungsleugnung."

[6]Pearson, *Terminology;* Sellin, *Streit;* A. J. M. Wedderburn, *Baptism and Resurrection* (WUNT 44; Tübingen: Mohr, 1987); Fee, *First Epistle,* 713–809; Horsley, *1 Corinthians,* 197–220; Hays, *First Corinthians,* 252–82.

[7]Schmithals, *Die Gnose,* 156–57; Bultmann, *Theology,* 1:169; E. Käsemann, *New Testament Questions of Today* (London: SCM, 1969), 126; A. C. Thiselton, "Realized Eschatology in Corinth," *NTS* 24 (1978): 510–26; C. M. Tuckett, "The Corinthians Who Say 'There Is No Resurrection of the Dead': 1 Cor 15:12," in *The Corinthian Correspondence* (ed. R. Bieringer; BETL 125; Leuven: Peeters/Leuven University Press, 1996), 247–75.

Against the second option, if bodily resurrection were the point, why is there no argument in 15.13–19 to show that immortality of the spirit is not enough?[8] There is no stress on Jesus' bodily resurrection in 15.1–11, and neither "he was buried" nor the discussion in 15.35–42 yields any emphasis on bodiliness. In fact, Paul's discussion in II,5.1–10 shows that he is quite relaxed with the perseverance of the "I," losing its "earthly tent" at death; there bodily resurrection seems dispensable provided we have a heavenly "house."

Finally, Wedderburn has combed ancient literature for instances of ἀνάστασις in a metaphorical sense but found none before 2 Timothy, which is too late for our text; thus, the opposition can hardly be held to assert a realized resurrection, however much they may have believed in a realized kingdom.[9] Nor does the Pauline wording correspond with such an interpretation. The τινες said, "There is no resurrection of the dead"; Hymenaeus (2 Tim 2.18) said that there was a resurrection and it had already taken place. The hypothesis would require ἀνάστασις νεκρῶν οὐκ ἔσται.[10]

But all three options are near to the truth. Schweitzer was right in thinking that the opposition denied the general resurrection, period; he was wrong in thinking that they believed in a return of the Lord. Sellin is right in thinking that they discounted the body and held that the spirit had already elevated Christians on to a level above death, but they did not speak of some spiritual resurrection. Bultmann was right in seeing all the stress as on present experience, but they said, "There is no resurrection of the dead," not, "There will be . . ."

A plain reading of I,15.12–19 leaves us with the firm impression that the Petrines denied the resurrection of the dead *tout court*. Despite Dan 12, Jewish tradition has always been in two minds about resurrection, and the failure of any general resurrection to take place after Easter may well have given rise to a negative response in Christian Jerusalem. With the gifts of the Spirit so impressive throughout the new community, the emphasis lay on present experience: death had been transcended, its power broken, and there was no ἀνάστασις νεκρῶν. Paul did not misunderstand this; he just thought it wrong—if there were no resurrection for the dead, their future was a thin one, in Hades.

But death was in fact a problem for the Petrines, and we see this problem already arising in 1 Thess 4.13–17. Paul was only briefly at

---

[8]Wedderburn, *Baptism,* 9; Tuckett, "The Corinthians," 254.

[9]Wedderburn, *Baptism,* ch. 3.

[10]Tuckett proposes a sophisticated version of the third theory, arguing that Col 3.1; 2.12 show that already around 60 C.E. people were speaking of "being risen with Christ," and suggesting that 15.12–19 is a prolonged statement of the Corinthian view. But, as he says himself, it would be a far longer statement of an opposition view than we find elsewhere, and his suggested parallel in Rom 7.14–25 is not quite the same.

Thessalonica, and the instruction of the church there may have been in the hands of Silas, a Jerusalem missionary, or some such person.[11] Paul's letter finds them grieving (λυπῆσθε) for those who have fallen asleep, and although other suggestions have been made, this probably means that they thought death was the end. Baptism was a magic rite that brought us eternal life; those who had been baptized would not die. But in fact some member of the Thessalonian church has "fallen asleep"; hence the grief and alarm. Paul's response fits this situation: "For if we believe that Jesus died and rose, so too will God bring those who fell asleep through Jesus with him." Those who believe the proclamation of the resurrection have no need to grieve "like the rest who have no hope." If Jesus rose again, so will those who have fallen asleep in him. Paul fills out this bare statement with a reassuring account of how the κεκοιμημένοι will join us who survive to the Lord's παρουσία. This is said to rest on a "word of the Lord," perhaps a prophetic revelation to Paul himself, like the "mystery" in I,15.51, but colored with traditional Jewish imagery: descent from heaven, thunderous angelic voices, the sound of the resurrection trumpet.

All this sounds like I,15:

1 Thess 4	*1 Cor 15*
the rest who have no hope	if in this life only we have been hoping in Christ
for if we believe that Jesus died and rose, so will God also bring those who have fallen asleep	you believed . . . Christ died . . . and has risen . . . so too those who fell asleep in Christ have perished
we the living who remain	we shall not all fall asleep
with the trumpet of God . . . and the dead in Christ shall be raised first	at the last trumpet, for the trumpet shall sound and the dead will be raised

What, then, did the Petrines think about Christians who had died? At first the Thessalonians were in despair, for they thought baptism was a guarantee against dying. But the Jerusalem missionaries who were teaching them were experienced people who knew this could not be so. Christians must have died in churches in Judea from early times. They thought that God would bring to nothing both food and belly (I,6.13), and this seems to imply that many of us will die and what perseveres after death is our spirit. There is no resurrection of the dead, and there is no παρουσία to inaugurate such an event; but the Christian is already πνευματικός, and his or her πνεῦμα will go marching on. So the Petrine position would have seemed to Paul not only

---

[11]See Goulder, "Silas in Thessalonica."

self-contradictory but also a recipe for suicide. But even if to us it is based on unreality, yet we cannot think it as weak as he makes out. It was obvious to them that the general resurrection had not happened and was not likely to, that with the Spirit, life was transformed and they were living in the glory of the kingdom, and this spiritual existence would continue after death for those who died. But they did not refer to this present exalted existence as "resurrection" or use the word in reference to perseverance after death—naturally, because it meant the rising of the body from the grave.

Such an idea would have been widespread in Jewish communities at the time. "It is probable that most Jews expected death not to be the end, though they may have conceived the future quite vaguely. The spread of Hellenistic culture meant, among other things, that acceptance of immortality was easy and, to many, self-evident."[12] Philo says of Moses, "The time came when he had to make his pilgrimage from earth to heaven, and leave this mortal life for immortality, summoned thither by the Father who resolved his twofold nature of body and soul into a single unity, transforming his whole being into mind (νοῦς), pure as the sunlight" (*Mos.* 2.288). Moses was, of course, special; then again, in their own view, so were the Jerusalem Christians. They would have used the word πνεῦμα where Philo prefers νοῦς, but they would have been happy to accept his dualism. The body, already but a snake's skin, a mortal coil, would be shuffled off at death; God would bring the belly to nothing but preserve the spirit. Sanders cites a number of texts from Josephus and from Qumran, some of them implying metempsychosis, others proclaiming the permanence of the soul in another world. It seems clear that there was a broad acceptance of the perseverance of the nonphysical part of humans, but with confusion and contradiction over what form it would take.[13]

I,15.20–28. Such a reconstruction of the Petrine position seems now to be confirmed by Paul's second wave of argument. Of course, the general resurrection had not taken place at Easter. Jesus was only "the firstfruits," and just as the sheaf of the firstfruits of the wheat harvest was offered in the temple on the day after the Sabbath in Passover week (Lev 23.10–11), while the full harvest thanksgiving was not until Pentecost (23.15–21), so Jesus' resurrection was the firstfruits of the full harvest, the general resurrection to come. Paul opens his new section: "But now has Christ been raised from the dead, the firstfruits of those who have fallen asleep."

But the relation between Christ's resurrection and the mass of humankind who have fallen asleep (τῶν καθευδόντων of Dan 12.2) needs some ex-

---

[12]E. P. Sanders, *Judaism: Practice and Belief, 63 BCE–66 CE* (Philadelphia: Trinity Press International, 1992), 298.
[13]Ibid., 298–303.

planation: "For since by a man came death, by a man too comes the resurrection of the dead." Here is the core of Paul's theology—to which we will return—explained by a second lapidary theologoumenon, pregnant with celestial fire: "For as in Adam all die, even so in Christ shall all be made alive." For Paul, Jesus' death and resurrection could only be understood as the reversal of Gen 2–3 (Rom 5.12–21). His resurrection was the beginning of the end: his obedience unto death reversed Adam's disobedience, which led to universal human death; his rising again was the first phase of the new world, in which there would be a universal rising, when "all will be made alive," some for eternity, some to be judged and to perish. But the Petrines have mistaken the phasing that God has laid down for us in Scripture. They have ignored what is said about the general resurrection and supposed that the kingdom of God has come already. That is wrong. There are four phases, like four formations (τάγματα) in the Roman army marching up behind one another: "But each in its own τάγματι." First there is "Christ as firstfruits, then," second, "those who are Christ's at his παρουσία." Paul is interested here only in the Christian dead, the κοιμηθέντες of 15.18, but he has mentioned in vv. 20–22 the great *massa perditionis* who will also be raised.

Opinion is divided whether "in Christ all shall be made alive" refers to all the dead or all the Christian dead. The Greek syntax implies the first, and the contrast with "in Adam all die" seems to require the same. First Thessalonians 4.16, "The dead in Christ shall rise first," suggests that the pagan dead are to follow, and Judaism had always been strong on the punishment of the wicked.

But even then we shall not have reached the kingdom of God. "Then [comes] the end, when [Christ] hands over the kingdom to the God and Father, when he has reduced to nothing every rule and every authority and power." In phase 3, Christ finally subjugates the powers; and in phase 4, he hands over the kingdom to God, and the kingdom of God begins. Christ may have been given the name above every name (Phil 2.10) and so the kingdom in heaven—not that we, as flesh and blood, are in a position to inherit it yet (15.50). But it will take some time, even after the παρουσία, before he subdues all the powers, and it will only be after this is completed that he will hand over the kingdom and "the kingdom of God" will continue into eternity.

Thus the whole paragraph, like the whole chapter, should be read as polemical. Christ's handing over "the kingdom to God" is to be set beside 4.8, "Without us you have begun reigning!" and 4.20, "for the kingdom of God is not in word but in power," and above all 15.50, "Flesh and blood cannot inherit the kingdom of God." Talk of a present kingdom of God is fantasy. It is countered by the sequence of phases that Paul introduces with temporal connections: ἀπαρχή . . . ἔπειτα . . . εἶτα . . . ἄχρι οὗ . . . τότε. Especially polemical is the reference to death, which is treated, as elsewhere in the NT, as a "power" (3.22; Rom 8.38). The Petrines are pretending that Death has been put down with the coming of the kingdom and that it has no power now to harm the spiritual. Nonsense, says the apostle: the powers will not be put down until phase 3, and then Death will be the last enemy to be subjugated. And the kingdom of God does not come until phase 4.

The powers were important to the opposition. The Petrines included visionaries, and angelic powers in the heavens were important features of visionary lore. In Phil 2.10–11 Christ's exaltation is to be greeted with the bowed knees of those in heaven and on earth and under the earth. In Col 1.16 the powers—thrones, lordships, rulers, authorities—are said all to have been created by (in) Christ. In Rom 8.38–39 Paul is persuaded that none of the powers can separate us from the love of God in Christ. It seems likely that the same thinking underlies our paragraph. Optimistic Petrines had revelations that God in his newly taken reign had overthrown the hostile powers, including Death itself. Hence the rather extended and elaborate argument Paul uses to prove that they are still around.

There is a striking parallel between I,15.20–28 and 2 Thess 2.1–12. There also an unreal fantasy world has taken over, with the belief that "the Day of the Lord has come (ἐνέστηκεν)" and the consequent decision by many to give up working. Paul counters this by setting out three phases that have to come first, following the book of Daniel: (i) Now there is a time of θλίψεις (Dan 7, etc.), as the restrainer (ὁ κατέχων) delays the end, like the princes of Dan 10 who withstand Michael. (ii) To come next is the revolt and the man of sin, the son of perdition, who will behave like King Antiochus in Dan 11, exalting himself against God. (iii) The Lord will destroy him with the breath of his mouth at his παρουσία (leading on to the general resurrection of Dan 12).[14] Paul follows exactly the same strategy here, but he draws his logic from Pss 110.1 and 8.6 instead of from Daniel; there has been less talk in Corinth of the Day of the Lord having come, and more of the subjection of the powers.

But there is a more important reason for appealing to these psalms. Paul is viewing history on the *Urzeit-Endzeit* principle: what happened with Adam in the beginning is reversed under Christ at the end (I,15.21–22). Before Adam's sin and death, reversed in Christ's cross and resurrection, God gave Adam dominion over the fish and birds and over every living thing (Gen 1.28; 2.19–20). This is celebrated in Ps 8.6–7: "You have given [man] dominion over the works of your hands; you have put all things under his feet," the sheep and oxen, the beasts, the birds, and the fish. This, then, needs still to be done; the closely similar phrasing in Ps 110.1 tells us by whom it is to be done, and when. God said to "my Lord," interpreted as

---

[14]Goulder, "The Phasing of the Future," sets 2 Thess 2.1–12 in a broader context.

"David" in the psalm's heading, and so Christ, "Sit at my right hand until I make your enemies your footstool." So Scripture tells us that it is Christ who will under God subjugate the enemy powers after his resurrection, and when this is done ("until"), Christ's reign will be over. Only when Christ (carefully excluded from the πάντα) subjugates himself to God will God's kingdom proper begin. The apostle ends with a characteristic "that God may be all in all" (I,15.28); such piety is not to be gainsaid and makes effective rhetoric.

We may represent the apostle's thought in a diagram:

2 Thess 2.1–12		*1 Cor 15.20–28*	
Christ has been raised from the dead		Christ has been raised from the dead	
Petrines *mistakenly think:*	**Paul** *reminds them that:*	**Petrines** *mistakenly think:*	**Paul** *reminds them that:*
• the Day of the Lord has already come		• the kingdom of God has already come • the powers have been overthrown • Death has been conquered	
• now they no longer need to work		• Believers now have glory	
	• there are still trials to come • the power of lawlessness is only under restraint • the lawless one will lead a revolt • the lawless one will be destroyed by the Lord at his παρουσία		• there are still trials to come • the παρουσία of those who belong to Christ is coming • Christ subjugates the powers • the kingdom of God begins

The phasing picked out by Paul differs according to the context in the two churches, but the strategy is the same: to rebut realized eschatology by inference, from Scripture, of future phasing.

In Paul's argument, the claim that Christ is the ἀπαρχή occupies a key place, and it explains what has long seemed a puzzle. Paul in 15.4 said that "Christ has been raised on the third day according to the Scriptures," and it has seemed from this that Paul had in mind some text that mentioned the third day. But the main candidates, Hos 6.2, Jonah 1.17, and Ps 16.10, all seem unconvincing. In his polemical context, however, Paul appeals to the biblical prescription of the ἀπαρχή as the foreshadowing of Jesus' rising. Leviticus 23.4–8 prescribes the sacrifices of Passover week and continues, "When you enter the land that I am giving you and you reap its harvest, you shall bring the sheaf of the first fruits of your harvest to the priest. He shall raise the sheaf before the LORD, that you may find acceptance; on the day after the sabbath the priest shall raise it" (Lev 23.10–11, NRSV). Paul thought of Christ as a Passover sacrifice: "Christ our Passover was sacrificed" (I,5.7). He died on a Friday. It was on the day after the Sabbath, on the third day, that he rose, as the priest raised (ἀνοίσει) the firstfruits sheaf. So Paul's "according to the Scriptures" in 15.4 is likely to be polemical, too, and probably his own elaboration of the παράδοσις. It might not be persuasive to cite Lev 23.10–11, but to Paul this text is God's foreshadowing of Christ's resurrection on the third day and a full justification for the "delay" in the general resurrection.

Hosea 6.2, although most often mentioned, is a weak candidate, for it prophesies only that "on the third day he will raise us up"; nor is it ever cited in the NT. Jonah 1.17 reports that Jonah was in the whale's belly for three days and three nights, which is a poor approximation to Paul's "on the third day." It is cited in Matt 12.40, but then the evangelist alters the length of Jesus' period in the tomb to fit. Peter in Acts 2 cites Ps 16.10, but it does not mention the third day, which has to be inferred from Jewish belief that corruption set in after the third day.[15]

I,15.29–34. Though not certain, it looks as if "those who are baptized for the dead" are members of the Petrine group. Paul's logic seems to imply this: "if the dead are not raised at all [ὅλως, as was implied in 15.18–19], why are they also baptized for them?" Such a practice would fit very well with the Petrine position as it has appeared. If there is no resurrection of the dead, what about our beloved parents who died before we heard the gospel? Can we do nothing to redeem them from Sheol? Baptism is a divine mystery that delivers us automatically from perdition (1.10–17; 10.1–13); why should God limit its saving effect to us? With a second baptism and intercession, they, too, may become πνευματικοί. We baptize our children and our slaves, the householder's faith counting for "all his house"; why not for dead members of the household also?

But to Paul's way of thinking, such an approach is transparently flawed. "For what are those who are baptized for the dead going to do [if things are so]?" They are going to look like complete fools. "If the dead are not raised at all," then they are stuck in Sheol, so what is the point? "Why are they also baptized for them?" Their position is obviously self-contradictory. Vicarious baptisms imply, as a corollary, the expectation of resurrection.[16]

---

[15]Cf. Fee, *First Epistle*, 726–28.

[16]It is sometimes said (De Boer, *Defeat of Death,* 96–97; Tuckett, "The Corinthians," 251–52) that the vicarious baptisms rule out certain interpretations of 15.12. But this is not justifiable: the deniers may hold a "hellenized" doctrine, including the perseverance of the spirit beyond death, while Paul thinks in more straightforward biblical terms. R. E. DeMaris, "Corinthian Religion and Baptism for the Dead— 1 Corinthians 15:29: Insights from Archaeology and Anthropology," *JBL* 114 (1995): 661–82, gives evidence of some obsession with death in first-century Corinth, with devotion to the dead hero Palaemon and to Demeter/Kore and Pluto. Such rites were in the hands of women and might shed light on our passage.

And what about Paul himself, who is not slow to mention his trials as an apostle (4.9–13) and whose dedicated and perilous life must have been familiar to many of them? "Why too are we at risk every day? I die daily, yes, by my boast in you which I have in Christ Jesus our Lord." Why should he expose himself to attacks by robbers, to delations, to frequent floggings at danger to his life, to perils on the sea? So far from the phony talk of death being put down, Paul suffers death in one form or another each day—he will not swear "by Christ Jesus," but he can solemnly assert by their community, which he is proud to have founded in Christ, that it is so. In particular, his mind goes to the "many adversaries" of 16.9, false brethren (as he would think of them) at Ephesus and hostile Jews, those later remembered as Hymenaeus and Philetus and Alexander the coppersmith. It was customary in the early church to speak of one's rivals as dogs, snakes, wolves, and so forth; so he says here, "If it was only on a human level that I fought with wild beasts at Ephesus, what profit would I have by that? If the dead are not raised, 'let us eat and drink, for tomorrow we die.'" Everything depended on the divine context, with resurrection as the crown of sufferings. If all these were merely κατὰ ἄνθρωπον, one might as well be a hedonist.

Paul could not have fought with wild beasts literally. Roman citizens were not liable to such ordeals, nor were there survivors from them. Ignatius, *Rom.* 5.1, borrows Paul's verb to refer to his soldier guards. κατὰ ἄνθρωπον occurs again in 3.3 in contrast to "spiritually": without Paul's faith in the resurrection, his many perils would have been merely on the human level and vain.[17]

Paul is fretted by many things: failure to stick firmly to the gospel as first delivered, denial of a central plank in his proclaimed structure of belief, but also, practically, the ethical disasters consequent on these errors. The church he left in the autumn of 51 had aspired to holiness, and look what has happened now, thanks to the coming of these Petrines! "Do not be deceived! Bad company corrupts the best of manners"; the old tag is applied to the Jerusalem visitors. "Sober up in virtue, and stop sinning [μὴ ἁμαρτάνετε, present], for some have no knowledge of God—I speak to your shame." What a state things have descended to, thanks to their muddles—quarrels and divisions, incest, lawsuits, barefaced idolatry, disgraceful behavior at worship! These τίνες credited themselves with γνῶσις, but in fact they have a gross ἀγνωσία of God. The same charge to sobriety and virtue that had followed the παρουσία passage in 1 Thess 5.1–11 comes over now much more briskly. All these things stem from the unreality of the kingdom-of-God-is-here party. Those who look forward to the Lord's coming, and the raising of the dead to meet him, know that they will have to look their judge in the eye.

---

[17]Cf. A. J. Malherbe, "The Beasts at Ephesus," *JBL* 87 (1968): 71–80.

I,15.35–41. Paul resumes his somewhat dyspeptic dialogue with the Petrines. Those who deny the resurrection have tried to lampoon the idea by asking, "How are the dead raised? With what body do they come?" As spiritual beings, they regard any such notion as crude and absurd; the ἔρχονται has an ironic note. Paul replies briskly with the analogy of a seed, which we also know from Jewish sources. The farmer puts a bare corn seed in the ground, and God miraculously clothes it with a new body, green and thriving; the same thing happens when we die. It is not our old flesh that will come back at the resurrection; we shall have a new and splendid body. Indeed, some created beings, the sun, moon, and stars, have radiant bodies, and we shall be like them hereafter. Daniel 12.3 foretold that the wise would shine like the brightness of the sky, like the stars, and Matthew says that the righteous will shine like the sun on judgment day (Matt 13.43).

Jewish tradition on postmortal life was vague. Paul adopted the line taken later by Rabbi Meïr: his new, glorious bodies were certainly more appealing than Ezekiel's dry bones. Rabbi Meïr was asked whether the dead would be raised clothed, and replied, "If a grain of wheat was buried naked, and comes up out of the ground abundantly clothed, how much more will the righteous be dressed in their clothes" (*b. Sanh.* 90b). The issue is different, but the common tradition ("a grain of wheat," "naked") is evident, and both theologians assume a physical resurrection. But Paul's opponents had an equally plausible picture of a persevering spirit, paralleled in Philo, Josephus, and the Qumran documents.

I,15.42–49. Genesis 1–2 contains two accounts of the creation of humans—a fact not first noticed in the modern period. Philo handles the matter differently in different passages, sometimes treating them as one, sometimes as a double creation, and this second possibility was discussed before him.[18] His account of it is as follows:

> After this he says that "God formed man by taking clay from the earth, and breathed into his face the breath of life" (Gen. 2.7). By this also he shows very clearly that there is a vast difference between the man thus formed and the man that came into existence earlier, after the image of God (Gen. 1.27); for the man so formed is an object of sense-perception, partaking already of such and such quality, consisting of body and soul, man or woman, by nature mortal; while he that was after the image was an idea (ἰδέα), or genus (γένος), or seal (σφραγίς), an object of thought, incorporeal, neither male nor female, by nature incorruptible. (*Opif.* 134; trans. F. H. Colson and G. H. Whitaker, LCL)

---

[18]He comments on Gen 2.8, "Some people, believing Paradise to be a garden, have said that since the moulded man is sense-perceptible, he therefore rightly goes to a sense-perceptible place." Tobin, *Creation of Man,* 102, cites the passage to show that the discussion of the two creation stories is pre-Philonic.

Similarly, Philo, *QG* 1.4, speaks of the Gen 1.27 creation thus:

> But the man made in accordance with [God's] form is intelligible and incorporeal and a likeness of the archetype, so far as this is visible. And he is a copy of the original seal. And this is the *Logos* of God, the first principle, the archetypal idea, the pre-measurer of all things.

There is a similar exposition of a double creation in *Leg.* 1.31–32. Philo has developed the exegesis of Gen 1.27 with the aid of his Platonism, but the idea of a heavenly original from which the earthly form was a copy was already in Scripture, with the archetype (תבנית) of the tabernacle that Moses is shown in Exod 25.8, and so forth.

We may infer from I,15.45–46 a knowledge of this tradition: "For thus it is written, 'The first man Adam became a living soul'; the last Adam became a life-giving spirit. But it is not the spirit-man (πνευματικόν) that was first but the soul-man (ψυχικόν), then the spirit-man." This is transparently polemical. Genesis has two accounts of the creation of man, and the Petrines are following Philo's double-creation interpretation: the first man is the incorporeal, incorruptible, asexual man of Gen 1, while Adam is the second, in Gen 2. Paul understands the two accounts to refer to a single creation (a view also found in Philo),[19] the second being an expansion of the first. He therefore contradicts the opposition—"But it is not the spirit-man that was first . . ."—and supports his contradiction by an amplified citation of Gen 2.7. The LXX said, "Man became a living soul," ἐγένετο ὁ ἄνθρωπος εἰς ψυχὴν ζῶσαν. Paul has deliberately amended the text to give the order he wants, by inserting first the word πρῶτος and then the name Adam, and the casual listener (especially a recently converted Corinthian Gentile) might be forgiven for thinking that the whole sentence, including the clause on the last Adam, was part of the citation. Paul would have felt that he was just clarifying the picture: as everyone knows, the first man was called Adam. *First* is in fact being used here in two senses: the Petrines mean that the Gen 1.27 ("earlier") creation precedes the Gen 2.7 creation, and Paul means that the two accounts both refer to the first human being, Adam.

We have thus a reasonable presumption that the Petrines worked their theology out on the same general principle that Paul did (and some of his contemporaries): the *Endzeit* was a reflection of the *Urzeit*. On the double-creation hypothesis, Gen 1 spoke of an incorporeal, incorruptible world that existed in the beginning, before the world of clay and ψυχή that is Adam's world and has been ours. With the coming of the Spirit, we have been transferred from the realm of the ψυχικόν to the realm of the πνευματικόν. Philo has much discussion of Adam's ψυχή and its limitations, but he does not use the adjective, and he uses ἄφθαρτος, like Paul, but not πνευματικός. But this

---

[19]Tobin, *Creation of Man,* 56–101.

is easily understood: the Spirit was the phenomenon of the church, Pauline as well as Petrine, and the adjective was in wide use, both of spiritual people and of spiritual gifts. The ψυχικός/πνευματικός antithesis was virtually inevitable. The Petrines thought: the kingdom of God has come, the last phase of this world's existence; we are in the carryover from the Adamic world to the Gen 1 world; other people, including those in the church who lack the apostolic baptism, are still ψυχικοί, but we are in the spiritual, glorified, incorruptible world of Gen 1; death came in Gen 3, and its power is now over.

It is striking that of the rather rare references to the Spirit of God in the OT, a prominent instance is in Gen 1.2: "The Spirit of God (πνεῦμα θεοῦ) moved over the water." If the Petrines justified their theology on the basis of Gen 1, as a return to the era of the first man (Gen 1.27), it would be surprising if they did not see their experience of the Spirit as a fulfillment of Gen 1.2.[20]

To Paul this was all gross error. The only thing correct was the contrast between the ψυχικόν and the πνευματικόν, but here they have the order wrong. The seed analogy shows that these adjectives refer to two forms of body: "it is sown a psychic body; it is raised a pneumatic body. If there is a psychic body, there is also a pneumatic [body]" (15.44). Adam was the first man, with his psyche and his psychic body; he was "from the earth, of dust," but "the second man" is Christ, who will come "from heaven" (v. 47). Adam just "became a living soul," but when Christ comes, he will be "a life-giving spirit"—he will literally give life to the dead (v. 22). Paul is taking up the brief statement of his theology in vv. 21–23. We have been, all of us, in Adam, and we shall not be out of the wood until Christ joins those who are his at the παρουσία. "As we have borne the image of the man of dust, we shall also bear the image of the heavenly man," Christ. But it will not be until then. All Petrine talk of the heavenly man of Gen 1.27 and the εἰκών of God as phenomena already here is just self-delusion.

In 15.49 there is strong attestation for φορέσωμεν (𝔓⁴⁶ ℵ A C D) against φορέσομεν (B). Fee prefers the aorist subjunctive, but UBS prefers the future indicative with a C rating. The future is to be preferred, as in line with the argument of the passage: we have not yet inherited anything (v. 50); we shall bear the image of Christ at his coming. An exhortation in v. 49 would be obscure and would interrupt the flow of thought; an unstressed ω was scarcely distinguishable from an ο, and dictation might easily have led to a change to exhortation.

I,15.50–58.   A new paragraph is customarily marked here, but the thought is continuous. What is fundamentally wrong with the Petrine eschatology is

---

[20]For Jewish speculations on the end time as a reversal of primal time, see C. K. Barrett, *From First Adam to Last* (London: Black, 1962). For the background of the πνευματικός/ψυχικός contrast, see Pearson, *Terminology.*

its unreality, leading to sin; as Paul said in 15.34, "Sober up in righteousness and sin no more." The denial of any resurrection of the dead goes with the vacuous talk of being glorified and incorruptible and reigning already in the kingdom of God. "Now this I say, brothers, that flesh and blood cannot inherit the kingdom of God, neither does corruption inherit incorruption." "Flesh and blood" means our present mortal condition, and φθορά is interpreted in v. 53 as τὸ φθαρτὸν τοῦτο. This corruptible being of ours cannot simply become incorruptible by baptism, simply move into Gen 1 mode as if by magic. Verse 50 crowns the whole series of negative comments on inheriting the kingdom of God in 4.8, 21; 6.9, 10; 15.24 and extending into Gal 5.21 and Rom 14.17. The other texts all speak of the kingdom by way of warning; 15.50 is the only clear statement that the kingdom is simply not available to us on this side of the παρουσία.

Joachim Jeremias's comments have been influential.[21] Barrett accepts his view:

> The Semitic word-pair "flesh and blood" is "only applied to living persons; the words flesh as well as blood exclude an application of the word-pair to the dead." In the parallel line *corruption* is used, as an abstract noun instead of a concrete, for "corpses in decomposition." Dr. Jeremias sums up: "The two lines of verse 50 are contrasting men of flesh and blood on the one hand, and corpses in decomposition on the other. In other words the first line refers to those who are alive at the parousia, the second line to those who died before the parousia. The parallelism is thus not synonymous but synthetic and the meaning of verse 50 is: neither the living nor the dead can take part in the Kingdom of God—as they are."[22]

But Fee is surely right to say that Jeremias is forcing too narrow a meaning on ἡ φθορά.[23] The parallelism is really just synonymous, as is shown by the continuing argument in vv. 52–54.

Verse 50 is an uncomfortable text for the many critics who have characterized Paul's theology as "already but not yet." In I,4.8–11 he shows how acid he can be about claims to "already." He knew that we had an ἀρραβών of the Spirit now, but he is clear that the kingdom will not be ours until the παρουσία.[24]

In 1 Thess 4.15 Paul could give an authoritative account of the παρουσία from a "word of the Lord." Here, similarly, he can say, "Behold I

---

[21]J. Jeremias, "Flesh and Blood Cannot Inherit the Kingdom of God," *NTS* 2 (1956): 151–59 (citation from 152).

[22]Barrett, *First Epistle*, 379.

[23]Fee, *First Epistle*, 798.

[24]See M. D. Goulder, "Already?" in *To Tell the Mystery: Essays on New Testament Eschatology in Honor of Robert H. Gundry* (ed. T. Schmidt and M. Silva; JSNTSup 100; Sheffield: JSOT Press, 1994), 1–18.

show you a mystery"—it has come to him by revelation, like the μυστήρια in the book of Daniel. Although some Christians may die, "we shall not all fall asleep, but we shall all be transformed." He is still hammering the point that the kingdom is not available in our present state. It will all happen "in a moment, in the twinkling of an eye," as Christ arrives with angels blowing "the last trump; and the dead will be raised incorruptible. We too will be transformed, for this corruptible being must put on incorruptibility." This takes us back to 15.42: "It is sown in corruption; it is raised in incorruption." The πνευματικοί, with the double-creation theology, supposed themselves already to belong to the world of the incorruptible spirit. Not so, says the apostle: we must be transformed first.

Ancient townspeople lived closer to the soil than we do, and Paul probably knew there was biological continuity between the "bare seed" that "died" in 15.36–37 and the glorious new body with which God miraculously endows it. Thus, although he compares our postmortal life to such a seed, he knows that there will have to be a continuity, a persevering element, our spirit. In this he is not so far from the Petrines, although he stresses the differences. "We," who are there at the Lord's coming, "will be transformed; this corruptible being must put on incorruptibility, and this mortal must put on immortality." The use of the verb ἐνδύσασθαι shows that a core element of our present being will carry on under its new and more glorious apparel.

It is not until this transformation takes place that the power of death will be at an end; this has not happened already, as the Petrines so vapidly proclaim. "But when this corruptible has put on incorruption . . . , then shall the word come to pass that is written. . . ." The whole argument is set out to counter the kingdom-already position, which denied any general resurrection of the dead and which we found hinted at in Paul's polemical "last enemy" (v. 26). The "word which has come to pass" (referring to Isa 25; Hos 13) is, like many of Paul's citations, somewhat adapted. According to LXX Isa 25.8, ὁ θάνατος is the subject and does the devouring (κατέπιεν), but the Hebrew more helpfully has, "[God] will swallow up death for ever (לנצח)." The LXX renders the last word with ἰσχύσας, and it is conjectured that in later Hebrew it carried the sense of "in triumph" and that this might justify Paul's εἰς νῖκος, "unto victory."[25] He wants a text that proclaims the defeat of death, its being put in subjection under Christ's feet—so much so that he introduces it a second time with a further text, Hos 13.14. Here the LXX had ποῦ ἡ δίκη σου, θάνατε; ποῦ τὸ κέντρον σου, ᾅδη; but Paul amends to ποῦ σου, θάνατε, τὸ νῖκος; ποῦ σου, θάνατε, τὸ κέντρον; There is no question but that he wants to prove that death's victory is going to be over when the Lord comes.

---

[25]G. B. Caird, "Towards a Lexicon of the Septuagint, II," *JTS* 20 (1969): 21–40, here 34; de Boer, *Defeat of Death*, 127.

A revealing text follows: "The sting of death is sin, and the power of sin is the law." The first half of the chapter closed with the demand for an awakening from drunken stupor (ἐκνήψατε) and from a life of sin (μὴ ἁμαρτάνετε), and the same thought is here. There is a plain corollary to a false eschatology with no day of judgment to come because of no resurrection of the dead: moral laxity, πορνεία, εἰδωλολατρία, and the rest. The Petrines proclaim that Death's power is over; very likely they cited Hos 13.14 themselves as a proof of this. But Death's power is visibly still with us, and you can see its sting at work in the rotten quality of their ethical living.

And what is it that gives such sin its driving power? It is paradoxically the appeal to the law. This is what dominated the discussion in I,1–2, when Paul contrasted his gospel, the word of the cross, with the words of wisdom, the interpretations of torah handed down by the Jerusalem sages and scribes. The Petrines felt they had this to hang on to for salvation, and so the god of this age was able to blind their minds so that the light of the glorious gospel of Christ should not enlighten them (II,4.4). It led to the arrogance of Rom 2 and the despair of Rom 7; it suggested sin in the first place (Rom 7.7–11). Paul has not had occasion to expound the shortcomings of the law in 1 Corinthians, partly because he wanted to appeal to it on ethical issues and partly because, for the moment, he was defending a distinction between "what is written" (I,4.6), the Torah text, and "words of wisdom," the learned applications of the text. But he has been thinking about the law as a false basis of salvation, and we get the full benefit of his thinking when he has leisure to write Romans.

With such a warning of things to come, Paul seals off his long discussion, first with a triumphant doxology, "But thanks be to God who gives us the victory . . . ," and finally with a charge, "So, my beloved brothers, be steadfast, unmovable, always overflowing in the work of the Lord, knowing that your labor is not vain in the Lord." Stick firmly to the gospel that I passed on to you four years ago, on which your salvation depends, and show its fruits in unbounded acts of charity. That is what will build up the church.[26]

---

[26]For a more detailed look at 2 Corinthians 5.1–10, see Appendix 3.

∼ 14 ∼

ANOTHER JESUS: I

PAUL WAS founding churches of disparate backgrounds, and it was inevitable that the first questions to arise would be practical: what can be said when church members die, when they give up work, marry their dead father's wife, attend dinners in pagan temples, and so on. It is only gradually that dogmatic differences surface, and these will also appear in practical forms: the validity of the law comes in question when the host at Antioch buys meat in the market, and those who think that the kingdom of God has already begun are heard maintaining that there is no resurrection of the dead. So also with Christology: a dogmatic cleft is first revealed with an excited exchange at the Corinthian Eucharist.

RELEVANT CHRISTOLOGICAL TEXTS

Our two letters yield enough evidence for us to know that the Petrines did not share the Pauline Christology, though not enough to make it clear what Christology they did hold. For that, it will be necessary to set them in a wider canvas. But it may be helpful to list the Corinthian texts that indicate that here, too, there is trouble:

I,1.12. "Each of you says, . . . I am of Christ." Chapter 2, above, has argued that there were indeed parties at Corinth, loyal to the missionaries who converted them or in whose name (in the case of Cephas) they were converted and baptized. This argument bypassed the problem of a Christ party, and to this we now turn. There were no converts at Corinth brought in by a missionary called Christ. The slogan, "I am of Christ," sounds as if it were upstaging professions of loyalty to human missionaries and may constitute some kind of christological claim.

I,8.6. "But to us there is one God the Father, from whom are all things, and we unto him, and one Lord Jesus Christ through whom are all things, and we through him." Some Petrines had claimed to have knowledge that there is no god but one, so idol meat could be eaten without harm. Paul concedes this as a principle, and 8.6a constitutes a formal agreement with it. But the second half of the verse, about Jesus Christ, prepares the way for a counter-argument ("the brother for whom [δι' ὅν] Christ died") and is probably Paul's own comment. The part in creation attributed to Christ is not likely to be an irrelevance.

I,10.4. "And the rock was Christ." As in 8.6b, we have the assertion of Christ's preexistence and activity in OT times: he was active not only in creation but also in the wilderness wanderings.

I,12.3. "No one speaking in the Spirit of God says, 'Damn Jesus.'"[1] This is a notorious crux, but the prima facie suggestion of the text is that some Christians, believing themselves to be speaking in the Spirit, uttered what seems a blasphemy. There are problems with all proposed solutions to the difficulty, but the apparent meaning deserves further consideration.

I,16.22. "If anyone does not love the Lord, let him be damned (ἀνάθεμα). Marana tha!" The first clause may be an echo of 12.3. It is difficult to see what specific failing, left so general, might lead to exclusion from the community of salvation. But if any one had said, "Damn Jesus," that person certainly did not love the Lord and might invite the same curse on his or her own head. Similarly, it is not easy to see how this leads on to an old Aramaic prayer, unless the title "Lord" (*mārē'* [מָרֵא]) is in dispute.

II,3.18; 4.4; 4.10–14. In a polemical passage, Paul twice speaks of Christ as the image of God (3.18; 4.4), and in the subsequent verses refers to him seven times as Jesus, without "Christ." This is out of seventeen times in all the Pauline writings, and some of the others are included in our present list (I,12.3; II,11.4).

II,10.7. "If anyone has confidence in himself that he is of Christ (Χριστοῦ εἶναι) . . ." While the point is disputed, it may be that we have here an echo of I,1.12: "I am of Christ." It might be that the Christ party was still active; if so, they seem to be closely identified with the "false apostles," and so the Petrines.

II,11.4. "For if the newcomer proclaims another Jesus whom we did not proclaim, or you are receiving a different Spirit, which you did not receive, or a different gospel, which you did not accept, you submit happily!" There

---

[1] I use this rather shocking translation because the original is rather shocking, and the effect is lost by the colorless "Let Jesus be cursed" (NRSV); likewise with I,16.22.

was a "different gospel" in Gal 1.6 and an appeal to the Spirit proclaimed by Paul in Gal 3.1–3, but this is the first time we hear of "another Jesus."

There may be other, more subtle hints of christological differences, but these are sufficient to suggest such a problem. It is noteworthy that here, too, it appears to reveal itself first in public scandal—people saying, "I am of Christ," or shouting out, "Damn Jesus"—and is only later attributed to the new missionaries' teaching (II,11.4).

Although critics have been hesitant about the relevance of each of these texts to a christological opposition, the case is strengthened by their cohesiveness. Thus II,10.7 suggests that there really was a Christ party, as seems to be implied by I,1.12, and that it was a persevering entity, active a year later. The name seems to stress its loyalty to "Christ," while several of the other texts seem to imply a denigration of "Jesus." II,11.4 does not suggest that the newcomer is far from Paul on the subject of Christ, but the newcomer holds a quite different view of Jesus. Perhaps, then, the newcomer made some distinction between a heavenly Christ and an earthly Jesus, which might explain the surprising comment in I,12.3 and its counterpart in I,16.22, the sudden emphasis on "Jesus" in II,4.1–17, and, for that matter, the "one Lord Jesus Christ" through whom God created the universe in I,8.6.

This chapter and that following will set the Corinthian Christology texts in a broader historical framework. First they will argue for a prophetic Christology in the early Jerusalem community. Then they will give evidence of two christological positions held by second-century Jewish Christians, both of them varieties of the view that Jesus was a prophet: the Pseudo-Clementine view and the Ebionite view. Only then will they offer an analysis of eight Corinthian texts, as implying a similar prophetic doctrine held by the Petrines. Finally, they will consider other relevant Pauline texts and other NT evidence.

A PRIMITIVE PROPHETIC CHRISTOLOGY

The Synoptic Gospels open their accounts of Jesus' ministry with uses of Isa 61.1 that are striking by being both shared and different. Isaiah 60 promises that Israel will repossess the land and will multiply, and closes, "κατὰ καιρόν I will gather them." Isaiah 61 then begins, Πνεῦμα κυρίου ἐπ᾽ ἐμέ, οὗ εἵνεκεν ἔχρισέν με· εὐαγγελίσασθαι πτωχοῖς, and in the next verse, παρακαλέσαι πάντας τοὺς πενθοῦντας.

Mark seems to be thinking of this passage when he has Jesus come into Galilee κηρύσσων τὸ εὐαγγέλιον τοῦ θεοῦ and saying, Πεπλήρωται ὁ καιρὸς καὶ ἤγγικεν ἡ βασιλεία τοῦ θεοῦ· μετανοεῖτε καὶ πιστεύετε ἐν τῷ εὐαγγελίῳ (1.15). The verb εὐαγγελίζεσθαι is the special preserve of the later chapters of Isaiah (40.9 [2x]; 52.7 [2x]; 60.6; 61.1), and Isa 60.22–61.1

is the only place where it is associated with καιρός. It is difficult not to think that Mark saw Jesus as expounding the latter passage. Jesus had just been baptized and seen the Spirit descending into himself (1.10). The Spirit had then driven him out into the wilderness for forty days (1.12). Mark began by telling the reader that this is the εὐαγγέλιον Ἰησοῦ Χριστοῦ. Jesus, Mark supposes, would have seen all this as the fulfillment of Isaiah. The Spirit of the Lord was upon him anointing him, and he now came with good news that the time was fulfilled. Indeed, the whole exordium of Mark is dominated by later Isaiah. He opens with a fulfillment of prophecy ascribed to Isaiah and containing Isa 40.3. The words from heaven ἐν σοὶ εὐδόκησα come from Isa 42.1. Jesus' proclamation, ἤγγικεν ἡ βασιλεία τοῦ θεοῦ, recalls Isa 56.1, ἤγγισεν γὰρ τὸ σωτήριόν μου (cf. Isa 46.13; 51.5), and Isa 52.7, εὐαγγελιζόμενος ἀγαθά . . . Βασιλεύσει σου ὁ θεός. Mark's πεπλήρωται ὁ καιρός is itself an appeal to the fulfillment of prophecy of the coming "time." Jesus' coming fulfilled later Isaiah, especially Isa 61.1.

Matthew follows Mark step by step, expanding as he goes—a sermon for the Baptist, hesitation over baptizing the sinless Jesus, three specified temptations in the desert. When Jesus comes to Galilee (Matt 4.12–13), there is a long citation from Isa 9.1–2, followed by Mark's "Repent, for the kingdom [of heaven] has drawn near" (Matt 4.17), referred to as τὸ εὐαγγέλιον in 4.23. Jesus' healing ministry (4.23–24) is later legitimated by the citation of Isa 53.4 (Matt 8.17). But Matthew's major insertion is the Sermon on the Mount, and this opens, Μακάριοι οἱ πτωχοὶ τῷ πνεύματι, ὅτι αὐτῶν ἐστιν ἡ βασιλεία τῶν οὐρανῶν. μακάριοι οἱ πενθοῦντες, ὅτι αὐτοὶ παρακληθήσονται (5.3–4). The inspiration is drawn from Isa 61.1–2, where the anointed one was to bring good news πτωχοῖς and to comfort all the mourners (παρακαλέσαι πάντας τοὺς πενθοῦντας). Matthew is a little anxious at the ambiguity of the prophecy: not every beggar will possess the kingdom, only the poor in spirit.

Luke treats Isa 61 twice. His Sermon on the Plain also opens μακάριοι οἱ πτωχοί (6.20) but abbreviates the Beatitudes to four, so there are no πενθοῦντες. But the influence of the prophecy comes through in the four balancing woes on the rich: they have their παράκλησιν and are told, πενθήσετε καὶ κλαύσετε (6.24–25). The Isaian passage is so significant to Luke that he cites seven lines of it in 4.18–19, making it the lesson that Jesus reads in the Nazareth synagogue and the text on which he founds his ministry. He begins his address, "Today has this Scripture been fulfilled in your ears" (4.21), and expounds his coming career in its light. The Spirit has anointed him to proclaim good news to the poor, as he does in the Sermon; release to the prisoners, such as the bent woman bound by Satan (and later Peter from prison); sight to the blind, as at Jericho; release for the oppressed more generally; and finally the Year of Jubilee.

Matthew may be seen as merely developing a theme latent in Mark, that of Isa 61.1, and Luke may be seen as merely developing Mark's use of the text in Luke 4.16–30 and Matthew's in Luke 6.20–26. But so minimalizing a view is hardly convincing. Both the later evangelists have taken the Isaian prophecy as a central theme of Jesus' proclamation, although it is only hinted at in Mark. It is likely that both knew a tradition of its importance in Jesus' ministry and that this tradition underlies Mark, too. Furthermore, when Paul visited the pillars in Jerusalem in 48, they asked him and Barnabas "only that we remember τῶν πτωχῶν" (Gal 2.10). The collection that Paul then took up at such pains was for the church at Jerusalem (Rom 15.26). Karl Holl suggested in 1921 the plausible hypothesis that the Jerusalem church called itself "the Poor People,"[2] and we might think that they derived the name from the עניים, the πτωχοί, of Isa 61.1 even before their common-purse policy brought them to actual poverty.[3]

It is commonly thought that Matthew and Luke have inherited the tradition of the Beatitudes from a common lost source, Q. If this were so, it would strengthen the present argument, that the use of Isa 61.1 is early and likely to go back to Jesus himself; but it is not so.[4]

Isaiah was "anointed" to bear good news (εὐαγγελίσασθαι) and to proclaim (κηρύξαι) release, and these are the terms (usually with the nominal form εὐαγγέλιον) used to describe Jesus' preaching. He sometimes speaks of himself as a prophet—in Luke's Nazareth sermon story, "no prophet is acceptable in his homeland" (4.24), and in the similar stories in Mark 6.4 and Matt 13.57. Luke seems to welcome the title in 7.16 when the crowd says, "A great prophet has arisen among us," and Matthew similarly tells of the crowd saying, "This is the prophet Jesus" (21.11), and says that they "regarded him as a prophet" (21.46). We may pause to speculate that quite likely this was how Jesus thought of himself, at least at first. "Prophet" was a category into which his ministry would fit smoothly, as "the Christ" was not. The language Mark uses implies that Jesus saw himself as the messenger of the later chapters of Isaiah. The coming of the Spirit on him in the baptism story could itself be a corollary of "The Spirit of the Lord is upon me" from Isa 61.1. Perhaps the Isaiah text first suggested his anointing (משׁח, ἔχρισεν), which theme was to have so great a future.

Equally significant is Luke's account of the preaching of the pre-Pauline church. To Cleopas and his companion, Jesus had been a prophet mighty in deed and word (Luke 24.19). In his temple sermon, Peter refers to

---

[2] K. Holl, "Der Kirchenbegriff bei Paulus in seinem Verhältnis zu dem der Urgemeinde" (1921; repr. in *Gesammelte Aufsätze zur Kirchengeschichte;* Tübingen: Mohr, 1933).

[3] M. D. Goulder, "A Poor Man's Christology," *NTS* 45 (1999): 332–48, elaborates Holl's thesis.

[4] I have argued the case against Q in a number of articles, and most fully in an eight-hundred-page commentary, *Luke—A New Paradigm* (JSNTSup 20; Sheffield: Sheffield Academic Press, 1989).

Jesus as "the holy and righteous one . . . the author of life . . . the anointed one appointed for you" (Acts 3.14–15, 20), but the last title is then glossed in 3.22–23: "Moses said, 'A prophet will the Lord your God raise up for you from among your brethren, like me: to him you shall hearken, according to all that he says to you. And it shall be that every soul that does not hearken to that prophet will be rooted out of the people' "—a long citation from Deut 18.15, 18–19. This text is important to Luke, for he quotes it again in Stephen's mouth in Acts 7.37. The church gathers for prayer as the rulers take counsel against the Lord and against his anointed (4.25–26), then specified as "your holy servant Jesus, whom you anointed [4.27, ἔχρισας, following Isa 61.1/Luke 4.18, ἔχρισεν]." Peter similarly identifies Jesus' anointing with his baptism in Acts 10.38: "God anointed Jesus of Nazareth with the Holy Spirit and with power; he went about doing good"; ἔχρισεν . . . πνεύματι once more recalls Isa 61.1.

Luke is a paid-up Pauline: he thinks that Jesus is the Son of God (Luke 1.35), Lord of all (Acts 10.36), and Christ in the highest sense. But he does his best to give his hearers some flavor of the individual heroes of his story. He ascribes a form of justification by faith to Paul in Acts 13.39 and of the cross as atonement in Acts 20.28. And in the early chapters we catch echoes of the church's first groping after a Christology: Jesus was God's servant, his holy and righteous one, his anointed prophet foretold in Deuteronomy and in Isaiah.

Modern writers on Christology have faced a problem. The title "the Christ" is first found in late-first-century Jewish writings *2 Baruch (Syriac Apocalypse)* and *4 Ezra*. Related expressions, "the Messiah of Israel," "the Messiah of the Lord," occur earlier in the Qumran writings[5] and in *Pss. Sol.* 17–18. Where the Messiah has any function in these texts, it is a military and regal one. He is of the line of David, and his calling is to lead Jewish armies, win victories, and establish a Jewish empire of miraculous fruitfulness. But Jesus did none of these things. The Messiah is never foretold as going about doing good and healing. This, then, leaves a conundrum: how did it come about that all Jesus' followers spoke of him as the Christ? An answer is suggested by Luke. Jesus saw himself as anointed with the Spirit at his baptism to proclaim the good news of the kingdom of God. Gradually it dawned on him and his followers that he was not just a prophet but *the* prophet of the end time, the prophet foretold by Moses. This was but a short step to the Anointed One of popular expectation, and so to the ride into Jerusalem to fulfill Zech 9.9, to the cross, and to the heavenly kingship of Christian faith.

---

[5]The best-known passages about the two Messiahs at Qumran are CD 7.18ff.; 19.7ff.; 1QSa 2.12ff.; 1QSb 5.20ff. The (Davidic) Messiah of Israel always takes second place to the (priestly) Messiah of Aaron.

Ferdinand Hahn discusses the problem and concludes that Jesus had in no way acted as a political messiah and that the Jewish authorities accused him of this "quite falsely." Sanders gives a more realistic political scenario: the chief priests took action because Jesus had, in an enacted parable, attacked temple worship and had assumed messianic pretensions by his Palm Sunday ride. This is a more convincing explanation of the authorities' motivation, but it leaves unexplained (i) why Jesus does not aspire to messiahship until the very end of his life and (ii) why the church took up so inappropriate a title for normative use. Also, Jesus' action against the temple is that of a prophet rather than a Messiah, since he cites Isaiah and Jeremiah. Anthony Harvey suggests a first step via Isa 61.1 and this seems rather convincing.[6]

JEWISH-CHRISTIAN PROPHETIC CHRISTOLOGIES

Jewish Christianity has been troublesome to define, but two streams of it have been broadly accepted. The one, already identified by Baur, has left its ideas in the Pseudo-Clementine writings, the *Homilies* and the *Recognitions,* and, underlying them, in the *Preaching of Peter (Kerygmata Petrou),* a supposedly second-century account of Peter's preaching. The other is found in the Jewish-Christian heresies identified by Irenaeus and later Epiphanius. Irenaeus lists a number of heresies in *Haer.* 1, but the only clearly Jewish form of Christianity is the Ebionites (אביונים, the Poor People). He associates these with one Cerinthus, and with the Nicolaitans, about whom he knows little. Epiphanius gives some detail about the Ebionites, including seven citations from their Gospel, which he knew, in *Pan.* 30. In *Pan.* 29 he describes another Jewish-Christian sect, the Nazoraeans, about whom he knows less and who seem to be a compromise with orthodoxy.

Jewish Christians of the *Preaching of Peter* tradition sometimes spoke of Jesus as the Teacher (*Ps.-Clem. Hom.* 2.51.1; 3.12.3; *Ps.-Clem. Rec.* 2.28; 6.5), or the Lord (*Ps.-Clem. Hom.* 11.35.3; *Ps.-Clem. Rec.* 3.5.3), or the Christ (*Ps.-Clem. Rec.* 1.59–60), but the normal title he enjoys is "the Prophet." Peter declines such a title for himself, "being a disciple of the true Prophet, not a prophet" (*Ps.-Clem. Hom.* 18.7.6); Jesus is the Prophet (*Ps.-Clem. Hom.* 3.13.1; 10.4.3; 11.26.2; 11.35.3; 13.14.3; *Ps.-Clem. Rec.* 1.37.2–3), the True Prophet (*Ps.-Clem. Hom.* 3.13.2; 10.3.3; *Ps.-Clem. Rec.* 3.41.4; 5.2.5, 9–10; 6.14), the

---

[6]F. Hahn, *The Titles of Jesus in Christology: Their History in Early Christianity* (trans. H. Knight and G. Ogg; New York: World, 1969), 148–61, here 159; Sanders, *Jesus and Judaism;* A. E. Harvey, *Jesus and the Constraints of History* (London: Duckworth, 1982), 140–42. For a broadly documented account, see W. Horbury, *Jewish Messianism and the Cult of Christ* (London: SCM Press, 1998).

Prophet of Truth (*Ps.-Clem. Hom.* 7.6.2; 11.19.1; 12.29.1; *Ps.-Clem. Rec.* 1.44.5–6), the sole Prophet of Truth (*Ps.-Clem. Hom.* 7.8.1), God's right-hand Prophet (*Ps.-Clem. Hom.* 7.11.3), the infallible Prophet (*Ps.-Clem. Hom.* 11.33.1), the good Prophet (*Ps.-Clem. Rec.* 1.40.1), the One Prophet (*Ps.-Clem. Rec.* 1.50.7; 1.54.5), and other similar phrases.[7] In particular, there are constant references to Jesus as the prophet promised in Deut 18.15, 18 (*Ps.-Clem. Rec.* 1.36.2; 1.39.1; 1.40.4; 1.49.1; 1.54.5; 1.56.2; 1.57; 2.48); he says, "I am he of whom Moses prophesied, saying, 'A prophet will the Lord God raise up for you' " (*Ps.-Clem. Hom.* 3.53.3, cf. *Ps.-Clem. Rec.* 1.43). His signs and wonders are seen as similar to those of Moses and as proving the point (*Ps.-Clem. Rec.* 1.57). Gerhard Friedrich is justified in saying, "In the early Church Jesus was still regarded as a prophet in Jewish Christianity."[8]

According to the *Preaching of Peter* tradition, the True Prophet was not a single person but a power that lighted on a series of people—Adam, Abraham, Isaac, Jacob, Moses, and so forth, and finally Jesus, in whom it came to rest. In his lesser way, Peter is in the same tradition. But the True Prophet is always opposed by the power of false prophecy, and each incarnation of the True Prophet has its pair, its συζυγία: Eve with Adam, Ishmael with Isaac, Esau with Jacob, Aaron with Moses, the Baptist with Jesus. Often the false prophet comes first, the true second. In the same way, Peter has his counter in the false prophet Simon Magus, who is a code for Paul. Thus God has never been left without a witness. An account is given of a singular element in the group's creed, the refusal of sacrifices. This can be credited to Adam, who lived as a vegetarian, and explained by the Moses-Aaron syzygy: it was Aaron, the archpriest, who carried the responsibility for the sacrificial system, which Moses only condoned for fear of worse.[9]

The situation from which the *Preaching of Peter* comes is to be inferred from its polemics. It is embattled against followers of the Baptist, who claimed that he was the True Prophet, a claim we find echoed in John 1.21 and in the Fourth Gospel more generally. It is also embattled against the Gentile church, as is shown by its covert attacks on Paul; they are *covert* attacks, for Paul has to be camouflaged as Simon Magus. The assault on sacrifices probably arises from the group's becoming vegetarian, perhaps because of the uncertainties of meat outside Palestine. But such teachings did not draw the wrath of heresiologists. The *Preaching of Peter* Christians do not

---

[7]See G. Friedrich, "προφήτης," *TDNT* 6:781–861.

[8]Ibid., 6:858.

[9]O. Cullmann, *The Christology of the New Testament* (rev. ed.; trans. S. G. Guthrie and C. A. M. Hall; Philadelphia: Westminster, 1963), 38–42; G. Strecker, *Das Judenchristentum in den Pseudoklementinen* (TUGAL 70; Berlin: Akademie-Verlag, 1958); H. J. Schoeps, *Theologie und Geschichte des Judenchristentums* (Tübingen: Mohr, 1949).

feature in Irenaeus and were probably assimilated into the Great Church with time.[10]

There was, however, a second group of Jewish Christians who did make the heresy catalogues, the Ebionites. We first hear of them in Irenaeus, *Haer.* 1.26.2:

> They use the Gospel according to Matthew only, and repudiate the Apostle Paul, maintaining that he was an apostate from the Law. As to the prophetical writings, they endeavour to expound them in a somewhat singular manner: they practise circumcision, persevere in the observance of those customs which are enjoined by the Law, and are so Judaic in their style of life that they even adore Jerusalem as if it were the house of God. (trans. W. Harvey, *Ante-Nicene Fathers*)

We have here unquestionably a group of Jewish Christians—indeed the only group in Irenaeus for which such evidence is offered. The practice of circumcision and other customs prescribed by the law are normal Judaism; prayer toward Jerusalem is found among the pious (Dan 6.10; Tob 3.11; Ps 28.2; 138.2; 1 Kgs 8.48); Matthew is the most Jewish of the Gospels; and Paul's reservations about the law, especially in Galatians, may certainly be read as apostasy. The somewhat singular exposition of the prophets only means that it differs from that normal in Gentile Christendom.

Irenaeus adds that "their opinions with respect to the Lord are similar to those of Cerinthus and Carpocrates." Cerinthus's Christology is presented in the previous paragraph, *Haer.* 1.26.1:

> He represented Jesus as not having been born of a virgin; he was the son of Joseph and Mary, conceived like the rest of mankind, and excelled mankind in justice, prudence and wisdom. And after his baptism Christ entered into him in the form of a dove from the highest power; and then he proclaimed the unknown Father, and performed miracles. In the end the power recalled Christ from Jesus, and Jesus suffered and rose again, while Christ continued untouched by suffering, as a spiritual being. (Author's translation)

This Cerinthian-Ebionite position is a striking departure from orthodoxy. First, it maintains a natural conception for Jesus, in defiance of the account in Matt 1. Hence Jesus is not the Son of God by his birth but is possessed by a heavenly power, Christ, which "entered him" after his baptism, in view of his great virtue and wisdom. Jesus is thus aligned with the prophets upon whom the word of the Lord came—Ezekiel, for example, who saw the heavens opened by the River Chebar and who was carried by the Spirit hither and thither. Jesus was now able to proclaim "the unknown Father," like the prophets who were privileged to stand in the divine council. And he could perform miracles, as the prophets Elijah and Elisha could,

---

[10]Cullmann, *Christology*, 42.

and Moses before them. But we notice a humbler origin for Jesus' ministry than that supposed in our NT: "Christ" is sent by "the highest power" (αὐθεντίας) rather than by God ("the unknown Father").

Jesus' possession by the heavenly Christ is for a limited period only; it begins after the baptism and ends before the passion. As a spiritual being, Christ could not suffer; hence, Jesus was left to suffer on the cross on his own. The Ebionites included Jesus' resurrection in their creed, no doubt from tradition; all the apostles, including Peter and James, had witnessed to it, so it was firmly embedded in the community's belief. There are prophetic figures in Judaism who are in heaven: Moses, Isaiah by his assumption, Jeremiah (2 Macc 15.13–16). But the limited period of inspiration is the normal prophetic experience—a moment of dramatic call followed by a series of revelations and signs.

Our main amplification of Irenaeus's account comes from Epiphanius, two centuries later. Epiphanius had access to a Gospel used by some Ebionites in his time, called by him the *Gospel of the Hebrews* (Epiphanius, *Pan.* 30.13.4) but usually referred to as the *Gospel of the Ebionites*. It did not open with any equivalent to Matt 1–2 but with the ministry of the Baptist.[11] Its account of Jesus' baptism is as follows:

> And when the people were baptized, Jesus too came and was baptized by John. And when he came up from the water, the heavens were opened and he saw the Holy Spirit in the form of a dove, coming down and entering him. And there was a voice from heaven saying, You are my beloved Son, in you I am well pleased, and again, Today I have begotten you. (*Gos. Eb.* 4; Epiphanius, *Pan.* 30.13.7)

This account supports Irenaeus's report on Ebionite doctrine: Jesus is not conceived as Son of God but becomes such upon his baptism. This follows from the omission of any birth narrative; from the phrase "entering him" (εἰσελθόντα εἰς αὐτόν), implying possession by the heavenly power; and from the addition of the phrase from Ps 2.7, "Today . . ." In two other ways, however, the passage contradicts Irenaeus. Its wording does not follow Matthew alone but is a compound of the three synoptic versions with additions, even though Epiphanius says the Gospel "is called according to Matthew,"[12] and the possessing power is not "Christ" but "the Holy Spirit."

No doubt, we should allow for development over time and for variety among different Ebionite communities. It would be natural to think that the use of the Jewish Matthew preceded that of a combination of details. But we

---

[11]Epiphanius, *Pan.* 30.13.6, on the baptism, opens, "And the beginning of their Gospel runs . . ."

[12]Epiphanius, *Pan.* 30.13.2; but Epiphanius may have inserted this from his knowledge of Irenaeus.

may think that the *Gospel of the Ebionites* tradition of the Holy Spirit is older than the Irenaean power, "Christ." It is the Spirit that features in the possession of OT prophets, and "Christ" is not found as the name of a heavenly power before the gnostics of the second century.[13] It could have arisen among Gentile converts to Jewish Christianity from the widespread use of the combination "Jesus Christ."

A further stress in the *Gospel of the Ebionites* is its vegetarianism. In the Gospels John the Baptist eats locusts (ἀκρίδες), but in *Gos. Eb.* 2 (Epiphanius, *Pan.* 30.13.4–5) these become cakes (ἐγκρίδες). Jesus is said to have proclaimed, "I am come to do away with sacrifices, and if ye cease not from sacrificing, the wrath of God will not cease from you" (*Pan.* 30.16.5). When the disciples ask about preparing the Passover, Jesus replies, "Do I desire at this Passover to eat flesh with you?" (*Pan.* 30.22.4).[14]

We seem thus to have two branches of Jewish Christianity, which are linked by two common features, vegetarianism and a prophetic Christology. The vegetarian emphasis is new, being largely absent from Judaism; but it is implied in Rom 14 as a practice of Jewish Christians at Rome. But the prophetic Christology is a strong theme in Acts 1–12 and is easily understood from a Jewish matrix. It has been developed in two slightly different directions in the two branches. For the *Preaching of Peter,* Jesus was the prophet like Moses promised in Deut 18, the ultimate prophet, but space has been made for the same prophetic power to have been incarnated in a line of earlier prophets, from Adam on. This power has now come to rest in Jesus. We have no indication that such a development was known to the Ebionites, although their "singular exposition of the prophets" could mean that. For them the inspiration of Jesus by the Spirit, and soon by "Christ," has been thought over and elaborated: the coming and departure of the heavenly power have been specified, with its effects in preaching and miracle, and a clear line has been drawn between the earthly Jesus and the celestial possessing power.

The new missionaries of II,10–13 proclaim themselves Hebrews, Israelites, the seed of Abraham, and we have seen reasons for thinking that they are successors to the Petrine party of I,1.12. If, then, we have a prophetic Christology in the primitive Jerusalem church and a prophetic Christology in two differing branches of second-century Jewish Christianity, it is

---

[13]Christ is among the first syzygies of the Barbelo gnostics, described in Irenaeus, *Haer.* 1.29, and in the *Apocryphon of John.*

[14]For more detail on the Ebionites, see M. D. Goulder, "The Jewish-Christian Mission, 30–130," *ANRW* 2:26.3, 1979–2037; "Poor Man's Christology," which gives fuller details of Epiphanius's account of the Ebionites; and "Ignatius' 'Docetists,'" *VC* 53 (1999): 16–30, which argues that the opposition faced by Ignatius in the twelfth decade in Asia were Ebionites.

proper to inquire whether, among the Jewish-Christian opposition in Corinth also, there are hints of a prophetic Christology.

THE NEW MISSIONARIES' CHRISTOLOGY IN CORINTHIANS

An unresolved enigma has been the fourth slogan of I,1.12, Ἐγὼ δὲ
Χριστοῦ. The first three slogans proclaim loyalty to the leaders of the suc-
cessive missions to the city, and so three parties, but a Christ party would be
different, and in the discussion in I,3–4, such seems to disappear. First Corinthians 3.22–23 runs, "Whether Paul or Apollos or Cephas, or the world
. . . all are yours, and you are Christ's, and Christ is God's," as if there were
three parties, though a fourth is here imaginable. But 4.6 speaks clearly of
those who are puffed up for the one (Cephas) against the other (Paul)—a
confrontation that Paul smoothes over by "transforming" it on to himself
and Apollos.

So there were three groups. But Paul could not have made up the
fourth slogan, since the Corinthians knew whether it was in use or not. It
would make sense if the Petrines, being Jewish Christians, held a Christology similar to Irenaeus's Ebionites. They could have believed in a human
Jesus possessed for a crucial period by a divine Christ; what would be dis-
tinctive, then, in their creed would be a faith in "Christ," and some of
them might be proud to proclaim their loyalty to him, "I am of Christ."
There would be an element of triumphalism in the slogan—"I am not just
loyal to some human missionary: I am loyal to Christ." We would have a
parallel in one of the early gnostic sects, which called itself after another
heavenly power, the supposed image of the ultimate god, Barbelo (Irenaeus,
Haer. 1.29).

Such a profession of loyalty to Christ as the monopoly of a Jewish-
Christian group seems to reappear in II,10.7. Paul has been heavily criticized by the new missionaries: he throws his weight about when he is a few
hundred miles away; he changes his plans all the time, as he walks according to the flesh. The apostle is angry; he has powerful spiritual weapons for
the overthrow of strongholds—arguments—and of all the pride that lifts itself against the knowledge of God, and he takes every thought prisoner
(10.4–5). This then leads to 10.7: "If anyone has confidence in himself that
he is of Christ (Χριστοῦ εἶναι), let him turn this over again with himself, that
as he is of Christ, so too are we."

It is difficult to believe that Corinthian Christians could ever have denied, or forgotten, that Paul was a Christian in the normal sense of the word.
The wording sounds more like the party rivalries of I,1–4. Now people
"have confidence" (πέποιθεν) that they are of Christ, and this leads into a
long assault on "boasting" (καυχᾶσθαι, II,10.8–12.13), with the citing of Jer
9.24, ὁ καυχώμενος ἐν κυρίῳ καυχάσθω (10.17). We had the same boasting

and being puffed up (φυσιοῦσθαι) in I,3.21; 4.6–8, where people boasted of being Petrine Christians, and in I,1.31 the same verse was cited from Jeremiah. We had the same response, too. Here Paul will not allow the term Χριστοῦ to be monopolized by one group: "If anyone is confident in himself that he is of Christ . . . so are we"—of course in a different, Pauline sense. He said something very similar in I,3.22–23, "Whether Paul or Apollos or Cephas . . . all is yours, and you are Χριστοῦ"; all three groups are "of Christ," not just one that has taken over the name.

The new missionaries not only attack Paul (II,10.1–3); they also advocate ideas of their own, notions (λογισμούς), arrogance (ὕψωμα) lifting itself against the knowledge of God, thoughts (νόημα) that must be taken prisoner. The second phrase probably reflects the claims to γνῶσις that featured so largely in 1 Corinthians (cf. I,8), but the λογισμοί and ὕψωμα remain undefined. But νοήματα recurs in II,11.3, where Paul fears that "your νοήματα be corrupted from the simplicity that is toward Christ," and it is likely that the λογισμοί and the ὕψωμα are the corrupting agents of the following verse, the proclamation of "another Jesus," "a different gospel," "a different spirit." Since the last-named is associated with the claims to γνῶσις in 1 Corinthians, we may think that the λογισμοί were about Jesus and the gospel.

The Ebionites proclaimed a different Jesus from that of the Pauline gospel. For all its problems, the Pauline Jesus-Christ was a real person, the same from birth to death, with a functioning personality, free and able to obey or disobey the divine will. The Ebionite Jesus was an unreal figure. For thirty years or so he had been a normal man, exceptional in his virtue and wisdom, and he had been the same, gasping to an agonized death, in his last hours. For the length of his ministry, however, he had been like a medium possessed by a "control" from another world, and his death could achieve nothing, since he must be God's Son to stand and plead effectively for the redemption of Christians. So a proto-Ebionite opposition gives good sense to the whole context of II,10–11 and to I,1.12. The Petrines believed that Jesus was a prophet, possessed like the prophets of old by the Spirit or by a spirit called Christ. They therefore tended to speak of themselves as "of Christ" when rivalries arose with other Christian groups, since they alone believed in a heavenly spirit, "Christ," who was Jesus' control. Paul could then properly say that they "proclaimed another Jesus."

It is likely that the same Christology underlies the Petrine missionaries' claims in II,11.22–23 to be Hebrews, Israelites, the seed of Abraham, διάκονοι Χριστοῦ. These predicates are theologically aggressive. The missionaries are not just Jewish ('Ιουδαῖοι) but belong to the elect people of God, which Gentile Christians need to join. They are authorized "ministers of Christ," the spiritual power that possessed Jesus through his ministry, and neither Paul nor Apollos nor any other self-appointed preacher has any right to such a title. People like them do not even believe in Christ's existence independently of Jesus. The Petrines do not speak of themselves here as "authorized ministers of Christ," in contrast with the unauthorized Paul; they are the only ones there are. Again Paul responds as he did in I,3.22–23 and II,10.7, quietly changing the definition: "Are they 'ministers of Christ'? I speak as one out of his wits, I am more" (II,11.23).

Pauline and Jerusalem Christians could be at one in their reverence for Jesus Christ, who had proclaimed and instituted the kingdom of God and in whose Spirit they lived a transformed life. It was not necessary for any christological tensions to arise in their early interactions. There were enough problems over the law and Paul's acceptance as an apostle. But the cracks were deep, and it was inevitable that they would soon become noticed. For, fundamentally, Paulines believed that Jesus Christ was a divine being, while Jerusalem Christians saw Jesus as a human being, a prophet, temporarily possessed by Christ, his divine control.

~ 15 ~

ANOTHER JESUS: II

FIRST CORINTHIANS 12.1–3

THE SPARK first flew at a gathering of the Corinthian church one Saturday night. The supper is over, and the atmosphere may be gauged by reading I,12 and 14. Different members are simultaneously speaking in tongues or prophesying, delivering messages from the Spirit. Others are interpreting the glossolalia as best they can or attempting to argue the meaning of some Scripture. The tensions rise as frustrations increase. The noise gets louder as people compete for audibility, and there are feelings of resentment as those converted by a different mission seize the floor.[1]

Eventually there is a cry from a Pauline convert, κύριος Ἰησοῦς, "Jesus is Lord"; the predicate is the familiar name of God in the LXX, the name that is above every name and that was bestowed on Jesus Christ by the Father in token of his self-emptying, his life and death of obedience. Very likely the cry is taken up by a group of like-minded Paulines, feeling excluded by the prolix and disordered babel around them, a sense aggravated by the awareness that many of the contributors are the new Petrine members and, worse, women. But to the Petrines such a cry is blasphemous. Jesus was a normal human being, a prophet like one of the old prophets. Elijah was not Yahweh, and it would be blasphemy to speak of him as such. And so one of the Petrines calls out in the Spirit, ἀνάθεμα Ἰησοῦς, "Damn Jesus! To hell with Jesus!" The inspired speaker is not hostile to Jesus, a revered prophet, but only to claims that he is divine. An innovative theologian

---

[1] I was present some time ago at a black Pentecostal church service that was being televised. Here the church was well disciplined, with an excellent minister (chief apostle), and no division known to me. But the presence of the cameras acted to raise the temperature. The prophetesses spoke first in English, but soon the Spirit prophesied in Fanti, and the cameras were trundled down the aisle to enable the viewer to enter the experience more closely. Their approach caused the prophetess to speak faster and faster, and at considerable length, and one could not but sense some impatience among the male prophets, who normally held center stage on these occasions. It was easy to think of I,14.

of modern times, told that "the bishop will not like this," might feel moved to say, "Damn the bishop!" or some such hasty impropriety.

The incident is a scandal to the Paulines and was no doubt reported to Paul by Chloe's party, even if it was not in the Corinthian letter. But the apostle, a σοφὸς ἀρχιτέκτων, knows better than to make a great fuss over a few unhappy words uttered in the heat of the moment under so-called inspiration. Besides, he will achieve nothing by severity. The Petrines think his disciples are blasphemous, just as he thinks the Petrines are. A heavy hand will merely lead to confrontation and, worse, division.

The Corinthians' letter has asked his advice about spiritual things, πνευματικά, by which they mean spiritual gifts, χαρίσματα. Paul is intent to downplay these colorful, personal gifts and to stress that all true Christians have the Spirit. The last clause in his introduction of the subject runs, "No one can say, 'Jesus is Lord,' except in the Holy Spirit." He then breaks off to discuss the place of the various χαρίσματα (12.4–31a) before pointing to a still more excellent way, attainable by all true believers—love.

Paul, however, needs to write carefully, of *true* Christians, because he has just been told of an instance where the inspiration was, in his view, certainly not from the Holy Spirit. So he begins with his somewhat standard phrasing, περὶ δέ . . . οἴδαμεν . . . (8.1, 4), . . . οὐ θέλω ὑμᾶς ἀγνοεῖν . . . (10.1). As Gentile converts, they have no experience of the living, speaking God, so the "common knowledge" (οἴδατε) from which he can start the argument is that "when you were Gentiles, you were seduced to voiceless idols, however you were led"—to Isis, Mithras, or whomever. The apostle is a little nervous on so delicate a subject, and his syntax lapses somewhat, omitting a second ἦτε perhaps. Since they have never encountered the God who speaks in his Spirit, Paul needs to make them understand (διὸ γνωρίζω ὑμῖν) one basic criterion for distinguishing the Holy Spirit from other spirits: "no one speaking in the Spirit of God says 'Damn Jesus.' " He carefully does not say, "No one holding a prophetic Christology can be in the Spirit." It is only a public attack on the Pauline doctrine that shows the inspiration to be demonic. Arguments from Scripture, messages from the angels, miracles, tongues, and the rest are all from God, whichever party people come from, and everyone in the church is in the Holy Spirit if they can say, "Jesus is Lord."

This seems to give a plausible account of both the implied incident and Paul's handling of it. In the history of exegesis, it has been most common to treat the anathema clause as stemming from a real incident and as offering a criterion for the activity of the Spirit.[2] The most common criticisms have been the following:

---

[2]J. S. Vos, "Das Rätsel von I Kor 12:1–3," *NovT* 35 (1993): 251–69, here 252–56.

Ecstasy. The text is often explained in terms of "ecstasy," but ecstasy is not mentioned either for the former idol worship or for the scene in the church at Corinth. Ecstasy is often spoken of rather loosely, but I have not referred to it; the atmosphere of excited disorder is implied in ch. 14. The speakers are clearly not in a trance, as they are speaking Greek suited to a believable context.[3]

ἀνάθεμα 'Ιησοῦς. It is difficult to believe that any Christian would ever say ἀνάθεμα 'Ιησοῦς, or that Paul would need to give instruction about such a thing, or that if such words were spoken, he would have thought it adequate to deal with them in a single sentence. But such a scenario as I have described above seems easily credible: the Pauline Christology, ascribing divinity to Jesus, must have seemed blasphemous to anyone holding a prophetic view. The acceptance of inspiration by superhuman spirits, with an atmosphere of indiscipline, frustration, and resentment, may lead easily to aggressive cries. Throughout 1 Corinthians, Paul avoids confrontation with the Petrines, and it was sensible of him to do the same here. He knows that no Christian really wishes to speak ill of Jesus, and he ignores the outburst, like a wise parent ignoring swearwords brought home by a schoolchild.[4] Also to be noted is the parallel passage in 1 John 4.1–3, where there are spirits not from God speaking in Christian worship through false prophets, who do not confess Jesus.

The Activity of the Holy Spirit. If 12.2–3 is treated as offering a criterion for the activity of the Holy Spirit, it does not lead on into the argument following in the rest of the chapter. This is indeed so, but it does link on to the scandals at the Eucharist in ch. 11. Furthermore, the passage makes a central point of Paul's concern before he deals with the Corinthians' interests: *all* true Christians can speak in the Spirit, and they do so when they say, "Jesus is Lord." We find the same concern in his introduction of ἀντιλήμψεις and κυβερνήσεις into the list of gifts (12.28, cf. Rom 12.6–8); but above all, it prepares the ground for ch. 13 on faith, hope, and supremely, ἀγάπη, fruits of the Spirit borne by all true Christians.[5]

---

[3]T. Callan, "Prophecy and Ecstasy in Greco-Roman Religion and I Corinthians," *NovT* 27 (1985): 125–40, distinguishes carefully between ecstatic, entranced religious experience and non-trance prophecy; he concludes that prophecy in chs. 12–14 was non-ecstatic.

[4]Norbert Brox, "ΑΝΑΘΕΜΑ ΙΗΣΟΥΣ. 1 COR. 12:3," *BZ* 12 (1968): 103–11, follows Walter Schmithals in citing the Ophites in Origen, *Cels.* 6.28, as having required their initiates to curse Jesus, but the force of this passage has been disputed.

[5]T. Holtz, "Das Kennzeichen des Geistes: I Kor 12:1–3," *NTS* 18 (1972): 365–76, similarly sets 12.1–3 in the broader context of chs. 12–14.

Hitherto a plausible scenario has been lacking, of the kind offered by the Ebionite Christology, and this has resulted in numerous suggestions criticized by Vos, Holtz, and others. The closest proposals have been of gnostic oppositions who again divided a heavenly Christ,[6] or Sophia,[7] from the earthly Jesus. But definitions of Gnosticism have become more strict, and it is not viable to equate the γνῶσις of the Corinthian letters with the systems of the second century. Theories that make the anathema clause hypothetical or rhetorical seem to reduce it to banality. Those setting the words in contexts of the Jewish synagogue, or the Roman demand for recantation, or of Paul's early life, strip them from their context in the letter, where chs. 11–14 are concerned with the conduct of Christian worship. Vos turns 12.3 into a positive form, "Every charismatic confesses the same Lord," but he underplays the link of thought between ἄφωνα and λαλῶν and imports an unnecessary missing link between vv. 2 and 3.

FIRST CORINTHIANS 16.21–24

We find a surprising echo of the anathema clause in the last verses of the letter: "The greeting of Paul in my own hand. If anyone does not love the Lord, let him be cursed (ἤτω ἀνάθεμα). Marana tha. The grace of the Lord Jesus be with you. My love be with all of you in Christ Jesus." Even for so businesslike a correspondent as Paul, this seems a little stark. The closest parallel, the last verses of Galatians, 6.11–18, suggests that, pen in hand, the apostle tends to the telegraphic and authoritarian, but the contiguity of blessing and curse in so few final words is unique.

What have the people done who do not "love the Lord," that Paul should curse them? Perhaps he is thinking of the man living with his father's wife, whose flesh is to be destroyed, and those whose selfishness subverts the church's unity at the Eucharist, and those whose idolatry excludes them from the kingdom. But the context raises hesitations. Why is the curse followed immediately by a prayer in Aramaic for the Lord to come?

The repetition of κύριος in the context of the ἀνάθεμα, "does not love the Lord, . . . [Our Lord, come!] The grace of the Lord Jesus," suggests that we have an echo of 12.3. There the true Christian confessed Jesus as Lord and spoke in the Holy Spirit as he or she did so. Anyone saying ἀνάθεμα Ἰησοῦς was not speaking in the Spirit of God at all. Paul similarly says of those who proclaim a different gospel from his own in Gal 1.8, ἀνάθεμα ἔστω. So it might well be that those in mind who do not love the Lord are especially those who do not accept that Jesus is Lord, that the "grace of the

[6]Schmithals, *Die Gnose;* Brox, "ΑΝΑΘΕΜΑ."
[7]Wilckens, *Weisheit; TDNT* 7:465–528.

Lord Jesus" is accordingly restricted to those who do, and that anyone who cursed Jesus clearly did not love him and deserved to suffer the same fate.

Such a line of thought would then explain the puzzling *Marana tha*. A major error of the Petrines was their fantasy that the kingdom of God had arrived already (4.8–20), with the consequent loss of concern for the future, when the Lord would come (4.5). This unreal world, where the believer is already reigning, is glorified, and has transcended death, caused a crisis at Thessalonica (1 Thess 4.13–18) and produced such statements of unbelief in the resurrection of Christians as we find in I,15.12, 35. But the first disciples believed in the resurrection of Jesus (15.5–11) and prayed in their own language, "Our lord, come," *Marana tha*. Paul, then, is invoking an old Petrine formula to gloss over a major crack in the foundations. As is often observed, the vocative "Lord" (*mar* [Aramaic], κύριε) is not the same as the nominative. Jesus is frequently addressed as κύριε in Matthew and Luke without the least suggestion of his divinity, but when Luke refers to him as ὁ κύριος, something different has happened. So here. Jerusalem Christians had hoped for Jesus' coming within a brief period and had invoked him, *Marana tha!*, but with no more sense of worshiping him as divine than an instructed Catholic has who prays to St. Anthony or to the Virgin Mary. But Paul does believe Jesus to be divine. The wise master builder spreads a little gravel over the nasty fissure: perhaps the simple will not notice that *Lord* is being used in two quite different senses.

In this way we have an understandable sequence of thought. Underlying the lapses of conduct at Corinth lay a false gospel with a false Christology. This led Petrines in moments of heady excitement to cry out ἀνάθεμα Ἰησοῦς, and although Paul wisely passes over the scandal briefly in 12.3, he is prepared to curse the cursers in 16.22, as he cursed the false missionaries in Gal 1.8. The root of their trouble was that they would not confess Jesus as divine Lord. They did not love the Lord, and the grace of the Lord was not for them. The best hope was an appeal to the ambiguity of the old Jerusalem prayer "Our Lord, come"; lost sheep need to be led by the nose.

First Corinthians 8.6

Twice in 1 Corinthians Paul refers to the preexistence of Christ: once in 10.4, "the rock that followed them was Christ," and once in 8.6. The rock text reveals little about the christological controversy, but the passage in ch. 8 is more helpful.

The opposition have justified eating εἰδωλόθυτα on the ground that "there is no idol in the world and that there is no God but one" (8.4). Paul cannot but agree with this; although there are many so-called gods and lords, "yet to us there is one God, the Father, from whom is the universe and we for him, and one Lord, Jesus Christ, through whom is the universe and

we through him" (8.6). The verse is often alleged to be a pre-Pauline formula, but the only part of it that was clearly in circulation before Paul was
the εἷς θεός (Deut 6.4, etc.; familiar to every Jew from recital in the Shema).
There is a similar praise of God in Rom 11.36, ἐξ αὐτοῦ καὶ δι' αὐτοῦ καὶ
εἰς αὐτὸν τὰ πάντα, and Paul speaks of God as the end of all things in
I,15.28. The pairing of God the Father and the Lord Jesus Christ stands at
the head of several of Paul's letters (1 Thess 1.1; Gal 1.3; II,1.2; Phil 1.2;
Phlm 3), and all Christian action is εἰς Χριστόν in Phlm 6.

The verse fits its context in a way not always noticed. Paul cannot but
agree with the Petrines that there is one God who has made the universe
from nothing (Gen 1) and who is the goal of the lives of Christians. From this
it follows that "the earth is the Lord's and its fullness"—nothing is unclean
(I,10.26). But what, then, of the corollary that Christians may therefore eat
idol food? This is the last thing Paul believes; he thinks Christians should
flee from idols lest they partake of the table of demons (10.14–22). But how
is he to avoid the exemplary logic of 8.4: heathen gods do not exist, so what
is wrong with idol food? The trouble is the offense caused to the conscience
of lately heathen converts, he replies, on account of whom (δι' ὅν) Christ
died. So the statement about God the Father, which seems to concede the
purity of all food, is balanced by the parallel statement about Christ. Everything came into existence through him (δι' οὗ), and we exist for him. Naturally, we shall respect the needs of the fellow believer on account of whom
he died. Once again there has been some fast footwork: if the preposition
διά is the same, who cares if the relative pronoun has moved into the accusa-
tive case?

Most commentators assert that 8.6, or at least its second clause, is "a
formula Paul had used before" (Barrett), "a Christian confession . . . the basis
of the old Roman creed" (Conzelmann), "an early Christian formula"
(Schrage).[8] Little evidence is offered for these claims, which rest upon the
apparent irrelevance of 8.6b and on the poetry-like balance of the clauses,
so often invoked to justify speculations on pre-Pauline hymns. Conzelmann's comment that the language is not Pauline is surprising in view of the
parallels above, which Fee cites; the latter thinks the verse is "probably a
Pauline construct."[9]

The verse, then, is Paul's own writing, fresh for the context; and it
gives a helpful hint that, from the beginning, his Christology was derived
from speculations on Gen 1. We hear from Philo of "God's first-born, who
holds the eldership among the angels, their ruler as it were; and many
names are his, for he is called Beginning, and the Name of God, and his

---

[8]Barrett, *First Epistle,* 192; Conzelmann, *1 Corinthians,* 143–44; Schrage, *Der
erste Brief,* 2:241.

[9]Conzelmann, *1 Corinthians,* 144 n. 86; Fee, *First Epistle,* 374.

Word, and the Man after his Image" (*Conf.* 146), and of the Wisdom that has many names, including Beginning and Image (*Leg.* 1.43). So Paul's δι' οὗ is based on Gen 1.26, בצלמנו, "through our image,"[10] or Gen 1.1, בראשית, "through Beginning" (taken to be the name of the angel of creation), to whom God said, "Let us make man." Here is the origin of the Pauline Christology of II,4.4, "the gospel of the glory of Christ, ὅς ἐστιν εἰκὼν τοῦ θεοῦ."

Paul's was not a static Christology in the way that Philo's angelology was: his Christ was promoted. Philippians 2.6–11 tells the story. Christ was at first "in the form of God," like the Wisdom, the Image, the Glory, the Word and the rest, "equal to God." But he emptied himself of such divine powers, humbled himself in the incarnation, was obedient to death, death on a cross. Because of such self-giving, God exalted him and gave him the name Lord, κύριος, which is above every name, and all creatures now kneel in worship to him—angels, humans, and demons. Christ Jesus was thus, in some sense, an extension of God's being from the beginning but is now given divine honors, with the divine name from the Greek Bible, and universal adoration.

It is often thought that the Philippian Christology is at odds with another "pre-Pauline" text in Rom 1.3–4. But there is no need to think that Paul contradicted himself on so central a matter, with or without the citation of an alien formula. The gospel of God is about "his Son who was born of the seed of David according to the flesh" (Rom 1.3); but Rom 8.3 says that "God sent his own Son in the likeness of sinful flesh." Paul sees Christ as God's Son from eternity; God sent him into the world. Paul had not thought about Isa 7.14 and the virginal conception, and in any case, there were promises in Samuel and the Psalms about an anointed one of the seed of David. He does not speculate about the mystery of the mode of God's action, which is just as well, as theologians still dispute it.

Philippians 2.9 says that God "highly exalted" (ὑπερύψωσεν) Christ, rather than the normal "raised," because Paul is associating the resurrection with the awarding of the divine name κύριος and the worship by angelic and demonic powers, as well as humans. But Rom 1.4 is concerned with this world only: "who was defined as Son of God in power according to the spirit of sanctification by the resurrection from the dead, Jesus Christ our Lord." It was the resurrection/exaltation that declared Christ to be κύριος in both passages, to be God's Son, which, unknown to us, he had been from the beginning. Now, however, he is Son of God ἐν δυνάμει and wields majestic power. The incarnation involved him in our fleshly world; he was born κατὰ σάρκα, sent in the likeness σαρκὸς ἁμαρτίας. The resurrection took him back into the spiritual world κατὰ πνεῦμα. Paul wishes to stress the ethical

---

[10]So Barrett, *First Epistle,* 192, following Schlatter.

consequences of faith in the resurrection, as in Rom 8.4–11, so he speaks not of the Holy Spirit, πνεῦμα ἅγιον, as he normally does, but of the spirit of sanctification, πνεῦμα ἁγιωσύνης.

Paul is not always a clear thinker, and it might be that he was in a fog over his Christology or that he was tactfully citing someone else's view in Rom 1.3–4. But the text does not compel us to that conclusion, and when the matter is in doubt, the exegete may incline to charity.

We must be cautious in adducing the evidence of Colossians. Many scholars do not think Paul wrote the letter, and his opinions might have changed if he did. But it cannot be excluded from the discussion. As already observed, it is written to oppose Jewish-Christian demands (pp. 69–71), with references to σοφία, and if it is post-Pauline, its date is likely to be early. Furthermore, its Christology is dramatically close to that of the Corinthian letters. The phrase ὅς ἐστιν εἰκὼν τοῦ θεοῦ of II,4.4 recurs in Col 1.15. The δι' οὗ τὰ πάντα of I,8.6 is echoed by the ἐν αὐτῷ ἐκτίσθη τὰ πάντα . . . τὰ πάντα δι' αὐτοῦ καὶ εἰς αὐτὸν ἔκτισται of Col 1.16. The underlying references in Gen 1 to בראשית and בצלמנו, "through whom" (Hebrew *b*ᵉ) God created the universe, Philo's archangel who is called Beginning and Image, are now expounded in full. Christ is the firstborn of all creation, before all things, the head (ראש) of the body, the church, the beginning (ἀρχή), the firstborn from the dead. Whoever wrote Col 1.15–20 seems to have understood the implications of the Corinthian Christology texts, I,8.6 and II,4.4.

Our interest, however, is not only in Paul's Christology but in that of his Jewish-Christian opponents, and here Colossians is suggestive. There is an insistent use of πάντα, often in association with the angelic powers, and the latter are repeatedly said to be subject to Christ, whether as created through him or as overcome in the cross:

> He is the firstborn of *all* creation, for in him *all things in heaven* and on earth were created, things visible *and invisible, whether thrones or dominions or rulers or powers—all things* have been created through him and for him. He himself is before *all things,* and in him *all things* hold together . . . that he might have the first place in *all things.* For in him *all* the fullness of God was pleased to dwell, and through him God was pleased to reconcile to himself *all things,* whether on earth or *in heaven,* by making peace through the blood of his cross. (1.15–20)

> See to it that no one takes you captive . . . according to *the elemental spirits of the world* and not according to Christ. For in him *all* the fullness of the Godhead dwells bodily, and you have come to fullness in him, who is the head of *all rule and authority.* . . . He divested himself of *the rulers and authorities, and made a public show of them, triumphing over them in* [the cross]. (2.8–10, 15)

The issue is partly about the law, over which the στοιχεῖα are understood to preside (2.8, 20), but it is also about Christology (1.19; 2.9), by means of which Paul means to undercut the demand for law observance. For him all the fullness (πᾶν τὸ πλήρωμα) of the Godhead took its dwelling in Christ physically (σωματικῶς); Paul believed in the incarnation. But his opponents, it would seem, did not believe in the incarnation. They had some more elaborate system in which the heavenly powers were involved—στοιχεῖα, θρόνοι, κυριότητες, ἀρχαί, ἐξουσίαι. He is so insistent that these powers owed their existence (and their humiliated reconciliation) to Christ that we are driven to suspect that Jewish Christians held an opposed position, with Christ as an inferior power, not the Image/Beginning of Gen 1.1, 26.

How, then, may we envisage their Christology? As Jews, they are heirs to the same exegesis of Gen 1 that we find in Philo and in Paul himself, so they would have seen God's agent in creation as Philo's "ruler of the angels, so to speak" (*Conf.* 146), the power of many names, רֵאשִׁית, צֶלֶם, and perhaps, so often associated with εἰκών in Paul, δόξα, כָּבוֹד. The Petrines were emphatic on the Glory in II,3: the law was delivered to Moses by the Glory, and they themselves had been privileged to see the Glory, which transformed them as it had him. Paul is anxious to trump this ace. The ministry of the Spirit excels in glory; in the gospel we behold the glory of the Lord and are transformed into the same image from glory to glory; the gospel is of the glory of Christ, who is the image of God. In I,2.8 the rulers of this age in their ignorance crucified the Lord of glory. Later works in the NT seem to persist in the same battle. The Word became flesh, and we beheld his glory; Isaiah saw Christ's glory; in Ephesians, much was done to the praise of Christ's glory.

If, then, in Jewish-Christian eyes, Christ was not the Glory/Image/ Beginning, he must have been one of the lesser powers in the πλήρωμα, and we may think this to be implied by Paul's repeated assertion that all the πλήρωμα of the Godhead was present in Jesus. Christ would have been one of the thrones, dominions, principalities, and powers against whom Col 1.15–20 polemicizes, and with so many categories from which to choose, imagination may have free play. Furthermore, Paul's stress on the bodiliness of his Christology (σωματικῶς, 2.9) suggests a non-incarnational theory. As we would expect from Jewish Christians, this sounds like prophetic possession for a temporary period of Jesus' life.

In this way, we end with a Christology difficult to distinguish from that of Irenaeus's Ebionites. For them, Christ was not the unique figure of Pauline orthodoxy but was sent by "the supreme power" (αὐθεντία). The latter figure is distinguished from "the unknown Father" and sounds like Philo's "ruler of the angels, as it were"—in other words, the divine Glory or Image. The Christ of the Jewish Christians at Colossae is not a bodily Christ and hence would be a spirit. How would this differ from the inferior spirit-Christ who possessed Jesus for a time, in Ebionite thought?

We may suspect the same background to underlie Philippians. Paul is anxious that the church members there "think the same thing . . . thinking the one thing, in no way with wrangling or vain opinion (κενοδοξίαν), but in humility taking each other to be better than yourselves" (Phil 2.2–3). But the one thing is going to be Pauline teaching, not the views of those who proclaim Christ in envy and rivalry (1.15), who are no doubt the Jewish-Christian dogs, the enemies of Christ's cross in ch. 3. Now we find the same combination of *all* with the submission of the angelic powers in 2.9–11: God "gave him the name that is above every name, that at the name of Jesus every knee should bow, of things in heaven . . . and every tongue should confess that Jesus Christ is Lord." With Colossians so close in date and setting, we cannot but descry a similar dim outline of a Jewish-Christian Christology. Like the Ebionites, the Jewish Christians at Philippi exclude the cross from their gospel. They have an excess of reverence for a world of angelic and demonic powers. Paul's stress on their united worship of Jesus Christ and their united confession of his lordship suggests that, like those at Colossae, they gave Christ too spiritual a being. It would, then, have been surprising to them to find Jesus-Christ/Christ-Jesus so often hyphenated and particularly scandalous that heavenly knees would be asked to bow at the name of a mere human, Jesus.

The Pauline Letters offer us but hints and shadows of the Christology of the Jewish-Christian opposition. We can see that it is sharply different from Paul's own Christology (I,12.3; II,11.4), but we would not have been able to reconstruct its probable outline without a larger historical framework. As it is, we can make out a prophetic Christology in the early Jerusalem church (Acts 3.22; 7.37 and the development of Isa 61.1), and we find two forms of prophetic Christology among Jewish Christians in the late second century (Pseudo-Clementine and Ebionite). Between the latter evidence and that for Jerusalem in the first decades stretch the NT documents. The discussion here has been limited to the Paulines, including Colossians. Elsewhere I have argued that the same Ebionite view underlies the Markan portrait of Jesus as a figure like Elijah or Elisha performing miracles, or like Moses giving an extension to the law. I have also suggested that it is being contested in the Johannine literature, especially 1 John (4.1–3; 5.6–8) and the Johannine account of Jesus' death (John 19.30, 34–35), and that the so-called Docetist opposition faced by Ignatius were none other than Ebionites.[11]

It seems, then, that we can form a consistent picture of a Jewish-Christian Christology developing from Jesus' lifetime and on for a century and a half. Jesus saw himself as a prophet, anointed by the Spirit, as in Isa

---

[11]Most recently, Goulder, "A Poor Man's Christology" and "Ignatius' 'Docetists.'"

61, and as the prophet like Moses foretold in Deut 18. The primitive Jerusalem church was content with this understanding. Jesus' brothers knew that his father was Joseph and had never heard of any descent from David: he had left home in his late twenties to join the Baptist movement, and thereafter there had been tales of marvelous healings and authoritative teaching. The Spirit of God had clearly anointed him at his baptism and would have left him before his death. So there is a straight line through from Peter and James to Cerinthus and the Ebionites. The Pseudo-Clementine Christology is a compromise between this thoroughgoing prophetic view and the Pauline incarnation Christology. Jesus remains a prophet, the True Prophet, but we hear no more of the Spirit's coming at the baptism or leaving before the passion. We may almost speak of the Spirit's being incarnate in its series of human resting places. There is still a resentment of Paul, but his teachings are cloaked as being those of Simon Magus. By 180 the Ebionite view, that of the Jerusalem pillars, has become a heresy, but like old soldiers, the Pseudo-Clementine communities never die; they just fade away.

∼ 16 ∼

A SCENARIO OF THE CORINTHIAN
CHURCH, 50–56 C.E.

AS IS often said, we do not have enough evidence to write a history of the first years of the Corinthian church; still, we have enough evidence to want to try. Two solutions to the dilemma are normal. One may declare the project impracticable and withdraw, or one may attempt the project, inserting the word *perhaps* into every sentence. Both policies seem misguided. If we cannot write a history, we can at least write a scenario, a web of possibilities that can be argued to be likely. It is only by weaving such a web that the story of the Corinthian community can be brought into three-dimensional focus. Not all of my judgments will be correct, but by setting them out clearly, I may hope that others will improve on them. We shall not advance our picture of the church by declining to consider possibilities. So this chapter is a scenario, not a history; this will save my readers the tedium of many *mays* and *mights*. But I ask them not to accuse me of wildness: my speculations, where important, are supported by cited evidence; where I have given my imagination rein, they are not significant.

A well-known and honorable attempt to reconstruct the early history of the Corinthian church is John Hurd's *Origin of 1 Corinthians*.[1] Those familiar with that work will notice the points at which I concur with, and diverge from, his reconstruction.

The first problem facing an account of the Corinthian church is the historical value of Acts, an issue that continues sharply to divide NT scholars.[2] I take it as a criterion of reliability that a historian can repeatedly de-

---

[1] J. C. Hurd, *The Origin of 1 Corinthians* (London: SPCK, 1965).
[2] There is a notable contrast, in two well-known commentaries on Acts, between the skepticism of E. Haenchen, *The Acts of the Apostles: A Commentary* (trans. B. Noble and G. Shinn; rev. R. McL. Wilson; Oxford: Blackwell, 1971), and the more open acceptance of Barrett, *Acts;* and between the robust conservatism of Martin Hengel and Anna Maria Schwemer in *Paul between Damascus and Antioch* (trans. J. Bowden; Louisville: Westminster John Knox, 1997) and the radicalism of Gerd Lüdemann's *Early Christianity according to the Traditions in Acts: A Commentary* (trans. J. Bowden; Minneapolis: Fortress, 1989).

scribe details that are confirmed in contemporary sources. One may get other matters wrong, and one may tell the story with a spin on it, but one cannot be repeatedly accurate unless one is well informed. Now, the following assertions in Acts seem to be confirmed by remarks of Paul:

> Paul and Barnabas had been co-pastors of the church in Antioch. (Acts 11.25–26; 13.1; Gal 2.1–14)

> Paul and Barnabas were bracketed as missionary travelers with a policy distinct from the Jerusalem apostles. (Acts 13–14; I,9.6)

> The missionaries who founded the Corinthian church were Paul, Silvanus (Silas), and Timothy. (Acts 18.1, 5; II,1.19)

> They came via Macedonia, where they founded the church at Thessalonica. (Acts 17.1–9; 1 Thess 1.1; etc.)

> There were attacks on both the missionaries and the local Thessalonian Christians. (Acts 17.5–9; 1 Thess 1.6–7; 2.14)

> Paul had come ahead of the others and began the Corinthian mission on his own. (Acts 18.1–4, 1 Thess 3.1, 6)

> He attempted a mission at Athens en route, but not for long. (Acts 17.15–34; 1 Thess 3.1)

> Paul earned his living at Corinth. (Acts 18.3: I,9; etc.)

> One of his early converts was a man of note called Crispus. (Acts 18.8; I,1.14)

> After Paul left Corinth, a like-minded missionary called Apollos came to Corinth. (Acts 18.24–28; I,1.12; etc.)

> Paul then spent a protracted period at Ephesus. (Acts 19; I,16.8–9)

> He made a final visit to Corinth, traveling through Macedonia. (Acts 20.1–2; II,1–2)

We have also to consider the probable historicity of the hearing before Gallio and, in both Acts and Paul, the link with Priscilla and Aquila and the mention of Sosthenes. In view of all these points, it seems that Luke was well informed, and his account should be treated with respect. Naturally, he has his own interests to forward, and we need to proceed with caution; however, in principle we should honor Acts and not, in Hengel's words, treat it as a novel.

We should observe incidentally the difference between Luke's story of the Corinthian mission and the account of the Ephesian mission in Acts 19. The contrast is marked between his detailed and coherent account of the Corinthian church and his vague and self-contradictory description of Paul's time at Ephesus.

PAUL AT CORINTH, 50–51

Paul spent the winter of 49 in Macedonia (Acts 17.10–14) and came in the spring to Athens. He reached Corinth in May 50 and was happy to find a Christian couple there; the man, Aquila, was of his own trade. They worked as a partnership and as fellow missionaries, at some peril to them all (Rom 16.3–4; Acts 18.2–3). Paul spoke effectively in the synagogue and made some significant converts, Stephanas and his family (I,1.16; 16.15) and Titius Justus (Acts 18.7), God-fearers. Soon afterwards they were joined by Crispus, who was on the synagogue committee (Acts 18.8; I,1.14), and by a wealthy man named Gaius (I,1.14), who was to be a major figure in the community's future. There was thus an encouraging nucleus of the church before Silas and Timothy arrived.

Their coming had two immediate consequences. Paul felt the church now needed its independence of the synagogue, so he ceased attempting to convert the hostile Jews and held meetings in Titius's house (Acts 18.7). But he also felt that the other two could look after the pastoring of the new community while he set forth around Achaia founding additional Christian groups. He was not in Corinth so much now, and therefore further baptisms were done by Silas and Timothy; he had been sent not to lead baptism classes but to evangelize (I,1.17). We know of a church he began in Cenchreae (Rom 16.1). His policy was to go to towns, especially towns with Jewish communities, and so we may think of him in Nauplion, Patras, and Nicopolis. In the First Letter, he greets the Corinthians "with all who call on the name of our Lord Jesus Christ in every place [in the province]" (I,1.2); in the Second Letter, he greets the church "with all the saints in the whole of Achaia" (II,1.1). Shortly afterwards he could say, "from Jerusalem and as far round as Illyricum I have completed the gospel of Christ" (Rom 15.19). Titus 3.12 mentions Nicopolis on the Adriatic, toward the Illyrian border.

Less happily, however, relations began to turn sour between the two leaders. Silas had been a "leading man among the brothers" at Jerusalem (Acts 15.22), a prophet (15.32) sent to Antioch to supervise the enforcement of the decree. Paul and he had got on well and had set off on the second missionary journey together (15.40), but Silas had Jerusalem ideas, and Paul agreed to circumcise Timothy at his urging (16.3). He had been in charge of the Thessalonians' church after Paul left Macedonia for Achaia (17.14). Paul never hints in 1 Thessalonians that Silas was responsible for their belief that baptism would save them from dying, but he does use the word *we* in a very insistent way throughout the epistle, as if to emphasize that he and Silas were at one on the matter. In 2 Thessalonians he is vexed to find that they have received "a letter as from us saying that the Day of the Lord has come" (2.2); this was not a forgery but a pastoral letter such as Paul would write himself but beginning, "Silvanus and Paul and Timothy."[3]

The errors at Thessalonica bear a strong family resemblance to those at Corinth. "The Day of the Lord has come" sounds like reigning already in I,4.8 or inheriting the kingdom of God in I,15.50. To be beyond the power of death through baptism is the creed opposed in 1 Thess 4.13–18, just as death is the last enemy to be destroyed in I,15.26, not swallowed up in victory until the παρουσία. Too much talk about the Spirit and the kingdom leads to people giving up work; only so is there time for healing services, prayer meetings, and the organizing of church life. Paul strongly urges the Thessalonians to follow their own trade and work with their hands (1 Thess 4.11–12) and to cease such nonsense on pain of shunning (2 Thess 3.6–15), just as he stresses his own labors, working with his own hands in I,4.12. There were no other missionaries in Macedonia in 49–50 but Paul, Silas, and Timothy, and these things were not taught by Paul or Timothy.

The irenic Luke does not like to mention these tensions, and he allows Silas to vanish into the sunset after reaching Corinth in Acts 18.5; nor does Paul co-author any more letters with him after 2 Thessalonians. That letter was written a few months after its predecessor, and we may sense a deepening rift in the apostolic partnership as the two leaders realize how different their theologies are. Silas wintered at Corinth and left for Jerusalem in the spring of 51; the report he carried to the pillars was not reassuring. Paul had kept the letter of the Jerusalem/Antioch agreement, and the meat at the church suppers was bought from kosher butchers, but there was no real intention to teach observance of torah, enthusiasm for the gifts of the Spirit was halfhearted ("Quench not the Spirit!" 1 Thess 5.19), and the kingdom was constantly spoken of as in the future, at the so-called παρουσία.

In the meantime, the Corinthian church continued to grow (Acts 18.8–11); Luke twice says that many believed there, and we have to think of perhaps fifty members. So many could not be accommodated in Titius's house, and Paul was lucky to have made a wealthy convert in Gaius, who became host to the whole church (Rom 16.23). Even rich people did not have rooms with space for fifty people to eat together, and we have to think of the church as meeting in his garden, under the trees in summer, in the portico in winter. Juvenal (*Satires,* 1.12–13) bemoans the tedium of *recitationes* in Fronto's porticoed garden:

---

[3]See Goulder, "Silas in Thessalonica."

Frontonis platani convulsaque marmora clamant
Semper et adsiduo ruptae lectore columnae.
"Fronto's plane trees cry out constantly,
and his shattered marble statues,
and his columns broken by the ceaseless declamation."

Saturday evenings at Gaius's were certainly more lively and enjoyable. Also Gaius had been a friend of Crispus (I,1.14) and understood about Jewish scruples, so there was no difficulty over the meat.

Luke ascribes Paul's departure from Corinth to tensions with the Jews, in which Paul was vindicated by Gallio, but he takes Paul back to Jerusalem, via Ephesus and Caesarea, for a visit not described. Paul in fact reacted to Silas's departure as he had reacted to the "false brethren" at Antioch in Gal 2. He knew there would be trouble brewing; he did not want his mission undercut or the church divided; he therefore sailed from Cenchreae (Acts 18.18) in September 51, taking a vow in the vain hope of impressing the pillars with his Jewish piety. This time he did not receive even the guarded welcome of three years before. James and Cephas had heard from Silas what was happening, and they determined to stop it. Paul got short shrift and left to spend the winter in Antioch with his old friends, feeling uncomfortable.

CORINTH WITHOUT PAUL, AUTUMN 51–SPRING 54

Paul was not to see his Corinthian converts for three years. "Having spent some time [at Antioch] he set out, passing in order through the Galatic region and Phrygia, encouraging all the disciples" (Acts 18.23). Luke makes it sound like winter in Antioch and summer in the Anatolian highlands. For him the Galatic region means the little line (καθεξῆς) of churches of Acts 13–14— Derbe, Lystra, Iconium, Pisidian Antioch—and there are now some daughter foundations westwards into Phrygia. Paul had nearly a thousand miles to walk, and Acts 20.1–21.15 suggests a missionary pattern of a week in each church (Troas, Miletus, Tyre).[4] With occasional delays for illness, or with trouble from the authorities or bandits, or with pastoral problems, the summer of 52 would have gone. Paul would be pleased to reach Ephesus in October 52, where he was able again to join forces with Aquila and Prisca (I,16.19).

In the meantime, life had not been dull in Corinth. The fiery Apollos had appeared in Ephesus soon after Paul's fleeting visit there, had been welcomed and befriended by Priscilla and Aquila, and had been turned into a

---

[4]Dio Chrysostom describes Diogenes' pattern of life as alternating between Corinth and Athens: "By spending the night at Megara he could very easily be in Athens on the following day" (*Tyr.* 6). Megara is twenty-five miles from Corinth, and Athens a further twenty-six miles, "both average hikes for walkers of the period" (Murphy-O'Connor, *St. Paul's Corinth*, 94). By this computation, it would take forty days of walking to cover a thousand miles.

thoroughgoing Pauline (Acts 18.24–26). He was bound for Corinth, so they sent him on with a commendatory letter in the spring of 52. His leadership, biblical learning, and speaking ability were a gift to the somewhat rudderless church there, and once more there were new faces each Saturday night in Gaius's garden (Acts 18.27–28; I,1.12; 3.5–6).

But sweetness and light were not to continue long. The Jerusalem leadership had at its disposal a good number of able and devoted members, some of apostolic status, like Barnabas and Silas, some men of character like the "false brethren" or the "certain from James" of Gal 2. James and Peter had finally made their minds up after Silas's report and Paul's failure to satisfy them, and in the spring of 52 they, too, were sending emissaries to Corinth, two men with clear convictions who could reclaim the distant community for the one apostolic metropolitan church. They were not given apostolic status themselves; they were to join the Corinthian church, bring it into obedience to Jerusalem, and report after a year or so. If there were any resistance, they should appeal to the authority of Cephas, Jesus' leading disciple (I,1.12–4.7).

The Jerusalem missionaries were sensible. They did not alienate the Corinthians by requiring circumcision; many of the local people had been attached to the synagogue earlier without being circumcised. The newcomers were Christians from the mother church, sent to show its care for all church-people everywhere and to aid in the missionary endeavor. They were, naturally, welcomed with open arms. They stressed the leadership of Cephas, bestowed on him by Jesus, and the superior knowledge of Jesus' teachings that came through Cephas and the other disciples. They were plainly devout men who understood the meaning of the biblical commandments better than Paul, who appeared to have been rather lax. They made new converts, including Jews, to whom they were more conciliatory than Apollos (Acts 18.28); when these were baptized, there was emphasis on their transformation into spiritual people, with a full apostolic baptism. Saturday evenings increased in excitement with revelations, visions, and other charismatic happenings. And Jesus had laid down that the church should pay toward its missionaries' living. Had Paul never mentioned that? How strange!

With such diplomacy, the new mission was grafted on to the old without obvious tension, and in time the church was left to itself again. Apollos resented the newcomers with their presumption of authority and their pro-Jewish stance and their knowledge of Palestinian halakah; early in 53 he left for Ephesus, where he had heard Paul was at work. The Jerusalem missionaries felt that things were going their way and left for home soon afterwards, in time for Pentecost perhaps, like Paul in 56. They were able to reassure the pillars that their mission had been successful: what was needed now was to appoint two full apostles to take the Achaean province over, to insist on a proper observance of torah and, in time, circumcision. Thus would Paul's unhappy influence be at an end.

Meanwhile, Paul's ministry in Ephesus was flourishing, at first in partnership with Priscilla and Aquila, later with Apollos as a further colleague (I,16.12). He was now in contact with Corinth through occasional visitors on commercial or other business. But with a wide and effective door open in Asia, and many opponents (16.9), some of them wild animals (15.32), he had his hands full.

With the departure of the visiting missionaries, fervor receded at Corinth, and with it discipline. The Jerusalem mission had even succeeded in convincing some young men of the call to celibacy: if they were now spiritual, they should be above fleshly needs. This was fine in the first flush of conversion, but with increasing normality, some of them had paid visits to the brothel. This divided the church. Their friends and relatives shook their heads. Youth will have its fling, they said; we should be patient and pray for them. But some of the old Paulines were scandalized: where was the sanctity of the church if this was tolerated? In the resulting impasse, Stephanas made an important proposal: If they were divided, why not write a letter and take it to Paul across the Aegean? He had founded the church and knew the people. Other voices suggested writing to Cephas as a higher authority still, but it was felt that he was too far away, did not know the church, and was probably too busy.

The message therefore came to Ephesus, and Paul came to write the "previous letter" (I,5.9), the precedent for future interactions. He was as scandalized as Stephanas expected. The purity of the church was paramount; a little leaven soon leavens the whole lump; the unfaithful must be immediately shunned. Paul unfortunately used the word ἄπιστοι, as he did in II,6.14, an ambiguous term that sometimes means faithless Christians, as Paul intended in these two places, and sometimes unbelievers. The church accordingly found difficulty understanding their apostle's instructions: surely they could not cut off relations with all unbelievers (I,5.10)?

FIRST CORINTHIANS

The seeds of discord, sown with such skill by the Jerusalem emissaries, took time to germinate, but by the winter of 53–54, it was evident that the church was divided and with increasing bitterness. People were openly declaring their loyalty to one leadership or the other (I,1.12; 4.6), some with the arrogant presumption that Cephas was the senior apostle and Paul counted for nothing. Worship was pandemonium: everybody shouting at once; women praying and prating barefaced; cliques coming early and taking food and wine in excess, while working people came late and found the tables empty. Discipline had gone: one wealthy brother going to bed with his dead father's wife, others going to law in secular courts for their money. Unrealism was everywhere: talk of the kingdom having come, of being transformed into spiritual beings; pressure on married people to live without sex and even to divorce. The claims of visionaries seemed to undercut the most basic principles: if you had knowledge, you could know that there were no other gods, so you could commit idolatry!

The move to write a fuller letter to Paul was made by Chloe, a wealthy widow, the manager of whose estates was Stephanas.[5] She suggested raising the three most contentious issues: Did a Christian's aspiration to holiness require giving up the fleshly pleasures of sex, and if so, did this mean celibacy for all, no remarriage for widows, continence within marriage, divorce for the married, or what? If there was only one God, did it follow that eating food offered to an idol and even eating in a temple restaurant did not matter? And what limits were there on the expression of spiritual experiences in worship? It would also be helpful if Paul could be a little more specific about arrangements for the collection that had been started for the Jerusalem church—the funds had dried up, as there seemed to be no urgency about the matter.

By the time Chloe made this proposal, the Corinthian church was more than a hundred strong. It contained converts from three missions. Paul says that there were not many powerful or upper-class (εὐγενεῖς) members, but we may count at least five: Chloe herself, who can afford to send three members of her staff across the Aegean for a month (I,1.11); Crispus, who had been a synagogue committee member (I,1.14; Acts 18.8); Gaius, with a house big enough to host the whole church (Rom 16.23); Erastus, the city treasurer (Rom 16.23);[6] and the man with his father's wife, who has enough connections to defy public opinion. The man who reclines in the εἰδωλεῖον is also probably well-to-do, as the assimilated were usually the better off, but he may be one of the four men just mentioned. All these people would have brought considerable households with them into the church. Chloe, Crispus, and Gaius were Paulines; the man in I,5 was with the γνῶσις wing of the Petrines.

Apart from these, we know of Stephanas and his household (I,1.16) and Titius Justus, who was a householder (Acts 18.7). There were some Jews in the church (I,7.18), some slaves (v. 21), some men with pagan wives (v. 12) and women with pagan husbands (v. 13), some freedmen (Fortunatus

---

[5]It is usually thought that two groups came to Ephesus independently—the Chloe party, which told Paul what was happening at Corinth, and Stephanas and his colleagues, who were the official delegation with the church's letter. But it seems rather a large coincidence that two such groups would have come from Corinth at virtually the same time. My suggestions of Chloe's initiative, and of her relation to Stephanas, are informed guesswork.

[6]J. Meggitt, "The Social Status of Erastus: Rom. 16.23," *NovT* 38 (1996): 218–23, has cast doubt on the widely held theory that Paul's Erastus was the aedile whose name is inscribed as donor of the city paving: the inscription may be much later, and the name Erastus is common (and might be Eperastus). Paul may mean only that his Erastus was treasurer of the church in the city.

and Achaicus), some poor but free workers who came late to the agape (11.21); some were married, some single, of both sexes, and some widowed (ch. 7). The church counted nine different gifts of the Spirit (12.8–10), and Paul varies the list with the addition of apostleship, teaching, (financial) assistance, and leadership; he tries to limit the prophets to two or three in a session (14.29), but we have the impression that several times this number were competing for a hearing. Of course, these groups overlap, but the First Epistle seems to portray a considerable and varied membership. For the breakdown between the different groups, those loyal to Paul and Apollos must have been a majority; otherwise they could not have won the proposal to ask Paul to arbitrate. But the Petrines must have been a considerable force; otherwise they would not have been able to press their radical claims. There must also have been an uncommitted minority. And so, when Luke has the Lord say to Paul in Corinth, "There are many in this city who are my people" (Acts 18.10), he is thinking of three figures.

With a letter describing such disarray, it is difficult to think that Paul did not answer it within a fortnight, and it would be surprising if a second, independent delegation of Chloe's people happened to arrive with the latest gossip in the same period. Stephanas is Paul's first convert and his nominee to run the church (I,16.15–16), and the church's letter was sponsored and written by Paulines. Chloe was an artful woman. The letter, written as a neutral request for guidance, was carried by her Pauline staff, who were authorized to tell the apostle verbally the real state of affairs: the divisions, the attacks on Paul's authority, the scandals, the chaos at worship. When she generously offered to pay for the delegation, all hands were raised in favor.

The deputation's account of things took Paul by surprise, his first shock of many in an *annus horribilis,* 54. He had been only mildly disturbed by the report of fornication by church members. He had sent Timothy with two companions to see that things were being handled properly (I,4.17), but not direct across the sea; they had gone via Macedonia and could not be expected to arrive before Chloe's party (16.10–11). In any case, Timothy was young and without standing (16.11). But a long evening with Stephanas and his friends soon opened Paul's eyes to the seriousness of the situation. The greater part of this study has been given to exploring the details of what had gone wrong and Paul's response to it. First Corinthians is a masterpiece, hard to fault: it is fair-minded, diplomatic, straightforward, dignified, principled, vigorous, fatherly, conciliatory. 'Tis not in mortals to command success, but Paul did more, good reader; he deserved it.

A Pastoral Visit, Autumn 54

Many parents have written good counsel to their children, advocating harder work, more regular habits, and so forth. If the relation is good, the child will mend his or her ways a little but not too much. But the wise parent will make some things obligatory and final: in future there is to be no more Ecstasy. The issue is then clear: either there is obedience or there is defiance, and if there is defiance, there will be an "Otherwise . . ." In the same way, 1 Corinthians urged the church to better ways in many respects, but only one thing was directly required of it—a unanimous vote at the church meeting to excommunicate and shun the man with his father's wife. Paul had already decided this, and the church was commanded to enforce his decision. People could behave slightly less selfishly at the eucharistic meal and say they were sorry about the lawsuit or the temple dinner without expecting to behave differently in the future, but on the issue of ch. 5, it was obedience or defiance. Since Paul found the church defiant when he visited it later in 54, it is likely that the man in question had refused to give the woman up and had got away with it. It is difficult to think of any other reason a church with a Pauline majority and a profound affection for their founder would have treated him so unkindly.

A scenario is not hard to imagine. The apostolic letter was read out one Saturday night, and one or another of the man's family and friends rose to say, "I take the very strongest exception to this. The authority for our church is the apostles in Jerusalem, not this Paul who is not an apostle at all—we were not even asked to pay for him. Our brother has been a faithful member for more than a year, and many members can testify to his generosity. This alleged sin is not so awful; his father is dead, after all, and there is nothing promiscuous about it. Christianity is supposed to be about forgiving people, not driving them out of the church. All I can say is that if this is done, I and many others will be joining him, and we shall form a proper apostolic church." No one who has been a member of the clergy or a minister will be a stranger to the sense of rising panic as the possibility of schism appears, and the urgent need to find some middle way. So Gaius said, "Beloved, let us do nothing hasty. I suggest that we hold a novena of prayer/ask Paul to come and meet us/write to St. Peter." The meeting broke up with the relieved decision to do nothing for the moment and hope the problem would go away.

Stephanas had underestimated the power of the Petrines, and Paul had felt no urgency when he wrote the First Letter. He said, "I shall be coming to you soon, God willing" (I,4.19), but by "soon" he meant settling affairs in Ephesus until Pentecost, making a pastoral tour through Macedonia, and reaching Corinth in six months, in time to spend the winter (16.5–9). Whether he had news of the reverse at Corinth at once or after some weeks, he would not have found it easy to disengage himself from his thriving and threatened Ephesian mission (16.9). He left for Achaia as he had planned in September, "cane" in hand (4.21).

But life was not so easy. Paul's reception caused him much distress and anguish of heart, many tears and grief (II,2.4–5); someone (τίς) wronged him (τοῦ ἀδικήσαντος, II,7.12), and he was wronged (τοῦ ἀδικηθέντος). But the depth of the hurt came from the congregation, who did not support him. He later wrote them a painful letter (7.8) and did not come on a third visit, a painful visit, so as to spare them (1.23–2.3).

This was not the last time that the church of God would be faced with the unpleasant choice between compromise and principle. Paul spoke first— of his authority as founding apostle, of the need for the purity of the church, of the unparalleled heinousness of the sin. Against him were stacked two powerful influences: first, the work of the Jerusalem emissaries that had undermined his authority, and second, the sinner's social position. With a network of relations and friends and business colleagues and clients and freedmen and slaves, he could take a third of the church with him if he went; not many were willing to divide the church for a fuss over a woman. Agamemnon did it with Achilles, but he nearly pushed his luck too hard.

So Paul went back to Ephesus to lick his wounds and to write one of his most eloquent and effective letters, the tearful letter (II,2.4), which the shamed recipients wisely destroyed in toto. He had been treated with injustice and ingratitude, and he was hurt; however, he had the power to move the human heart in such a plight. This time, when the letter was read out, there was a profound silence, and then Gaius said, "Beloved, I think we have made a mistake. Paul is quite right, and we have done badly in not supporting him. The church cannot be holy while one of us is living in scandal. I call upon our brother to send his concubine away; if he will not, then I propose that we do as we were told to in the First Letter, and damn the consequences." He was speaking for the community. Paul was greatly heartened by this response: "your yearning, your sorrow, your zeal for me" (II,7.8); he had hurt them κατὰ θεόν and had brought about "earnestness, no, eagerness to clear yourselves, no, indignation, no, alarm, no, zeal, no, retribution!" (7.11).

Paul knew about the final result when he wrote the Second Letter, but he did not hear about it quickly. He had sent Titus with the tearful letter (II,7.5–16), and Titus was so slow in returning that Paul was worried sick that something had happened to him (2.13; 7.5–6). Perhaps Gaius turned the tide of opinion in November, but the sinner may have been slow to mend his ways. Negotiations and prevarications can take months, and Titus stayed to make sure the issue was finally decided as Paul had ordered. Eventually it was clear that the sinner was obdurate, and in the spring of 55, the church voted to hand him over to Satan, not to speak to him or eat with him.

But now the strength of his social network was tested. Some of his associates had made strong friendships in the church that they did not wish to be broken, and few were willing to start a breakaway group based on scandal and defiance. The wretched man found himself isolated socially and in a state of religious dread; to be handed over to Satan for the destruction of the flesh was no vacuous superstition in the first century. After a few weeks of defiance, the young woman was sent away, and he petitioned for readmittance to the church. But reference to 1 Cor 5 disclosed no possibility of re-pentance and readmission: once handed over to Satan, your only hope was for your spirit on the Day of the Lord Jesus (I,5.5).

THE COUNTERMISSION

Silas had reported to the Jerusalem leadership in 51 about the three prov-inces where the noxious herbs of Pauline heterodoxy were taking root—Galatia, Macedonia, and Achaia. The pillars decided to follow the same pol-icy that had borne fruit at Antioch: first, to send fact-finding emissaries to join the churches, bring them, if possible, into line with the mother church, and in due course bring back word; then, if necessary, to impose their own authority. A group of Christians saying, "I am of Cephas," did not arise in Corinth without some encouragement from without, and there would have been similar groups with encouragement from similar emissaries in Galatia and Macedonia in 52–53.

This sensible policy had disappointing results. The Corinthian counter-mission made only limited headway, and a majority of the congregation were still loyal to Paul and Apollos. Galatia and Macedonia were even less rewarding, and Paul himself was now operating successfully in Asia (I,16.9). The pillars therefore decided that they must put their foot down. They sent pairs of apostles to each of the four centers, armed with letters of authoriza-tion to take the churches over and impose Jerusalem practices and the Jeru-salem creed. These apostles left Jerusalem in the spring of 54.

The most zealous of them went to the nearest area, Galatia, where they reproached the congregations for their failure to observe torah. Those who wished to serve God in the Spirit must accept God's sacrament, circumci-sion, without which no man could belong to the people of God (Gen 17.13–14). But here the same forces that were weighing against Paul in Cor-inth told in his favor in Anatolia. The churches wanted to postpone the evil day; they had more reverence for their founding apostle than for distant names making unpleasant demands, and the richer members did not fancy the knife themselves. So there was a meeting of leaders from the various churches, and it was agreed to write to Paul for advice. This missive arrived at Ephesus soon after his return from his unhappy trip to Corinth, and our angry, rattled, defensive, contorted Epistle to the Galatians is the apostle's response.

The Petrines made little ground in Macedonia, the final fortress to which Paul withdrew in 55 (II,2.13; 7.5). Even in Macedonia there were ἔξωθεν μάχαι (II,7.5), which probably means a serious attempt to undermine his position. But the Philippians and Thessalonians were among his most loyal and affectionate disciples (II,8.1; 9.4; Phil 1.5). Still, the Jerusalem

apostles did not give up lightly; they are the dogs, the κατατομή, the enemies of the cross of Christ of Phil 3 six years later.

It was at Ephesus, however, that the Jerusalem apostles had their most
dramatic success. Already in the spring Paul had been feeling the pressure:
there were "many adversaries" (I,16.9), some of whom he had to fight as
wild beasts (I,15.32). Throughout the summer, there were major distractions—the letter from Corinth, the disquieting report of Stephanas, the need
to write 1 Corinthians with some urgency, the intelligence that things were
not going well there, the visit and its bitter failure, the return and writing of
the tearful letter, the arrival of a deputation from Galatia with further disturbing news, the writing of an emotional response. With Paul out of
Ephesus or beset with other business, the new apostles had things their
own way, and at a meeting in the winter of 54–55, a vote was carried
to hand the care of the church over to the metropolitan-orthodox-catholic-
apostolic authority whose representatives had now arrived. Paul found himself voted down, and not only in Ephesus; the capital's lead was followed in
daughter church after daughter church. A later Pauline was to write in the
apostle's name, "You are aware that all who are in Asia have deserted me"
(2 Tim 1.15).

Heartbroken, Paul withdrew northward; he had intended to start a
mission in Troas in Pontus and had arranged with Titus to meet him there
(II,2.12–13). But unsurprisingly, he now had a breakdown of health. The trials of 54 had been too much for him: the defection of two of his major missions, Corinth and Asia, to the Petrines; and threats to the other two, a
serious threat in Galatia. He speaks of "our affliction (θλῖψις) that befell in
Asia, for we were utterly crushed, beyond our powers, so that we despaired
even of living. Indeed, we have ourselves received within ourselves the sentence of death" (1.8–9). His life's work crumbling about him, his normal natural vigor at an end, his back was to the wall. Without the support of the
faithful Timothy, who joined him in his hour of crisis (1.1), he might well
have succumbed.

Meanwhile, the fourth pair of Jerusalem apostles had arrived in Corinth, where they were faced with a dilemma. On the one hand, there was a
thriving anti-Pauline minority trumpeting its loyalty to Cephas; on the other
hand, the principle they were defending was the right of a leading member
to sleep with his father's wife in defiance of the repeated prohibition in the
Torah. It was wise to remain silent on the second issue and to stress the first.
They were true apostles, authorized with letters from Jerusalem, gifted with
visions of God that had transformed them like Moses of old. Paul was a
mountebank, a man who changed his plans with every whim, constantly in
trouble with the authorities, without any true spiritual powers—without
speaking ability, without courage, without presence, without ability to discipline, without visionary experience, without a record as a miracle worker.
He was not even straight with money: he never lived at church expense,

as Jesus ordained apostles should, but he was making up for it with a huge collection that he was going to embezzle.

Despite their uncharity, these apostles were honest men, laboring to maintain a united church and exposing what appeared as evident flaws in a self-appointed schismatic leader. We may spare them some sympathy, for they arrived at the wrong moment. They could not support the Petrine sinner, and their lack of backing would have helped to drive him out. At the same time, Paul's tearful letter had brought about a revulsion of feeling in his favor, which they were powerless to stem. Titus left Corinth in the summer of 55, the bearer of mixed tidings for Paul. The good news was that the church had voted the sinner out, as Paul had required in I,5.4–5, and he was begging to be readmitted. The bad news was the presumption and the growing influence of the so-called apostles from Jerusalem.

SECOND CORINTHIANS

Paul survived his breakdown of health through the winter of 54–55, and in the spring he set out for his intended mission to Troas. There was a good response (II,2.12), but as the weeks passed, his anxiety increased at Titus's failure to appear. Finally, he felt so disturbed that he suspended his preaching and moved over to Neapolis, through which Titus should come (2.13; 7.5). When at last he did arrive, Paul was transported with feelings both of happiness and of anger. Primary was the sense of triumph: his disciple was alive and well; his church was loyal after all; the defiant sinner was repentant; thanks be to God. But at the same time, Satan was doing his best to seduce the church through his false apostles and their slanders. It is out of this ambivalent situation that our two-toned Second Letter was written.

Paul begins with the note of triumphant thanksgiving that will dominate the letter. God has comforted him after all his affliction in Asia and the worries thereafter; Titus has come safely; the tearful letter has done its godly work; the church has shown its zeal in supporting Paul (1.1–14; 2.3–13; 7.2–16).

Early in 54 Paul had intended a counterclockwise tour of his Greek churches—Macedonia, Achaia for a prolonged visit, and then on, perhaps, to Jerusalem (I,16.3–7). The bad news from Corinth in the summer made Paul reverse this plan. When he arrived for his ill-starred visit in the autumn, he told the Corinthians that he had changed his mind: he had come direct to Corinth because of the trouble; he would go north to Macedonia on leaving them and would return for "a second benefit" before moving on with the collection for Judea (II,1.15–16). But when the atmosphere turned sour and he was forced to leave in humiliation, it became obvious that a third visit would issue in nothing but mutual reproaches and frustration. To spare the church this, he called off the return visit (1.23). This change of plan was thrown in his face by the new apostles as vacillation between yes and no and as "planning according to the flesh" (1.17)—an unfair charge, as he was merely responding to the clear will of God, whose "yes" stands behind the whole mission (1.19–22).

But what about the man with his father's wife? Paul agreed with Virgil: *parcere subiectis et debellare superbos* ("spare the submitting and fight down the proud"). While the man was obdurate and contumacious, Paul fought him down; now he was penitent (7.10) and eaten up with excessive sorrow (2.7). In the end, the church had bowed to Paul's demand and had handed the man over to Satan for the destruction of the flesh; at least, most of them (τῶν πλειόνων, 2.6) had excommunicated and shunned him. In victory magnanimous, Paul revokes the punishment: let the church forgive and reinstate him in their love (2.7–10). The hurt to him was nothing (7.12)[7]

The reference to the successful mission at Troas leads on to the first rebuttal of the claims of the new apostles and to the vindication of Paul's own apostleship (2.14–4.6), extending indeed into a defense of his ministry of "weakness" to 6.10. This sore subject is later resumed in 10.1–12.13 and has been sufficiently expounded above.

There are still some matters of discipline to be set straight. Paul yearns for a total response to his affection for the church, but this will mean a firm line with those who are still eating food that has been offered to idols (6.11–7.1; pp. 228–30). He is hoping that the shunning policy will bring back the erring sheep here also. But there are lesser sins that will also have to be dealt with when he comes: quarreling, jealousy, and disorder (II,12.20, cf. I,1.11; 11.18), and sexual misdemeanors that caused trouble before (I,5.9; II,12.21). He speaks severely of holding a court with proper witnesses, but the severity is in the hope that they will repent quickly and be in a state of grace to greet him (II,12.19; 13.5–12).

Paul had agreed with the pillars back in 48 that he would raise money for the home churches, but he had not pressed the matter on his new converts, feeling that such action would be counterproductive. First Corinthians 16.1–4 shows that the idea has been on the back burner: the Corinthians knew of the collection but have done nothing about it, and have written to ask what they should do. Paul for the first time, in spring 54, suggests the practical notion of every member saving a little each week for the fund; he is already nervous that there will be a last-minute collection, with an inadequate total.

But even this was wishful thinking. With the poor reception of the First Letter, the ugly mood at his second visit, and the prolonged tensions through the winter of 54–55, Paul knew that no one had been thinking about

---

[7]Most modern critics refuse the identification of ὁ ἀδικήσας (II,7.12) with the incestuous man of I,5, but the sketch I have set out above seems best to account for all the details given.

his fund. Hence the urgency of the issue: four verses had covered the question in I,16, but he gives two chapters to it now. Foremost in his mind is the embarrassment he is going to feel when he has told the Macedonians how keen the Achaeans were about it and then they arrive with him and find that nothing whatever has been done. As so often, he deals with the matter generally (II,8.1–15), digresses to stress the reliability of his three collectors (8.16–24), and then returns to the topic more specifically (9.1–15)—his standard A-B-A' pattern, beginning both appeal sections with the Macedonians (8.1–5; 9.1–4). In the first exposition, he proceeds with flattery (8.6–7), emulation (v. 8), theological profundity (v. 9), sweet reasonableness (vv. 10–14), and a proof text (v. 15; Exod 16.18). In the second, he develops the line he used in Gal 6: the one who sows generously will reap generously (9.6–11). This dubious appeal to self-enrichment is completed with a more attractive thought of the thanksgiving generated all around by a good response (vv. 12–15).

Paul pulls out every stop because he sees the collection as a vital element in his hope of acceptance by Jerusalem. Relations have deteriorated with the countermission, and if he turns up with a nugatory amount, his efforts may be rejected (Rom 15.30–31). But they will find it harder to refuse a large amount. He has evangelized in four provinces, Galatia, Asia, Macedonia, Achaia. We may think that he has established four sizable churches in each province, with perhaps fifty earners in each. If they saved a tithe each from a laborer's income—about thirty dinars a year—he could think of taking four or five talents to Jerusalem (1 talent = 6,000 dinars). But a quarter of this money must come from Achaia, and the fund there has hardly started.

PAUL'S LAST VISIT, WINTER 55–56

Paul would have liked to go to Corinth straightaway, but his wise old heart counseled delay. He wrote the Second Letter instead and sent it with three of his most trusted lieutenants: Titus, Luke, and Aristarchus (cf. Acts 27.2; Col 4.10, 14). They left Paul in July 55, and he followed them in October. They were to get the collection moving in a big way (II,8.6–7; 9.3–5) and to persuade the church to set its house in order over any factiousness or sexual looseness (12.20–21). He did not want any trouble this time.

Luke says Paul stayed in Greece three months (Acts 20.2–3); he means that Paul passed the winter there, no doubt successfully. He wrote his Letter to the Romans while he was there, a document full of relaxed confidence and hope. There was a contribution from Achaia to the fund (Rom 15.26), though not perhaps a very large one. Paul had originally thought of sending a group of Corinthians to take their share of the collection to Jerusalem (I,16.3), but Luke mentions no Achaean among the party who take the fund to Palestine. There are three delegates from Macedonia (Sopater from

Beroea and Aristarchus and Secundus from Thessalonica), two from Galatia (Gaius and Timothy), and two from Asia (Tychicus and Trophimus) (Acts 20.4). With such recent bitter divisions at Corinth, Paul may have felt it expedient to keep his supporters there.

So the apostle took ship in March 56, bound for Jerusalem, to rendezvous with the other church representatives at Troas after the Feast of Unleavened Bread (Acts 20.3–6). If there were tears and embraces, grief and joy, at Miletus (20.36–38) and Tyre (21.13), we may picture the scene at Cenchreae without hesitation: a crowd of more than a hundred, weeping and laughter, the heartfelt prayers of the humble kneeling on the sand. The old hero who had come so far to bring them the message of salvation, and at the cost of so many afflictions, who had defied the pretensions of Jerusalem single-handedly, was now setting out in the fragile hope of a reconciliation, armed with what little money they had put together. They had inflicted on him some of his worst trials, but now overflowing affection burst, as he had hoped, from many a warm Levantine heart. They would not see his face again, and his hopes of reconciliation would turn to ashes. What awaited him was betrayal, riot, prison, false justice, chains, and execution. But thus was done the will of the Lord, and the blood of the martyr was the seed of the Great Church.

Robert Jewett sets the last journey to Jerusalem in 57. This enables him to synchronize three chronological data: (i) Paul's party left Troas on a Monday (Acts 20.6–7, 13), after a week in the town (Tuesday–Monday), and before that a five-day journey (Friday–Tuesday) beginning directly after the Feast of Unleavened Bread, which would then itself have begun on a Friday. By astronomical calculations, the feast began on a Friday only in 54 and 57, of possible dates.[8] (ii) We do not know the date when Festus took the governorship over from Felix; 58, 59, and 60 are possible, but 59 is the most likely.[9] (iii) Paul spent three months on Malta, following the shipwreck that took place a fortnight after "the Fast" of Atonement (Acts 27.9).[10] If Paul was to set sail from Malta even as early as February, he would need to have arrived there in November; we thus need a late date for Atonement. Atonement fell on September 16 in 58 and on October 5 in 59, so the later year is again preferable. Jewett therefore brings Paul to Jerusalem in 57, has him in prison in 57–59 (two years, Acts 24.27), tried by Festus on his arrival in 59, shipwrecked the same winter, and in Rome in 60–62.

Jewett earns the reader's gratitude for gathering much varied information, but the argument often seems perilously thin. The Eucharist at Troas was probably on a Saturday night ("the first day of the week" [Acts 20.7], a formula rooted in Jewish reckoning of the day from sundown), so the party

---

[8]R. Jewett, *Dating Paul's Life* (London: SCM Press, 1979), 48–50.
[9]Ibid., 40–44.
[10]Ibid., 50–52.

may have left on a Sunday; the five-day journey from Philippi need not have overlapped on the Tuesday with the seven-day stay at Troas; Luke does not say that they left the day after Unleavened Bread; we cannot tell on which day the new moon was sighted; we do not know in which year an intercalary month was declared. All calculations of this kind are bricks without straw. Similarly, Luke's three months on Malta (Acts 28.11) should not be taken *au pied de la lettre:* the party sailed in a ship that had wintered on the island, and the time span given means the winter, give or take a few weeks, as it does with Paul at Corinth (20.3).

It is almost impossible that Paul would have been around in the Aegean later than the spring of 56. He reached Jerusalem in time for Pentecost, escaped lynching, was arrested, and spent 56–58 in prison at Caesarea. Festus took over from Felix in the summer of 58, and the shipwreck happened the following winter. Paul reached Rome in 59 and was executed in 61.

APPENDIX 1: THE INTEGRITY OF 2 CORINTHIANS

ALTHOUGH THE integrity of the First Letter is now widely conceded, the same is not true of the Second Letter.[1] Four main proposals have been made to subdivide it.

PROPOSALS TO SUBDIVIDE 2 CORINTHIANS

Second Corinthians 2.14–7.4. This text has been inserted into a letter, 1.1–2.13 and 7.5–16 (–9.15). Verse 13 of ch. 2 speaks of the delay in Titus's coming, οὐκ ἔσχηκα ἄνεσιν τῷ πνεύματί μου . . . ἐξῆλθον εἰς Μακεδονίαν, and 7.5 begins, Καὶ γὰρ ἐλθόντων ἡμῶν εἰς Μακεδονίαν οὐδεμίαν ἔσχηκεν ἄνεσιν ἡ σάρξ ἡμῶν.

The texts 1.1–2.13 and 7.5–16 would make a joyful letter, full of comfort and happiness that the church has now turned to support Paul; it is only concerned that the man who had caused such offense during his disastrous visit in 54 should be forgiven and reinstated. On the other hand, there are passages in the much less happy 2.14–7.4 that, so far from rejoicing at the church's new loyalty, in fact appeal for it (6.11–12; 7.2–4).

Second Corinthians 6.14–7.1. This text likewise appears to be an intrusion. It interrupts the two appeals just mentioned: πλατύνθητε καὶ ὑμεῖς . . . Χωρήσατε ἡμᾶς (6.13; 7.2). The intervening verses seem to be concerned with avoiding relations with non-Christians (ἀπίστοις) and not to belong in the context; rather, they seem to be related to the problems of the "previous letter" of I,5.9.

---

[1]There have been numerous *Teilungshypothesen* for 1 Corinthians; for an outline, see Sellin, "Hauptprobleme," *ANRW* 25.4:2964–82. None of these has won general agreement, however, and the integrity of the First Letter is well defended by Schrage, *Der erste Brief,* 1:63–71.

Second Corinthians 8–9.   Since these verses cover the topic of the collection at length, and with some repetition, it has been thought that they may be doublets and perhaps parts of further independent letters.

Second Corinthians 10–13.   The most serious problems concern II,10–13, which is widely thought to belong to a letter separate from 1–9.[2] The dominant spirit in 1–9 has been of comfort, joy, and conciliation, and this has reached its natural climax in the long appeal to contribute to the collection, a visible symbol of the church's unity, its loyalty to Paul, and its concern for the metropolitan church in Jerusalem. But then from 10.1 the tone changes to harsh and bitter altercation; there is sarcasm ("superapostles") and abuse ("emissaries of Satan"). So sharp a change of mood is not to be attributed to a bad night's sleep. It would wreck any hope of success for the collection appeal.

Nor is the difference to be explained as a change of address, from the church as a whole to the incoming missionaries. It is still the church (ὑμεῖς) that is being spoken to, distinguished from the newcomers (τινές, ὁ ἐρχόμενος). In addition, whereas there had been extravagant praise of the Corinthians' faith and obedience to Paul in 2.9, 7.16, and 8.22, these things are in doubt in 12.20–21 and 13.5, and 11.2–4 expresses fears of the total corruption of their faith. Again, in 1–9 the dominant first-person pronoun is plural, ἡμεῖς, whereas in 10–13 it is singular—Paul himself is embattled. These contrasts are often explained by the fusion of the greater part of two letters—probably an earlier, polemical 10–13 followed by an irenic 1–9— even if there is no manuscript support for such a hypothesis.

THE INTEGRITY OF 2 CORINTHIANS

Reimund Bieringer has written a series of articles[3] listing and criticizing the principal theories on the integrity of the Second Letter, both those proposing subdivisions and those defending its unity. I do not need to repeat his work, to which I am indebted, but will set out a brief answer to the problems raised.

A Weak Literary Argument.   As Bieringer says, the literary argument is weak. There is no obvious motive for anyone to divide an original 1.1–2.13 and

---

[2]Barrett, *Second Epistle,* 10–14; Furnish, *II Corinthians,* 35–41; Thrall, *Second Epistle,* 1:2–11; and many others, but not R. Bieringer and J. Lambrecht, *Studies on 2 Corinthians* (BETL 112; Leuven: Leuven University Press/Peeters, 1994), passim; also see J. Lambrecht, *Second Corinthians* (SP 8; Collegeville, Minn.: Liturgical, 1999).

[3]Now assembled in Bieringer and Lambrecht, *Studies,* 67–179.

7.5–16; the καὶ γάρ at 7.5 would have to be credited to the editor; the change from the singular ἐξῆλθον to the plural ἡμῶν needs explaining; there is no obvious parallel in Paul to a statement followed by the same in the genitive absolute. So the whole of the opening phrase of 7.5 would have to be the editor's, and the evidence for the hypothesis would disappear. Further, Lietzmann drew attention to considerable linguistic echoes in 7.4 with the rest of the chapter—θλίβειν, χαρά/χαίρειν, παράκλησις, καύχησις ὑπὲρ ὑμῶν, and so forth.[4] Bultmann comments, "This proves only the intelligence of the redactor," but on this basis, it is difficult to see how Bultmann could lose the argument. It would appear more natural, therefore, to treat 7.5 as a resumption of 2.13 after the long digression—Paul's customary A-B-A' pattern.[5]

The long digression is due to a second element in Titus's report. The good news was that there had been a strong revulsion of feeling in Paul's favor: the man who had insulted him was being shunned. But there was also bad news: men had arrived from Jerusalem with letters authorizing them to act as apostles and to take over the churches (3.1–3). Paul is already exercised in 1.15–22 over slanders about his plans κατὰ σάρκα to visit the church, a criticism voiced by the new apostles (10.2). Thus, when he comes to speak of Titus's long-looked-for coming, he launches into a thanksgiving for God's triumphal progress in the great Gentile mission (2.14); Titus's success (and spiritual maturity) was again to draw a heartfelt thanksgiving at 8.16. But the triumphal image recalls the bloody scenes at the end of a Roman triumph, the sparing of some prisoners, the slaughter of others. This leads to a preliminary defense against the new missionaries: they are the ἀπολλύμενοι in God's procession, and the Paulines are the σωζόμενοι (pp. 79–81).

L. L. Welborn defends an original 1.2–2.13 and 7.5–16 as corresponding with contemporary literary theory, but it is questionable whether Paul was familiar with such theory, let alone followed it in his letters.[6] In short, there is no reason to think that 1.2–2.13 and 7.5–16 were divided by the insertion of 2.14–7.4.

Paul's Paradoxical Glorying in His Sufferings.   With some further digressions Paul's paradoxical glorying in his sufferings continues until 6.10, where the phrase ὡς λυπούμενοι ἀεὶ δὲ χαίροντες brings him back to the λύπη and the χαρά that had been the first subject of the letter. He therefore seals off the defensive section 2.14–7.4 with an appeal to the Corinthians to come with him all the way in loyal affection and to separate themselves from the

---

[4]Lietzmann, *An die Korinther,* 131.
[5]Bultmann, *Second Letter,* 52.
[6]L. L. Welborn, "Like Broken Pieces of a Ring: 2 Cor. 1.2–2.13; 7.5–16 and Ancient Theories of Literary Unity," *NTS* 42 (1996): 559–83. See below, p. 248.

newcomers and their local following. The latter are ἄπιστοι, not unbelievers but faithless Christians, who, as in I,8, 10, have partaken (μετοχή, κοινωνία) in idol food (εἰδώλων), on the spurious ground that, since there is only one God, idols do not exist (I,8.4–5).[7] Furthermore, they allege libelously that Paul is embezzling money in his great collection (οὐδένα ἐπλεονεκτήσαμεν, II,7.2), a charge that Paul again rebuts in II,12.14–18 (ἐπλεονέκτησα, ἐπλεονέκτησεν).[8]

Two recent articles defend the integrity of 6.14–7.1 in its present context. G. Sass notes that the vocabulary is Pauline; there are closer parallels to the passage in *Jub.* 1 than those alleged from Qumran and Philo, and Paul may be drawing on a well-known theme.[9] F. Zeilinger observes that Paul elsewhere closes with a warning (Rom 16.17–20; I,16.22), but much of the argument is based on literary theory of *conquestio* followed by *indignatio*, a less dependable base.[10]

The "Problem" of Second Corinthians 8–9.   The collection was a basic plank in Paul's policy of forming good relations with Jerusalem (Gal 2.10), and he had been pushing it for some time (I,16.1–4; Gal 6.6) with increasing nervousness (Rom 15.25–27, 30–32). But he had made a late start at Corinth (I,16.1); nothing would have been set aside during the greater part of 54, when relations were strained, and he had indulged in some idle talk to the Macedonians about how zealous the Achaeans were, so unless something was done quickly, there would be red faces when he and his Macedonian friends arrived. The collection chapters thus form the climax of Paul's appeals, and do not constitute a serious problem. As so often, there is an A-B-A′ structure to the argument: 8.1–15 is the first appeal; 8.16–24, the practical arrangements; 9.1–14, the renewed appeal.

Betz treated II,8 and 9 as constituting two independent letters, but D. A. deSilva argues persuasively that the collection passage makes a climax to II,1–9.[11] DeSilva regards II,10–13 as distinct.

---

[7]See below, p. 247.

[8]I have argued this case more fully in "2 Cor. 6:14–7:1 As an Integral Part of 2 Corinthians," *NovT* 36 (1994): 47–57, the substance of which is on pp. 244–46 of the present book. There are (partially) similar conclusions in G. Fee, "II Corinthians VI.14–VII.1 and Food Offered to Idols," *NTS* 23 (1977): 140–61, and, on different grounds, by Lambrecht, *Second Corinthians,* 531–49, and Bieringer, in Bieringer and Lambrecht, *Studies,* 551–70.

[9]G. Sass, "Noch einmal 2 Kor 6,14–7,1: Literarkritische Waffen gegen einen 'unpaulinischen' Paulus," *ZNW* 84 (1993): 36–64.

[10]F. Zeilinger, "Die Echtheit von 2 Cor. 6:14–7:1," *JBL* 112 (1993): 71–80.

[11]H.-D. Betz, *2 Corinthians 8 and 9* (ed. G. W. MacRae; Hermeneia; Philadelphia: Fortress, 1985); D. A. deSilva, "Measuring Penultimate against Ultimate Reality: An Investigation of the Integrity and Argumentation of 2 Corinthians," *JSNT* 52 (1993): 41–70.

Paul's Situation.   Paul's situation may be compared to that of an Allied military officer in 1943 with a Greek resistance group that he has encouraged and armed. There was a "misunderstanding" when they nearly went over to the communists, but this has happily now been put straight. On the other hand, the latest news is that two members of a communist cell have joined the group and are conducting classes on *Das Kapital.*

As elsewhere, Paul's instinct is to open a tricky topic with kid gloves, move off into easier areas as may seem suitable, and then come back to the fight with the gloves off. In 2.14–7.4 he addresses the opposition gingerly: their letters of authorization, their claims to being transformed, their superior attitude to his life of suffering apostleship. He had no doubt that they would end up in "death" (2.16) and that they proclaimed a travesty of the word of God (2.17), being blinded by the god of this age (4.4), but he restrains himself and keeps to a dignified (and eloquent) apologia for his paradoxical apostleship. In the same way, he had in general restrained his emotions in Galatians, and he would do the same in splendor in Phil 1–2.

But it is not sensible to go on wrapping up the point when the whole mission is at stake and the opposition are ruthless as well as wrongheaded. At Gal 6.11 Paul takes the pen in his own hand and gives his converts a plain statement of how things are: these Judaizers merely want to force circumcision on you so that they do not get criticized by Jews themselves. Similarly, at Phil 3.1 he turns to "write the same things" to the Philippians. He has been so diplomatic in the first two chapters that we might not have known they were the same point, but from 3.2 the issue is markedly clearer: "Beware of the dogs, beware of the evil workers, beware of those who mutilate the flesh!"; κακοὺς ἐργάτας recalls the ἐργάται δόλιοι in II,11.13. Likewise, our Allied officer might begin a talk to his partisans by showing that his own behavior had always been trustworthy and only later reply to some communist slanders and even say, "These people do not really want to fight the Germans; they want to hand the country over to Stalin after the war."

In the same way, Paul takes a more direct hand in the letter, beginning at II,10.1: "Now I, Paul, myself charge you." It is no surprise that he moves into the first-person singular, because the slanders have been largely aimed at him personally; he is aggressive about them, partly because they are unfair and partly because he is frightened for the faith of his converts (11.3). The charges in 10–13 boil down to four: (a) He is not a proper apostle, whereas the newcomers boast of their being Jews, ministers of Christ (11.22–23), apostles of Christ (11.13), [super]apostles (11.5; 12.11); indeed, Paul has confessed as much by not having the church pay for his living (11.7–11; 12.13). (b) He overreached himself by trying to run missions in Europe that he could not supervise (10.12–18). (c) He lacked the Holy Spirit in every way—he had no presence (10.1), no oratorical power (10.10), no authority (11.16–21), no visions (12.1) or miracles (12.12). (d) He is dishonest and means to embezzle the collection (12.16–18).

These reproaches are more specific than we have met before, but in substance they are hinted at in II,1–9 and in 1 Corinthians:

(i) The letters of commendation of 3.1–3 gave the newcomers apostolic authorization (ἱκανότης, ἱκάνωσεν), and they boasted ἐν προσώπῳ (5.12), with reference to those who had known Christ in the flesh (5.16); so the references to superapostles and so forth in 10–13 are nothing new. Indeed, the same altercations go back to I,1–4. The trouble that has arisen now—about why Paul paid his own living expenses—was also running in I,9.1–5.

(ii) The complaint about Paul's disorganization and consequent cancellation of visits is rebutted formally in 10.14 (οὐ γὰρ . . . ὑπερεκτείνομεν ἑαυτούς), but it took the form of a gibe that he walked κατὰ σάρκα (10.2–3), and it was precisely this choice of words in this context that infuriated Paul in II,1.17.

(iii) The attack on Paul's lack of spiritual stature seems often to have used the word ἀσθένεια, and he is content, paradoxically, to boast in his weaknesses, especially in the great catalogue of his sufferings in 11.23–33. But we have had similar lists of "weaknesses" in II,4.7–15 and 6.4–10 and even in I,4.9–13. Paul did not think that an apostle was a church dignitary; it was by publicly sharing Christ's sufferings and resurrection that he lived the life of apostleship. Other differences on what makes someone spiritual are also in evidence in 1 Corinthians. Impressive glossolalia seemed to his critics to be important, though here Paul felt he could beat off competition (I,14.18). Still, his stress on ἀγάπη over against γνῶσις in I,13 shows that he was felt to be lacking in the more sparkling gifts. Chapter 7, above, argued that "knowledge" comes from visions, the area of Paul's deficiency in II,12.1–5.

(iv) The suspicions over the collection in II,12.16–18 are in evidence earlier in the epistle. The ironic "Being a πανοῦργος I took you δόλῳ" (12.16) is echoed in 4.2: μὴ περιπατοῦντες ἐν πανουργίᾳ μηδὲ δολοῦντες. In 8.16–24 Paul distances himself from the money, describing carefully the qualifications of Titus's companions, one of whom has been appointed by the (probably) Macedonian churches to administer this generous undertaking (8.19). "We intend that no one should blame us about this generous gift which we are administering" (8.20).

The movements of Titus have been a source of suspicion over the epistle's integrity, a suspicion that would never have arisen but for other factors. Paul sent Titus to Corinth twice, first (before 2 Corinthians) to find the church's response to the tearful letter and the troubles of 54, then as the bearer of 2 Corinthians.

Rebutting the charge of embezzlement, Paul writes, "Did I defraud you through any of those whom I sent to you? I urged Titus, and I sent the brother with him: did Titus defraud you at all? Did we not walk in the same spirit? In the same tracks?" (II,12.17–18). Paul sent Titus and a companion on the recent visit, and they never touched any of the church's money—any more than Paul did during his period of mission there. He had behaved with exactly the same disinterest as they did a few weeks back.

Paul usually speaks of Titus alone in connection with this past visit (2.13; 7.6, 13; 8.16), but 12.18 shows that Titus was accompanied; in any case, Christian emissaries almost always traveled in twos and threes for security. Titus is mentioned specially because he is "my brother Titus" (2.13), "my partner and co-worker in your service" (8.23). He had been promoted into the kind of relation Paul once shared with Barnabas, while the others were "apostles of the churches, the glory of Christ" (8.23). Titus's companion on the recent visit was probably just a local Christian from Assos or some such place; it sounds as if Paul cannot remember his name. Paul "urged" (παρεκάλεσα) Titus, whereas he "sent the brother."

Titus was as delighted as Paul by the positive Corinthian attitude (7.13) and dead keen to capitalize on it (8.16). He did not need Paul's "urging" (παράκλησιν), and Paul is sending along with him (συνεπέμψαμεν, epistolary aorist) "the brother whose praise in the gospel runs through all the churches" (8.18) and also "our brother whom we have often tested and found eager in many matters" (8.22). This party of three are to go ahead of Paul and make sure the money arrangements go smoothly when he arrives with the Macedonian delegates (9.3–5). Paul speaks tactfully of "you being ready, as I said you would be," but what he is really worried about is a refusal to hand over the funds amid accusations of his dishonesty.

Furnish argues that "the mission of Titus (and a brother) to Corinth referred to in 12:18 is most probably to be identified with the mission of Titus (and two brothers) to Corinth which is in view in 8:16–24; 9:3–5. But the context of 12:18 requires that the aorist tense verbs in that verse be interpreted as real aorists."[12] Furnish is clearly right that 12.18 refers to the visit just completed, but the context in chs. 8–9 shows that it is a second visit that is now in mind. The common use of παρακαλεῖν in 8.6, 16 and 12.18, and of the accompanying brother(s), is a weak basis for dividing the letter.

It is difficult to see any difference in Paul's attitude to the incoming missionaries between II,1–9 and II,10–13. In the early chapters, they water down the word of God, the gospel (2.17), and the god of this age has blinded their thinking (4.4). In the later chapters, they purvey another Jesus, another gospel, and another spirit, and they may corrupt the thinking of the church from its simplicity and holiness (11.2–4). In 1–9 they are not straightforward (2.17), commending themselves and boasting in surface matters (5.12); in 10–13 they are deceitful workers (11.13) and boast in the flesh (11.18). From the start, they are perishing (2.15; 4.2), bound for death (2.16), deprived in their faithlessness of seeing the light of the gospel by the god of this age (4.4). By the end, they are seen as transforming themselves into apostles of Christ,

---

[12]Furnish, *II Corinthians,* 38, cf. 559, nn. 17–18.

ministers of Satan, and their end will be according to their works (11.13–15). There is no change or development of attitude, only a little clarification.

The same is true of Paul's attitude to the Corinthian church. In II,1–9 he is full of affection. His sufferings are for their consolation (1.6); they are his boast, and he theirs (1.14); he works with them for their joy (1.24); they are his letter of commendation (3.2); everything is for their sake (4.15); if he is in his right mind, it is for them (5.13); his heart is wide open to them, there is no restriction in his affections, and he addresses them as children (6.11–12); they are in his heart (7.3); he often boasts about them (7.4); he writes of their longing, their mourning, their zeal, their indignation (7.5–11). The tone throughout these chapters is of a genuine and profound warmheartedness toward his erring flock. But the same feeling is equally manifest in 10–13. What is different is that the denial of his apostleship is now being taken seriously. God knows he loves them (11.11); it is they who should have been commending him (12.11); he never burdened them for his living (12.13); he wants not their money but them; he is like a parent spending his own for his children; he loves them the more and should not be loved by them the less (12.14–15); everything he does is for the sake of building them up (12.19).

When Paul speaks of their acceptance of his teaching, there is an understandable wavering. A wise parent may feel that a child will respond better to a few words of optimistic encouragement than to another toasting, and Paul is a wise parent, not a martinet. The church has made the major move, accepted his authority, and acted to punish the offender. So he can be happy that they stand firm in the faith (1.24); he is confident about all of them, that his joy would be theirs (2.3); he has complete confidence in them (7.16); they excel in everything—in faith, in word, in knowledge, in eagerness (8.7; 9.2). Wise parents do not feel they need be too exact when appreciating what obedience they can secure, and Paul similarly rather overstated the progress of the collection in Achaia when speaking to the Macedonians.

But the real situation is not quite so rose-tinted. Jerusalem envoys nearly wrecked the church before (I,3.17), and the situation is more perilous now with the coming of the so-called apostles. Besides, there is still unfinished business to be settled. So Paul entreats his converts to be reconciled to God, even in II,1–9 (5.20), and not to receive the grace of God in vain (6.1). The point of these appeals becomes clear at 6.14 when he begs them not to carry an alien yoke with faithless Christians who consort with idols, but to separate from them (6.14–7.1). This sense of peril is then aggravated as he reflects on the newcomers' attacks. He feels a divine jealousy for his converts, for he promised them in marriage to Christ, and he fears that Satan may seduce them (11.2–4). The harder tone in 10.1–12.13 is a function of this anxiety: those who become absorbed in *Das Kapital* may soon give up the partisans' struggle.

But there is also a subsidiary anxiety. The church has been corrupted in the past by sexual peccadilloes, about which Paul had spoken before (12.21; 13.2), and it has been riven with quarreling and backbiting over the last year (12.20). Paul is coming in a few weeks with an escort of Macedonian Christians, and he does not want a bad atmosphere ("I fear that when I come . . . ," 12.20, 21); on the contrary, he wants a happy, united church, with an edifying amount of money set aside for the collection. So 12.19–13.11 is his charge to have things in order or expect an uncomfortable series of scenes. In face of the charges of his weakness, it is not surprising if he puts on his stern face, but then it was the same in his First Letter: "I will find out not the talk of these arrogant people but their power. . . . Am I to come to you with a cane, or with love in a spirit of gentleness?" (I,4.19, 21).

Argument continues for the independence of II,10–13. N. H. Taylor still thinks of five letters that have been combined (and edited) to make our present 2 Corinthians. Welborn thinks that II,10–13 is an edited version of the tearful letter.[13] But such speculations seem unnecessary: there is no substantial reason to deny the integrity of the letter.

---

[13]N. H. Taylor, "The Composition and Chronology of 2 Corinthians," *JSNT* 44 (1991): 67–87; L. L. Welborn, "The Identification of 1 Corinthians 10–13 with the 'Letter of Tears,' " *NovT* (1995): 138–53.

APPENDIX 2: ACTS OF POWER

SECOND CORINTHIANS 12.1–10 marks the climax of Paul's rebuttal of his opponents' charges, but there is also a brief further point raised in 12.11–12 about his lack of signs (σημεῖα) or acts of power (δυνάμεις). The issue has a history going back to the First Letter. In the course of I,12–14 we learn what gifts the church counted and what Paul did, and we gain further insight into the issues between the two.

In I,12 Paul gives two lists of the gifts of the Spirit, the first apparently those prized by the church, the second his own list with a different selection and a different order. Paul's order is emphasized by numbering, "first . . . second . . . third." Both lists contain nine gifts, set out here in columns:

1 Cor 12.8–10	*1 Cor 12.28–30*
A word of wisdom	Apostles
A word of knowledge	Prophets
Faith	Teachers
Gifts of healings	Miracles
Working of miracles	Gifts of healings
Prophecy	Subsidies
Discrimination of spirits	Administration
Kinds of tongues	Kinds of tongues
Interpretation of tongues	Interpretation of tongues

The variations are instructive. Paul does not want to deny that learned exegesis of Scripture ("words of wisdom") or the insights of visionaries ("words of knowledge") are gifts bestowed by the Spirit (I,1.5), but he has shown his lack of enthusiasm for them in 1.17–2.16, and chs. 8–10, and he drops them both from his own list. In their place come some down-to-earth but indispensable gifts for a healthy church life. In the first place, there is apostleship; the church would not have been founded without Paul, their apostle. Then good teachers are invaluable for giving catechumens a sound foundation. There are poor widows and other church members, and it is important that some generous person put some money in the kitty. And the community needs some sensible and efficient organization. These four normal matters are gifts of the Spirit just as much as the paranormal practices that seemed so impressive at Corinth.

Paul's introduction of these four practical gifts is a reflection on the unreal world inhabited by his opponents. The first list contains no practical charism; they thought that a spiritual church did not need to think about organization, and the result of this neglect is the chaos of church worship revealed in chs. 11–14—women praying and prophesying barefaced, cliques at the supper, greed, drunkenness, blasphemous shouting, several people trying to speak simultaneously. With a bit of teaching and proper administration and a fund, things would run better.

Both lists give some emphasis to miracle working. The first list seems to mention this three times: "to another faith in the same spirit, and to another gifts of healings in the one spirit, and to another working of acts of power." They follow directly on the words of wisdom and of knowledge. In 13.2 Paul mentions "faith so as to move mountains," so it is miracle-working faith that is at issue. It is not clear where the boundaries were felt to lie between the three, but it is likely that "faith" comprised the other two. Paul includes healings and miracles in his own list and omits faith (which has a different connotation for him, 13.13), but in 13.2 faith seems to stand for the other two. "Healings" will be the same sort of events that are ascribed to Jesus (and, incidentally, the apostles) in the Gospels and Acts. "Acts of power" (δυνάμεις) may cover exorcisms, curses on the wicked (Ananias and Sapphira, Elymas), or prayers answered in time of need.

As we have so strong a tradition of Jesus performing healings and exorcisms, there can be little doubt that the tradition goes back to the Jerusalem church for both sides. Explanations for them naturally vary, but belief in the power of the spiritual to heal perseveres into the modern church, especially its charismatic wing. Probably a large majority of those prayed for were unaffected,[1] but there are many psychosomatic troubles that may be responsive to a word of power, there are cases of natural remission, and we cannot exclude instances of fraud. Still, in a community convinced that the Spirit was at work in a dramatically new and powerful way, healings were attempted regularly and were thought often to have been achieved.

Unfortunately, this was less true for Paul than for his opponents, who gave less energy to evangelism and more to church gatherings. He says regretfully, "Jews require signs" (I,1,22), whereas to him Christ crucified is the power (δύναμις) of God. Luke does recount three healing miracles at Paul's hands in Acts, but he gives the impression that Paul is keeping up with Peter: he heals a lame man at Lystra as Peter did in the temple; he raises

---

[1]W. Hollenweger, Professor of Mission in the University of Birmingham in the 1980s, once said in my hearing that, of those prayed for personally in black-led healing services, 9 percent claimed to be better.

Eutychus to life as Peter raised Dorcas; and he also heals Publius's fever and dysentery (Acts 28.8). There is, in addition, the exorcism of the woman with the Python, but no reader of Acts feels that Paul is a great miracle worker.

The new apostles felt the same and added it to his list of weaknesses; Paul responds in II,12.11–13 to this final charge: "for I fell behind the superapostles in nothing, even if I am nothing. The signs of the apostle were wrought among you in all endurance, in both signs and wonders and acts of power. For in what have you been worse off than the other churches, except that I did not burden you?" The superapostles said, "Paul is nothing. A sign of a true apostle is that he can work a miracle, as Peter does in Jerusalem. When did Paul do a miracle in Achaia? Not one!"

Here again the apostle shows his forensic brilliance, by quietly changing the meaning of the words in the same way that he did in I,1.22–24. There Jews asked for σημεῖα, that is, they required evidence that Paul could perform miracles, but what Paul produced was the proclamation of the true δύναμις of God, the cross. Now the (true) σημεῖα τοῦ ἀποστόλου have indeed been performed by Paul among them—that is, his tribulations (II,11.23–33), which he has faced ἐν πάσῃ ὑπομονῇ. We had the very similar phrase in II,6.4, where Paul commended himself as a minister of God ἐν ὑπομονῇ πολλῇ. What really shows a man to be an apostle is his perseverance in proclamation at the cost of floggings and shipwreck. It is his endurance of anything that is the apostolic σημεῖον; indeed, such trials endured are the real signs and wonders and acts of power spoken of in Scripture. Paul's response is not a sophistry. σημεῖα καὶ τέρατα is a common pair in the OT, usually referring to the deliverance from Egypt. Jeremiah and other prophets showed themselves to be God's ministers by courageous speaking, not by healings. We are better not to render δυνάμεις with "miracles"; the suggestion of transcending the laws of nature is alien to the biblical world of thought, which does not draw a line between Providence and miracle.

Commentators understand Paul to be asserting that he had indeed performed some signs and wonders, that is, healings, at Corinth.[2] But this seems to be excluded by two features: (i) Healings and other signs are not performed "in all endurance." No doubt they take energy out of the healer (Mark 5.30), but what is required is power, not endurance. Paul associates ὑπομονή with his tribulations. (ii) It is not very likely that the opposition would have raised the matter if Paul was well known to have performed some healings in Achaia; but if they did, it would be quite inadequate simply to deny the accusation. We would have expected "Did I not heal Sosthenes

---

[2]So Barrett, *Second Epistle,* 320–22, with caution; Furnish, *II Corinthians,* 553–56; P. Barnett, *The Second Epistle to the Corinthians* (NICNT; Grand Rapids: Eerdmans, 1997), 579–81; Lambrecht, *Second Corinthians,* 211–12.

when he was beaten?" or some such example. Also, I,1.22 suggests that Paul was unable to meet Jewish demands for signs.

The same point is made in Romans, in a passage often mistranslated: "So I have occasion of boasting in Christ Jesus in my work for God—οὐ γὰρ τολμήσω τι λαλεῖν ὧν οὐ κατειργάσατο Χριστὸς δι᾽ ἐμοῦ εἰς ὑπακοὴν ἐθνῶν, λόγῳ καὶ ἔργῳ, ἐν δυνάμει σημείων καὶ τεράτων, ἐν δυνάμει πνεύματος—so that I completed the gospel preaching" (Rom 15.17–19). Paul does feel a proper pride in his achievement, in Christ, in the task God gave him; he has carried the word from Jerusalem round the Mediterranean to Illyria. He will not presume to boast of anything that Christ has *not* worked through him, whether by speaking power (II,10.10; 11.6) or by acts of power. Eloquence and miracle have not been his gifts, but he has had the power in Christ to proclaim the cross.

The context in Rom 15 is remarkably close to that in II,10.12–18. "We will not boast unlimitedly (εἰς τὰ ἄμετρα), but according to the measure of the area (κανόνος) that God has apportioned as our measure, that we reach as far as you . . . not boasting unlimitedly in other men's (ἀλλοτρίοις) labors, but having hope . . . to proclaim the gospel in the regions beyond you, not to boast of work already done in another man's (ἀλλοτρίῳ) area" (10.13, 15–16). Paul had agreed with the pillars that he should go to the Gentiles (Gal 2.9), and no doubt he appealed to this compact when Jerusalem emissaries invaded his territory. This then evoked complaints that he "boasted unlimitedly" (the same phrase twice, in 10.13, 15), that is, claimed that the whole Gentile world was his archdiocese, and that he overextended himself (ὑπερεκτείνομεν ἑαυτούς, v. 14). Not at all, says Paul: we did reach as far as you without overextending ourselves, and we do mean to carry the work beyond you, but other people have planted the gospel elsewhere, and we make no claims about their work (vv. 15–16).

Romans 15.31 shows how nervous Paul feels about his reputation with Jewish Christians: they may even refuse the money he has so carefully collected for them. He knows that the Jewish Christians in Rome will have heard ill of him, and he goes into his tactful mode: "I am persuaded that you are filled with all knowledge" (cf. I,1.5!), "I have written to you rather daringly" (Rom 15.14–15). God made him a priest to offer the Gentile mission to God, so he has a καύχησιν in that he has proclaimed the gospel as far as Illyricum. It is the same limited boast that he made in II,10.13, 15, and here again it excludes building on other people's foundations (ἀλλότριον θεμέλιον, 15.20). The Roman church was founded without Paul, and he would not dare to boast about work that he did not do himself, with its attendant wonders. He only wants to see the church there and to be sent on by it in his further mission to Spain. It is the same cycle of thought as in II,10.12–21.

τι . . . ὧν οὐ κατειργάσατο (Rom 15.18) does not mean "except what Christ has accomplished" (NRSV), which would require εἰ μὴ ἅ or something similar. It is alarming to see how many commentaries force the Greek at this point;[3] the honest Barrett is a rare exception (followed by NRSV mg.). The passage has to be taken as a main clause, vv. 17, 19b, interrupted by a parenthesis. The ὥστε clause (v. 19b, continuing in fact to v. 21) is dependent on v. 17, "So I have occasion of boasting in Christ Jesus in things referring to God . . . so that I have completed the gospel preaching from Jerusalem and round as far as Illyria." No doubt the work has been forwarded by the gifts of others in word and deed, but Paul will not presume to boast of them. He will speak only of what Christ wrought through him (δι' ἐμοῦ), in his zeal to proclaim the gospel not where Christ was already named (v. 20) (the phrasing is close to II,10.15, "not boasting beyond the limit in other men's labors"). As in I,12, Paul is happy to credit other people's gifts to the Holy Spirit; he is more relaxed than in the tensions of II,12.11–12 and is content to speak of "signs and wonders" in their usual NT sense.

For the remaining gifts, it is a matter of priority. First Corinthians 14 shows that Paul is seriously concerned about edification in worship and that he wishes to restrain and downgrade tongues and to promote the more rational prophesying. As in OT use (and in Revelation), the latter would have consisted partly in foretelling the future and partly in homiletic matter. It is not an accident that prophecy is advanced in Paul's list to the second position or that tongues languish at the bottom of both lists. He knows that people soon get bored with streams of unintelligible verbiage but that they can profit from something appealing to reason. So he ends I,12 with "Be zealous for the higher gifts" (12.31) and begins I,14 with "Be zealous for spiritual gifts, but especially that you may prophesy" (14.1).

The wise pastor is never content, however, to take sides in a practical controversy. Paul knows that battles are won by holding the higher ground, so before moving from his lists of gifts in I,12 to his judgments in I,14, Paul "shows [them] a still more excellent way." There are gifts of the Spirit— some Christians have some, and others, others. But there is also the fruit of the Spirit (Gal 5.22), which grows naturally in each Christian's heart. Neither tongues (of humans and angels), nor prophecy, nor knowledge (with the knowing of all mysteries), nor faith (to work marvels), nor the devotion of one's possessions and one's time ("body"), are of any use without love. These other things all too easily end in boasting (ἵνα καυχήσωμαι, I,13.3); they are provisional and partial. What is permanent is the fruit of the Spirit: "faith, hope, love—and the greatest of these is love." As the apostle's eloquence reaches its crescendo, the angels rise to give their ovation, and e'en the ranks of Tuscany could scarce forbear to cheer.

---

[3]F. Leenhardt, *The Epistle to the Romans* (trans. H. Knight; London: Lutterworth, 1961), 369; E. Käsemann, *Commentary on Romans* (trans. and ed. G. W. Bromiley; Grand Rapids: Eerdmans, 1980), 393–94; Dunn, *Romans,* 2:862; J. A. Fitzmyer, *Romans* (AB 33; New York: Doubleday, 1992), 713.

APPENDIX 3: 2 CORINTHIANS 5.1–10

FIRST CORINTHIANS 15 was a controversial chapter, written to confound the error that denied the general resurrection; this rested on a false confidence that the kingdom had come already and that the spiritual were living in a renewal of the world of Gen 1. Paul has not changed his beliefs about the resurrection when he comes to write 2 Corinthians, but the atmosphere is different.[1] Titus has reassured him that the church as a whole has come over to his side, and in general, except when Paul thinks of the Petrine missionaries, his tone is affectionate and pastoral.

But the Petrines' charges cannot be forgotten, of course, and an answer has to be made to their slanders. In II,3.1–4.6 Paul has commented on their exalted claims of visions and transformation on the model of Moses. From 4.7 he begins the paradoxical exposition of the suffering apostolate. God had committed to him the great treasure of the gospel ministry (4.4–6), but this treasure was in earthen vessels, and it involved a daily dying with Christ (4.10, 12, 16; cf. 11.23), reminiscent of I,15.31, "I die daily." Such daily dying was only rational if one believed in a resurrection hereafter: "if the dead are not raised, let us eat and drink" (I,15.32); "knowing that he who raised the Lord Jesus will also raise us with Jesus" (II,4.14). This then leads to a contrast between the outer person, Paul's physical body, which is being destroyed, and his inner person, his spirit, which is being renewed daily (4.16), between the immediate light afflictions of a few floggings and shipwrecks and the permanent glory hereafter (4.17). As so often, Paul's paraenesis is effective because he brackets his converts with himself, and his sufferings, aspirations, and affections are transparently genuine. The language is a little more penetrated by Hellenistic dualism than in the discussion of I,15, but forms of dualism were widespread. Wisdom 9.15 speaks of a

---

[1]The exegesis of II,5.1–10 is controverted; Thrall, *Second Epistle,* 1:356–400, in a masterly exposition, discusses as many as nine different interpretations of some problem phrases. I have followed her most of the way, though not entirely over γυμνοί, and I have gone further than her in postulating polemics, e.g., with διὰ εἴδους.

perishable body weighing down the soul and of "this earthly tent" burdening the teeming mind; the image is probably a cliché.[2]

So the apostle lifts his own eyes, and those of his flock, to what cannot be seen but is eternal: "For we know that if our earthly tent-home is broken up, we have a dwelling from God, an eternal home not made with hands in heaven." The recent afflictions in Asia had brought him face-to-face with death (II,1.8–9), and survival to the παρουσία was no longer so certain. Never mind: "if" the tent is broken up and he dies, he has nothing to worry about—there will be a permanent and glorious home to replace it. The old σῶμα ψυχικόν will be replaced by a σῶμα πνευματικόν.

First Corinthians 15.36–44 presented an ambiguous image. There, at first it seems that our death and burial are compared to a bare seed that dies (ἀποθάνῃ, v. 36) and rots (ἐν φθορᾷ, v. 42): "we" are the Hebraic psychosomatic unity, sown in weakness, raised in power. But then there is the problem of continuity: we are sown a σῶμα ψυχικόν and raised a σῶμα πνευματικόν—what, then, links the two? By v. 53 the question has forced its natural solution: "this corruptible must put on incorruption and this mortal must put on immortality"; Hellenistic dualism is moving in. There is a core element to us that needs clothing (ἐνδύσασθαι, vv. 53–54 [4x]) with a body; a lowly body here, a glorious body hereafter; an "earthly tent-home" here, "a building of God, a home made without hands, eternal in heaven," hereafter (II,5.1).

The destiny of a true apostle is to suffer, but his suffering is a matter for rejoicing in view of the glories that shall be revealed: "For in this [body] we groan, yearning to be clothed over with our dwelling from heaven." A life of θλίψεις is not a bed of roses, but it is set in a splendid context of the future. Our οἰκία τοῦ σκήνους may be broken up at death, and we—our "inner man"—clothed over (ἐπενδύσασθαι). The clothing image has slipped in alongside the tent/house image. But the careful apostle will never count himself to have attained already; he presses on, knowing that otherwise he may find himself disqualified. So here he adds, "if indeed when we have actually dressed (εἴ γε καὶ ἐνδυσάμενοι), we shall not be found naked."[3] There are eternal homes of glory for the faithful, but there can be none for those judged faithless. How terrible for those who lose the protection of their "tent" and then have no covering for eternity! As already mentioned,

---

[2]Thrall, *Second Epistle,* 1:357–58, cites similar uses of σκῆνος from Ps.-Plato, *Ax.,* 365E, 366A, and from *Corp. herm.* 13.15, and of the body as the οἰκία of the soul from Philo.

[3]NA[26] prints ἐκδυσάμενοι with a United Bible Societies rating of D. But this reading is attested only by D* and a few Old Latin MSS against 𝔓[46] ℵ B C and many authorities reading ἐνδυσάμενοι. The latter reading is preferred by Barrett, Furnish, and Thrall and seems to be the harder text.

Rabbi Meïr commented, "How much more will the righteous be raised in their clothes" (*b. Sanh.* 90b), and Jewish tradition consigned sinners to Gehenna naked,[4] the better to feel the tormenting flames. The wily apostle is not just thinking modestly of himself; good pastors have in mind their erring sheep, whose confidence in eternity can always do with a mild shaking. Besides, there are false apostles, emissaries of Satan, at Corinth, who certainly have no permanent home awaiting them.

The text resumes: "For we who are in the tent groan, being weighed down, inasmuch as we do not want to be unclothed but clothed over, that our mortal element may be swallowed up by life." Paul had been weighed down (ἐβαρήθημεν, II,1.8) by his tribulation in Asia and thought he might die. His groaning is compared in Rom 8.22 to that of a woman in childbirth (συστενάζει καὶ συνωδίνει), groans of pain that will lead to a happy issue. But as in Phil 1.22–24, he does not want to die, to be unclothed (ἐκδύσασθαι), to lose his present "tent." It would just be marvelous ("far better") to move into his new, permanent home when the present mortal body will be transformed, "swallowed up by life."

Such an understanding is suggested by the linguistic elements common to I,15.53–54. There also our present self is spoken of as τὸ θνητόν, and it is repeatedly said that it must be clothed (ἐνδύσασθαι). A prophetic text was amended to read κατεπόθη ὁ θάνατος; here our mortality must be swallowed up (καταποθῇ) by life. There the new body was spoken of as ἄφθαρτον having ἀθανασία, here as being ἀχειροποίητον, αἰώνιον. The same stress emerges as in I,15: the apostle's daily dying only makes sense in the context of future resurrected being, and some account of this will be helpful in a community that has recently disputed it.

Paul's natural image was clothing. The mortal person had to be clothed with the new, glorious body to come. In II,5.1–4 he has slipped into the tent/house image, familiar from Wis 9 and common usage, but there is then a clumsy overlap as we are said to yearn to be clothed in a dwelling. A second clumsiness arises from Paul's drift between Hebraic monism and Hellenistic dualism. In I,15.53 "this mortal [unity] must put on immortality," but in II,4.16 there is an inner person being renewed while the outer person is destroyed. τὸ θνητὸν τοῦτο, then, has a present clothing, its corruptible body, and will need an overclothing, an incorruptible body; so the doubled preposition is suitable in II,5.2, 4, ἐπενδύσασθαι. But in II,4–5 Paul is thinking more of an inner person, our spiritual core, whose tent, the outer person, will soon collapse and be replaced by the permanent house. No one builds a permanent house around a collapsing tent, and the doubled preposition is actually unsuitable. Paul never thought of the new body as an overcoat.

---

[4]A. Oepke, "γυμνός," *TDNT* 1:773–76.

So far it has not been necessary to suppose any directly polemical note to the discussion; but the whole context is polemical, and the battle is resumed openly in 5.11–12. We should therefore be wary of possible reflections on Petrine doctrine, especially where Paul uses negatives. Thus, "insofar as we do not wish to be unclothed" may well signal the claims of Petrine πνευματικοί: God would soon bring their belly to nothing, and they would die and become pure spirit, no longer clad in flesh or weighed down by this earthly tent. This is still more likely with 5.5, which fits somewhat uneasily into its context: "And he who has prepared us for this very thing is God, who gave us the down payment of the Spirit." Why the ἀρραβών, here and at 1.22, and not just "the Spirit," as so often? The pneumatics claimed to have the Spirit, to be in the Spirit, to be above fleshly, psychic living, already reigning in the kingdom: what sort of an apostle is this Paul, looking like a tramp, a disreputable man punished by both Roman and Jewish courts? This is the pattern of true apostleship set out by God himself, replies the saint, a daily dying with Christ, and we are far from having the full Spirit as yet—all we have now is a first installment, an ἀρραβών, the firstfruits, ἀπαρχή (Rom 8.23). Flesh and blood cannot inherit the kingdom.

We can hear the grinding of axes even more clearly in the following verses. "So being always confident (θαρροῦντες) and knowing that as we reside in the body we are exiled from the Lord": Paul's mind is so full of competing thoughts and emotions that he drifts into anacoluthon. θαρρεῖν is part of his opponents' vocabulary of slander. Thus, the bitter ch. 10 opens, "I who am humble among you to your face but confident (θαρρῶ) towards you when absent. And I beg you that I shall not be confident (θαρρῆσαι) against some" (10.1–2). The Petrines were contemptuous of Paul's θαρρεῖν when he was living across the Aegean. All right, he says, it is not just that we do not lose heart (οὐκ ἐγκακοῦμεν, 4.1, 16); we positively "have confidence" (5.6, 8); like Carl Jung, we do not believe but "know": at present God bids us "reside in the body," and so for a while "we are in exile" from Christ in heaven, but this will not be for long.

The polemical undertone is reinforced by the parenthesis following: "for we walk by faith and not διὰ εἴδους." The last word has been a puzzle. The traditional rendering, "by sight," makes good sense, but there is lacking any parallel usage with this meaning. εἶδος normally has a passive meaning, "appearance," but attempts to interpret Paul's contrast as "not by faith but by appearance, form" seem forced.[5] The closest approximation to an active meaning is Num 12.8, where Moses is said to speak with God mouth to mouth, ἐν εἴδει καὶ οὐ δι' αἰνιγμάτων, but here εἶδος means "vision" rather than "sight." This text is indeed significant, for the final phrase is echoed in

---

[5]So Thrall, *Second Epistle,* 1:389: "the form of the glorious exalted Christ who dwells in heaven, not visible to believers who still dwell on earth."

I,13.12, "now we see by a reflector ἐν αἰνίγματι," in the context of knowledge by vision (ch. 7). The Petrine leaders reckoned that they already had access to the divine presence in visions and that they furthermore, in some cases, had penetrated to the third heaven ἐν σώματι (II,12.2–3). Paul is deeply distrustful of such claims (12.1–5). He is confident and knows that we have to walk by faith alone while we are here; we cannot both reside in the body and visit heaven, except by very special providence. Claims to combine the two are delusions—"we walk by faith, not by vision."

With 5.8 Paul returns to what he meant to say at 5.6: "But we are confident and are happy rather to be exiled from the body and to reside with the Lord." He is not afraid of dying. He is confident of what is to come thereafter and welcomes the thought of departing and being with Christ, for it is far better (Phil 1.23). "Wherefore also we strive, whether resident or in exile, to be pleasing to him." As in I,15.34, 56, his care is never far from the aspiration to holy living. While he is here (ἐνδημοῦντες), he is zealous to live by grace, and the hint is that his hearers should share his ambition. The εἴτε ἐκδημοῦντες is just rhetorical; he is not thinking about ethical behavior after death.

The cutting edge is again in evidence with 5.10: "For we must all be exposed before the judgment seat of Christ, that each may be rewarded for actions in the body, according to what they have done, whether good or bad." Paul's mind throughout the paragraph has been on the church, and τοὺς πάντας ἡμᾶς means all of us Christians. Although he has given major consideration to the possibility of his death ("if our earthly tent-home collapses"), he still expects most Christians (including himself) to be alive at the παρουσία, and it is then that Christ will take his place on the judgment throne and the secrets of all (Christian) hearts will be revealed (φανερωθῆναι). Christians will rise first (1 Thess 4.16); the full day of judgment, when God himself will take the throne and judge all humankind, is (for the present discussion) to come later. In I,4.5 Paul thought of the Lord coming and revealing (φανερώσει) the counsels of Christian hearts, and Christ as judge comes also in Matt 25.31; Acts 10.42; and John 5.27. Elsewhere God is judge, as in Rom 2.16; 8.33; 14.10.

Again the somewhat surprising syntax is our indication of a polemical undertone: why both τὰ διὰ τοῦ σώματος and πρὸς ἃ ἔπραξεν? It is in the face of claims to be πνευματικοί, to have risen above the bodily with an apostolic baptism, already to have passed beyond judgment into glory. There may be a number of ordinary Corinthian church members who have taken such vapid talk seriously, but certainly these are the doctrines of the Jerusalem missionaries. In I,3.10–17 Paul warned of two possible fates for those who built unworthily on his foundation: some would be disgraced, seeing their life's work go up in flames, but others who destroyed God's temple would themselves be destroyed. Feelings have hardened since those days, and there is little doubt with which group Paul would class the emissaries of Satan.

How far have Paul's teachings developed since early days? Not very much. He still thinks most Christians will be alive when the Lord comes in judgment, although he does take more seriously the prospect of prior death for himself, a change we can easily understand in the light of the many afflictions he has been suffering, especially his brush with death in II,1.8–9. He still thinks that all Christians will be embodied hereafter with a σῶμα πνευματικόν, a house not made with hands, eternal in heaven. He still thinks that the παρουσία will mean a judgment by Christ (I,3.10–17; 4.5; II,5.10) and that this will involve the resurrection of dead Christians (1 Thess 4.16; I,15.23; II,5.1–4). The only noticeable change is that the interim state of the dead is no longer stressed. The κοιμηθέντες who were such a feature of 1 Thess 4.13–18 and I,15 are no longer mentioned. The expectation now is that Paul at least would at once receive his eternal body at death: if his earthly tent-home collapses, he has (ἔχομεν, II,5.1) a building from God and expects to depart and be with Christ forthwith (Phil 1.23). But an interim state is still presupposed for ordinary Christians. How can they move into their glorious eternal quarters before they have been judged worthy of them? They may still be found naked.

Paul writes letters as a pastor, not as a systematician. In 1 Thessalonians he had two concerns—the false belief that baptism was a guarantee against dying, and the low level of morals. Hence the stress in 4.13–18 on the resurrection of the κοιμηθέντες on a parity with the rest of us, and in 5.1–11 on the possibility of the Lord's coming any time. In 2 Thessalonians, he has a slightly developed situation in view: it is being claimed that the Day of the Lord has come (2.2), and so people have given up work. Hence the necessity of setting out a series of events, inferred from Dan 7–12, that must happen before the resurrection (2.1–12) and the requirement to work or be shunned (ch. 3). Logically minded modern scholars notice a contradiction between the two letters and infer a different author for 2 Thessalonians, but we may think that for Paul systematics was the handmaid of pastoral theology.

Likewise with the developing situation in Corinth. In 1 Corinthians Paul is shocked to find a denial of the general resurrection and an assertion that in baptism Christians have already overcome death and are reigning (a position all too similar to that being proclaimed at Thessalonica). He again uses an argument of phases inferred from Scripture: Christ the firstfruits, then the resurrection of Christians at the παρουσία, then the reign of Christ with the final overcoming of death, finally the kingdom of God. All this still needs repeating in 2 Corinthians, but the approach of death has taken on a more immediate feel, and the emphasis in II,5.1–10 has shifted a little. Egalitarians may be scandalized that Paul should expect the privilege of immediate postmortal reclothing while other Christians have to await the Lord's coming, but I think that anyone who has read the lists of his trials in the epistle will have sympathy with his confidence.

APPENDIX 4: 2 CORINTHIANS 5.14–15

IT HAS been possible to infer in chs. 14–15 an outline of the Petrine gospel, with its different Christology and its emphasis on the arrival of the kingdom and the Spirit upon those who have become "spiritual." But 2 Corinthians contains a statement of Paul's own gospel that is almost equally obscure, in 5.14–15.

Paul set out his κήρυγμα in his three major epistles, the Corinthian letters and Romans, which are generally thought to have been written within two years of each other, between 54 and 56; only a few months separate 2 Corinthians from Romans. The main statements of Paul's creed do not come until some way into these letters—not until 1 Cor 15; 2 Cor 5.14–21; and Rom 5–6 and 8.

First Corinthians 15 is brief, even staccato. The basic creed, shared (Paul says) by all the apostles, includes Christ's death for our sins and his resurrection; this is then expounded in 15.21–22: "For since by a man [came] death, by a man also [comes] resurrection of the dead: for as in Adam all die, so also in Christ shall all be made alive." These two brilliant sentences enable us to see the force of the theory in a moment. Adam's sin involved all humankind in the divine judgment of death. Christ reverses the work of Adam at the end of history: his resurrection brings about the resurrection of all humankind. The myth (if we may use such a word in a neutral sense) is not accidental to Paul's thought; he returns to it in vv. 44–49. Christians have borne the image of the first Adam, the man of dust, and at his coming will bear the image of the second, last Adam, the man from heaven.

Romans is the most leisurely of the three letters and gives a fuller version of the theory in 5.12–21: "Therefore as by one man sin entered the world and through sin death, and so death passed through on to all human beings." The contrast is set out at length between the trespass of Adam and the obedience of Christ, between death and grace, condemnation and making righteous. We may therefore feel ourselves justified in thinking that the last-Adam theory was central to Paul's gospel, his understanding of what God had done in Christ, and we are not surprised to find that Barrett entitled his Hewitt lectures *From First Adam to Last* or that Dunn has given an important chapter of his *Theology of Paul the*

Apostle to the subject.[1] The only problem is that there is no mention of Adam in 2 Corinthians.

Preachers and lecturers tend to expound their thought in similar order to different audiences, and the expositions in II,5 and Rom 5–8 are markedly parallel, as shown in the following.

ENDURANCE IN HOPE

In II,4.7–5.10 Paul describes the apostle's life as a sharing in Christ's death, but in the expectation of a share in his risen glory; this theme is resumed in II,6. The same themes are sketched in Rom 5.1–5 and more fully in 8.18–39. We may notice in particular these similarities:

For our immediate light affliction (θλίψεως) works for us (κατεργάζεται) . . . an eternal weight of glory (δόξης). (II,4.17)

We boast in hope of divine glory (δόξης). And not only so, but we boast too in tribulations (θλίψεσιν), knowing that tribulation (θλῖψις) works (κατεργάζεται) endurance (ὑπομονήν). (Rom 5.2–3)

. . . as we look not at what is visible (βλεπόμενα) but what is invisible (μὴ βλεπόμενα); for the visible (βλεπόμενα) is temporary but the invisible (μὴ βλεπόμενα) is eternal. (II,4.18)

Hope that is seen (βλεπομένη) is not hope, for who hopes for what he sees (βλέπει)? But if we hope for what we do not see (βλέπομεν), we are awaiting in endurance (ὑπομονῆς). (Rom 8.24–25)

For in this [body] we groan (στενάζομεν), yearning to be clothed. . . . we groan (στενάζομεν) being weighed down. (II,5.2, 4)

All creation groans together (συστενάζει). . . . we ourselves groan (στενάζομεν), expecting adoption, the redemption of our body. (Rom 8.22–23)

God, who has given us the down payment of the Spirit . . . (II,5.5)

And not only so, but we too, having the firstfruits of the Spirit . . . (Rom 8.23)

---

[1] J. D. G. Dunn, *The Theology of Paul the Apostle* (Grand Rapids: Eerdmans, 1998), ch. 3, esp. n. 4.

These are not the only passages that speak of apostolic tribulations, but they are the only ones that use the verb στενάζειν or that so strongly contrast the visible with the invisible, and in the context of the (limited) gift of the Spirit.

DIVINE LOVE IN THE CROSS

Paul is the least dry of theologians; his convictions are felt passionately because they rest on emotional experience:

> For the love (ἀγάπη) of Christ constrains us, who make this judgment. (II,5.14)

> . . . because the love (ἀγάπη) of God has been poured out in our hearts. (Rom 5.5)

What II,5.14 hints at is set out more fully in Rom 5. Hardly anyone would give his or her life for someone else unless the latter were a fine person, but Christ died for us when we were sinners, his enemies, to save us from the divine wrath, to reconcile us. It is this divine love that has taken us over, been poured out in our hearts, constrains us, and convinces us of the truth of the gospel of the cross.

RECONCILIATION

> For all things are from God, who reconciled (καταλλάξαντος) us to himself through Christ and gave us the ministry of reconciliation (καταλλαγῆς), that God was in Christ reconciling (καταλλάσσων) the world to himself, and placing in us the word of reconciliation (καταλλαγῆς). . . . be reconciled (καταλλάγητε) to God. (II,5.18–19)

> For if being enemies we were reconciled (κατηλλάγημεν) to God by the death of his Son, much more having been reconciled (καταλλαγέντες) we shall be saved in his life . . . through whom we have now received reconciliation (καταλλαγήν). (Rom 5.10–11)

In no other passage of the Paulines is there so concentrated an emphasis on reconciliation. The reconciliation text in Rom 5.10–11 leads on immediately into the Adam/Christ exposition of 5.12–21; that in II,5.18–20 stands in the middle of an account of the atonement in 5.14–21.

ONE MAN FOR ALL

Paul begins his atonement passage in II,5.14–21 with an enigmatic state-ment: "One man (εἶς) died for all, so all died." This is indeed puzzling: we would have expected "so all were saved from death."[2] Nor is it clear who the "all" are. Barrett, Bultmann, and Thrall take it in its natural comprehensive-ness, "for all humankind"; F. F. Bruce, Ralph Martin, and Robert Tannehill limit it to all Christians. But what, then, about "so all died"? Perhaps "died" is here being used spiritually, "died to self"—unlike the "died" in "one man died," which is meant literally. But it is not true that all humankind has died to self, so we would have to add "potentially." Even if we limit the "all" to Christians, Paul elsewhere uses unglossed *die* to mean either actual dying or suffering trials that will lead to death; when he is speaking metaphorically, he uses adverbial phrases to say so: "die to self," "die to the law," "die to sin." All these suggestions seem forced and unsatisfying.

Barrett is an example of the contorted exegesis to which one is driven if the natural meaning of *all* is maintained: "Perhaps it is best to be content with the statement that, on account of the death of Christ, all men became potentially dead in the sense about to be described in the next verse. 'He died for us that we might die to ourselves' (Calvin). . . . To have died is 'to have become free for a new life with new aims and new purposes' (Windisch)." Similar to Barrett (and Calvin and Windisch) is Bultmann: "Für alle die Möglichkeit gegeben ist sich den Tod Christi anzueignen, was freilich nur im Glauben aktualisiert wird." Or Gerd Delling says, "So far as dying with Christ is realized for [a person], it is realized in baptism. . . . The saving action of God on the cross for all is recognized as such—on the basis of the preaching—by faith,"[3]

Thus, the universality of *all* has to be glossed by "potentially" or "as re-alized by faith." Others restrict it to all Christians. So Tannehill: "The basis for the direct inference from the death of one to the death of all is the idea of dying with Christ"—which has happened only for Christians. Bruce says that "[5.14] probably means that *one has died* as the representative of *all* his people" (note the intrusive "his"). Martin will have no beating about the bush: "πάντων can speak only of those who have accepted the message. . . . *All died* signifies those who accept Jesus—cf. Rom 6.1–11." Dunn recognizes the central difference made by faith and solves the problem with ingenuity: all die either because they identify with Christ's death and so are saved or

[2]So Windisch, *Der zweite Korintherbrief,* 182; R. Tannehill, *Dying and Rising with Christ: A Study in Pauline Theology* (BZNW 32; Berlin: Töpelmann, 1967), 65.
[3]Barrett, *Second Epistle,* 168; Bultmann, *Second Letter,* 153; G. Delling, "Der Tod Jesu in der Verkündigung des Paulus," in *Apophoreta* (ed. W. Eltester et al.; BZNW 30; Berlin: Töpelmann, 1964), 91, 94, (author's translation).

because they do not and "die their own death." If this were Paul's meaning, he would have to say it a little more clearly.[4]

It is important to note how carefully Paul glosses *die* when he means the word metaphorically: die to sin (Rom 6.2, 10), die with Christ (Rom 6.8; Col 2.20; 3.3), die to the law (Gal 2.19; Rom 7.6), die to oneself/to the Lord (Rom 14.7–8). Without such interpretative phrases, *die* means *die* or *be on the way to death.*

We may note two features of the expositions in 1 Corinthians and Romans. First, both open with a statement about Adam that does not mention him by name:

> For since by a man (δι' ἀνθρώπου) [came] death . . . (I,15.21)

> Therefore as through one man (δι' ἑνὸς ἀνθρώπου) sin entered the world, and death through sin . . . (Rom 5.12)

Indeed, Rom 5.12–21 uses the expression "one man" ([ὁ] εἷς [ἄνθρωπος]) no less than eight times to refer to Adam.

Second, both passages stress the universal consequence of Adam's sin in the death of all humankind:

> For as in Adam all die (πάντες ἀποθνήσκουσιν) . . . (I,15.22)

> . . . and so death passed on all human beings (πάντας ἀνθρώπους). (Rom 5.12b)

> . . . by the trespass of the one the many died (οἱ πολλοὶ ἀπέθανον). (Rom 5.15)

The echo with II,5.14 is noticeable:

> εἷς ὑπὲρ πάντων ἀπέθανεν, ἄρα οἱ πάντες ἀπέθανον.

If the εἷς were Adam, like the εἷς ἄνθρωπος in Rom 5.12 or ὁ εἷς in Rom 5.15, we would have perfect sense for the logic. Adam acted on behalf of (ὑπέρ) all people in his sinning and dying, "and so all died." This is exactly what is said in I,15.22 and Rom 5.15, in virtually the same words, πάντες ἀποθνήσκουσιν, οἱ πολλοὶ ἀπέθανον.

---

[4]Tannehill, *Dying and Rising,* 69; F. F. Bruce, *1 and 2 Corinthians* (NCB; London: Oliphant, 1971), 207; R. P. Martin, *2 Corinthians* (WBC 40; Waco, Tex.: Word, 1986), 131; J. D. G. Dunn, "Paul's Understanding of the Death of Jesus," in *Reconciliation and Hope: New Testament Essays in Atonement and Eschatology* (ed. R. Banks; Grand Rapids: Eerdmans, 1974), 125–41, here 130–31, 141.

The solution seems so obvious that one wonders that it has not been (to my knowledge) thought of before. There are apparently two reasons for this. One is that normally ὑπέρ has the meaning "for the benefit of." Martin asks, for example, "Does [Paul] mean 'for' in the sense of 'instead of' (substitution) or in the sense of 'for the benefit of'?"[5] But ὑπέρ is often used in the papyri in a neutral sense: one person acts *as agent for* others, and it may be that he or she does so to their ruin.[6] (In Britain, Arthur Scargill declared the miners' strike of 1984 as agent for the miners' union but brought many of its members to poverty and unemployment; a few years later, Tony Gooda acted as agent for his Names on Lloyd's of London, that is, his financial backers, at the cost of their fortunes.)

Nevertheless, an agent acts normally in the intention of benefiting his or her principal, and it is uncomfortable to speak of Adam "dying for all" his descendants with the meaning *involving them all* in death. But there is a second feature at work, which is Paul's willingness to stretch his prepositions for the sake of a rhetorical parallel. "As in Adam all die" is not natural Greek. Paul uses ἐν Χριστῷ regularly for a Christian's membership in Christ's body, and he writes the phrase ἐν τῷ Ἀδάμ as a rhetorical parallel. We are baptized εἰς Χριστόν, and this leads to Israel having been baptized εἰς τὸν Μωϋσῆν in the sea and the cloud (I,10.2), an expression never found in the rabbis. Romans 5.12–21 is filled with the more natural contrasts using διά—"through one man," "through Jesus Christ," "through the trespass of the one man," "through the obedience of the one man." Paul has used the expression "Christ died for us (ὑπὲρ ἡμῶν ἀπέθανεν)" in Rom 5.8, and he uses the same phrase by extension of the one man, Adam, in II,5.14.

Good sense then follows for II,5.15. One man, Adam, died as agent for all, and so all humankind died; "and he [Adam] died as agent for all [humankind] in order that [in the providence of God] those who are alive [today] might no longer live to themselves, but to him who died and rose for them [Christ]." The contrast is the same as in I,15.21–22: all die in Adam, all come to life again in Christ. We may notice that it is normal to translate "who died and rose for them," that is, the resurrection of Jesus as well as his death is for us. But then Jesus did not rise with the intention of benefiting anyone. God raised him; he rose as the unwitting agent of our rising to new life, just as Adam was the unwitting agent of universal death.

Standard exegesis has found the ἵνα clause problematic, too. If it was Jesus who died for all in II,5.14, who are οἱ ζῶντες in 5.15? They have to be glossed as those who are alive spiritually, in Christ. But in 4.11 ἡμεῖς οἱ

---

[5]Martin, *2 Corinthians,* 129.
[6]MM 651, s.v. ὑπέρ, offers instances of representation in business and law and refers to the larger corpus in L. Wenger, *Die Stellvertretung im Rechte der Papyri* (Leipzig: B. G. Teubner, 1906).

ζῶντες means we Christians who are literally alive now, and in 1 Thess 4.15, 17 the same phrase means οἱ περιλειπόμενοι, those who are alive at the Lord's coming. So here they are more naturally just "those who are alive today." Paul is a thorough providentialist and often attributes divine purpose (ἵνα) even to bad events. In 4.7–15 Paul's sufferings are "all for you that (ἵνα) grace may abound." In Rom 8.20–21 God has subjected creation to vanity in the hope that it will be liberated from corruption. In Rom 11.32 God shut up all into disobedience that (ἵνα) God might have mercy on all.

"All died . . . the living" suggests that a contrast is being drawn, but Barrett makes them the same: "*The living,* a descriptive subject, where 'men' or 'all men' might have sufficed, brings out the fact that the death all died in the death of Christ was not like his physical death."[7] Paul sometimes uses *live* metaphorically, like *die,* but again he makes it clear by the context, "live to God," "to oneself," "eternally," and so forth.

No Longer to Ourselves

Romans continues to expound more fully the thought of II,5 to the end. Paul is constrained, moved by the love of Christ so demonstrated on the cross; it drives him, and all who accept his gospel, to a different pattern of living:

> . . . that those who are alive should no longer live (μηκέτι ζῶσιν) to themselves but to him who died and rose for them. (II,5.15)

> . . . so that we should no longer (μηκέτι) be slaves to sin. (Rom 6.6)

> Christ being raised from the dead dies no longer (οὐκέτι) . . . so you too reckon yourselves to be dead to sin but alive to God (ζῶντας τῷ θεῷ) in Christ Jesus. (Rom 6.9, 11)

This new quality of life is possible because we are now "in Christ":

> If anyone is in Christ, he is a new (καινή) creation. (II,5.17)

> So we were buried with [Christ] in baptism into death, that as Christ was raised . . . we too might walk in newness (καινότητι) of life. (Rom 6.4)

> Romans 6 is given to expounding our incorporation into Christ's body, and our consequent transfer from a life of sin to one of righteousness.

---

[7]Barrett, *Second Epistle,* 170.

So, amid the welter of practical issues, Paul finds opportunity to state his central Adam/Christ theology in each of his three major letters. In 1 Corinthians, the first two chapters speak of the word of the cross, but this and the resurrection do not receive any exposition until the Adam passages in ch. 15. In the fuller Roman letter, the correspondence of Adam and Christ is set out at more leisure in Rom 5–6, 8. And the same basic myth, in almost the same contrasting phrases, provides the mainspring of the Second Letter in II,5.14–21: the one man who died and brought about the death of all, and the one who died and rose again to transform our lives.

APPENDIX 5: NEW CRITICAL APPROACHES

THE READER will be aware, and perhaps disappointed, to find little reference in this work to novel critical approaches. The last two decades have seen a blooming of nontraditional lines of study, and these have concentrated especially on the Corinthian letters, as giving the most detail from the Pauline correspondence. There have, in particular, been aspirations to forms of sociohistorical and rhetorical criticism.

SOCIOHISTORICAL CRITICISM

Traditional commentaries treated the Corinthian letters, as I have done, as being motivated by religious concerns, and the attempts of Marxist writers to turn Christianity into a proto-proletarian movement were not taken up. It is obvious, however, that there is a social and economic aspect to any religious community, and from the 1960s studies were produced of this side of life in the church.[1] E. A. Judge refused the identification of the churches with the poor, but he tried to set them in a real context of first-century life.[2] A church was structured in the same way as a Greco-Roman household; Paul was a wandering preacher who would be seen as somewhat like a Sophist, so his churches would seem like "scholastic communities," devotees of a new, deviant philosophy. At the same time, Paul could not be reduced to any kind of stereotype. He had to fit into the world of the influential and the less influential, but he gave no ground to worldly values.

In the 1970s Gerd Theissen, in a series of articles, concentrated on the Corinthian church, on which there is the most information, and suggested

---

[1] J. K. Chow, *Patronage and Power: A Study of Social Networks in Corinth* (JSNTSup 75; Sheffield: Sheffield Academic Press, 1992), 12–14, mentions writings by Engels and Kautsky.

[2] E. A. Judge, *The Social Pattern of the Christian Groups in the First Century* (London: Tyndale, 1960).

criteria for discerning social stratification in the community.[3] There are rich people as well as poor; educated ("wise") people with households, able to travel; and so forth. Most of those named in the letters are from the upper strata, and Paul baptized only such people and their households— Stephanas, Crispus, Gaius. It would be the richer people who caused the trouble in 1 Corinthians, going to law for money, being involved in business dinners or giving occasional free meals, both of which would include prayers to heathen gods over the meat. The tensions at Corinth must be seen therefore as primarily between the richer, wise, strong group and the poorer, weak Christians. Paul refuses to be identified with either party and tries to reconcile them.

Theissen's work was original and interesting, and it has generated much discussion. Some helpful criticisms were made by Wayne Meeks: for instance, we have evidence of quite poor farmers going to law for their rights.[4] It is not so surprising if more independent people are the first to espouse a new creed, but an important doubt arises over Theissen's understanding of the wise and the strong. The discussion of wisdom is limited to I,1–3, and the σοφός of I,1.20 is associated with the γραμματεύς as a pundit of Jewish learning, not an educated person. The antithesis between the strong and the weak similarly turns on "knowledge" of the application of Jewish law (I,8.1–6). In Rom 14 the same terms are applied but are reversed: there the weak are the Jewish Christians who will eat only vegetables, whereas the "strong" are Gentile Christians, whose consciences do not balk at meat from the market.

The 1990s have seen further studies of the social background to the Pauline mission. Both John Chow and Andrew Clarke have examined the Roman system of patronage as an inevitable feature of the Corinthian church.[5] Wealthy men such as Erastus and Gaius were patrons of the church, providing houseroom and finance for the community. They would have had groups of friends, relatives, and associates, freedmen and slaves, who were their clients, dependent on them for favors in everyday life. Hence they, and other patrons, were in a position to call on a network of support for their preferences. So it is not surprising if they do such scandalous things as taking one's father's wife or eating in a temple restaurant. They could depend on their clients to support them if there were criticisms by the apostle.

---

[3]The articles are collected in G. Theissen, *The Social Setting of Pauline Christianity* (trans. J. H. Schütz; Philadelphia: Fortress, 1982), with a second series, *Social Reality and the Early Christians* (Edinburgh: T&T Clark, 1993).

[4]W. A. Meeks, *The First Urban Christians: The Social World of the Apostle Paul* (New Haven: Yale University Press, 1983).

[5]Chow, *Patronage and Power;* A. D. Clarke, *Secular and Christian Leadership in Corinth: A Socio-historical and Exegetical Study of 1 Corinthians 1–6* (Leiden: Brill, 1993).

It has been difficult, however, to be sure of our perspectives in a world so vast and so distant, and few points have remained unchallenged. For instance, A. C. Mitchell claimed that there was no evidence of the rich suing the poor.[6] Justin Meggitt has questioned a series of widely agreed conclusions.[7] We have to be cautious about the Greco-Roman social background even more than about the Jewish culture that is more directly mirrored in our texts.

Clarke and Chow are right about the influence of the influential; perhaps no one who has been a parish cleric would doubt their conclusions. All churches contain more confident, wealthy, gifted, or active members whose friends and relatives tend to support them. What has been disappointing about the sociohistorical enterprise is the little novel light it has shed on Pauline Corinth. The church does not divide into the rich and the poor. There are a number of well-to-do Paulines, and there are well-to-do people in the opposition. It is a help to understand that prosperous people would find it hard to avoid meals in temple restaurants, but if Erastus was one of them, was he a Pauline or a Petrine?

RHETORICAL CRITICISM

The study of Greco-Roman rhetoric has seemed to offer a promising insight into the background of Paul's mind. Betz's work on Galatians in the 1970s gave the impetus for this new approach. Here follow some comments on a well-received book by one of his students, Margaret M. Mitchell, *Paul and the Rhetoric of Reconciliation* (1992), a study of 1 Corinthians. Other works on the same letter are by Litfin and Anders Eriksson.[8]

Ancient critics divided speeches into three categories: deliberative, epideictic, and forensic. Mitchell places 1 Corinthians in the deliberative (συμβουλευτικόν) category; its aim is to persuade, and the persuasion is throughout to one end, the union or reconciliation of the church. Ancient deliberative addresses commonly had four foci: they advocated policies for the future; they stressed what was to the hearers' advantage (σύμφορον); they offered examples (παραδείγματα); and they opposed factionalism. All these four features are hallmarks of 1 Corinthians. Paul is persuading the

---

[6]A. C. Mitchell, "Rich and Poor in the Courts of Corinth: Litigiousness and Status in 1 Cor. 6.1–11," *NTS* 39 (1993): 562–86.

[7]J. Meggitt, "Meat Consumption and Social Conflict in Corinth," *JTS* 45 (1994): 137–41; "Social Status."

[8]M. M. Mitchell, *Paul and the Rhetoric of Reconciliation: An Exegetical Investigation of the Language and Composition of 1 Corinthians* (Louisville: Westminster John Knox, 1992); Litfin, *St. Paul's Theology;* Eriksson, *Tradition as Rhetorical Proof.*

community to alter their attitudes in the future. Five times he uses the συμφερ– root, appealing to his hearers' innate desire for what is in their best interest. Much of the letter is given to examples, sometimes from Scripture but most often with Paul taking himself as the case to be imitated. The entire letter is against factionalism.

The theme of the letter is set out in I,1.10, which uses four phrases that belong to the technical vocabulary of deliberative addresses. The Corinthians are bidden τὸ αὐτὸ λέγειν, a phrase used in Polybius (twice), in Thucydides, in Dio Chrysostom, and in Aelius Aristides (five times), all in the sense of agreeing, coming to a common mind. σχίσμα is from the σχιζ– root, which Lucian and Plutarch use for a divided community. ἐν τῷ αὐτῷ νοΐ is synonymous with ὁμόνοια, the standard term for being *of the same mind;* and to be of the same γνώμη is a common phrase, sometimes even paired with ὁμόνοια.

Mitchell follows the same technique throughout the epistle, picking out significant words and images, such as building, and showing that they recur in Greek and Latin deliberative addresses. This enables her to set out the whole letter as an instance of Greco-Roman rhetoric. It has an epistolary format, with prescript and thanksgiving (1.1–9) and closing (ch. 16). But the body of the letter can be arranged in line with the deliberative speech: the πρόθεσις (1.10), the διήγησις (1.11–17), the πίστεις (*proofs,* 1.18–15.57), the ἐπίλογος (*summation,* 15.58). Paul had imbibed the pervasive rhetorical patterns of his time, and this yields an important conclusion: the letter is not a conflation of different communications but a single composition with a single theme, the church's reconciliation.

To show that Paul was influenced by Greco-Roman rhetoric, it is necessary either to give evidence from his letters that this is so or to provide external testimony. Murphy-O'Connor argues from Paul's upbringing at Tarsus that he is likely to have gone to school there and to have become familiar with Homer, Euripides, and other standard Greek educational texts.[9] This is a frail reed indeed. There is no echo of either Homer or Euripides in all the Pauline Epistles. Paul's father was a Pharisee and may not have thought much of Achilles and Medea; perhaps he sent his boy to attend the synagogue school and to read Leviticus instead.

Litfin advances a more widely employed argument. Oratory was the key to success in the Roman world, and education was largely education in public speaking. Even those who had not been taught the techniques of such speaking would hear them practiced at public meetings addressed by civic officials, politicians, philosophers, and so on. One could not escape them. There is a minimum of truth in this. Paul plainly knows how to ask a series

---

[9]J. Murphy-O'Connor, *Paul: A Critical Life* (Oxford: Clarendon, 1996), 48.

of rhetorical questions in the manner of a diatribe; he can cite a popular tag from Menander; he can play with words such as ἀσύνετος/ἀσύνθετος. He has indeed snapped up some trifles at street corners. But this is a long way from the hypothesis that he knows the structure (*the* structure?) of a Greek speech and can or would wish to reproduce it. We are all used to hearing the standard political oratory, with its repetitious dogmatic crescendos, but my readers will not find them reproduced in my writings: I attended a different school.

Rhetorical critics need to show a much more impressive and detailed correspondence between 1 Corinthians and the models proposed. It is rather obvious, for example, that a letter or speech urging a community to action will refer to the future. It may be a regular theme of leaders to plead for a common front or to argue from examples. But then, as Eriksson concedes, such generalities might be found in a speech by President Clinton, who has probably not studied Quintilian. When we come to something specific, such as the use of συμφερ–, we find the issue less clear. Is Paul really arguing primarily from the Corinthians' self-interest? Surely he commends the word of the cross because this is the divine wisdom; other missionaries' wisdom is not less advantageous but declared by God to be folly; he and Apollos taught the principle "Not beyond what is written," because that was the truth. He condemns incest with one's father's wife because it is wrong, it is πορνεία. And going to law is wrong, too; it is πλεονεξία. And so on through the letter. Paul was not a utilitarian. The mentions of what is σύμφορον are incidental.

It is the same with the "technical" phrases in I,1.10. Not surprisingly, a number of authors, like Paul, urge their audiences to say the same thing, think the same thing, speak the same thing, or share the same opinion. These are among the commonest of Greek phrases. More impressive would be the use of specialized expressions such as ὁμόνοια, but this does not occur in the epistle, unfortunately, nor in the Pauline corpus. Nor does the word σχίσμα occur in the Greek speeches. Mitchell cites two instances for the use of the verb σχίζεσθαι, but neither of them refers to a faction: in one an assembly is divided (ἐσχίζετο) between two opinions; in the other the parting of friends is like a (limb of a) body that is broken or split (σχισθέντος).[10] When it comes to anything approaching the genuinely technical, the evidence is missing.

Paul is indeed trying to persuade the church to unite, but the letter is not written against factionalism but against the Cephas faction. Probably all appeals for unity are for unity on the speaker's terms, and this is certainly so here. Paul would not be satisfied if the Corinthians united in honoring

---

[10]Mitchell, *Paul and Rhetoric,* 73.

words of wisdom. But a letter covering so many particular issues cannot be proven to be a single composition by its general demand for unity: Mitchell's omnibus "proofs" ("1:18–15:57 πίστεις" in her outline analysis) are too multifarious, and too unlike proofs in the normal sense. The same feature applies to 2 Corinthians, which she thinks to consist of five subunits while Frances Young used a different rhetorical argument to prove its unity.[11] Neither argument is valid.

---

[11]F. M. Young and D. F. Ford, *Meaning and Truth in 2 Corinthians* (BFT; London: SPCK, 1987).

BIBLIOGRAPHY

Addinall, P. "Why Read the Bible?" *ExpTim* 105 (1994): 136–40.

Barclay, J. M. G. *Jews in the Mediterranean Diaspora: From Alexander to Trajan (323 BCE–117 CE)*. Edinburgh: T&T Clark, 1996.

Barker, M. *The Great Angel: A Study of Israel's Second God*. London: SPCK, 1992.

Barnett, P. *The Second Epistle to the Corinthians*. NICNT. Grand Rapids: Eerdmans, 1997.

Barrett, C. K. *The Acts of the Apostles*. 2 vols. ICC. Edinburgh: T&T Clark, 1994–1998.

———. *A Commentary on the Epistle to the Romans*. BNTC. London: Black, 1957.

———. *A Commentary on the First Epistle to the Corinthians*. 2d ed. BNTC. London: Black, 1971.

———. *A Commentary on the Second Epistle to the Corinthians*. BNTC. London: Black, 1973.

———. *Essays on Paul*. London: SPCK, 1982.

———. *From First Adam to Last*. London: Black, 1962.

———. *The Gospel according to St. John*. 2d ed. Philadelphia: Westminster, 1978.

Barth, G. "Zur Frage nach der in 1 Korinther 15 bekämpften Auferstehungsleugnung," *ZNW* 83 (1992): 187–201.

Baur, F. C. "Die Christuspartei in der korinthischen Gemeinde, der Gegensatz der petrinischen und paulinischen Christentums in der ältesten Kirche, Petrus in Rom." *Tübinger Zeitschrift für Theologie* 4, no. 3 (1831): 61–206.

———. "Die Einleitung in das Neue Testament als theologische Wissenschaft." *Theologische Jahrbücher* 9 (1850): 463–566; 10 (1851): 70–94, 222–53, 291–329.

———. *Paul, the Apostle of Jesus Christ*. 2d ed. 2 vols. Vol. 1 translated and edited by E. Zeller; revised by A. Menzies. Vol. 2 translated by A. Menzies. Edinburgh: Williams & Norgate, 1876). Translation of *Paulus, der Apostel Jesu Christi: Sein Leben und Wirken, seine Briefe und seine Lehre. Ein*

Beitrag zu einer Kritischen Geschichte des Urchristenthums. 2d ed. Stuttgart: Becher & Müller, 1845.

Bernard, J. H. "The Connexion between the Fifth and Sixth Chapters of I Corinthians." *Expositor* 7.3 (1907): 433–43.

Betz, H.-D. *Der Apostel Paulus und die sokratische Tradition.* BHT 45. Tübingen: Mohr, 1972.

———. *2 Corinthians 8 and 9.* Edited by G. W. MacRae. Hermeneia. Philadelphia: Fortress, 1985.

Bieringer, R., and J. Lambrecht. *Studies on 2 Corinthians.* BETL 112. Leuven: Leuven University Press/Peeters, 1994.

Boer, M. C. de. *The Defeat of Death: Apocalyptic Eschatology in 1 Corinthians 15 and Romans 5.* JSNTSup 22. Sheffield: Sheffield Academic Press, 1988.

Borgen, P. *Early Christianity and Hellenistic Judaism.* Edinburgh: T&T Clark, 1996.

Brown, P. *The Body and Society: Men, Women, and Sexual Renunciation in Early Christianity.* Boston: Faber & Faber, 1988.

Brown, R. E. *The Gospel according to John.* 2 vols. AB 29–29A. New York: Doubleday, 1966–1970.

Brox, N. "ΑΝΑΘΕΜΑ ΙΗΣΟΥΣ. 1 COR. 12:3." *BZ* 12 (1968): 103–11.

Bruce, F. F. *The Epistle to the Galatians: A Commentary on the Greek Text.* NIGTC. Grand Rapids: Eerdmans, 1982.

———. *1 and 2 Corinthians.* NCB. London: Oliphant, 1971.

Bultmann, R. *The Second Letter to the Corinthians.* Translated by R. A. Harrisville. Minneapolis: Augsburg, 1985.

———. *Theology of the New Testament.* 2 vols. Translated by K. Grobel. New York: Scribner, 1951–1955.

Caird, G. B. "Towards a Lexicon of the Septuagint, II." *JTS* 20 (1969): 21–40.

Callan, T. "Prophecy and Ecstasy in Greco-Roman Religion and I Corinthians." *NovT* 27 (1985): 125–40.

Carr, W. "The Rulers of This Age—I Corinthians II.6–8." *NTS* 23 (1976): 20–35.

Chadwick, H. " 'All Things to All Men' (1 Cor. ix. 22)." *NTS* 1 (1954–1955): 261–75.

Chester, S. "The Secrets of the Heart Laid Bare." Paper presented at the British New Testament Conference, Leeds, September 12, 1997.

Chow, J. K. *Patronage and Power: A Study of Social Networks in Corinth.* JSNTSup 75. Sheffield: Sheffield Academic Press, 1992.

Clarke, A. D. *Secular and Christian Leadership in Corinth: A Socio-historical and Exegetical Study of 1 Corinthians 1–6.* Leiden: Brill, 1993.

Collins, J. N. *Diakonia: Reinterpreting the Ancient Sources.* Oxford: Oxford University Press, 1990.

Conzelmann, H. *1 Corinthians.* Translated by J. W. Leitch. Edited by G. W. MacRae. Hermeneia. Philadelphia: Fortress, 1975.

Cullmann, O. *The Christology of the New Testament.* Rev. ed. Translated by S. G. Guthrie and C. A. M. Hall. Philadelphia: Westminster, 1963.

Dahl, N. "Paul and the Church at Corinth according to 1 Corinthians 1–4." Pages 313–35 in *Christian History and Interpretation: Studies Presented to John Knox.* Edited by W. R. Farmer et al. Cambridge: Cambridge University Press, 1967.

Davis, J. A. *Wisdom and Spirit: An Investigation of 1 Corinthians 1:18–3:20 against the Background of Jewish Sapiential Traditions in the Greco-Roman Period.* Lanham, Md.: University Press of America, 1984.

Delling, G. "Der Tod Jesu in der Verkündigung des Paulus." Pages 85–96 in *Apophoreta.* Edited by W. Eltester et al. BZNW 30. Berlin: Töpelmann, 1964.

Delobel, J. "Coherence and Relevance in 1 Cor 8–10." Pages 177–90 in *The Corinthian Correspondence.* Edited by R. Bieringer. BETL 125. Leuven: Leuven University Press, 1996.

DeMaris, R. E. "Corinthian Religion and Baptism for the Dead—1 Corinthians 15:29: Insights from Archaeology and Anthropology." *JBL* 114 (1995): 661–82.

Deming, W. "The Unity of 1 Corinthians 5–6." *JBL* 115 (1996): 289–312.

DeSilva, D. A. "Measuring Penultimate against Ultimate Reality: An Investigation of the Integrity and Argumentation of 2 Corinthians." *JSNT* 52 (1993): 41–70.

Duff, P. B. "Metaphor, Motif, and Meaning: The Rhetorical Strategy behind the Image 'Led in Triumph' in 2 Corinthians 2:14." *CBQ* 53 (1991): 79–92.

———. "The Mind of the Redactor: 2 Cor. 6:14–7:1 in Its Secondary Context." *NovT* 35 (1993): 160–80.

Dunn, J. D. G. *The Epistle to the Galatians.* BNTC. London: Black, 1993.

———. *I Corinthians.* NTG. Sheffield: Sheffield Academic Press, 1995.

———. "Paul's Understanding of the Death of Jesus." Pages 125–41 in *Reconciliation and Hope: New Testament Essays in Atonement and Eschatology.* Edited by R. Banks. Grand Rapids: Eerdmans, 1974.

———. *Romans.* 2 vols. WBC 38A–38B. Dallas: Word, 1988.

———. *The Theology of Paul the Apostle.* Grand Rapids: Eerdmans, 1998.

Engberg-Pedersen, T. "1 Cor. 11.16 and the Character of Pauline Exhortation." *JBL* 110 (1991): 679–89.

Eriksson, A. *Tradition As Rhetorical Proof: Pauline Argumentation in 1 Corinthians.* ConBNT 29. Stockholm: Almqvist & Wiksell, 1998.

Fee, G. D. "Εἰδωλόθυτα Once Again: An Interpretation of 1 Corinthians 8–10." *Bib* 61 (1980): 172–97.

———. *The First Epistle to the Corinthians.* NICNT. Grand Rapids: Eerdmans, 1987.

———. *New Testament Exegesis.* Philadelphia: Westminster John Knox, 1983.

————. "II Corinthians VI.14–VII.1 and Food Offered to Idols." *NTS* 23 (1977): 140–61.

Feuillet, A. "L'homme 'gloire de Dieu' et la femme 'gloire de l'homme': 1 Cor. XI.7ᵇ." *RB* 81 (1974): 161–82.

Fiore, B. "'Covert Allusion' in 1 Corinthians 1–4." *CBQ* 47 (1985): 85–102.

Fisk, N. "ΠΟΡΝΕΥΕΙΝ As Body Violation: The Unique Nature of Sexual Sin in 1 Corinthians 6.18." *NTS* 42 (1996): 540–58.

Fitzmyer, J. A. "A Feature of Qumran Angelology and the Angels of 1 Cor 11:10." *NTS* 4 (1958): 48–58.

————. "Glory Reflected on the Face of Christ: 2 Cor 3:7–4:6." *TS* 42 (1981): 630–46.

————. *Romans.* AB 33. New York: Doubleday, 1992.

Furnish, V. P. *II Corinthians: A New Translation with Introduction and Commentary.* AB 32A. New York: Doubleday, 1984.

Georgi, D. *The Opponents of Paul in Second Corinthians.* Philadelphia: Fortress, 1986. Translation of *Die Gegner des Paulus im 2. Korintherbrief.* WMANT 11. Neukirchen-Vluyn: Neukirchener Verlag, 1964.

Goulder, M. D. "Already?" Pages 1–18 in *To Tell the Mystery: Essays on New Testament Eschatology in Honor of Robert H. Gundry.* Edited by T. Schmidt and M. Silva. JSNTSup 100. Sheffield: JSOT Press, 1994.

————. "Ignatius' 'Docetists.' " *VC* 53 (1999): 16–30.

————. "The Jewish-Christian Mission, 30–130," *ANRW* 2:26.3, 1979–2037. Part 2, *Principat,* 26.3. Ed. H. Temporini and W. Harse. Berlin and New York: de Gruyter, 1996.

————. *Luke—A New Paradigm.* 2 vols. JSNTSup 20. Sheffield: Sheffield Academic Press, 1989.

————. "The Pastor's Wolves." *NovT* 38 (1996): 242–56.

————. "A Pauline in a Jacobite Church." Pages 859–76 in vol. 2 of *The Four Gospels 1992: Festschrift F. Neirynck.* 3 vols. Edited by F. van Seghroeck et al; Leuven: Leuven University Press/Peeters, 1992.

————. "The Phasing of the Future." Pages 391–408 in *Texts and Contexts: Biblical Texts in Their Textual and Situational Contexts.* Edited by T. Fornberg and D. Hellholm. Boston: Scandinavian University Press, 1995.

————. "A Poor Man's Christology." *NTS* 45 (1999): 332–48.

————. "2 Cor. 6:14–7:1 As an Integral Part of 2 Corinthians." *NovT* 36 (1994): 47–57.

————. "Silas in Thessalonica." *JSNT* 48 (1992): 87–106.

————. "So All Died: 2 Cor 5.14." Pages 141–48 in ΕΠΙ ΤΟ ΑΥΤΟ: *Studies in Honour of Petr Pokorný.* Edited by J. Mrazek, M. Dvořákova, and S. Brodskyl. Prague: Mlyn, 1998.

————. "Σοφία in 1 Corinthians." *NTS* 37 (1991): 516–34.

————. *A Tale of Two Missions.* London: SCM Press, 1994.

————. "Vision and Knowledge." *JSNT* 56 (1994): 51–69.

————. "The Visionaries of Laodicea." *JSNT* 43 (1991): 15–39.

Gundry, R. H. *SOMA in Biblical Theology*. SNTSMS. Cambridge: Cambridge University Press, 1970.

Haenchen, E. *The Acts of the Apostles: A Commentary*. Translated by B. Noble and G. Shinn under the supervision of H. Anderson, with the translation rev. and brought up to date by R. McL. Wilson. Oxford: Blackwell, 1971.

Hafemann, S. J. *Suffering and the Spirit: An Exegetical Study of II Cor. 2.14–3.3 within the Context of the Corinthian Correspondence*. WUNT 2.19. Tübingen: Mohr, 1986.

Hahn, F. *The Titles of Jesus in Christology: Their History in Early Christianity*. Translated by H. Knight and G. Ogg. New York: World, 1969.

Hall, D. R. "A Disguise for the Wise: ΜΕΤΑΣΧΗΜΑΤΙΣΜΟΣ in 1 Corinthians 4.6." *NTS* 40 (1994): 143–49.

Harris, G. "The Beginning of Church Discipline: 1 Corinthians 5." *NTS* 37 (1991): 1–21.

Harvey, A. E. *Jesus and the Constraints of History*. London: Duckworth, 1982.

Hays, R. B. *First Corinthians*. Interpretation. Louisville: John Knox, 1997.

Hengel, M., and A. M. Schwemer. *Paul between Damascus and Antioch*. Translated by J. Bowden. Louisville: Westminster John Knox, 1997.

Hodgson, P. C. *The Formation of Historical Theology: A Study of Ferdinand Christian Baur*. New York: Harper & Row, 1966.

Holl, K. "Der Kirchenbegriff bei Paulus in seinem Verhältnis zu dem der Urgemeinde." Repr., 1921.

Hollander, H. W., and J. Holleman. "The Relationship of Death, Sin, and Law in 1 Cor 15:56." *NovT* 35 (1993): 270–91.

Hollander, H. W., and G. E. van der Hout. "The Apostle Paul Calling Himself an Abortion: 1 Cor. 15:8 within the Context of 1 Cor. 15:8–10." *NovT* 38 (1996): 224–36.

Holtz, T. "Das Kennzeichen des Geistes: I Kor 12:1–3." *NTS* 18 (1972): 365–76.

Hooker, M. D. " 'Beyond the Things Which Are Written': An Examination of I Cor. IV.6." *NTS* 10 (1963): 127–32.

Horbury, W. *Jewish Messianism and the Cult of Christ*. London: SCM Press, 1998.

Horn, F. W. "1 Kor 15,56: Ein exegetische Stachel." *ZNW* 82 (1991): 88–105.

Horsley, R. A. *I Corinthians*. ANTC. Nashville: Abingdon, 1998.

———. " 'How Can Some of You Say That There Is No Resurrection of the Dead?' Spiritual Elitism in Corinth." *NovT* 20 (1978): 203–31.

———. "Wisdom of a Word and Words of Wisdom at Corinth." *CBQ* 39 (1977): 224–39.

Horst, P. W. van der. *Hellenism–Judaism–Christianity: Essays on Their Interaction*. Kampen: Kok Pharos, 1994.

Hurd, J. C. *The Origin of 1 Corinthians*. London: SPCK, 1965.

Jastrow, M. *A Dictionary of the Targumim, Talmud Babli, Yerushalmi, and Midrashic Literature.* New York: Judaica, 1975.

Jeremias, J. "Flesh and Blood Cannot Inherit the Kingdom of God." *NTS* 2 (1956): 151–59.

Jervell, J. *Imago Dei: Gen. 1,26f in Spätjudentum, in der Gnosis, und in den paulinischen Briefen.* FRLANT 58. Göttingen: Vandenhoeck & Ruprecht, 1960.

Jewett, R. *Dating Paul's Life.* London: SCM Press, 1979.

Judge, E. A. *The Social Pattern of the Christian Groups in the First Century.* London: Tyndale, 1960.

Jülicher, A. *Einleitung in das Neue Testament.* Freiburg im Breisgau, 1894.

Käsemann, E. *Commentary on Romans.* Translated and edited by G. W. Bromiley. Grand Rapids: Eerdmans, 1980.

———. "Die Legitimität des Apostels." *ZNW* 41 (1942): 33–71. Repr. as independent booklet. Darmstadt: Wissenschaftliche Buchgesellschaft, 1956.

———. *New Testament Questions of Today.* London: SCM, 1969.

Kempthorne, R. "Incest and the Body of Christ: A Study of I Corinthians VI.12–20." *NTS* 14 (1968): 568–74.

Köpf, U. "Ferdinand Christian Baur als Begründer einer konsequent historischen Theologie." *ZTK* 89 (1992): 440–61.

Kuhn, T. S. *The Structure of Scientific Revolutions.* 2d ed. Chicago: University of Chicago Press, 1970.

Kümmel, W. G. *The New Testament: The History of the Investigation of Its Problems.* Translated by S. M. Gilmour and H. C. Kee. Nashville: Abingdon, 1972.

Lambrecht, J. *Second Corinthians.* SP 8. Collegeville: Minn.: Liturgical Press, 1999.

———. "Structure and Line of Thought in 2 Cor 2,14–4.6." *Bib* 64 (1983): 344–80.

Lampe, P. "Das Spiel mit der Petrus-Namen—Matt. XVI.18." *NTS* 25 (1978–1979): 227–45.

Lautenschlager, M. "Abschied vom Disputierter: Eine Exegese von συζη-τητής—1 Kor 1,20." *ZNW* 83 (1992): 276–85.

Leenhardt, F. *The Epistle to the Romans.* Translated by H. Knight. London: Lutterworth, 1961.

Lietzmann, H. *An die Korinther I, II.* 5th ed. Supplemented by W. G. Kümmel. HNT 9. Tübingen: Mohr, 1969.

Lincoln, A. T. " 'Paul the Visionary': The Setting and Significance of the Rapture to Paradise in II Cor. XII.1–10." *NTS* 25 (1979): 204–20.

Lindars, B. *The Gospel of John.* London: Oliphant, 1972.

Lindemann, A. "Paulus und die korinthische Eschatologie: Zur These einer Entwicklung im paulinischen Denken." *NTS* 37 (1991): 373–99.

Litfin, D. *St. Paul's Theology of Proclamation: 1 Corinthians 1–4 and Greco-Roman Rhetoric.* SNTSMS 79. Cambridge: Cambridge University Press, 1994.

Lüdemann, G. *Early Christianity according to the Traditions in Acts: A Commentary.* Translated by J. Bowden. Minneapolis: Fortress, 1989.

Lütgert, W. *Freiheitspredikt und Schwarmgeister in Korinth: Ein Beitrag zur Charakteristik der Christuspartei.* BFCT 12.3. Gütersloh: Bertelsmann, 1908.

Malherbe, A. "The Beasts at Ephesus." *JBL* 87 (1968): 71–80.

Manson, T. W. "The Corinthian Correspondence. 1." Pages 190–207 in *Studies in the Gospels and Epistles: Essays in Memory of T. W. Manson.* Edited by M. Black. Manchester: Manchester University Press, 1962.

Martin, R. P. *2 Corinthians.* WBC 40. Waco, Tex.: Word, 1986.

Meeks, W. A. *The First Urban Christians: The Social World of the Apostle Paul.* New Haven: Yale University Press, 1983.

Meggitt, J. "Meat Consumption and Social Conflict in Corinth." *JTS* 45 (1994): 137–41.

———. "The Social Status of Erastus: Rom. 16.23." *NovT* 38 (1996): 218–23.

Meier, J. P. "On the Veiling of Hermeneutics: I Cor 11:2–16." *CBQ* 40 (1978): 212–26.

Miller, G. "ΑΡΧΟΝΤΩΝ ΤΟΥ ΑΙΩΝΟΣ ΤΟΥΤΟΥ—A New Look at 1 Corinthians 2:6–8." *JBL* 91 (1972): 522–28.

Mitchell, A. C. "Rich and Poor in the Courts of Corinth: Litigiousness and Status in 1 Cor. 6.1–11." *NTS* 39 (1993): 562–86.

Mitchell, M. M. *Paul and the Rhetoric of Reconciliation: An Exegetical Investigation of the Language and Composition of 1 Corinthians.* Louisville: Westminster John Knox, 1992.

Morgan, R. C. "Ferdinand Christian Baur." Pages 261–89 in vol. 1 of *Nineteenth Century Religious Thought in the West.* 3 vols. Edited by N. Smart et al. New York: Cambridge University Press, 1985.

Morray-Jones, C. R. A. "Paradise Revisited—2 Cor. 12.1–12: The Jewish Mystical Background of Paul's Apostolate." *HTR* 86 (1993): 177–217, 265–92.

———. "Transformational Mysticism in the Apocalyptic-Merkabah Tradition." *JJS* 43 (1992): 1–31.

Moulton, J. H., and G. Milligan. *The Vocabulary of the Greek Testament, Illustrated from the Papyri and Other Non-literary Sources.* London: Hodder & Stoughton, 1930.

Müller, K. "1 Kor 1,18–25. Die eschatologisch-kritische Funktion der Verkündigung des Kreuzes." *BZ* 10 (1966): 246–72.

Munck, J. *Paul and the Salvation of Mankind.* Translated by F. Clarke. Richmond, Va.: John Knox, 1959.

Munier, C. "Où en est la question d'Ignace d'Antioche? Bilan d'un siècle de recherches, 1870–1988." *ANRW* 27.1:359–484. Part 2, *Principat,* 27.1. Edited by H. Temporini and W. Haase. New York: de Gruyter, 1993.

Murphy-O'Connor, J. "I Corinthians V,3–5." *RB* 84 (1977): 239–45.

———. "1 Corinthians 11:2–16 Once Again." *CBQ* 50 (1988): 265–74.

———. *Paul: A Critical Life*. Oxford: Clarendon, 1996.

———. *St. Paul's Corinth: Texts and Archaeology*. Good News Studies 6. Wilmington, Del.: Glazier, 1983.

———. "Sex and Logic in 1 Corinthians 11:2–16." *CBQ* 42 (1980): 482–500.

———. *The Theology of the Second Letter to the Corinthians*. New Testament Theology. Cambridge: Cambridge University Press, 1991.

Neill, S., and N. T. Wright. *The Interpretation of the New Testament, 1861–1986*. 2d ed. New York: Oxford University Press, 1988.

Oepke, A. "γυμνός, κτλ." *TDNT* 1:773–76.

Oosterdorp, D. W. *Another Jesus: A Gospel of Jewish-Christian Superiority in II Corinthians*. Kampen: Kok, 1967.

Osler, R. E., Jr. "Use, Misuse, and Neglect of Archaeological Evidence in Some Modern Works on 1 Corinthians: 1 Cor. 7:1–5; 8:10; 11:2–16; 12:14–26." *ZNW* 83 (1992): 52–73.

Pearson, B. A. *The Pneumatikos-Psychikos Terminology in 1 Corinthians*. SBLDS 12. Missoula, Mont.: Scholars Press, 1973.

Plutarch. *Moralia*. 15 vols. Translated by F. C. Babbitt. LCL. Cambridge: Harvard University Press, 1927–1969.

Pokorný, P. *Colossians: A Commentary*. Translated by S. Schatzmann. Peabody, Mass.: Hendrickson, 1991.

Pratscher, W. *Der Herrenbruder Jakobus und die Jakobustradition*. FRLANT 139. Göttingen: Vandenhoeck & Ruprecht, 1987.

Pritz, R. A. *Nazarene Jewish Christianity: From the End of the New Testament Period until Its Disappearance in the Fourth Century*. StPB 37. Leiden: Brill, 1988.

Räisänen, H. "The Nicolaitans: Apoc. 2; Acta 6." *ANRW* 26.2:1602–44. Part 2, *Principat*, 26.2. Edited by H. Temporini and W. Haase. New York: de Gruyter, 1995.

Ritschl, A. *Die Entstehung der altkatholischen Kirche*. Bonn, 1850.

Robinson, J. A. T. *The Body*. SBT 1.5. London: SCM Press, 1952.

Rosner, B. "Temple Prostitution in 1 Corinthians 6:12–20." *NovT* 40 (1998): 336–51.

Rowland, C. C. *The Open Heaven: A Study of Apocalyptic in Judaism and Early Christianity*. London: SPCK, 1982.

Rudolph, K. *Gnosis: The Nature and History of Gnosticism*. Translated by R. McL. Wilson. San Francisco: Harper & Row, 1983.

Sandelin, K.-G. *Die Auseinandersetzung mit der Weisheit in 1. Korinther 15*. Åbo, Finland: Åbo Akademi, 1975.

Sanders, E. P. *Judaism: Practice and Belief, 63 BCE–66 CE*. Philadelphia: Trinity Press International, 1992.

———. *Paul*. New York: Oxford University Press, 1991.

Sass, G. "Noch einmal 2 Kor 6,14–7,1: Literarkritische Waffen gegen einen 'unpaulinischen' Paulus." *ZNW* 84 (1993): 36–64.

Schäfer, P. "New Testament and Hekhalot Literature: The Journey into Heaven in Paul and in Merkavah Mysticism." *JJS* 35 (1984): 19–35.

Schenk, W. "Der Kolosserbrief in der neueren Forschung." *ANRW* 25.4: 3327–64. Part 2, *Principat,* 25.4. Edited by H. Temporini and W. Haase. New York: de Gruyter, 1987.

Schlatter, A. *Die korinthische Theologie.* BFCT 18.2. Gütersloh: Bertelsmann, 1914.

Schlier, H. "βάθος." *TDNT* 1:517–18.

Schmidt, J. E. C. *Bibliothek für Kritik und Exegese.* 2 vols. 1797–1803.

Schmithals, W. *Die Gnosis in Korinth: Eine Untersuchung zu den Korintherbriefen.* FRLANT 2.48. Göttingen: Vandenhoeck & Ruprecht, 1956. Translated as *Gnosticism in Corinth: An Investigation of the Letters to the Corinthians.* Translated by J. E. Steeley. Nashville: Abingdon, 1971.

Schnackenburg, R. *The Gospel according to St. John.* 3 vols. Translated by K. Smyth. New York: Herder & Herder, 1968–1982.

Schnelle, U. *Antidoketische Christologie im Johannesevangelium: Eine Untersuchung zur Stellung des vierten Evangeliums in der johanneischen Schule.* FRLANT 144. Göttingen: Vandenhoeck & Ruprecht, 1987.

Schoeps, H. J. *Theologie und Geschichte des Judenchristentums.* Tübingen: Mohr, 1949.

Schrage, W. *Der erste Brief an die Korinther.* 3 vols. to date. EKKNT 7. Zürich/Neukirchen-Vluyn: Benziger/Neukirchener Verlag, 1991–.

Schrenk, G. "θέλω, θέλημα." *TDNT* 3:44–62.

Schweitzer, A. *The Mysticism of Paul the Apostle.* London: A. & C. Black, 1931.

Scott, W., ed. *Hermetica: The Ancient Greek and Latin Writings Which Contain Religious or Philosophical Teachings Ascribed to Hermes Trismegistus.* 4 vols. Oxford: Clarendon, 1924–1936.

Segal, A. F. *Paul the Convert: The Apostolate and Apostasy of Saul the Pharisee.* New Haven: Yale University Press, 1990.

Sellin, G. "Hauptprobleme des ersten Korintherbriefes." *ANRW* 25.4:2940–3044. Part 2, *Principat,* 25.4. Edited by H. Temporini and W. Haase. New York: de Gruyter, 1987.

———. *Der Streit um die Auferstehung der Toten.* FRLANT 138. Göttingen: Vandenhoeck & Ruprecht, 1986.

Söding, T. " 'Die Kraft der Sünde ist das Gesetz'—1 Kor 15:56: Anmerkungen zum Hintergrund und der Pointe einer gesetzkritischen Sentenz des Apostels Paulus." *ZNW* 83 (1992): 74–84.

South, J. T. "A Critique of the 'Curse/Death' Interpretation of 1 Corinthians 5.1–8." *NTS* 39 (1993): 539–61.

Spörlein, B. *Die Leugnung der Auferstehung.* BU 7. Regensburg: Pustet, 1971.

Strecker, G. *Die Johannesbriefe.* KEK. Göttingen: Vandenhoeck & Ruprecht, 1989.

————. *Das Judenchristentum in Pseudoklementinen.* TU 70. Berlin: Akademie, 1958.

Tabor, J. D. *Things Unutterable: Paul's Ascent to Paradise in Its Graeco-Roman, Judaic, and Early Christian Contexts.* SJud. Lanham, Md.: University Press of America, 1986.

Tannehill, R. *Dying and Rising with Christ: A Study in Pauline Theology.* BZNW 32. Berlin: Töpelmann, 1967.

Taylor, N. H. "The Composition and Chronology of 2 Corinthians." *JSNT* 44 (1991): 67–87.

Theissen, G. *The Social Setting of Pauline Christianity.* Translated by J. H. Schütz. Philadelphia: Fortress, 1982.

————. *Social Reality and the Early Christians: Theology, Ethics and the World of the New Testament.* Translated by Margaret Kohl. Edinburgh: T&T Clark, 1993.

Theobald, M. *Die überströmende Gnade: Studien zu einem paulinischen Motivfeld.* FB 22. Würzburg: Echter, 1982.

Thiselton, A. C. "Realized Eschatology in Corinth." *NTS* 24 (1978): 510–26.

Thrall, M. E. *The Second Epistle to the Corinthians.* ICC. Edinburgh: T&T Clark, 1994–2000.

Tobin, T. H. *The Creation of Man: Philo and the History of Interpretation.* CBQMS 14. Washington: Catholic Biblical Association of America, 1983.

Trevett, C. *Montanism: Gender, Authority, and the New Prophecy.* Cambridge: Cambridge University Press, 1996.

Tuckett, C. M. "The Corinthians Who Say 'There Is No Resurrection of the Dead': 1 Cor 15:12." Pages 247–75 in *The Corinthian Correspondence.* Edited by R. Bieringer. BETL 125. Leuven: Peeters/Leuven University Press, 1996.

VanderKam, J. C. *The Dead Sea Scrolls Today.* Grand Rapids: Eerdmans, 1994.

Vaux, R. de. "Sur le voile des femmes dans l'Orient ancien." *RB* 44 (1935): 397–412.

Vielhauer, P. *Geschichte der urchristlichen Literatur.* Berlin: de Gruyter, 1975.

————. "Paulus und die Cephaspartei in Korinth." *NTS* 21 (1975): 341–52.

Vos, J. S. "Der ΜΕΤΑΣΧΗΜΑΤΙΣΜΟΣ in 1 Kor 4,6." *ZNW* 86 (1995): 154–72.

————. "Das Rätsel von I Kor 12:1–3." *NovT* 35 (1993): 251–69.

Vos, C. S. de. "Stepmothers, Concubines, and the Case of Πορνεία in 1 Corinthians 5." *NTS* 44 (1998): 104–14.

Wagner, J. R. " 'Not beyond the Things Which Are Written': A Call to Boast Only in the Lord." *NTS* 44 (1998): 279–87.

Watson, F. *Paul, Judaism, and the Gentiles: A Sociological Approach.* Cambridge: Cambridge University Press, 1986.

Wedderburn, A. J. M. *Baptism and Resurrection.* WUNT 44. Tübingen: Mohr, 1987.

Weiss, J. *Der erste Korintherbrief.* 9th ed. KEK. Göttingen: Vandenhoeck & Ruprecht, 1910.

Welborn, L. L. "A Conciliatory Principle in 1 Cor. 4:6." *NovT* 29 (1987): 320–46.

———. "The Identification of 2 Corinthians 10–13 with the 'Letter of Tears.' " *NovT* 37 (1995): 138–53.

———. "Like Broken Pieces of a Ring: 2 Cor. 1.2–2.13; 7.5–16 and Ancient Theories of Literary Unity." *NTS* 42 (1996): 559–83.

Wenger, L. *Die Stellvertretung im Rechte der Papyri.* Leipzig: B. G. Teubner, 1906.

White, L. M. "Baur, Ferdinand Christian, 1782–1860." Pages 112–13 in *Dictionary of Biblical Interpretation.* Edited by J. H. Hayes. 2 vols. Nashville: Abingdon, 1999.

Wilckens, U. *Weisheit und Torheit: Eine exegetisch-religionsgeschichtliche Untersuchung zu 1 Kor 1 und 2.* BHT 26. Tübingen: Mohr, 1959.

———. "σοφία, κτλ." *TDNT* 8:465–528.

Willis, W. L. *Idol Meat in Corinth: The Pauline Argument in 1 Corinthians 8 and 10.* SBLDS 68. Chico, Calif.: Scholars Press, 1985.

Windisch, H. *Der zweite Korintherbrief.* 9th ed. KEK. Göttingen: Vandenhoeck & Ruprecht, 1924.

Wire, A. C. *The Corinthian Women Prophets: A Reconstruction through Paul's Rhetoric.* Minneapolis: Fortress, 1990.

Young, F. M., and D. F. Ford. *Meaning and Truth in 2 Corinthians.* BFT. London: SPCK, 1987.

Zeilinger, F. "Die Echtheit von 2 Cor. 6:14–7:1." *JBL* 112 (1993): 71–80.

INDEX OF MODERN AUTHORS

INDEX OF SUBJECTS

Index of Ancient Sources

2 Kings
22:14–20   145

1 Chronicles
22:14   22n.9
22:16   22n.9
29:2   22n.9

2 Chronicles
3:6   22n.9
24   180

Job
1:12   116
2:6   116
28   51

Psalms
2:7   206
8:6–7   187
16:10   188, 189
28:2   205
106:20   49
106:28   152
110:1   187
138:2   205

Proverbs
1:7   51, 100
1:20–33   51
8   51
8:25   52
9   51
9:10   100

Song of Songs
3:6–7   79n.8

Isaiah
6:9–10   84
7:14   217
9:1   88n.29, 89
9:1–2   200
11:2   100
11:9   100
25   195
28:11–12   71
29:13   66, 70
29:14   62, 66
40:3   200
40:9   199
42:1   200
43:6   173

46:13   200
51:5   200
52:7   199, 200
52:11   90, 172
52:15   97
53   180
53:4   200
54:11–12   22n.9
56:1   200
60:6   199
60:22–61:1   199
61:1   201, 202, 220
61:1–2   200
64:3   97, 98
65   98

Jeremiah
8:13–9:24   62n.26
9:23   63, 66, 68
9:23–24   62
9:24   208
31:31   34
38:31   84

Ezekiel
1   100
1:1   106
11:19   82
20:34   173
36:26   82
44:18   136n.26

Daniel
2:44   181
5   67n.1
6:10   205
7   187
7:9–18   181
10   106, 187
12   183, 187
12:2   185
12:2–3   181
12:3   191

Hosea
4:1   100
6:2   188, 189
6:6   100
13   195
13:14   196

Jonah
1:17   188, 189

Haggai
2:8   22n.9

Zechariah
9:9   202

Malachi
3:2   106

APOCRYPHA

Tobit
3.11   205

Wisdom of Solomon
7.26   86n.18
9.15   254
14   49

Sirach
1.10   98
24.8   52
24.8–10   77n.3
24.11   52
24.15   79
24.22–23   52
24.23   54
38.31–39.11   53
39.1   53
39.6   53, 65
43.16   106

Baruch
3.9–4.3   52

2 Maccabees
7:37–38   180
8:2–7   180
15   180
15.13–16   206

4 Maccabees
1.17   54, 65
5.2   152
17:20–22   180

NEW TESTAMENT

Matthew
1–2   206
4:12–13   200

4:17   200
4:23–24   200
5:3–4   200
5:4–5   133
5:17–20   54
5:32   122
5:48   94
6:16–18   143
7:24   53
7:28   53
8:17   200
12:11   72
12:40   189
13:43   191
13:57   201
15:19   122
16:18   22
17:17   81
18:14   32
19:1   53
19:12   146
19:21   94
21:11   201
21:46   201
23:2   53, 96
23:23   53
23:34   58
25:31   258
26:1   53
27:9–10   97

Mark
1:10   200
1:12   200
1:15   199
5:30   251
6:4   201
7:6–7   66
8:11   60
9:19   81, 172
13:17   127
13:22   60
14   10, 29
16:7   29

Luke
1:22   106
1:35   202
2.36–38   142
4:16–30   201
4:18   97, 202
4:18–19   200

4:21   200
4:25–26   147
6:20   200
6:20–21   133
6:20–26   201
6:24–25   200
7:16   201
7:41   25
8:3   145
9:41   81
11:50–51   180
12:41   81
12:46   81, 172
16:13   25
18:10   25
21   132
24:19   201

John
1:14   77
1:16–18   77
1:17–18   101
1:21   204
3:13   101
5:27   258
6:46   101
14:9   101
19:30   220
19:34–35   220
20:27   81, 172
21   132

Acts
1–12   207
2   189
2:38   20
3:14–15   202
3:20   202
3:22   220
3:22–23   202
4:25–27   202
7:37   202, 220
7:56   180
8:16   20
9:22   89n.30
10   10, 171
10:36   202
10:42   258
10:48   20
11:25–26   223
11:29–30   168
12:15   144
13–14   223

13:1   223
13:15   68
13:39   202
13:45   60
14:8–10   59
14:11–18   60
15   5, 165, 167, 168, 170, 176
15:1   60
15:1–5   3
15:2   43
15:20   169
15:22   224
15:29   169
15:32   224
15:40   224
16:3   224
16:16–18   59
17:1–9   223
17:3–5   60
17:10–14   224
17:15–34   223
18   27
18:1–4   223
18:2–3   224
18:4–6   68n.7
18:5   223, 225
18:7   224, 229
18:8   223, 224, 229
18:8–11   225
18:10   230
18:11   20
18:18   226
18:23   226
18:24   26
18:24–26   227
18:24–28   19, 223
18:25   21
18:26–27   21
18:27–28   227
19   46, 223, 224
19:21–21:15   44
19:35   58
20:1–2   223
20:1–21:15   226
20:2–3   237
20:3   239
20:3–6   238
20:6–7   238
20:9–12   59
20:13   238
20:16   45